SUPERPOWER ILLUSIONS

JACK F. MATLOCK, JR.

Superpower Illusions

HOW MYTHS AND FALSE IDEOLOGIES
LED AMERICA ASTRAY—AND HOW
TO RETURN TO REALITY

YALE UNIVERSITY PRESS   NEW HAVEN & LONDON

Set in Scala and Scala Sans types by
The Composing Room of Michigan, Inc.
Printed in the United States of America.

Library of Congress Cataloging-in-Publication Data
Matlock, Jack F.
Superpower illusions : how myths and false ideologies led America
astray—and how to return to reality / Jack F. Matlock
p.   cm.
Includes bibliographical references and index.
ISBN 978-0-300-13761-3 (alk. paper)
1. United States—Foreign relations—1989–   2. United States—
Foreign relations—1980–1989.   3. United States—Foreign relations—
Philosophy.   4. United States—Military policy.   5. United States—
Foreign relations—Soviet Union.   6. Soviet Union—Foreign
relations—United States.   7. Cold War—Influence.   8. Unilateral acts
(International law)   9. Intervention (International law)
10. International cooperation.   I. Title.
E895.M38   2009
327.73009'048—dc22   2009027152

A catalogue record for this book is available from the British Library.

This paper meets the requirements of ANSI/NISO Z39.48–1992
(Permanence of Paper).

10 9 8 7 6 5 4 3 2 1

For my grandchildren
John Graham Anderson Benton
Nicholas Hugh Matlock
Cristina Maria Matlock

CONTENTS

PART THREE. THE TASKS AHEAD

PREFACE

HOW IS IT THAT WE HAVE MOVED, IN less than two decades, from the confidence that enveloped America when the Cold War ended, the Berlin Wall came down, and President George H. W. Bush proclaimed a "new world order," to the division and widespread fear prevalent today? The world faces a deepening recession; American armed forces are fighting two wars that have lasted longer than World War II; the United States has become the world's largest debtor, with a fraying infrastructure and educational system and an economy dangerously dependent on imports of energy from some of the most unstable parts of the world.

By 2008, dissatisfaction with the Bush-Cheney administration had reached such intensity among American voters that the candidates of both major political parties ran on platforms of "change." Barack Obama's election has altered for the better much of the world's perception of the United States. Nevertheless, admiration for the United States could be short lived if the Obama administration fails to reorient both domestic and foreign policy. In 2009, as I write these words, America's problems, both at home and abroad, are so profound that successful change is far from assured. There is a danger that the justified pride in the nation's choice of its first African-American president will lead its people and the world to underestimate the forces standing in the way of the policy reorientation our crisis requires.

There are many reasons for the predicament we find ourselves in, but one of the most fundamental is our failure as a nation to understand the lessons the Cold War and the collapse of the Soviet Union should have taught us. To judge from the superficiality—sometimes even irrelevance—of much of our political debate on foreign policy issues, neither the Democratic nor Republican party leadership has a clear idea of what we should have learned from the Cold War and the way it ended, the reasons the Communist Party lost control of the Soviet Union, and why that empire suddenly shattered into fifteen independent countries.

These events rearranged the political map of the world, but too many American politicians looked at the end of the Cold War as if it were a quasi-military victory rather than a negotiated outcome that benefited both sides. They seemed to think that the disappearance of the Soviet Union left the United States as the sole remaining "superpower," able to police the world —if necessary without international sanction or the help of allies. Armchair strategists with illusions of power never seemed to understand that the disappearance of the Soviet Union *decreased* American leverage over other countries, which no longer needed U.S. support to fend off the communist threat. Many pundits inflated the importance of potential "enemies" to justify maintaining American military forces at a level far higher than needed for the nation's defense.

And many were misled by the term "Cold War." It was not a war in the normal sense of armed hostilities between nations. If it had been, we would very likely not be here today to think about it. "Cold War" is a metaphor, akin to the "wars" on drugs, poverty, and terrorism. A metaphorical war cannot be won by the same methods as a real one. When we act as if it can, we make a dangerous mistake. Misunderstanding the nature of the Cold War —treating it as if it ended with the military victory of one country over another, rather than a negotiated conclusion that benefited all countries—induced a false sense of security, a giddy triumphalism that blinded us to the growing threat of terrorism and led American leaders to involve the nation's armed forces, for humanitarian reasons, in a growing number of local and regional conflicts.

Intervening to protect human rights was done with the best intentions, but it has too often led where roads paved with good intentions usually lead. The end of the Cold War gave the United States the opportunity to help build a new international system, just as American leadership after World War II created alliances in Europe and the Far East that avoided the mistakes that followed World War I. This system of alliances survived the tensions of the Cold War, while the parallel system organized by the USSR, based on force and compulsion, collapsed. The "new world order" proclaimed by George H. W. Bush in 1991, in which aggression by one country against another would be deterred or reversed by collective action, seemed close at hand.

With no further need to worry that local insurgencies might be exploited by an expansionist Soviet Union, the United States had the opportunity to trim back security commitments to far-flung areas of the world. The door was open to share more of the responsibility for peacekeeping with regional powers—including those from both sides of the Cold War divide—as their economic and military capacity grew. America had the opportunity to cooperate with Russia and other nuclear powers to continue on the path Ronald Reagan, Mikhail Gorbachev, and George H. W. Bush had set, to reduce reliance on nuclear weapons and resist further proliferation.

But instead of working to create an international order that would address the issues most important to its own security—an order in which power and responsibility would be shared, local conflicts contained, and weapons of mass destruction brought under reliable control—the United States allowed itself to be distracted. It involved its military forces in struggles hardly relevant to American well-being, and did so in a way that engendered the hostility of countries whose cooperation was in the long run essential to American security. The Clinton administration's decision to expand NATO to the east rather than draw Russia into a cooperative arrangement to ensure European security undermined the prospects of democracy in Russia, made it more difficult to keep peace in the Balkans, and slowed the process of nuclear disarmament started by Presidents Reagan and Gorbachev.

In campaigning for the presidency in 2000, George W. Bush promised a "humble" foreign policy that would eschew the sort of "nation-building" President Clinton had attempted. But when hijacked aircraft destroyed the World Trade Center in New York, damaged a significant portion of the Pentagon, and killed nearly three thousand people, he announced that the "world has changed," and his policies became even more assertive, unilateral, and ambitious than Clinton's had been. After using military action against Al-Qaeda in Afghanistan and the Taliban regime that had harbored it—actions approved by the United Nations and supported by the NATO alliance—he ordered an attack on Iraq without either United Nations sanction or the support of some key allies.

The United States invited others to participate, but only on American terms, and we proclaimed ourselves ready and willing to take on hostile forces alone if necessary. These attitudes severely damaged the international institutions that President Bush's predecessors, Republican and Democrat alike, had built to augment American power. They weakened the efforts to establish rules of law for international relations. At times it seemed that our leaders entertained the illusion that, as the world's sole remaining "superpower," America could remake the world in what it perceived as its own image if only it applied enough force with enough persistence.

The war in Iraq has damaged the United States in many ways. By tying down our military forces, particularly the army and marines, it has reduced the leverage America's military strength could otherwise provide our diplomacy. It has boosted the recruitment of terrorists by the likes of Osama bin Laden. It has raised further doubts about our intentions in a world already made suspicious by America's contempt for international law and its walking away from treaties that gave other countries a voice and role in keeping order in the world. To many, it has seemed that the United States is determined to rule as an imperial power. That does not dispose them to cooperate with the United States, even—sometimes—when cooperation is in their best interests.

No foreign policy can be effective in the long run unless it is built on and flows from domestic policies that provide the means to carry out strategic objectives, in other words the strength to back up diplomacy. Strength is not just military might; it also embraces economic strength, political cohesion, the health of alliances, and a sound strategic vision based on realities in the world, not on some theoretical construct pushed to logical but quite unrealistic extremes. George W. Bush's administration embarked on a risky, adventurous foreign policy without the domestic strength necessary for success, even if that policy had been competently executed. A country that allows itself to sink deeper and deeper in debt to the rest of the world will inevitably find itself acting from a position of weakness, not strength. If it persists in a war opposed by the majority of its people, it will be extremely difficult to maintain political cohesion at home. And if it has no strategy to reduce its dependence on foreign oil or head off the ravages of global warming, it will be impossible for even a superpower to maintain an independent foreign policy.

It does not help anyone's understanding that debate on these issues is often couched in terms of "conservative" versus "liberal" politics. There is nothing conservative about invading a country that has not attacked you, and nothing liberal about devastating another country in the belief that doing so will promote democracy. There is nothing conservative about huge budget deficits, and nothing liberal about putting up barriers to trade. The real harm of these labels, however, goes deeper: our loudly polarized debate is one of the things that prevents us from seeing our true position in the world over the past generation. This book argues that America and Russia have both fundamentally misunderstood how and why the Cold War ended, and it shows how that crucial misconception gave rise to misconceived policies that continue to this day. Our current troubles arise directly from our distorted view of history.

One lesson to be derived from the collapse of the USSR (an event that occurred after the Cold War was over) is that the Soviet Union failed as a state because it was based on an ideology that caused its leaders to look at the world in theoretical rather than realistic terms. The Soviet ideology divided the world into opposing camps and postulated that only Communist-ruled states could be reliable allies. It was permissible to impose communism by force because, as Marxist doctrine made clear, communism was the inevitable future.

The American desire to spread democracy in the world is laudable, but not because democracy elsewhere increases American power. Whether a foreign democracy supports U.S. policy will depend on what the policy is and how that country and its leaders are treated—whether they are considered partners who have interests that must be respected, or pawns in some grand design for a world ruled by the United States. Furthermore, Americans of all people should understand that democracy cannot be spread by force. Government "of the people, by the people, for the people" is a contradiction in terms when a foreign occupier holds the ultimate levers of power. The best way—probably the only way—to spread democracy is to show how it works at home to the benefit of all.

I observed much of the Cold War from a privileged vantage point. I was in Washington when President Reagan's policies were being formulated, and in Moscow when Mikhail Gorbachev began to open up the Soviet Union and cooperate with the United States. I watched the process from the inside, drafting key speeches for Reagan and most of his correspondence with Gorbachev, coordinating his talking points, taking notes in his meetings, organizing and commenting on intelligence reports, even playing Gorbachev in rehearsals for summit meetings. From 1987 I was in Moscow, meeting frequently with Gorbachev and other Soviet leaders, getting to know the opposition to him as it developed, traveling to most of the Soviet republics to give speeches, not only in Russian but also in Ukrainian, Georgian, and Armenian, and short passages in several other languages.

When I was named U.S. ambassador to the Soviet Union in 1987, I had already spent three tours of duty at the American embassy in Moscow. The first was in the early 1960s when Nikita Khrushchev headed the Communist Party. I watched the reaction of Soviet citizens as he denounced Stalin in public (he had already done so in secret earlier, in 1956), as people were released from the gulag, and as Khrushchev authorized publication of Alexander Solzhenitsyn's story of life in Stalin's prison camps, *One Day in the Life of Ivan Denisovich*. Together with my friend and colleague Herbert Okun (later ambassador to East Germany and to the United Nations), I translated Khrushchev's messages to President Kennedy during the Cuban missile crisis. Before leaving Moscow in 1963, I drafted a message to the State Department advising that my unofficial Soviet contacts were telling me that opposition to Khrushchev was rising and that it seemed to be led by Leonid Brezhnev—which drew a complaint from State Department officials that the embassy was indulging in "too much kremlinology." A few months later, Khrushchev was removed by a group led by Brezhnev.

As director of the Office of Soviet Union Affairs in the State Department, I attended all of President Richard Nixon's summit meetings with the Soviet leaders and took part in negotiating the agreements that eased relations for a time. Then, again at the American embassy in Moscow in the mid-1970s, this time as the ambassador's deputy, I saw that détente was coming under pressure from Soviet adventurism in what was then called the Third World and from a refusal of the Brezhnev regime to honor its commitments to protect human rights. After Brezhnev signed the Helsinki Final Act in 1975,

I organized an official dialogue on specific human rights problems with my counterpart in the Soviet Ministry of Foreign Affairs, but this was terminated after President Jimmy Carter took office, despite his public criticism of Soviet abuse of human rights.

When Ronald Reagan became president, I was sent back to Moscow as chargé d'affaires to run the American embassy for most of 1981, before going to Prague as ambassador to Czechoslovakia. The Solidarity trade union was growing ever more popular in Poland, and as demonstrations against the government expanded, there was growing fear that Soviet forces would intervene, as they had in Hungary in 1956, Czechoslovakia in 1968, and Afghanistan in 1979. I reported that the Soviet leaders, despite huffing and puffing, would probably try to avoid military intervention—quick victory was eluding them in Afghanistan—and suggested that they would probably bring pressure on the Polish government to crack down. In November, Polish prime minister Wojciech Jaruzelski declared martial law and suppressed Solidarity—for a time.

Although much of my career was spent in the Soviet Union or in Washington dealing with Soviet affairs, I also served for seven years in Africa in the 1960s, in Ghana, on Zanzibar, and in the Tanzanian capital, Dar es Salaam. Those years, along with the time I spent in Central Europe, convinced me that Communists were not winning the hearts and minds of people anywhere. When African leaders resorted to communist methods or took support from communist countries to stay in power, they stimulated widespread opposition. Kwame Nkrumah was overthrown as president of Ghana by a rebellion of military and police leaders in 1966. Zanzibar's Abeid Amani Karume, who had placed East German advisers in his security apparatus, was assassinated in 1972.

The years in Africa brought me into direct contact with Islamic communities and impressed upon me the need to understand the thinking of people who come from cultures different from those of the United States and Europe. Living in sub-Saharan Africa during the American civil rights struggle of the 1960s concentrated my attention on the importance of correcting injustice at home if America was to be successful abroad. Domestic policy and foreign policy are not separate branches of statecraft but a whole, with each element influencing the other.

When I returned to Moscow as ambassador in 1987, we had the benefit of the finest, most capable, most dedicated staff ever assembled at an American embassy. As Soviet society opened up to contacts, American diplomats were everywhere, meeting everyone they could. Together, we had a better feel for what was happening in the country than even President Gorbachev, who was the victim of misleading intelligence reports. We advised Washington to plan for a possible Soviet collapse eighteen months before it happened.

Since retiring from the Foreign Service in 1991, I have been able to return repeatedly to the countries where I served and also to visit other areas in Europe, the Far East, Central Asia, and Latin America. This has sensitized me to the impact that American foreign and domestic policies have on U.S. relations with countries throughout the world.

Because memories are not always accurate, I have sought verification as I assess past happenings. For my previous books describing the Soviet collapse and the end of the Cold War, I interviewed Gorbachev and other former Soviet officials many times, reviewed the records of high-level meetings—most now declassified—and was given access to notes on Politburo meetings, which provided important insight into the internal workings of the Soviet government. I have studied the memoirs of senior officials and the work of journalists and historians dealing with the Cold War and its end. When some turn what happened on its head and use false images to support a dangerous political agenda, I feel obligated to protest.

This book arises out of my experiences and research, not from any partisan spirit. As a Foreign Service officer I took an oath to support the Constitution of the United States, not a political party or an individual. We diplomats were expected to provide support to our elected leaders regardless of party affiliation. In all of my postings, I never thought of foreign policy as Republican or Democratic, however I might mark my ballot in November. We diplomats thought about the interests of the country and how best to support the president and the secretary of state in defining and defending these interests.

It happens that my most responsible and influential positions were with two great Republicans, Ronald Reagan and George H. W. Bush. I voted for both, Reagan in 1984 and Bush in 1988, though I was a registered Democrat, because I believed they were better able than their opponents to lead the country. I did not change my party affiliation, because it was irrelevant. We were working as Americans.

After I retired from the Foreign Service, I left the Democratic Party early in the Clinton presidency. I felt that President Clinton's foreign policy was too much driven by domestic political considerations, and that he lacked both the vision and the competence to take advantage of the opportunity the end of the Cold War and the breakup of the Soviet Union provided. That opportunity was nothing less than the chance to create a world in which security tasks could be shared, weapons of mass destruction reduced rapidly, and barriers to nuclear proliferation raised. With the Cold War behind us, there was the possibility of a realistic strategy to reduce America's dependence on imported energy and to cooperate with other countries to limit the human contribution to environmental degradation and global warming. But more often than not, the Clinton administration played politics rather than attempting to move American policy in a new direction.

It would be unfair to place nothing but blame on the Clinton administration. It had some signal successes: balancing the budget was a notable achievement, and one that contributed directly to America's power and capacity for leadership. It reformed welfare to make it more acceptable to the majority of Americans, without forcing our poorer citizens even deeper into poverty. Furthermore, after 1994 Clinton was confronted with a Congress dominated by Republican leaders who were quite different from Ronald Reagan and George H. W. Bush, even though they pretended to wear the Reagan mantle. A remarkably large proportion of the representatives who elected Newt Gingrich Speaker of the House in 1995 did not even have a U.S. passport; they were ignorant of the world outside the United States, and proud of their ignorance. Careful not to let exposure to the rest of the world color the simplistic certainties of their philosophy, they saw it as their primary task to hobble the federal government, not to make it more effective. Any chance for the Clinton administration to have a bipartisan foreign policy that would fulfill America's potential to help remake the world simply went out the window. A domestic political struggle was all that was left.

Under such circumstances, I could not in conscience register as a Republican. The Republican Party was no longer the party of those Republican presidents I had worked for and respected: Dwight Eisenhower, Richard Nixon (whose achievements in foreign policy should be recognized despite his faults in other respects), Gerald Ford, Ronald Reagan, and George H. W. Bush. I changed my registration from Democrat to independent.

If the Clinton administration missed opportunities, its successor turned them into dangerous threats. In its sixteen years under Bill Clinton and George W. Bush, America went from being the most admired country on the planet in many opinion polls to the most feared. As the Bush-Cheney administration came to an end, the majority of people in many countries considered the United States the most dangerous country in the world. Nobody likes a bully, even if he is on your side—and you really worry if you have the feeling he's only out for himself and has no regard for you.

That view was, of course, unfair. We Americans are really not like that, and we don't deserve a government that makes us seem like bragging, insensitive bullies. But so long as this is the image of America that prevails in much of the world, it will be much harder—sometimes quite impossible— for us to ensure our own security, let alone that of our friends and allies.

President Barack Obama's election gives us hope that America will embark on a new course and regain the respect and support of responsible governments the world over. Nevertheless, key members of President Obama's foreign policy team have, in the past, entertained some of the myths about the end of the Cold War and the breakup of the Soviet Union that have led U.S. policy astray. The United States no longer has the margin of superiority and worldwide respect that allowed the Clinton administration to veer off course largely unnoticed, and it will be the joint task of President Obama and his team to chart a course that does not repeat the errors of his two predecessors.

Our failures are bipartisan. Administrations led by both political parties have squandered the political capital America had accumulated at the end of the Cold War. Neither party has served us as well as it should have. The generation of leaders who landed us in our current dangerous mess must not leave to our children and grandchildren the burden of correcting their mistakes. I have written this book for thinking Americans, whether they consider themselves conservative, liberal, or somewhere in the middle, to explain why so much has gone wrong since the end of the Cold War and to offer concrete suggestions for steps that can, in time, restore America's strength and leadership in the world.

PART ONE

GETTING HISTORY RIGHT

1

Myths and Realities

IN 1998, CNN BROADCAST A DOCUMENTARY series on the Cold War produced by Sir Jeremy Isaacs.[1] It concluded with scenes showing the USSR's hammer-and-sickle-emblazoned red flag being replaced with the new Russian tricolor. A truly dramatic ending to the Cold War, right?

When President Ronald Reagan died, the *Economist* described him on its cover as "The Man Who Beat Communism."[2] He had called the Soviet Union an "evil empire," and a few short years later it was gone.

During his losing bid for reelection in 1992, President George H. W. Bush bragged, "We won the Cold War!" It didn't help him win the election—not because people doubted what he said but because they wished to move on; the issue in 1992 was the economy.

This tiny sample of the myriad distortions and misrepresentations about the end of the Cold War shows that the mythmaking began almost as soon as the Soviet Union fell, and it did not spare our highest leaders and most trusted opinion makers. Since 1991, these distortions have created a set of beliefs as widespread as they are unfounded. This is not merely an abstract problem for historians to argue about. Our beliefs affect how we vote and how our leaders govern; their decisions affect our lives. We expected the end of the Cold War to bring us a safer, more peaceful world, but it has not. In fact, it is precisely our false interpretations of how the Cold War ended that have fueled attitudes and policy decisions that deprived us of many of the benefits the end of the Cold War promised.

Let us start with the most important of these false interpretations—bearing in mind that there will be more to come later in the book—and some of their destructive implications.

Myth 1: The Cold War ended with the collapse of the Soviet Union.

No!

The Cold War ended well before the collapse of the USSR; if it had not, the USSR would probably still exist. Moreover, if this was truly the end of the Cold War, then the Soviet Union was the defeated power, and its breakup was comparable to the collapse of Nazi Germany and the Japanese empire in 1945. This belief has given rise in Russia to the myth that Mikhail Gorbachev was tricked by Reagan and Bush Sr. to give away the store, and that ever since, the United States has been set on turning Russia into a colony fit only for supplying cheap energy and raw materials. We shall see how American actions in the 1990s seemed to confirm in the minds of many Russians this illusion of American duplicity and malignity.

In the United States, the Soviet collapse was viewed by many as the result of a military victory. This led to a spirit of triumphalism, as if the United States were a champion boxer with the habit of shouting, "I'm the greatest!" A feeling of omnipotence seemed to envelop an influential segment of public opinion: as the world's sole remaining "superpower," the United States could accomplish whatever it chose. The history of competing political systems was at an end, as Francis Fukuyama opined, and democratic capitalism had proven to be the irresistible wave of the future.[3] There were no viable competitors to American dominance in the world, and the care of alliances, so important in bringing the Cold War to a peaceful end, was seen as no longer necessary.

Myth 2: Western (especially U.S.) military pressure defeated Communism.

No!

Communist rule ended in the Soviet Union because Mikhail Gorbachev, the leader of the Communist Party of the Soviet Union, maneuvered it out of exclusive power. He did this in the Soviet Union's own interest, when the CPSU tried to block the reforms Gorbachev supported.

If the USSR had indeed been brought to its knees by American military pressure, then this would mean that the United States, as the greatest power in history, has the means to take down any ideology or political system it finds dangerous or repugnant. The only requirement would be to keep a strong military establishment and be willing to use it.

Much of the rest of the world would draw the same conclusion. If a country had a problem, it would expect the United States to set it right. A failure to do so would mean that America was indifferent at best—or more likely ill disposed, maybe even an enemy.

Myth 3: The Cold War was in effect World War III (and the "War on Terror" can thus be considered World War IV).

No way!

If the Cold War was, like World War I and World War II, an "existential struggle" (in today's propaganda) that ended in the defeat and collapse of the Soviet Union, and if other challenges to American security that pop up around the world are World War IV, then they require the same sort of all-out military effort that was needed to win World Wars I and II. But in fact, the Cold War was totally unlike the two world wars: there was no direct conflict between the principal antagonists and no surrender by one side. The "War on Terror" is totally unlike either of the world wars or the Cold War.

Myth 4: Russia was defeated in the Cold War.

No!

The Russian Federation of today was not a party to the Cold War because it was at that time part of a Communist empire, the Soviet Union, and therefore not an independent actor. This myth conflates Russia and the old Soviet Union.

If Russia was defeated in the Cold War—and if the Cold War was comparable to the world wars—then the victors had the right to determine Russia's security environment as they saw fit. For example, during the debate over the enlargement of NATO, which Russia opposed, some pundits said bluntly, "We won the Cold War, so we can do as we please. The Russians will just have to get used to the fact that they are no longer a Great Power, and we have no need to pay attention to their views." This attitude led many Russians to conclude that "the West" would not accept Russia as a partner but only as a subservient appendage. Therefore, Russia needed a stronger central government to mobilize its resources and prove to the world that its interests could not be ignored. Enter Vladimir Putin.

Half-truth: We won the Cold War.

Yes, but so did everybody else! The Cold War ended on terms the United States and its allies set, but these were formulated so that they served the interests of a Soviet Union willing to live in peace with its neighbors. It was therefore in the Soviet interest to accept these terms. Gorbachev is right when he says that we all won the Cold War.

But winning a war usually implies that somebody was defeated, and in addition to the misperceptions already listed, the boast that "America won" has helped perpetuate the zero-sum thinking that prevailed during the Cold War itself. Each side has been suspicious of the other's motives even when there is no good reason to be.

In Russia, the Soviet collapse was followed by runaway inflation that destroyed all savings, even worse shortages of affordable goods than existed under communism, a sudden rise in crime, and a government that, for several years, was unable to pay even the miserable pensions on time. Conditions resembled anarchy much more than life in a modern democracy, but the rest of the world talked as if Russia, having thrown off communism, was already a democracy. Many Russians concluded that they had in fact been defeated, and that the pseudo-democracy that was foisted on them resulted from the machinations of a hostile West.

The myth that the United States, or the West, destroyed the Soviet Union to gain an advantage in the world is now widespread and influential among Russians. It not only affects attitudes on foreign policy but also is applied to personal behavior in respect to Westerners. Russia has a disproportionate share of clever software hackers engaged in various criminal schemes to extract credit card and banking information from databases in the West. The nation's law enforcement officials have done little to curb this activity. When the problem was discussed in a Russian Internet forum, one Russian commented: "I don't see this as a big tragedy. . . . Western countries played not the smallest [that is, a large] role in the fall of the Soviet Union. . . . As for the West, you are getting what you deserve."[4] In other words, it's payback time.

Against these and other myths and half-truths I will put forward two realities.

Reality 1: *Negotiation backed by strength brought the Cold War to an end, not military and economic pressure alone.* This will be clear when we take a close look at Ronald Reagan's diplomacy and Mikhail Gorbachev's response to it.

Reality 2: *The Cold War would not have ended if the United States had insisted on "regime change" rather than a change of behavior.* Gorbachev helped end the Cold War because he was convinced that the Soviet Union needed internal reform and he knew that this would be impossible so long as the East-West military confrontation continued. If the West had demanded a Soviet surrender rather than a mutual reduction of arms and a fair settlement of other disputes, Gorbachev would have had no option but to continue Cold War policies.

These are some of the lessons we should have learned from the end of the Cold War, rather than thinking of it as a military victory. My purpose in trying to change the common understanding of this era is not only about the past but also about the future. This book starts with the past, examining misconceptions and attitudes that have weakened our country, but it ends by suggesting what we can do to put the United States back into a position of acknowledged leadership in our dangerous world.

The Cold War

One can argue, as revisionist scholars have, that the Cold War was not inevitable, that the United States was at fault for initiating an arms race with the Soviet Union, and that once it had started, the United States missed opportunities to end it.[5] Historians will doubtless continue to debate such questions long after those of us who lived through the events have passed from the scene. I do not intend to debate them here.* The Cold War took

---

*Except to observe that, given Stalin's actions at the end of World War II and immediately thereafter, no American president could have summoned the necessary political support to maintain a cooperative relationship with Stalin. Stalin imposed Communist governments on those parts of Eastern and Central Europe the Soviet army had occupied, forced millions of refugees into Western Europe, and closed off the parts of Europe and Asia he controlled from normal interaction with the rest of the world. The only politically viable choice any post–World War II president had was between a policy of "containing" the Soviet Union and efforts to "liberate" the countries that Stalin and his successors controlled. Despite occasional rhetoric to the contrary, in practice all presidents chose containment.

place, and it ended. Let us put aside questions of blame and try to discover what we should have learned from the way the Cold War was conducted, and particularly from the way it ended. Let's start at the end and work back from there.

Three Seismic Events

Between 1988 and 1991, three events occurred that transformed the geopolitical globe and changed the nature of international relations.

First, the war ended. With his speech to the United Nations on December 7, 1988, Mikhail Gorbachev signaled an ideological end to the Cold War. He then took actions over the next two years, in cooperation with George Bush and the other Western leaders, to end the division of Europe and the arms race.

Second, Gorbachev undermined the Communist Party to the point that, by late 1990, its control over the country was weaker than at any point since the Bolsheviks prevailed in the Russian Civil War of 1918–1921.

Third, at the end of 1991, the Soviet Union broke apart into fifteen independent countries, the largest of which, the Russian Federation, had about half the population of the Soviet Union.

These three events happened so rapidly, and for most observers so unexpectedly, that they have become conflated in people's minds and memories. Most now think the Cold War ended with the breakup of the Soviet Union. But in fact it ended *before* the Communist Party lost its grip on the Soviet Union, and both of these events occurred before the Soviet Union collapsed. The three events are connected but separate: Communist rule would not have ended as it did if the Cold War had still been dividing "East" and "West"; the Soviet Union would not have collapsed if the Communist Party had still been able to keep the country together by force.

Think of it this way: the Cold War confrontation and the arms race acted on the Soviet Union and the Warsaw Pact as the walls and top of a pressure cooker, restraining rising internal pressures. The Soviet leader was able to begin opening up his country to the outside world and tolerating similar reforms in the Soviet satellites only when the military competition with the West subsided.

Was Gorbachev forced to "open up" the Soviet Union by U.S. and Western pressure? Not really. When Gorbachev came to power, in 1985, it was apparent that the Soviet Union's economic problems were worsening and that people's expectations of a better life were not being met. Growth rates were declining and spot shortages were becoming more frequent, but there was no actual recession. Gorbachev could have stabilized the situation, though not improved it much, by cutting back on military spending and trimming commitments abroad (such as withdrawing from Afghanistan and ending military support to insurgencies) without attempting to carry out fundamental reforms. The Soviet economy would likely have gone into a slow decline, but there would not have been a sudden collapse such as occurred in 1991.

If the Cold War ended between 1988 and 1990, when did it start?

It Started with an Idea

Most recent histories of the Cold War start with the end of World War II, when the competition between the Soviet Union and the United States became the world's biggest military and geopolitical rivalry. So far the most concise and lucid of these accounts is the one by John Lewis Gaddis, *The Cold War: A New History*. But the histories of the Cold War published in the 1960s started much earlier—back in 1917, when the Bolsheviks seized power in Russia. If we want to understand the roots of the Cold War and the ideology that drove it, we must begin there.

The Bolshevik Revolution was not, as some would have it, a revolt of Russians against tsarist autocracy. It was a revolt against a liberal government that had already removed the tsar and was planning to introduce parliamentary democracy to Russia. The Bolshevik leaders, Vladimir Lenin first of all, saw their seizure of power in Russia as the spark that would bring about a revolution in Germany, then in the rest of Europe, and eventually in the entire world. A few months before seizing power, Lenin told a Bolshevik Party congress, "It is an absolute truth that we will be condemned to perish if the revolution does not break out in Germany."[6]

The Bolshevik aim was never just to rule Russia but to lead a revolution that would create a communist utopia throughout the world. The goal was not democracy but dictatorship—in theory, a dictatorship of the proletariat, but in practice a dictatorship of the Communist Party, as the Bolsheviks eventually renamed themselves. The Communist Party defined itself as the

"vanguard" of the proletariat, and Karl Marx had predicted that the proletariat would eliminate the ruling bourgeoisie and create a communist paradise on earth. History was moved, Marx argued, by the struggle of antagonistic economic classes. Just as the bourgeoisie had earlier replaced the
aristocracy, the proletariat would now replace the bourgeoisie. Then class
struggle would end, the state would "wither away," and all would live without force or compulsion in a society of equals dedicated to the principle
"from each according to his ability, to each according to his needs."

The Bolshevik seizure of power in Russia was therefore a declaration of
ideological war against all the existing governments at that time. It is not
surprising that Western governments opposed it, particularly since the Bolsheviks had vowed to take Russia out of the Allied coalition then fighting a
war against Germany and Austria-Hungary. Desiring a weak Russia more
than it feared a revolution at home, the German government permitted
Lenin, who had been in exile in Switzerland, to cross its territory by train and
enter the political fray in Petrograd. On December 5, 1917, less than a month
after seizing power, the Bolsheviks signed an armistice ending their war
against Germany.

None of the Allied powers accepted the Bolshevik regime as legitimate. To
different degrees and for different reasons, Britain, France, the United
States, and Japan all intervened with military force during the Russian Civil
War that followed the Bolshevik seizure of power. France and Britain actively supported the "White" armies that for a time occupied southern Russia and Ukraine. The United States and Great Britain sent a military force
to Archangel to prevent military supplies that had been sent to Russia from
falling into German hands, and cooperated with anti-Bolshevik forces there.
For a time the Japanese and Americans occupied much of the trans-Siberian
railroad and thereby controlled Siberia and the Russian Far East. When the
Bolsheviks prevailed in the Russian Civil War, the Western powers refused
to recognize the Communist government and closed their embassies.[7]

The United States withheld recognition not only because it considered
the Communist regime illegitimate and objected to the renunciation of
Russia's foreign debts but also because it feared the influence of the Bolsheviks' revolutionary ideology. In 1919, American authorities conducted
widespread arrests and deportations of persons who had been organizing

workers and agitating for aid to the Soviet government. The campaign against "radicals and communists" was dubbed a "Red Scare" by journalists, a term historians have retained.[8] Although the reaction by U.S. authorities was excessive and unfair to many individuals, it illustrates the ideological underpinning of the Cold War that eventually developed. The United States was not as vulnerable to Communist subversion as the Red hunters imagined, but the Bolshevik government was genuinely intent on fomenting revolution throughout the world. It created the Communist International (Comintern) in March 1919 to organize and control revolutionary movements worldwide.

When it became clear to the Bolshevik leaders that successful revolutions elsewhere were not imminent, they proclaimed a goal of "socialism in one country" and downplayed their support for world revolution. But they did not abandon the dream; they saw their mission as establishing a base for Marxist revolutions wherever possible. While they were weak, they were willing to work with "bourgeois" governments, for instance by initiating military cooperation with Germany's Weimar Republic in 1924. Such cooperation with the ideological enemy was always considered limited and temporary.

Most Western countries granted diplomatic recognition to the Soviet government in the mid-1920s, but not the United States. Although Americans provided substantial humanitarian aid during the Russian Civil War and the famines that followed, their government withheld recognition of the Soviet government until 1933, following Franklin D. Roosevelt's election. There was a substantial expansion of trade with the United States in the 1930s under Stalin's policy of rapid industrialization, but the widespread famines brought on by the confiscation of food from farming areas and mass deportations, followed by bloody purges of supposed "wreckers" and "traitors," convinced most Americans that Stalin's Soviet Union was an unbridled tyranny.

In the 1930s, as Hitler gained control of Germany and, in concert with Mussolini's Italy, embarked on an imperialist course, Stalin proposed a "united front" with Britain and France to oppose fascism. His price was high: he wanted a free hand in the three Baltic countries, Finland, and Poland, all of which had become independent following World War I. When

Britain and France were unwilling to betray their principles to gain a questionable ally, Stalin turned to Hitler and made a deal with him.

The Nazi-Soviet Nonaggression Pact of 1939 shocked the world. The mere fact that Stalin would conclude a cooperative agreement with an enemy who had systematically destroyed the Communist Party in his own country disillusioned many leftists, who considered communism (viewed as a left-wing ideology) the natural opposite of fascism (supposedly a right-wing ideology). But the Nazi-Soviet pact was only the tip of the iceberg. It was accompanied by a secret protocol that, in effect, divided Europe between Hitler and Stalin. This protocol remained secret until the end of World War II, when the U.S. Army captured microfilm copies of German documents, but its effects were immediate and obvious: Soviet troops occupied the three Baltic countries and eastern Poland, as German troops invaded Poland from the west. Estonia, Latvia, and Lithuania were forcibly incorporated into the Soviet Union, as were parts of eastern Poland. When World War II began in Europe with Hitler's invasion of Poland, Stalin was Hitler's ally.

It was the Nazi-Soviet pact that prompted Winston Churchill's famous description of Russia as "a riddle, wrapped in a mystery inside an enigma."[9] The riddle, however, was not Russia but Stalin and communist ideology. In Stalin's eyes, Hitler, Churchill, Roosevelt, and the other Western leaders were all class enemies, representatives of the bourgeoisie. Since the Soviet Union was too weak to take them all on, it had to make temporary alliances with some—divide and conquer, as it were. Siding with Great Britain against Germany was ideologically no different from siding with Germany against Great Britain. Stalin would make a deal with anyone who offered the most. The idea that Nazism and Communism stood at opposite poles was absurd; they were as kindred as Siamese twins. The real mystery was not Stalin's and Hitler's behavior but that anybody could take the left-right dichotomy seriously after the Nazi-Soviet pact.

World War II: Stalin's Fear of Ideological Contamination

Hitler's decision to attack the Soviet Union in June 1941 surprised and shocked Stalin, but not because he trusted Hitler.[10] He was surprised because Leninist ideology held that the "imperialist" powers would first fight each other, weakening their societies and making them vulnerable to revolution. Thus he assumed that Germany's conflict with Great Britain would take precedence over an attack on the Soviet Union. Hitler might someday turn on the Soviet Union, but he would not do so, Stalin thought, until he had subdued Great Britain. Had not Napoleon's mistake in 1812 been invading Russia? The German General Staff would never allow Hitler to plunge the country into the same two-front war that had brought it defeat in World War I, even though the Eastern Front had collapsed almost a year before the armistice. Stalin was thus misled by a combination of ideology and an accurate grasp of history. What escaped his comprehension was that Hitler did not think like a Leninist or a rational "realist."

The initial near-collapse of Soviet resistance to the Nazi invasion convinced Stalin that the Soviet Union could not survive without massive material assistance from its ideological enemies, Britain and the United States, and without another military front against Germany on the continent of Western Europe. In calling for this "second front," Stalin conveniently ignored the fact that the *first* front against Nazi Germany had been in Western Europe during the Battle of France in 1940, at which time he had refused to open a second front in the east. Nevertheless, both Churchill and Roosevelt recognized that Soviet resistance was vital to the war against Nazi Germany and provided as much assistance as they could. But a successful invasion of France's Atlantic coast was three years distant.

In the meantime—and even after D-Day in June 1944, when the Western Allies stormed the beaches of Normandy—Stalin harbored a persistent fear that Britain and the United States would make a separate peace with Germany. After all, that is exactly what Stalin would have done—in fact had done when the shoe was on the other foot. If his ideological concepts were sound, it would have been natural for Britain to consign the continent of Europe to Germany, and thereby snuff out the threat of Bolshevism, in return for preservation of the British Empire. He was unable to imagine that moral constraints had any force in Western political thinking, since they had none in his own.

Equally, he feared that the Soviet people's contact with Westerners and "bourgeois" societies would weaken his control of the country. Thus he generally refused to publicize Western aid in the Soviet media and did everything he could to minimize contact between Soviet citizens and those few Westerners who were stationed in the Soviet Union. When the tide of battle turned with the German defeat at Stalingrad in December 1942, he even sent to the gulag Russian women who had dated Westerners in Moscow. One of these was Nikita Khrushchev's daughter-in-law, whose husband had been killed early in the war. After the war was over, most of the Soviet prisoners of war who were returned (many against their will) to the Soviet Union were sent to labor camps. Exposure to the West, even under the unspeakably difficult conditions of German prison camps, was considered potentially seditious.

The Soviet people paid an immense price for Stalin's unique combination of paranoia, ideological rigidity, and bad judgment.[11] The rest of the world owes the Soviet people an immense debt for the sacrifices they made to defeat Hitler. But the Soviet people owed Stalin absolutely nothing; it was he who weakened the Soviet armed forces before the Nazi invasion, distrusted his most capable generals, and pursued the war in ways that maximized casualties. Nevertheless, he was able to manipulate the Soviet propaganda machine so effectively that many Soviet citizens came to attribute their victory to Stalin's leadership, instead of blaming him for their near defeat.

Europe Divided: The Roots of Containment

To be effective, Stalin's propaganda machine required a monopoly. Since it put forward versions of events that were often the precise opposite of reality, it could be effective only if it had no competition. To stay in power, Stalin needed not only to maintain the terror he had used before World War II but to make sure Soviet citizens heard only the version of events that glorified him and his rule. This required cutting his people off from any effective communication with the "capitalist" world.

During the war, many Americans had hoped that once Nazi Germany was defeated, Stalin would open up the country, "soften" his rule, and allow more democracy. Had not the Soviet people showed their loyalty and their mettle in overcoming the Nazi juggernaut? Didn't they deserve a free and democratic government? But foreigners who knew the reality of Stalin's tyranny understood that this was not his goal. George Kennan, a Russian-speaking Foreign Service officer, was in charge of the American embassy in Moscow in February 1946 when the Treasury Department in Washington asked the embassy why the Soviet government was not cooperating to establish a stable international monetary system. Kennan, who had long worried about the tendency in Washington to think of Stalin as a potential liberal, sent a detailed explanation of why it was an illusion to think that the Soviet Union would be a willing partner in the reconstruction of Europe on democratic principles.[12]

The message arrived in Washington at a propitious time. Officials had been increasingly frustrated by Soviet foot-dragging on proposed cooperation and by signs that Stalin intended to use the Red Army to establish puppet regimes in Soviet-occupied countries. Kennan offered not only an explanation but a rationale for going ahead with the reconstruction of those parts of Europe not occupied by the Soviet Army, without waiting for Stalin's approval or expecting his cooperation.

Kennan advised that while true cooperation with the Soviet Union would not be possible, there was no need to think that war was either inevitable or desirable; he described such thoughts as "sheerest nonsense." With the Soviet Union gravely weakened by the war, Stalin would try to close off the country in order to perpetuate his total rule. Contradictions in the Soviet system itself would eventually bring it down. Until that happened, it was sufficient for the United States to contain the Soviet Union so that further expansion would not be interpreted as validation of the system.

Kennan's message, which became known as the "long telegram," laid out the basic rationale for American policy toward the Soviet Union from 1948 until Gorbachev began to change the Soviet system in the late 1980s. The "containment" strategy that Kennan proposed was not always acknowledged, either by politicians who argued that the United States should act to liberate Eastern Europe, or by Kennan himself, who when out of government believed that American presidents' ideas about containment relied too heavily on military pressure. But in fact, this doctrine was the foundation of every postwar American president's policy. Dwight Eisenhower used the slogan "Roll Back the Curtain!" during his campaign for the presidency in 1952, but when he was president and the Hungarians revolted against their Soviet-imposed government in 1956, he did nothing to support their revolution. He was wise not to, since by then the Soviet Union had nuclear weapons.

The Marshall Plan

Containment was never just a military concept, though at times that aspect seemed to dominate. The most successful and long-lasting effort to prevent the expansion of communism was the Marshall Plan, announced in 1947. The economies of continental Europe were prostrate from the destruction of the war; most countries were flooded with penniless refugees, and famine and disease were serious threats. In France and Italy, Communist parties thrived on the economic dislocation and the popular illusion that communism was the opposite of the fascism they had experienced under Pétain and Mussolini. If economic conditions continued to deteriorate, there was a serious danger that France and Italy would fall under Communist governments by popular election, with no direct military help from the Soviet Union.

The Marshall Plan was one of the most successful geopolitical moves in all of human history. It succeeded because it departed from the normal behavior of victors following a war—the tendency to place all the burden on the defeated parties, and to exact vengeance—and instead treated all the devastated countries alike, including the Soviet Union. Stalin, not unexpectedly, rejected the offer of help and also forced the Poles and Czechoslovaks to retract their original acceptance. But he could not claim that the USSR was excluded as a matter of Western policy.

Another novel feature of the Marshall Plan is the degree to which decisions and leadership were left to the Europeans. The United States encouraged reconciliation of previous enemies, but it was up to French and German leaders to take the lead in healing the historic hostility between their countries. The perceived Soviet menace helped concentrate minds, but it was the Europeans who made the Marshall Plan work, and American willingness to refrain from micromanaging encouraged them to take responsibility for the results.

Soviet behavior in its zone of occupation was in many ways the opposite. "Class enemies," members of the "bourgeoisie," were rounded up and sent to prison camps, or sometimes simply executed. Industrial plants, particularly those in German territory, were looted and their machinery shipped to the Soviet Union as reparations. Communist governments subservient to Moscow were installed and Soviet-style totalitarian systems were imposed, complete with the confiscation of all income-producing property and, except in Poland, collectivization of agriculture.

Containment Goes Global

The first containment line was drawn in Europe. When a serious Communist insurgency erupted in Greece, and Turkey came under Soviet pres-

sure for territorial concessions, President Truman decided to aid both countries to resist Communist domination. When Soviet troops continued to occupy Iranian Azerbaijan following the German surrender, the United States
brought sufficient diplomatic pressure to bear that Stalin took them out.

While the United States and European countries were grappling with the
near economic collapse brought on by the war, a revolution in China swept
Chiang Kai-shek's American-backed government off the continent and onto
the island of Taiwan, which the United States had returned to China after
fifty years of Japanese rule. Mao Zedong had received a lot of help from Stalin, including arms captured from the defeated Japanese occupiers, but it
was a Chinese-led and Chinese-controlled revolution. Nevertheless, given
the Soviet clampdown in Eastern Europe and Soviet attempts to expand elsewhere, most American political leaders considered it obvious that the rout
of Chiang Kai-shek's forces was the result of a giant conspiracy directed
from Moscow, and that China was now Stalin's pawn.

Before the Communist conquest of China had sunk fully into the public
consciousness, the Soviet-installed government of North Korea attacked the
American-installed government in South Korea. Within days, South Korean
forces were driven to a small enclave around Pusan. This time, the United
States did not wait; it got an immediate vote in the United Nations to condemn the invasion and authority to resist it under the U.N. flag. General
Douglas MacArthur, who had commanded the forces that defeated Japan,
was placed in charge of the U.N. forces. A daring amphibious landing on the
Inchon Peninsula cut off the North Korean troops in the south. It would
have been a simple matter at that point to reestablish the previous border,
but MacArthur decided (and received Washington's approval) to push north
and try to eliminate the North Korean regime. Within days, American troops
occupied Pyongyang and sped toward the Chinese border. As they approached, Chinese forces poured across the Yalu River and overwhelmed
the smaller numbers of U.S. and allied troops. By July 1953 the front had stabilized not far from the border along the 38th parallel that had separated
the Soviet and American occupation zones. Both sides settled down to a
heavily armed cease-fire that endures to this day—except that the Chinese
troops have long since been replaced by North Koreans.

Another shock to American opinion occurred in 1959 and 1960, when
Fidel Castro, who had led an insurgency that swept away Fulgencio Batista's

dictatorial regime in Cuba, forced a communist-style system on the island. Although Batista had been a brutal dictator, he had protected American property and interests in Cuba. Even so, the United States probably would have learned to live with Castro if he had not declared himself a Communist, nationalized property, forced middle-class Cubans into exile, and sought aid from the Soviet Union. With this alliance the pattern of Soviet expansion seemed serious indeed—first Europe, then Asia, and now within a few miles of Florida.

The costly American military involvement in Vietnam was yet to come. In 1954, following a defeat at Dienbienphu, the French decided to leave Vietnam, and the country was divided roughly midway in its waist into separate zones in the north and south. The north was left to the Communists—the Viet Minh—led by Ho Chi Minh, and a non-Communist regime, under French protection, was established in the south. The United States helped those Vietnamese who did not wish to live under the Viet Minh to relocate to the south. This arrangement was supposed to be temporary, with free elections throughout Vietnam within two years. The elections, however, never occurred because neither the North nor South Vietnamese government was willing to permit them.

Gradually, the United States replaced France as the principal supporter of South Vietnam—first with military equipment and advisers, then with increasing numbers of combat troops. Between 1965, when U.S. forces were first authorized to conduct offensive operations, and 1973, when the last Americans were withdrawn from Vietnam, more than 58,000 Americans were killed there and over 150,000 were wounded. The number of Vietnamese killed during the long war is unknown but was certainly in the millions. As helicopters lifted the last Americans and Vietnamese from the roof of the U.S. embassy in Saigon, it was clear that the United States had suffered the most humiliating military defeat in its history.*

It is difficult now, two decades after the Cold War, to recapture the alarm felt in the 1950s and 1960s in the face of what seemed an expanding juggernaut. Not only Americans were alarmed. I was assigned to the American

---

*The British occupation of Washington, D.C., during the War of 1812 was humiliating, but eventually the United States won the war.

embassy in Vienna, Austria, in the late 1950s. Even though most of the war's physical damage had been repaired and the economy was beginning to soar as a result of the Marshall Plan, many Austrians clearly felt that communism—which most had learned to hate during the postwar years when Soviet troops occupied Austria's eastern provinces—was the more dynamic system. "What is the difference between an optimist and a pessimist?" the joke would go, and the answer was, "The optimist learns Russian; the pessimist, Chinese."

It is very likely that some military confrontation growing out of the U.S.-Soviet geopolitical rivalry would have turned the Cold War into World War III if not for another powerful element. Nuclear weapons, which appeared on the world stage only in the closing days of the war against Japan, turned out to be at once the most destructive and dangerous weapons ever created, and also the most stabilizing, caution-inspiring weapons the world had yet known.

The Nuclear Factor

Not everyone shared George Kennan's judgment that thoughts of military intervention in the Soviet Union following World War II were the "sheerest nonsense." Throughout the late 1940s and 1950s, prominent voices asserted that war with the Soviet Union was inevitable and that it would be better to get it over sooner than later. *Colliers,* a popular American weekly magazine, ran a special issue in 1951 predicting an easy conquest.[13] Calls for "preventive war" persisted even after the Soviet Union exploded its first atomic device; the argument then was that the United States must strike before the USSR had the means to attack American soil. (Soviet aircraft did not have the range to attack the United States and return; there were as yet no intercontinental missiles.) The logic seemed obvious: we failed to stop Hitler when he was weak; we must not repeat that mistake.

Despite considerable public clamor, neither President Truman nor any of his successors ever seriously planned *starting* such a war. The worry was that the Soviet Union, emboldened by its growing nuclear arsenal and its rapid advances in missile technology (by 1953 it had tested a hydrogen bomb, and in 1957 it put *Sputnik,* the first artificial Earth satellite, into orbit), would increase its military pressure on other countries or even use its massive conventional forces to invade Western Europe.[14]

This fear led to the establishment of the North Atlantic Treaty Organization in 1949 and the rearmament of West Germany within that defensive alliance, which in turn led the Soviet leaders, in 1955, to create a counter "alliance" with the countries they controlled in Eastern and Central Europe. There was a fundamental difference between NATO and the Warsaw Pact. NATO was entirely voluntary, while the Warsaw Pact countries were forced to subordinate their military establishments to Soviet command. This fact was a source of weakness for the Soviet Union, not always appreciated by the governments (and publics) of NATO countries. For a time, American nuclear superiority seemed adequate to compensate for the Warsaw Pact's greater number of tanks, artillery, fighter planes, and men under arms. But the Soviet leaders rapidly closed the gap in nuclear capability, in both the number and destructiveness of their nuclear weapons and the reach, carrying capacity, and accuracy of their ballistic missiles.

When the United States placed nuclear missiles in Turkey that could reach the Soviet Union, Nikita Khrushchev countered by deploying Soviet nuclear weapons in Cuba. This produced the only confrontation during the Cold War that came close to a nuclear exchange between the principal adversaries. It ended when Khrushchev agreed publicly to remove Soviet missiles from Cuba and Kennedy pledged privately to withdraw the American missiles from Turkey.

After the Cuban missile crisis, both countries were more circumspect about threatening each other. But the arsenals grew. Like the sorcerer's apprentice, both governments seemed to have unleashed forces they could not control. No rational purpose could be served by increasing the power to destroy when each side had more than enough weapons to make the earth uninhabitable, or by using these weapons when the most probable result would have been national suicide. Fortunately, the leaders of both the United States and the Soviet Union came to understand this, at least by the early 1970s and probably earlier. But they were both riding tigers; if either got off first, his country might be doomed.

The focus of attention shifted to making sure the weapons were not used. The West's approach came to be called Mutual Assured Destruction (MAD): if you strike me, I will destroy you—and you can see that I have the means to do so! Neither side officially adopted this doctrine, but the actions of both were usually consistent with it.

MAD seemed to require both governments to have enough nuclear weapons to conduct a devastating retaliation on the other even after they had suffered a massive attack. In the 1970s, the United States started reducing the number of its warheads but also making the weapons it had more accurate and less vulnerable. Soviet leaders still depended more on numbers, but tended to close, within a few years, any technical gap the United States opened.

A generation of earnest arms control specialists—diplomats, soldiers, scientists, and security wonks—worked to discover formulas for arms reduction that would be fair to both sides and lower the danger posed by the existence of large numbers of nuclear weapons. The differences in the structure of the Soviet and American arsenals made it practically impossible to find a formula that both sides would accept. Each had powerful special interests defending any given weapons system. Repeated attempts by both sides to find ways to control the nuclear arms race began to resemble attempts to stuff toothpaste back into a leaky tube.

Détente—Its Concept and Its Demise

From the eighteenth century to the early twentieth, French was considered the language of international diplomacy. Among the French words adopted into other languages' diplomatic jargon during this period was *détente*, which originally meant either discharging or unloading a firearm, but in diplomacy came to mean a relaxation of tension. This was the term that Henry Kissinger, who started his career as a diplomatic historian, applied to the policy he and President Richard Nixon worked out with the Soviet leaders in 1972. They accepted the concept but used a Russian word, *razryadka* —with a derivation similar to the French—to express it.

For the Americans, détente was based on several logical propositions: (1) the countries would deal with each other as equals; (2) limits would be placed on the numbers and capacity of nuclear weapons; (3) each country would refrain from seeking "unilateral advantage" over the other; and (4) both would seek areas for cooperation where their interests coincided. Kissinger spoke of weaving a web of mutual dependence, by trade and other forms of cooperation, that would attenuate antagonisms. It was a serious attempt to escape from the zero-sum thinking that had stymied most negotiations up to then.

The Soviet leaders thought of razryadka somewhat differently. They wanted two things above all: to curb an arms race that was costing their economic development dearly, and to lock in the territorial gains they had made during and after the Second World War. They also wanted to increase trade in high technology goods with the West, since they recognized that the Soviet Union was behind in developing new technologies. But the Soviet leaders were wary of allowing Western influence to reach the Soviet people as a whole, and they had no intention of interpreting the commitment to refrain from "unilateral advantage" as inhibiting their "international duty" to assist insurgencies around the world.

Détente reached its high point between 1972 and 1975. President Nixon and General Secretary Brezhnev inaugurated it officially at a summit meeting in Moscow in 1972 when they signed the Anti-Ballistic Missile (ABM) Treaty, the Interim Agreement on the Limitation of Strategic Arms (SALT), a Declaration of Principles, and a series of agreements on cooperative projects. Brezhnev's visit to the United States in 1973 and Nixon's return visit to Moscow in 1974 helped create the appearance of steadily warming U.S.-Soviet relations.

It was perhaps not a coincidence that the 1972 Moscow summit meeting followed Nixon's visit to China, which led to a normalization of relations with Communist China. For over a decade, China had been more a competitor than an ally to Moscow. After Nixon's resignation, his successor, Gerald Ford, continued Nixon's détente policies by concluding the Vladivostok Agreement in 1974, which specified the main features of a treaty to limit strategic nuclear weapons, and by signing the Helsinki Final Act in 1975.

The Helsinki accord was controversial when it was signed: critics in the West claimed that it legitimized the Soviet hold on Eastern Europe in return for implausible promises regarding respect for human rights. The critics were wrong: the Final Act did not legitimize any borders not already recognized,* and while the commitments regarding human rights were ignored

---

*A point President Ford made explicit in a public statement before he signed the Final Act. The Final Act held that recognized borders could be changed only by mutual agreement of the parties in question, but it did not specify where these borders were. President Ford made clear, for example, that the United States did not recognize the incorporation of the three Baltic countries into the Soviet Union.

for a time, they encouraged the formation of opposition groups and eventually made a significant contribution to the loosening and subsequent downfall of the Communist systems in Europe.

After 1975, however, détente began to fray. Soviet expectations of freer trade had been frustrated by the Jackson-Vanik amendment to the Trade Act of 1974, which prohibited "most-favored-nation" (that is, non-discriminatory) tariff treatment to "non-market-economy" (i.e., Communist-ruled) countries that did not permit free emigration by their citizens. The amendment was intended to pressure the Soviet authorities to allow Jews to emigrate without the restrictions that had been placed upon their departure. At first the Soviet authorities tried to make a secret deal to allow the emigration of up to sixty thousand Jewish citizens a year, but when the matter was publicized, they drew back and increased their restrictions.

For the United States, disillusionment with détente came not only from the Soviet authorities' actions on Jewish emigration but also from their increased support of insurgencies in Africa and Latin America. Americans viewed what seemed to be a Soviet offensive in the Horn of Africa, in Angola, in Nicaragua, and elsewhere as blatant attempts to take advantage of the U.S. reluctance, following the fiasco in Vietnam, to involve American military forces in distant battlefields. Even in Europe, the Soviets seemed to be determined to change the balance of armaments: in 1976 they began to deploy a new, much more capable nuclear missile against the European NATO countries.*

Washington saw these Soviet moves as designed to secure the unilateral advantage Brezhnev had foresworn in the 1972 Declaration of Principles. The intertwined interests that Nixon and Kissinger had started knitting with the Soviet Union began to unravel.

*The RSD-10 missile was designated the "SS-20" by NATO, and because the Soviet name was secret at the time, the NATO designation was generally used in negotiations concerning these missiles. Their deployment was considered an escalation of the threat against European NATO countries because they were more accurate, had a greater range, and were less vulnerable (being mobile) than the missiles they replaced. The United States had no comparable missiles in Europe until it deployed Pershing II ballistic missiles and Tomahawk cruise missiles in November 1983, after the Soviet government refused to eliminate or greatly reduce the number of SS-20s.

President Carter tried, early in his presidency, to extend the nuclear agreements Nixon and Ford had made with Brezhnev. His ideas were good, and with careful diplomacy he might have persuaded the Soviet leaders to accept them. But his diplomacy—or rather lack of it—backfired. Carter began his presidency with loud public criticism of the Soviet human rights record. The criticism was well deserved, but it hardly put Brezhnev in a mood to accept new proposals on arms control. Then Carter worked out a plan for "deep cuts" and made it public before consulting the Soviet leaders, who interpreted the proposal as a challenge rather than an invitation to serve the interest of both countries. When Secretary of State Cyrus Vance brought the proposals to Moscow in March 1977, the response was a curt dismissal and an accusation that the United States was reneging on commitments made by President Ford in Vladivostok in 1974.

As negotiations on a strategic arms treaty continued in 1977 and 1978, the Carter administration became increasingly concerned with Soviet arms supplies to insurgencies in Africa. At one point in 1977, the State Department asked the American embassy in Moscow for suggestions on how the U.S. might deter Soviet support of these insurgencies. At the time I was the ambassador's deputy, and I drafted a message suggesting that the most effective leverage would be to make the conclusion of an arms control agreement, which Brezhnev needed, contingent on a scaling-back and eventual cessation of Soviet military aid to insurgencies. After a few weeks I was informed that arms control was so important that it had been decided not to link it with anything else.

Carter and Brezhnev finally signed an agreement to limit strategic nuclear weapons (SALT II) in May 1979. Though leading Republicans declared it "fatally flawed," it might have gained Senate approval if the administration had handled its ratification more competently. As it turned out, the Soviet invasion of Afghanistan in December 1979 made ratification unthinkable. Carter withdrew the treaty from Senate consideration and ordered a series of "retaliatory" moves, such as limiting American exports of wheat to the Soviet Union (when it was available elsewhere on the world market), ordering American athletes not to participate in the 1980 Moscow Olympics, and withdrawing U.S. diplomats from Kiev and Soviet consular officials from New York. This last action left no Americans in Kiev to keep an eye on increasingly restless Ukraine, but kept some seven hundred Soviet officials and family members attached to the United Nations in New York. Carter also refused to renew the U.S.-USSR Cultural Exchange agreement, in force since the Eisenhower presidency, when its term expired. It had been the main vehicle for connecting people across the Iron Curtain and injecting a feel for the outside world into the largely closed Soviet society.

President Carter's aims were laudable and reasonable, but the implementation of his policies was haphazard and poorly thought out. In part, this was a result of bickering between Secretary of State Cyrus Vance and Zbigniew Brzezinski, Carter's assistant for national security. But more broadly it was because Carter took an engineering approach to foreign policy issues, treating each major issue separately without building a coherent overall strategy. While he mastered the details of major negotiations, such as those on strategic arms, he seems to have given little thought to how they might be most effectively presented to the other side.

By the time Carter left office, détente had become a dirty word in Washington. Ronald Reagan, his successor, accused the Soviets of turning it into a "one-way street." That was probably the mildest comment to be heard in the American capital as the New Year dawned in 1981.

Some Cold War Realities

I have touched only a few highlights (or lowlights) of the issues that arose during the Cold War. But let us pause at the end of 1980, when Ronald Reagan was elected president of the United States, and—with the hindsight of decades—consider what conclusions we can draw regarding Cold War thinking and U.S.-Soviet interaction during the thirty-five years immediately following World War II.

1. *The concept of two "superpowers" was overdrawn.*

While the world seemed to be divided between two superpowers confronting each other in powerful alliances, in fact the two sides were not equal in any aspect except the size and effectiveness of their military establishments. The Soviet Union was much weaker in every other category—but neither the United States nor the Soviet Union could exercise complete control over other countries. The "superpower" label exaggerated the power of each.

Nor were the alliances equal. The Warsaw Pact had more conventional arms, but the Soviet Union's allies were captive nations, not willing partners; NATO, by contrast, was a voluntary alliance.* Sometimes, in their lighter and more candid moments, Soviet diplomats would joke that we Americans should have pity on the Soviet Union because it was the only nation in the world surrounded by hostile Communist countries.

2. *The arms race damaged both parties, but unequally.*

The arms race that developed between the United States and the Soviet Union reached absurd magnitudes. Both sides feared that the other would derive advantages—and perhaps even attack—if it gained clear superiority. The buildup of arms was a burden to both sides, not least because it created vast scientific and industrial establishments with vested interests in arms development and production. In the United States, President Eisenhower expressed concern about the influence of the military-industrial complex as he was leaving office, but the problem grew more serious under later presidents. The cost of the arms race brought more distortion and had a much greater impact on the smaller, less efficient Soviet economy than it did on the American economy, but it was a burden to both countries.

3. *Ideology produced a zero-sum mentality in negotiations.*

If the world had been locked in a historically inevitable struggle between antagonistic classes, as Marx, Engels, Lenin, and Stalin believed, there could be no long-term compromise. Every negotiation would be a test of the antagonistic parties' power and will. Any gain for one would be a net loss to the

---

*In the early 1980s I was given a classified briefing on military capabilities of NATO and the Warsaw Pact at NATO headquarters. The figures looked very one-sided, with the Warsaw Pact having substantially more tanks, artillery, aircraft, and men under arms. If one looked only at the numbers, the possibility that NATO could defend itself against a Soviet-sponsored invasion without using nuclear weapons looked questionable. But then I asked the American general who was briefing me what he would do with the non-Soviet forces in the Warsaw Pact if he were the Soviet commander. Would he put them on the front, so that, if war broke out and things went bad, they could defect to the West, or would he station them behind Soviet forces where, if things started going bad, they could turn on the Soviet forces from their rear? Poles, after all, would rather kill Russians than Germans or Americans, and one can imagine that East Germans might also harbor a similar preference. The briefer thought a moment, then commented, "My God, I hadn't thought of that! They would be crazy to start a war!"

other. This attitude made it extremely difficult to come to terms even when both sides wanted a settlement. By the late 1960s, both the American and Soviet leaders wanted to curb the nuclear arms race, but it was hard to reach agreements that both sides considered equal and balanced. The combination of domestic special interests and the ideology-driven zero-sum mentality obstructed practical deals that would have benefited both countries.

4. *Peaceful coexistence did not mean peace.*

After Nikita Khrushchev rose to power, Soviet foreign policy began to stress the concept of "peaceful coexistence." This seemed unexceptionable, even laudable, to many observers in the West. What could be more fair than to live and let live? The problem was that, in the pre-Gorbachev Soviet Union, "peaceful coexistence" did not mean what each word standing alone seemed to mean. It was a code phrase for a set of assumptions that was the antithesis of lasting peace between two ideological systems. The full formulation was "peaceful coexistence between states of different social systems."* A different principle applied if the states had the same social system. One "socialist" state could use force against another socialist state if socialism in the latter was threatened. This idea came to be called the Brezhnev Doctrine, and it provided the logic behind the Soviet interventions in Hungary in 1956, Czechoslovakia in 1968, and Afghanistan in 1979.

That was not the only flaw in the concept. Soviet ideologists held that peaceful coexistence was a necessary tactic for pursuing the international class struggle in a world with nuclear weapons. Since nuclear war would be suicidal, it was not a useful tool in the class struggle. But the struggle continued in every other area. During the détente period of the 1970s, Soviet domestic media frequently reminded the country that there could be no re-

---

*In 1972, when I was director of the Office of Soviet Union Affairs in the State Department, I was assigned the task of negotiating a joint statement to be issued by President Nixon and General Secretary Brezhnev at their upcoming summit meeting. Yuly Vorontsov, Ambassador Anatoly Dobrynin's deputy, handled the negotiations on the Soviet side. Vorontsov offered a draft from Moscow that included an endorsement of "peaceful coexistence." I amplified the statement to read: "peaceful coexistence, irrespective of the similarity or difference of social systems." Vorontsov accepted the change and sent it to Moscow for approval. A few days later he called to say that Moscow would not accept the change I made. "You really trapped me on that one!" he exclaimed, and added in jest, "Now I'll have to take a make-up course in Marxism-Leninism!"

laxation in the field of ideology. So long as that attitude prevailed among the Soviet leadership, the Cold War would have continued even if the arms race had been brought under temporary control.

5. *In the Soviet Union, ideological rigidity was destructive.*

The Marxist-Leninist ideology, combined with the conviction that the Communist Party was the repository of truth and morality, distorted perceptions to the point that the Soviet leaders had difficulty recognizing reality when it diverged from dogma. Not that all were enthusiastic ideologues —after Lenin and Stalin, most paid little attention to ideology as such. But ideology was built into their perception of the world, and "truth" became what fitted the Communist Party line of the day.

Inasmuch as communist ideology defined history as a death struggle of economic classes and predicted that the bourgeois class would be supplanted by a dictatorship of the proletariat, Moscow saw no point in seeking compromise except for short-term, tactical purposes. Even then, the ideology encouraged a zero-sum attitude toward negotiations.

This mentality also fed the conviction that only a Communist government could be a friendly one. The Soviet Union's security demanded that neighboring countries be ruled by Communists. When some Communists tried to assert their independence—first Marshal Tito in Yugoslavia, and then Mao Zedong in China—this was interpreted as apostasy, a falling away from the true socialist faith. Only a Communist-ruled government subservient to Moscow and controlled by Moscow could be a fit partner. Stalin and his successors, right up to Gorbachev's predecessor, Konstantin Chernenko, took the adage "either for us or against us" one step further. It became, in effect, "either our puppet or our enemy."

6. *In the United States, political partisanship was destructive.*

Whenever the nation's dealings with the Soviet Union became a partisan political issue, American interests were damaged. The excesses of McCarthyism and the destructive debate over "who lost China" deprived the United States government of every official with extensive experience in dealing with China. Adjustment to the Chinese Communist victory was much delayed; it took years for the U.S. government to recognize that a Sino-Soviet split had occurred and that it could better manage its relations with the Soviet Union and avoid bloody wars in Asia if it had normal relations with the People's Republic of China.

Throughout much of the postwar period, Republicans argued that Franklin Roosevelt had "sold out" Eastern Europe at the Yalta Conference in 1945. This was not true—the discussion concerned where temporary occupation zones would be established as Hitler's forces were defeated—but the allegation had deep resonance in Eastern Europe, particularly in Czechoslovakia. Edvard Beneš, the postwar Czechoslovak president, wrote in his memoirs that he was convinced there had been a secret deal between Roosevelt and Stalin to place Czechoslovakia under Soviet hegemony.[15] This conviction demoralized the democratic forces in Czechoslovakia and contributed to their capitulation to the Communist coup d'état of February 1948.* American politicians often forget that politically charged arguments at home can have effects abroad that they do not anticipate.

Like the Yalta agreement, the Helsinki Final Act of 1975 was also misrepresented. This time the split was not strictly partisan but primarily within the Republican Party. President Ford was accused of "selling out" Eastern Europe by signing the Helsinki agreement. Yet this agreement played a key role in generating open dissent in the Soviet Union and, once Gorbachev was in charge, in ending many human rights abuses.

Neither party was immune to the temptation to accuse the other of being weak on Communism. During the 1960 election, John Kennedy argued that the United States under Eisenhower had allowed the Soviet Union to open a "missile gap" by building more missiles than the United States. When he took office he found that, in fact, there was a missile gap, but it was actually in America's favor. Similarly, in the 1980 election, Ronald Reagan argued that the United States had fallen behind the Soviet Union in military strength, but the allegations on which he based that claim turned out to be mostly incorrect.

The distortions nurtured by American political campaigns were never as profound or pervasive as the ideology-driven imaginary world in which So-

*Czechoslovakia was the only Eastern European country that came under Communist control not as a result of Soviet occupation but through a seizure of power by Czechoslovak Communists from a divided and demoralized democratic government. When I was U.S. ambassador to Czechoslovakia (1981–1983) I found that Czech intellectuals were still laboring under the illusion that the United States had secretly made a deal with Stalin at Yalta placing them in the Soviet orbit. I undertook a vigorous campaign to set them straight.

viet leaders operated. But they were sufficient to handicap the U.S. government and to drive unnecessary defense spending.

7. *Hypersecrecy created more dangers than it prevented.*

Traditionally, Russians have been excessively secretive out of fear and a sense of vulnerability. Americans, who are inclined to be more open, insist on secrecy to protect technological advantages and the confidentiality of policy discussions. Both have valid reasons to keep some things secret, but both have often exaggerated both the possibility and the need to do so. The closure of much Soviet territory to foreign visitors was intended to cover weakness and to prevent contact between local citizens and foreigners. But the result was to raise unnecessary suspicion and—more important—to deprive Soviet citizens of the knowledge and stimulation that comes from contact with more dynamic and open societies.

In 1980, when Ronald Reagan was elected president of the United States, the Soviet leaders were not only growing older; they were also losing whatever intellectual vitality they might have once possessed. They looked at their society and the world outside with ideological blinkers and seemed incapable of doing more than repeating, as if by rote, the self-defeating policy formulations that had grown up in the give-and-take of Cold War diplomacy.

During his campaign for the presidency, Reagan accused Jimmy Carter of being too soft and trusting in dealing with the Soviets. He promised to increase the American defense budget to reverse what he considered a decline in military capability, and to be more demanding in negotiations with the Soviet Union. Much of the world worried that Reagan's election would bring even greater East-West tensions than those that followed the Soviet invasion of Afghanistan and the withdrawal of the SALT II Treaty from the U.S. Senate. Anyone who predicted that the Cold War would be essentially over when Reagan left office would have been considered utterly delusional.

Why did ending the Cold War by negotiation seem so far-fetched in 1980? There were two unquestioned assumptions: first, that no Soviet leader would be willing or able to change traditional Soviet policy and reform the Soviet system of governance; and second, that Reagan was making impossible demands and was unwilling to negotiate with the Soviet leaders. A close look at what happened between 1981 and 1988 reveals what was wrong with those assumptions—and others as well.

2

Framework Diplomacy:
Reagan's Approach to Gorbachev

WHEN RONALD REAGAN TOOK OFFICE IN 1981, the Cold War seemed as intense as it ever had been. The détente of the 1970s had gradually frayed, then ended abruptly with the Soviet invasion of Afghanistan in 1979. Reagan's anti-Soviet statements suggested to the Soviet leaders—and to much of the public in both countries—that he was not interested in reviving the sort of limited cooperation that had developed during the Nixon and Ford administrations.[1]

His aim was more ambitious. He wanted to put an end to the arms race and reduce weaponry substantially. But that would require a change, not only in Soviet policy, but also in the attitude of the Soviet leadership. Since it was clear that the Soviet Union needed respite from the arms race, Reagan thought that he could convince the Soviet leaders that it was in their own interest to come to an accommodation with the West. Many of his advisers disagreed, arguing that the Soviet system was so rigid that it was incapable of change. Without thinking much about the specifics at first—other than the need to keep America strong—Reagan set out to construct a framework for negotiation that would stress accommodation rather than confrontation. He was intent on negotiation, but determined to do so from strength, not weakness.

While still recovering from an assassination attempt during his first months in office, Reagan drafted a letter to Leonid Brezhnev appealing for "a meaningful and constructive dialogue which will assist us in fulfilling our joint obligation to find lasting peace."[2] Secretary of State Al Haig and many members of his staff advised against sending it, and also against lifting the partial grain embargo imposed by President Carter following the Soviet invasion of Afghanistan. Reagan, however, insisted on lifting the grain embargo because he had promised to do so during the election campaign. He also decided to send a personal letter, written by hand, along with a more formal and bureaucratic typed letter drafted by the State Department.

Brezhnev failed to take advantage of the personal appeal. As Anatoly Dobrynin, then Soviet ambassador in Washington, recalled in his memoirs, "Brezhnev's letter [sent in reply a month later] . . . was cast in the standard polemical form stressing their differences, without any attempt to emphasize the necessity of developing their personal relations. The tone could not possibly have built a personal bridge."[3]

Those who remember Reagan's harsh words about the Soviet Union (he called it an evil empire in one speech, delivered after Brezhnev had brushed off his appeal) and its leaders (who, he said, held to a philosophy that allowed them to lie and cheat to achieve their ends) may think that his rhetoric made accommodation impossible. There is no question that it upset the Soviet leaders, who were accustomed to launching verbal attacks on Western, especially American, leaders with impunity. Nevertheless, Reagan's critics and the Soviet leaders at the time ignored several salient facts:

- Reagan's characterization of the Soviet Union and the habits of its leaders was basically accurate; Soviet personal attacks on American society and its presidents were basically inaccurate.
- Reagan never attacked the Soviet leaders by name, even though he was subject to almost daily vilification in the Soviet media as a warmonger planning to start a nuclear war. Reagan never accused the Soviet leaders of planning to attack the United States, but rather of trying to derive political advantages from a superiority of arms.
- Reagan accompanied his criticism with assurances that "we share the planet" and must find a way to deal with each other in peace.

Nevertheless, Reagan's desire to find an accommodation with the Soviet Union evoked no interest from Moscow during the early years of his presidency.

Soviet Leaders Before Gorbachev

The fundamental problem in dealing with the Soviet leaders before Gorbachev was not Reagan's harsh words, but the dogmatic view those Soviet leaders held of the world, and of their own policy. Though not utter ideologues as Lenin and Stalin had been, they were nevertheless steeped in Marxist-Leninist thinking: the "bourgeois" world was inevitably hostile; insurgencies in the Third World were benign instruments of history leading inexorably to socialism; Soviet security depended on imposing socialist governments on neighboring countries; once a country was declared socialist, the Soviet Union had an obligation to use force to keep its regime in power (the Brezhnev Doctrine); peaceful coexistence was a policy applicable only to states with different social systems (between capitalism and socialism) and did not imply an end to the ideological struggle.[4]

At home, the ideology justified the totalitarian state the Soviet leaders headed: as the vanguard of the proletariat destined to create a socialist, then communist society, the Communist Party of the Soviet Union had a right to dictatorial power. Critics and dissidents were to be silenced, by arrest, or exile if necessary, since opponents of the regime were, by definition, counterrevolutionaries.* (The regime had mellowed since Stalin's time: it no longer executed critics, committed mass murder of innocents, herded millions into forced labor camps, or created mass famines.)

In short, Soviet leaders before Gorbachev were locked mentally in a vicious ideological circle that prevented their perceiving that Soviet policies were not serving the real interests of the Soviet Union. An attentive outsider could see that the regime's problems were growing: a slowing economic growth and—more important—a growing gap between new technologies being developed elsewhere in the world and the prewar technologies that still prevailed in Soviet civilian industries. Nikita Khrushchev had boasted that the Soviet Union would one day catch up with the United States in pro-

---

*This was true even after Nikita Khrushchev declared that the Communist Party of the Soviet Union had become "the party of the whole people" rather than that of the "proletariat" alone. But this formulation rested on the assumption that the bourgeoisie had been eliminated as a class in the Soviet Union. Soviet foreign policy, until 1988, still proceeded from the belief in an international class struggle, with the Soviet Union representing the interests of the proletariat.

duction of coal and steel. It did—but by then nobody cared. Economic destinies were determined by how much information could be stored on a silicon chip, and who could produce and design programs for them most efficiently. Meanwhile, the open-hearth furnaces of Magnitogorsk, built in the 1930s, were still belching orange-colored smoke into the atmosphere. Deteriorating public health—in large part caused by pollution, poor occupational safety, and alcoholism born of despair—was a growing problem despite a regime that promised universal free health care. Life expectancy began to fall—the first time in an industrialized country. When the Cold War ended, male life expectancy in Russia was only about fifty-eight years.

When Brezhnev died in 1982, Reagan tried to signal once again his desire to establish a dialogue with the Soviet leader. He sent Vice President Bush to Moscow for Brezhnev's funeral and went to the Soviet embassy in Washington himself to sign the official book of condolence. Yuri Andropov, the former KGB chief who became Brezhnev's successor, knew that the Soviet Union needed to improve its economic performance, but thought he could solve the problems with a bit of tinkering with management, without fundamental reform. He stubbornly resisted any change in the increasingly dysfunctional Soviet foreign policy, and rebuffed Reagan's suggestions for an improved dialogue.

In fact, U.S.-Soviet relations, at least on the surface, deteriorated sharply during Andropov's tenure as general secretary (1982–1984). Although negotiations had started to reduce both strategic and intermediate-range nuclear missiles, they were getting nowhere. Meanwhile, in March 1983, Reagan made a speech announcing a long-term research and development program to create a defense against ballistic missiles. He called it the Strategic Defense Initiative (SDI), but critics and much of the public referred to it as "Star Wars."* The Soviet leaders took immediate alarm. Although Soviet scientists were conducting similar research secretly, they feared that SDI was part of a strategy to build a defensive shield that would permit the United States to strike the Soviet Union and then defend itself from retaliation.

---

*An inaccurate sobriquet, since the defenses would not necessarily be based in space or utilize exotic technologies.

In September 1983, a Soviet fighter plane shot down a Korean airliner that had strayed into Soviet airspace while it was flying between Anchorage and Seoul. All passengers and crew members, 269 persons including an American congressman, were killed. At first the Soviet authorities denied knowledge of what had happened, and—once the U.S. produced evidence of the shoot-down—charged that the plane was on a spy mission. The accusation was a total fabrication. Reagan was furious. He returned from his ranch in California to deliver a speech he rewrote heavily from the draft I prepared, adding, for example, the charge that the Soviet pilot had committed a massacre.

When the Soviet government refused to accept responsibility for the loss of life, the United States sought and obtained a condemnation in the United Nations and temporary sanctions on Soviet commercial flights to other countries.

Soon after the Korean airliner was destroyed, Andropov withdrew all Soviet negotiators from arms control negotiations. His pretext was the stationing of American intermediate-range nuclear missiles in Europe. Years before, while Jimmy Carter was president, the NATO countries had resolved to react to the deployment of a new class of Soviet missiles in Europe, the SS-20—mobile nuclear-armed missiles, each with three warheads that could reach European NATO capitals in something like five minutes. This constituted an escalation of the potential threat against America's NATO allies and was also contrary to the Nixon-Brezhnev undertaking not to "seek unilateral advantage."

In response, NATO governments decided to initiate negotiations with the USSR in an effort to persuade the Soviet leaders to withdraw or severely reduce the number of these threatening weapons. The allies also decided that the United States should develop comparable weapons for deployment in Europe if the negotiations were not successful. When no agreement was reached by the predetermined date in November 1983, the United States proceeded with the deployment of American missiles. In response, Andropov withdrew from all nuclear arms negotiations and vowed not to resume them so long as American intermediate-range missiles remained in Europe.

Even before this, Andropov had ordered the KGB to conduct what it called "active measures" to prevent Reagan's reelection in 1984.[5] Of course, these orders were secret, but Andropov made his view public when he issued a statement in the fall of 1983 that if there had ever been illusions that the Soviet government could deal with the Reagan administration, it was then clear that the illusion had no foundation.[6] Meanwhile, Andropov, already on a dialysis machine because of a kidney ailment, had only a few months to live.

Andropov's successor, Konstantin Chernenko, a crony of Brezhnev who had few if any additional perquisites for high office, proved equally unable to shift Soviet policy to a more productive track. Soviet citizens, and the rest of the world, waited impatiently for a younger, more capable leader to take charge.

Reagan's Approach

Concerned with his inability to engage the Soviet leader in a substantive dialogue, and learning to his surprise that the Soviet leaders feared that he might be planning a nuclear attack, toward the end of 1983 Reagan asked me to draft a speech that would stress his desire to negotiate a substantial reduction of nuclear weapons, and to find ways to cooperate with the Soviet Union on issues of common interest.[7] Hitherto, most of his comments on U.S.-Soviet relations had been sporadic and the public had misunderstood his approach. The media had concentrated on his comments critical of the Soviet system and paid little attention to his statements revealing his desire to end the arms race, reduce substantially the number of nuclear weapons, and find ways to cooperate with the Soviet Union in areas where our interests coincided.

The speech Reagan delivered on January 16, 1984, identified four major areas where the United States and Soviet Union needed to improve cooperation in the interests of both countries.[8] While noting the various problems in the relationship, the speech emphasized the need to cooperate to reduce arms, to withdraw from proxy conflicts in third countries, to protect human rights, and to "improve the working relationship"—a euphemism for raising the Iron Curtain and allowing people and ideas to flow unimpeded across the East-West divide.

None of the specific goals cited in the speech were new to U.S. foreign policy, but three features distinguished it from previous statements by American leaders.

· The goals were designed to be consistent with the national interests of a peaceful Soviet Union.
· The goals were couched in terms of cooperation, not demands that the Soviet Union make unilateral concessions. Although the substance of the issues would require the Soviet Union to make more changes in its practices than the United States, the approach was reciprocal, an appeal to work together to improve human rights protection, reduce arms, diminish regional conflict, and improve communication.
· Reagan made no rigid linkage between issues, but he pointed out that progress on any one of the goals would be influenced by what happened on others; in other words, arms reduction—the principal Soviet interest —would not get very far until the other problems were addressed constructively.

Subsequently, using both public statements and direct communications with the Soviet leaders, Reagan provided further details on each of the points in the January 1984 speech, but that speech offered a capsule summary of his Soviet policy through the rest of his administration. Reagan's assumption was that the Soviet leaders were encountering increasing difficulties at home, particularly with the economy, and that Soviet commitments abroad to insurgencies and revolutionary regimes were sapping Soviet strength and creating dangers without tangible benefit. In short, much Soviet foreign policy was detrimental to the country's real interests. If the ailing Soviet leaders of 1983 and 1984 were unable to grasp that fundamental fact, it was hoped that a younger, more pragmatic leader would succeed them.

As it turned out, Reagan was, in effect, preparing for Gorbachev. Most American journalists, however, attributed what seemed to be a change in Reagan's Soviet policy to election-year politics. Those elements in the Reagan administration who opposed realistic negotiation with the Soviet Union, including the neoconservatives, leaked stories to the media that Reagan was not serious. Consequently, the American public gave the speech less attention than it deserved. The Soviet leadership chose to disregard it altogether. On Foreign Minister Andrei Gromyko's orders, the Soviet press dismissed it as containing "no indication of any positive changes in the Reagan administration's approach."[9]

The Gorbachev Difference

In 1985, when Mikhail Gorbachev came to power as general secretary of the Communist Party of the Soviet Union, most observers, in and out of the Soviet Union, recognized that Gorbachev, a generation younger and much healthier and better educated than his predecessors, would be a more active and effective leader. It was not hard for him to look like an improvement over his predecessors. As Dusko Doder, the correspondent of the *Washington Post* in Moscow, observed, "He walks, he talks, and his suits fit." Nevertheless, there was uncertainty whether this would be good or bad for the United States and its Western allies. Lacking some of his predecessors' weaknesses, would Gorbachev not be more dangerous than the leaders he replaced? If his goal was to make the Soviet Union more efficient and powerful in order to carry out its traditional foreign policy (as William Casey, the director of central intelligence, and Robert Gates, his deputy, argued), then there was no hope of a lasting accommodation; at best, one could aim to manage the competition so that it did not get out of hand and blow us all up. Margaret Thatcher, the prime minister of Great Britain, who had met Gorbachev a few months before he succeeded Chernenko in the top Soviet post, was of a different opinion. She announced to the world that Gorbachev was "a man we can do business with."

President Reagan hoped she was right, and as soon as he heard that Gorbachev had been selected by the Communist Party Central Committee to be its general secretary, he sent an invitation to Gorbachev to visit the United States. Vice President Bush, who traveled to Moscow to attend Chernenko's funeral, delivered it personally. Gorbachev agreed to meet, but not to come to Washington; subsequently it was decided that Reagan and Gorbachev would meet in Geneva, Switzerland, in November.

From March 1985 until his first meeting with Reagan in November, Gorbachev had to spend most of his energy consolidating his power in the Soviet Union. In order to gain control over Soviet foreign policy, he needed to replace Andrei Gromyko, the longtime Soviet foreign minister who had earned the sobriquet "Mr. Nyet," with someone who could put a smile on the face of Soviet diplomacy. This Gorbachev contrived to do by moving Gromyko up-stairs to the prestigious but powerless position of chairman of the Presid-ium of the USSR Supreme Soviet—the nominal chief of state. Gromyko had requested this "promotion," assuming that his principal deputy, Georgy Kor-niyenko, would be appointed to succeed him and that he would continue to control foreign policy decisions.[10] But instead of replacing Gromyko with Korniyenko, Gorbachev reached outside the Soviet foreign policy establish-ment and named his friend Eduard Shevardnadze, the Communist Party boss in Soviet Georgia, to take over the Ministry of Foreign Affairs.

From his first meeting with George Shultz, the American secretary of state, at the end of July 1985, Shevardnadze seemed personally reasonable and conciliatory, in sharp contrast to his predecessor. Nevertheless, the change in manner did not yet reflect a change of policy. It took time for Gor-bachev to consolidate his power in Moscow, to realize fully that the policies he had inherited did not serve Soviet interests, and to decide how to go about changing things.

While Gorbachev was dealing with his opponents in the Soviet leader-ship, Reagan was studying the Soviet Union and Gorbachev. Feeling that his knowledge was sketchy, Reagan made time, almost daily, for briefings and discussions. I organized for him the equivalent of a college course on the Soviet Union, with emphasis on relevant history, culture, and—espe-cially—the psychology of the Soviet leaders in general and of Mikhail Gor-bachev in particular. Reagan consulted not only his own staff and officials from the State Department and Central Intelligence Agency, but scholars including James Billington, the librarian of Congress and specialist in Rus-sian history, Suzanne Massie, the author of a cultural history of Russia, and Harvard professor Nina Tumarkin, who wrote about political imagery and the use of propaganda.

He also authorized negotiations with the Soviet Union on more than a score of cooperative projects, including renewal of the agreement on cul-tural, educational, and athletic exchanges that had lapsed during Jimmy Carter's presidency. Reagan requested a substantial expansion of contacts, especially those involving college undergraduates and high school students, who had been excluded (by the Soviet government) from earlier agreements.

Reagan considered his proposal a test of whether Gorbachev was willing to allow more contact between ordinary Soviet and American citizens.

In an attempt to bypass the zero-sum psychology that had come to predominate in U.S.-Soviet negotiations, Reagan made sure that ideas for expanded people-to-people contacts were first made to Soviet officials in private, with a request for their comment and additional suggestions. Only when there seemed to be general agreement did he announce his proposals to the public. He hoped to get all U.S.-Soviet negotiations on a confidential track, at least in their early stages, to avoid premature public disputes and the confrontational mindset that had doomed President Carter's "deep cuts" proposal in 1977. Too often, when opposing positions were publicized early in a negotiation, the negotiations were viewed as sporting events, with each side gaining or losing points—obviously not a propitious atmosphere for workable compromises.

Gorbachev turned out to be unexpectedly forthcoming regarding the proposals for expanded exchanges and more cooperative projects, but U.S. and Soviet positions on nuclear arms reduction remained far apart. Before he left Washington for the meeting with Gorbachev in Geneva, Reagan wrote out on a yellow legal pad his thoughts regarding the upcoming meeting.[11] In it he anticipated that Gorbachev would be a tough negotiator who would try to split the United States from its allies in Europe, but that negotiation should be possible because of Gorbachev's need to tame the arms race. Reagan considered protection of human rights extremely important, but something that should be pursued in private in order to facilitate Gorbachev's cooperation. He welcomed the anticipated agreement to expand contacts and cultural exchanges, but considered "security issues like arms control, the regional areas of conflict and the prevalent suspicion and hostility between us" the main topics with which he would be dealing.* He mused that he should let Gor-

---

*Lest these three priorities seem obvious, even anodyne, it should be recalled that the Soviet position was that an arms control agreement (on Soviet terms) was necessary before anything else in the relationship could be improved, that conflict in the Third World was not a proper subject for negotiation, or even discussion, since it was only the inevitable march of history, and that distrust and suspicion were also unavoidable between countries that represented the interests of opposing economic classes (proletariat versus bourgeoisie, in Marxist terms).

bachev know in private that, if they could not reach "a solid, verifiable arms reduction agreement," an arms race would ensue that the Soviet Union was bound to lose. But he concluded his notes by writing: "Let there be no talk of winners and losers. Even if we think we won, to say so would set us back."

Rocky Road to Mutual Trust

The first meeting did not remove the "suspicion and hostility" between Reagan and Gorbachev. In fact, Gorbachev reported to his colleagues when he returned to Moscow that Reagan came across as a "political dinosaur."* Reagan had expected Gorbachev to be a vigorous negotiator, but hoped to initiate a process of better communication with periodic meetings and private correspondence, backed up by frequent meetings of the foreign ministers, George Shultz and Eduard Shevardnadze. Therefore, Reagan was delighted when Gorbachev accepted his invitation to visit the United States in 1986 and invited Reagan to pay a return visit to Moscow in 1987.

These meetings, however, did not occur as agreed in Geneva. When Reagan tried to pin Gorbachev down on his promised visit to Washington, Gorbachev objected that they needed to make sure they could sign a major arms control agreement when he came. "One get-acquainted meeting is fine," he said, but the next meeting would be considered a failure if it did not produce a commitment to reduce arms. Reagan suspected that Gorbachev was trying to pressure him to sign a bad agreement and refused to modify the American negotiating position until he saw some Soviet concessions.

For the most part, Reagan and Gorbachev talked past each other in late 1985 and early 1986. Just after returning from the Geneva meeting, Reagan sent Gorbachev a letter I drafted inviting him to discuss two key issues: how to ensure that research on missile defense would not threaten the other country, and how to arrange a Soviet withdrawal from Afghanistan without creating insecurity on the Soviet southern border.[12] Gorbachev gave unyielding replies to both proposals, but in January 1986 he made a proposal for nuclear weapons reduction that seemed impractical. Reagan's staff drew

---

*Gorbachev jokes about this now. In January 2008, he remarked during a speech at Harvard University that after their first meeting he called Reagan a political dinosaur, while Reagan was convinced that Gorbachev was a dyed-in-the-wool Bolshevik.

the conclusion that the proposal was propaganda, not least because it was announced to the world before Reagan had a chance to consider it and react to it. It seemed to be the old game of public one-upsmanship rather than a serious proposal for negotiation.[13]

Gorbachev's staff also considered the proposal largely propaganda, but, along with several unacceptable proposals, it contained a new element that grabbed Reagan's attention: a stated goal of eliminating nuclear weapons by the end of 1999. Reagan overruled the initial staff recommendation to reject Gorbachev's proposal outright and insisted that the U.S. praise the idea of eventually eliminating nuclear weapons. Gorbachev had suddenly—and perhaps inadvertently—found the key to dealing with Reagan.

People who confined their attention to Reagan's statements about the dangers of communism and the threat of Soviet aggression missed a very important feature of his view of the world. One of his most deeply held convictions was an abhorrence of nuclear weapons. This was clear to all of us who worked closely with him on these issues, but you don't have to take our word for it. Here is how Reagan himself described his attitude toward nuclear weapons at the beginning of his presidency:

> Even if a nuclear war did not mean the extinction of mankind, it would certainly mean the end of civilization as we know it.
>
> *No one* could "win" a nuclear war. Yet as long as nuclear weapons were in existence, there would always be risks they would be used, and once the first nuclear weapon was unleashed, who knew where it would end?
>
> My dream, then, became a world free of nuclear weapons.[14]

Having stated his dream, Reagan pointed out in his memoirs that some advisers, including those in the Pentagon, "did not share this dream." But that did not deter him. "For the eight years I was president I never let my dream of a nuclear-free world fade from my mind," he wrote. Those of us who worked with him in developing and implementing his policy toward the Soviet Union can testify to the validity of that statement; his foreign policy had no greater goal than that of setting the world on a path that would free it from the danger nuclear weapons constitute by their very existence.[15]

It is hard to say how sincere Gorbachev was when he proposed that the U.S. and USSR eliminate their nuclear weapons before the twentieth century ended, but a few months after he made the proposal, an accident at a

Soviet nuclear power plant would have made him a true believer even if he had not been earlier.

Chernobyl: An Accident with Multiple Fallout

During the early morning hours of April 26, 1986, a reactor at the Chernobyl nuclear power plant in Ukraine exploded. A plume of highly radioactive particles rose and spread over the western Soviet Union and eastern and northern Europe, and then was detected even in North America. The first alarms that something serious had happened came from Scandinavia, not from the Soviet government or media. It took hours before the Soviet media mentioned that an accident had occurred, and for days no clear instructions were given to the hundreds of thousands of people living in the area of the greatest contamination.

It has been estimated that the Chernobyl explosion created thirty to forty times the radioactive fallout as that produced by the atomic bomb dropped on Hiroshima in 1945. According to Soviet statistics, more than three hundred thousand people had to be evacuated and relocated, and agricultural land was contaminated in a huge swath of territory extending right through Scandinavia.

Radioactive fallout from the power plant killed and shortened the lives of many people and changed for the worse that of many more. It polluted areas, particularly in Belarus, that could not be safely used for decades. But radioactivity was not the only fallout. For the Soviet leadership, damage from the political fallout was even more severe, even if longer delayed.

Chernobyl was a disaster for the regime in several ways. It demonstrated in the most painful form the weaknesses of central planning and unsafe work conditions that permeated Soviet industrialization. The Chernobyl reactor was faulty in design, with too few fail-safe features; the human errors that led to the explosion exposed sloppy work habits and disregard of safety that were widespread throughout the economy. Even more damning was the Communist Party's reaction to the disaster: silence, cover-up, followed by scraps of information doled out too late to help those most affected. In the past, the Soviet authorities had been able to hush up major man-made accidents, but the scale of this one and the fact that radioactivity escaped the borders of the Soviet Union made that impossible this time.

The failure of Soviet bureaucrats and Communist Party officials to deal promptly, efficiently, and openly with the tragedy brought home to Gorbachev as never before the country's desperate need for fundamental reform. For the population as a whole, it highlighted the incompetence and self-serving arrogance of their Communist masters. It was one of the important sparks that started the political conflagration that eventually brought down the Soviet Union.

Chernobyl also brought home to Gorbachev—even if he had not been convinced before—that a goal of eliminating nuclear weapons was in the interest of the Soviet Union and of humanity as a whole. Subsequently, in 1989 and 1990, General Dmitri Yazov, Gorbachev's defense minister, would explain why in private meetings. He said that before the Chernobyl accident, he had thought that if a nuclear war should occur, the Soviet Union could prevail. Chernobyl, however, convinced him that no one could prevail in a nuclear war. In fact, any war between nuclear powers should be unthinkable. One side would not have to use nuclear weapons to devastate the other—they could do so by simply bombing nuclear power plants.[16]

The Summit in Reykjavík

After several months of sparring in early 1986 and a few months to absorb the lessons of Chernobyl, Gorbachev proposed a short meeting to identify an arms reduction agreement he could sign in a subsequent visit to Washington. During the meeting in the Icelandic capital, Reykjavík, Reagan and Gorbachev came near to agreeing on what might have been the most sweeping arms control agreement in history: a 50 percent reduction of strategic weapons in five years, then the elimination of all strategic nuclear weapons—perhaps all nuclear weapons—in ten years.* But Gorbachev demanded that research on strategic missile defense be confined to laboratories, a condition Reagan rejected because he believed it would kill the program he had espoused. This was not the only disagreement: Gorbachev refused to consider Reagan's proposal to eliminate ballistic missiles. Reagan was willing to settle for a treaty incorporating those elements they had

---

*The transcript of the conversation is not entirely clear on this point; at times they spoke of strategic nuclear weapons, at other times of "all nuclear weapons."

agreed on (eliminating intermediate-range nuclear weapons in Europe and reducing strategic arsenals by half), but Gorbachev rejected the idea of any treaty that did not include his demand to confine missile-defense research to laboratories. The meeting broke up with both Reagan and Gorbachev angry at each other.

Within a few months, however, negotiations were resumed, not only on arms reduction, but on the other items on the American agenda. That agenda, in fact, became a joint agenda, and by December 1987, when Gorbachev finally visited the United States, he and Reagan signed a treaty to eliminate their nuclear-armed missiles with a range of five hundred to twenty-five hundred kilometers, and also to extensive on-site inspection to insure that both sides executed the agreement faithfully.

Agreements in other areas began to come to fruition. An agreement to remove Soviet troops from Afghanistan within a year was completed in April 1988. Equally important, Gorbachev's internal reforms began to affect some of the fundamental features of the Communist Party's totalitarian rule. Just before Reagan paid a return visit to Moscow in May 1988, Gorbachev issued a set of propositions for the upcoming Communist Party Conference. All were aimed at a democratization of the state structure; there was no whiff of Marxist-Leninist ideology in them. I read the Russian text of these proposals, called Theses, in Helsinki, where the Reagans had paused for two days before visiting Moscow. I told Reagan that the changes proposed were fundamental: if they were adopted and implemented, the Soviet Union would never be the same.[17] Something was occurring, the possibility of which virtually every Western specialist on the Soviet Union had long excluded: an attempt by the Soviet leader to alter the very basis of the Soviet system.

Reagan and Gorbachev's Perestroika

Reagan was able finally to visit Moscow officially in May 1988, during his last year in office. From his first term, he had dreamed of showing the Soviet leader the United States and then visiting the Soviet Union so that he could communicate his desire for peace to Soviet citizens. Now, this dream had come true. He was received by ordinary Soviet citizens, particularly the young, as a hero. His speech to the students at Moscow University, a paean to the virtues of freedom, elicited an ecstatic response.[18] Svetlana Savranskaya, who subsequently earned a Ph.D. at Emory University, was one of the students in the audience. She recalls the reaction of Reagan's listeners:

> Students were surprised to see a smiling, eloquent and very human U.S. President who was always portrayed by the official sources as an aggressive anti-Soviet ideologue. His speech was most impressive for us, unaccustomed to public discussion of human rights and democratic values. But most of all, talking to each other as we filed out of the room, we were touched by his obvious warmth and sense of humor, and the sparkle in his eyes as he answered the questions from the audience. For many of us, I know, the Cold War ended in that very room during Reagan's address to the students—after that experience nobody could persuade me that Reagan was a proponent of nuclear war, that U.S.-Soviet conflict was inevitable. Just the opposite, we were all enveloped in a new sensation of confidence and hope for the end of arms race, and for real friendship between our two countries.[19]

Reagan also made a deep impression on Soviet intellectuals when he spoke to a group of the most prominent at the Soviet Writers' Club, and to the Soviet people as a whole in several televised presentations. And then, inevitably, while strolling on Red Square with Gorbachev, he was asked by journalists if he still considered the Soviet Union an evil empire.

"No," he replied, "that was another time, another era."

"And who is responsible?" came the next question.

"Mr. Gorbachev. He's the leader of this country."

Gorbachev writes in his memoirs that this was a powerful endorsement of his reform plans, already called *perestroika*, or "restructuring."

The Party Conference that followed Reagan's visit approved most of the democratizing measures Gorbachev had proposed.

Parting as Partners

In December 1988, Gorbachev came to New York to address the United Nations and to have a last meeting with Reagan while he was still president. George Bush had been elected to succeed Reagan but would not be inaugurated until January 1989. On December 7, 1988, Gorbachev publicly called off the ideological Cold War. Most observers were struck by his promise to reduce Soviet armed forces by a half million men without seeking any reduction by the United States or NATO. But persons familiar with communist ideology noted that he also rejected a principle that had served as the foundation of Soviet foreign policy since the Bolshevik Revolution. In speaking of the "common interests of mankind" and proclaiming that there could be no limit on a country's right to choose its system of government, he discarded the concept of the international class struggle, and its corollary, the Brezhnev Doctrine.

Following his speech to the United Nations, Gorbachev met with Vice President Bush (then president-elect) and President Reagan on Governors Island in New York. The meeting was entirely harmonious, marred only by the news of a devastating earthquake in Soviet Armenia. Reagan wrote in his diary that evening that he had the feeling they left each other as "partners in making a better world."[20]

When he returned to Moscow, Gorbachev told his Politburo colleagues that Reagan had informed him that he prayed to God that his successor would follow his policies. Gorbachev was not certain President-elect Bush would do so, but he used that as an argument to insist that his promise to reduce the size of the Soviet armed forces be implemented without delay. The Soviet Union, Gorbachev argued, must preempt any attempt by the "military-industrial complex" in the West to revive the arms race.[21]

In 1989, Gorbachev acted on his promises to the United Nations with a rapidity and decisiveness that amazed the world.

How They Did It

No one can look closely at what happened in the negotiations between Reagan and Gorbachev without noting that, over time, despite repeated verbal tussles, sharp arguments, and occasional outbursts of real anger, these two very different people, the leaders of very different countries who had come to power in very different ways, developed a personal relationship not only of mutual respect but of genuine warmth. This fact may lead some to argue that international problems can be solved if only political leaders develop a personal friendship. That is not a conclusion I would draw. There are countless examples in history of political leaders whose cordial personal relations failed to prevent tension, even war, between their countries (most notably the close fellowship between Tsar Nicholas II of Russia and Kaiser

Wilhelm II of Germany before the outbreak of World War I). Personal relations can take leaders only so far. They are not decisive, and it is not always
possible or appropriate to seek warmth in ties with foreign dictators.

Nevertheless, leaders of countries that are at odds with each other have little hope of solving problems short of violence if they do not communicate
with one other, with personal respect and in good faith. Reagan was correct
when he wrote just before meeting Gorbachev for the first time that one of
the three big issues with the Soviet Union was the "distrust and suspicion"
that prevailed. He was determined to find a way to overcome that if he could,
without compromising America's vital interests.

Reagan knew very well that cordiality alone was not enough. He had to
convince Gorbachev, among other things, that the United States was not trying to break up the Soviet Union or to use arms reduction in order to create
a military advantage. Many of his advisers thought that the Soviet Union
was impervious to outside influence, incapable of reform, and therefore that
the U.S. should try to bring maximum pressure, military, political, economic, and ideological, on the regime until it cracked. They also thought
that the United States was strong and productive enough that it could create and maintain a military edge over the Soviet Union.

Reagan rejected both of these propositions. Toward the end of 1983, when
he was formulating his plans for negotiating with the Soviet leaders, he
asked me to make sure that U.S. officials did not question the legitimacy of
the Soviet regime. He wanted to change Soviet behavior and lower weaponry
to equivalent levels, as low as the Soviet Union would accept, but understood that Gorbachev could not accept inferiority. Also, as Reagan supervised development of a plan for negotiation, he frequently admonished his
staff not to ask the Soviet leader for any concession that would harm his
country's interest, so long as it was willing to live in peace with the rest of
the world.

Of course, trust did not come automatically. There was ample room for
misunderstanding, particularly since self-styled "hard-liners" in his administration kept leaking stories to favored journalists that Reagan was not really
serious.[22]

The turning point in the Reagan-Gorbachev relationship occurred at their
meeting in Reykjavík, Iceland, in October 1986. Though each was angry

with the other when it concluded, in time each looked back and realized that his counterpart was trying to achieve the same thing he sought: eliminating the threat of nuclear weapons. This was the overriding issue that eventually created a personal bond that persisted in spite of their disagreement over Reagan's Strategic Defense Initiative.

In his autobiography, Reagan summed up his view of Gorbachev as follows: "I liked Gorbachev even though he was a dedicated Communist and I was a confirmed capitalist. But he was different from the Communists who had preceded him to the top of the Kremlin hierarchy. . . . He was the first not to push Soviet expansionism, the first to agree to destroy nuclear weapons, the first to suggest a free market and to support open elections and the freedom of expression."[23]

Since the end of the Cold War, I have attended several conferences with Mikhail Gorbachev. If any participants made disparaging statements regarding Reagan—calling him an intellectual lightweight or worse—Gorbachev always leapt to Reagan's defense, pointing out that he was, in Gorbachev's view, a "man of vision and sound political judgment."

A Team Effort

An atmosphere of increasing respect and trust between the top leaders can help change the climate of an international relationship, but it is not likely to produce concrete results unless it penetrates the power structure of both countries. Reagan and Gorbachev both set an example for subordinates that helped transform the U.S.-Soviet relationship from a testy, zero-sum contest conducted, largely from a distance, by two impersonal bureaucracies, to one of growing understanding and cooperation by responsible officials in the upper reaches of both countries' governments.

George Shultz and Eduard Shevardnadze led the way, and in time others followed with their encouragement. Shortly after the first Reagan-Gorbachev meeting in Geneva, while I was responsible for Soviet affairs on the National Security Council staff, I suggested that the State Department establish regular meetings between assistant secretaries of state responsible for the various regions of the world and their Soviet counterparts. I did not expect immediate results, since U.S. and Soviet policies in most regions were in conflict. But I thought that frank discussions of the issues and of the policies both countries had adopted might in time reveal ways to diminish the confrontations.

Secretary of State Shultz accepted my recommendation, but when he asked his assistant secretaries to arrange regular meetings with their Soviet counterparts, some objected. The assistant secretary of state for American republic affairs strongly opposed dealing with his Soviet counterpart; he objected to any discussion of matters in "our" hemisphere with Soviet officials. Nevertheless, Shultz insisted, and the consultations began on a regular basis. A few years later, they produced an agreement to end the conflict in Nicaragua. Other regional consultations ended the Soviet occupation of Afghanistan and the Soviet and Cuban military involvement in the civil war in Angola. Once both countries accepted that their interests were best served by peace rather than providing military backing to one side or the other, constructive moves were possible. The consultations did not (and could not) solve all the local problems, but they progressively removed U.S.-Soviet military competition from Third World areas.

Subsequently, we established regular consultations on other sensitive topics as well, including protection of human rights. Assistant Secretary of State Richard Schifter met regularly with Deputy Foreign Minister Anatoly Adamishin to discuss and resolve human rights abuses.[24]

Extensive contacts, from the top to at least the middle level of the foreign affairs bureaucracies, bore fruit in another sense: they gave the leaders of both countries a more accurate understanding of their "adversaries" than their respective intelligence organizations were able to provide. The CIA leaders, but not all analysts, were still telling Reagan and Shultz in 1987 and 1988 that Gorbachev wanted to strengthen the Soviet Union to carry out its traditional aggressive policies more successfully.* But Reagan and Shultz sensed from the reports sent by the American embassy in Moscow and from

---

*Broadly speaking, those analysts and observers who had direct experience living and working in the Soviet Union were more alert to the possibility of change than were those whose careers had been largely elsewhere and whose knowledge, therefore, was more abstract and theoretical. Also, specialists in Soviet internal affairs often grasped the significance of changes more quickly than did those who directed their attention principally to Soviet foreign or military policy.

their personal contact with Gorbachev and Shevardnadze that, in fact, Gorbachev had different aims in mind.

Both Reagan and Shultz made sure that the United States had a strong embassy of capable, experienced Russian-speaking diplomats in Moscow. They might send to other countries political appointees whose principal virtue derived from their financial support of electoral campaigns, but not to Moscow. The embassy in Moscow was entrusted to professionals, and both Reagan and Shultz listened carefully to what their diplomats had to report and kept them in the policy loop so that they could serve as reliable American voices in the Soviet Union.

American diplomats in Moscow and Leningrad, observing the degree to which the Soviet Union was opening up and changing, reported that Gorbachev was a new sort of leader who should not be judged by stereotypes from the past. Reagan and Shultz placed more credence in the reports of their representatives in the Soviet Union—which reinforced their own instincts—than in the speculations of intelligence analysts sitting in Langley, Virginia, most with little direct experience living in or dealing with the Soviet Union.

Gorbachev and Shevardnadze followed a similar practice. Soon after taking over the Foreign Ministry, Shevardnadze began to rely primarily on those diplomats who knew the United States well, rather than on more senior officials who shared Gromyko's pattern of thinking. He placed American specialists Alexander Bessmertnykh and Yuly Vorontsov in key positions to advise him on dealing with the United States. Both had spent much of their careers in the Soviet embassy in Washington and were versed in American English, not just in the language but in the American way of thinking as well. He brought Sergei Tarasenko, a more junior American specialist, into his office as his personal assistant.

Gorbachev named Anatoly Chernyaev as his foreign policy assistant—roughly the counterpart (though with less bureaucratic authority) of the American president's assistant for national security. Chernyaev was not a specialist on the United States, but he was not an acolyte of traditional Soviet foreign policy. His memoirs reveal strong skepticism about the utility and morality of the usual Soviet way of conducting its foreign affairs. He proved to be a vigorous proponent of change.

Each in his own way, Reagan and Gorbachev organized the upper levels of their foreign affairs agencies to advise them how to emerge from the fruitless and dangerous competition that had plagued U.S.-Soviet relations and weakened both countries. Without creating new institutions or bureaucracies in either country, the American and Soviet leaders relied on a select group of officials dedicated to the task of putting the Cold War to rest, for the benefit of both countries.

After a few months of hesitation, George Bush followed Reagan's example, and his secretary of state, James A. Baker III, was as successful as George Shultz had been in bonding with Shevardnadze.

How Did the Myths Arise?

Before we return to an examination of what the end of the Cold War should teach us, we should take another look at the myths that have arisen. Widespread misunderstandings doubtless have multiple causes, but when it comes to the way the Cold War ended, distortions of events by those in the Reagan administration who opposed realistic negotiations, who doubted that the Soviet Union could change, and who ridiculed the idea that personal relationships could play a useful role have been major contributors to historical falsehoods.[25] Each time there was a crisis of some sort, they advised Reagan to terminate negotiations in order to "punish" the Soviet Union for impermissible behavior. In their eyes, merely talking to Soviet leaders directly was a form of endorsement. They considered Soviet leaders immune to reasonable discourse and feared that Communist adversaries would only draw strength from "recognition" by decent leaders of democratic countries.

Reagan rejected this approach. He believed in communication, and believed that refusing to talk was a sign of weakness, not of strength. After all, whenever the Soviet leaders pulled out of a negotiating forum, they lost. When Andropov withdrew Soviet diplomats from the arms control negotiations following the deployment of Pershing II missiles in Germany, he thought he was encouraging Reagan's defeat in the 1984 presidential election. As it turned out, it helped ensure Reagan's reelection, since it conveyed to the American people that it was not Reagan's fault that the United States was unable to reach an agreement to reduce arms.

I had my own direct experience, from time to time, with those who felt that communicating with the Soviet leadership—or even going to the Soviet Union in order to communicate with the Soviet public—was somehow a favor to Communists, a compromise with evil. In 1986, when I was still responsible for European and Soviet affairs on the NSC staff, I was invited to lead a group of American officials to a meeting in the Soviet Union where we would debate the issues in the U.S.-Soviet relationship before a large gathering of Soviet citizens, a few hundred visiting Americans, and television cameras. I accepted, considering the meeting a test of how far Gorbachev was willing to go in allowing Soviet citizens direct access to Western ideas. I planned a hard-hitting speech explaining why Soviet policies were blocking accommodation and cooperation between our countries.

The meeting had been planned by the Chautauqua Institution in upstate New York, which had sponsored two debates by Soviet and American officials on its own premises. The meeting in the Soviet Union—actually in Soviet-occupied Latvia—was a return invitation without precedent. Up to then, Soviet officials had not invited foreigners to come to the Soviet Union and speak on Soviet television unless they were considered sympathetic to Soviet policies. This time, they invited the Americans to express the views of their government frankly and guaranteed that the speeches would be televised.

For some Americans, the idea of going to a conference in Soviet-occupied Latvia was repugnant, but we decided that the opportunity to communicate directly with Latvians and other Soviet citizens was too important to pass up. Among other things, we could make clear to the Latvians and their Baltic neighbors that the United States did not recognize the legality of their incorporation into the Soviet Union. We made one condition to our Soviet hosts: we would go to Jūrmala only if the Soviets issued visas to three young Latvian Americans to accompany our group. They agreed, and it seemed in September that we might have the first opportunity since President Nixon's summit meetings to explain American policy on Soviet television.

The meeting, however, almost did not come off. When the Soviet authorities arrested Nicholas Daniloff, an American journalist, in retaliation for the arrest of a Soviet spy in New York, the American participants were outraged. Daniloff, we knew very well, was an innocent journalist, not a spy, and no one wanted to visit the Soviet Union while he was held in prison. A few days before we were to leave Washington, however, Daniloff was released to the custody of Richard Combs, the American chargé in Moscow. It seemed to most of us that boycotting the meeting in Jūrmala would serve no useful purpose—the Soviet authorities were running a certain risk in allowing us to come and express our views publicly; threatening to stay away provided no leverage to assist Nicholas Daniloff. Nevertheless, three of our group of speakers refused to go: Jeane Kirkpatrick, the former U.S. ambassador to the United Nations, Alan Keyes, an assistant secretary of state, and Richard Perle, an assistant secretary of defense.

As Kirkpatrick explained to me, she was unwilling to honor the Soviet Union with her presence so long as Daniloff was not allowed to leave the country. I explained that it was possibly a unique opportunity to communicate with the Soviet people—to make clear that much of the official propaganda was false. She was unbending. Merely going to the Soviet Union, in her view, was a favor to an evil regime. Perle took much the same line, arguing that his boss, Caspar Weinberger, would not understand his participation under the circumstances. The organizers quickly located prominent replacements, but they told me the trip would be canceled unless I agreed to go as the lead American speaker.

The issue suddenly became a subject of public debate inside the Washington Beltway. I felt that I should not go unless the president wanted me to, so I asked John Poindexter, the national security adviser, to check with him. The word came back that Reagan thought I ought to go. "It is an opportunity to communicate with the Soviet people that we shouldn't miss," he explained to Poindexter.

I told the group that I would go. That evening, Robert Novak complained on one of the Friday evening television talk shows that Jack Matlock, a senior official in the Reagan White House, was violating U.S. nonrecognition policy by going to a conference in occupied Latvia and also, by this trip, undermining efforts to secure Nicholas Daniloff's release.

So what happened? I went to Jūrmala, gave a speech partly in Latvian and partly in Russian, which among other things pointed out to the people in Latvia, Estonia, and Lithuania that the United States did not recognize their incorporation in the Soviet Union. It was televised locally and created a sensation, particularly the part I delivered in the Latvian language. Latvians, like Estonians and Lithuanians, were worried that they had been forgotten; many thought that Americans considered all Soviet citizens Russians. Now they heard a senior American official who was not of Latvian descent speaking their language. So Americans *did* understand that not everyone in the Soviet Union was Russian! And, more important, the United States did not recognize that they had legally been taken into the Soviet Union. This was the most sensational part for most who heard the speech.

Ten years later, Latvians who had attended the Jūrmala conference came to Chautauqua and explained that the movement that brought independence to Latvia in the final months of the Soviet Union got its start when they heard the American speeches in 1986. Dainis Ivans, the leader of the Latvian People's Front, explained: "We suddenly understood that we were not alone; if the United States did not recognize that we were legally part of the Soviet Union, we had a chance!"

Two of the most valued awards that I have received include one from the Association of Baltic Americans for my contribution to Baltic independence, and an honorary doctorate from the now independent Latvian Academy of Sciences, awarded on an anniversary of my speech in Jūrmala.*

Charges against Nicholas Daniloff were soon dropped and he was allowed to leave the Soviet Union as the result of negotiations between George Shultz and Edward Shevardnadze. Daniloff would have been released in any case, because Reagan made it clear that he would not meet Gorbachev again while Daniloff was held, and Gorbachev was eager for the meeting at Reykjavík.

I recount this experience because it illustrates the basic fallacy in the reasoning of those who confused communication with appeasement or capitulation. Every time a problem arose in the U.S.-Soviet relationship—a Korean airliner shot down, an American soldier killed in East Germany, an innocent American journalist arrested—there were those in the Reagan administration who argued that official contacts should cease until the of-

---

*I am not the only member of our Chautauqua delegation to look back in pride at our decision to go. Two of the young Latvian Americans in the Chautauqua delegation, Ojars Kalnins and Ints Silins, became ambassadors shortly after Latvia regained its independence, Kalnins as Latvian ambassador to the United States and Silins as American ambassador to Latvia.

fenders admitted they were wrong and apologized. That sounds like a very high-minded and moral approach. But it has a flaw: *it just doesn't work in the real world.*

This attitude was particularly common among those known as neoconservatives.[26] Reagan normally rejected their advice if it involved refusing to talk to adversaries. But when his policies actually worked, instead of conceding that Reagan was right and they were wrong, they have sought explanations for the end of the Cold War that bolster the myths that have plagued us. Thus the idea is perpetuated that it was U.S. force and threats, rather than negotiation, that ended the Cold War, and also that Reagan's rhetoric "conquered" communism, and that the collapse of the Soviet Union was the equivalent of a military victory. These claims are all distortions, all incorrect, all misleading, and all dangerous to the safety and future prosperity of the American people.

By defining goals that could benefit both countries, and by dealing with Gorbachev with respect but from a position of strength, Ronald Reagan put in place, with Gorbachev's assistance, the framework for the negotiations that brought the Cold War to a peaceful end.

3

Cleanup Diplomacy and Conclusions
We Can Draw

WHILE THOSE OF US OBSERVING EVENTS in the Soviet Union when George Herbert Walker Bush was inaugurated in January 1989 may have sensed that the Cold War was over in an ideological sense, it is not surprising that persons more distant from the epicenter of change had not yet recognized that fact. Agreements to reduce strategic and conventional arms still eluded us, and—most significantly—Europe continued to be divided between NATO and the Warsaw Pact. There were still two separate German states, with hundreds of thousands of American troops stationed in the Federal Republic and even more Soviet troops ensconced in bases in the German Democratic Republic. It was doubtless such facts that caused General Brent Scowcroft, President Bush's able national security adviser, to say in a television interview in January, "I think the Cold War is not over."[1]

In fact, if Gorbachev had not acted in 1989 in conformity with the ideological shift he had signaled in his December 1988 speech to the United Nations, the Cold War would not have been over. It was prudent for the Bush administration to see whether Gorbachev was serious about the course he had announced before it could declare the Cold War a matter of history. President Bush had an additional incentive for avoiding hasty judgment: he was aware that the right wing of the Republican Party had less than complete trust in him. Therefore, he had to make a show of reassessing U.S.-Soviet relations to demonstrate that he was more hard-nosed than Ronald Reagan in dealing with the Soviet leadership.

Actually, Bush did not need an intensive restudy of U.S.-Soviet relations. He was well briefed on all the issues. He had been intimately involved in the development of Reagan's policy and had been an enthusiastic supporter of Reagan's negotiating approach. However, he jettisoned most senior Reagan political associates when he made his appointments, and this intensified the suspicion of the Republican Party's right wing. Furthermore, Bush did not want his administration to look like a mere continuation of his predecessor's. That made the transition from the Reagan presidency to the Bush presidency more like a change of political parties than a change of administration within the same party.

Although Bush replaced most of the senior officials in Washington who were dealing with the Soviet Union, he asked me to stay on as ambassador in Moscow. Therefore, when he announced that he was embarking on a reassessment of policy toward the Soviet Union, I sent a series of three telegrams with my personal views and recommendations.[2] I reported that "we can plan our foreign policy with a high degree of confidence that the Soviet leadership's preoccupation with internal reform will continue throughout the first Bush administration," but that "perestroika will not bring marked improvements to the Soviet economy in this period." Soviet foreign policy, I predicted, would of necessity "conform to domestic demands and domestic capabilities," which would require "a reduction in international tension," and therefore Soviet policy would be "less threatening militarily."

As for U.S. policy, I pointed out that we had a "historic opportunity to test the degree the Soviet Union is willing to move into a new relationship with the rest of the world, and to strengthen those tendencies in the Soviet Union to 'civilianize' the economy and 'pluralize' the society." The old "four-part" agenda remained relevant (arms reduction, withdrawal from military confrontation in third countries, protection of human rights, and opening the Iron Curtain), but I suggested that we consider two additional areas: multilateral cooperation on transnational issues and economic cooperation designed to assist the Soviet Union in a transition to a market economy based on private property. The suggestion to expand active cooperation on transnational issues was accepted by the administration, but not, for a time, the suggestion to initiate more economic cooperation.

One of my predictions turned out to be incorrect: mindful that many in

Washington felt that Gorbachev risked removal at any time, I predicted that he was likely to stay in power for at least five more years. I was wrong; he actually stayed in power for slightly less than three, but those three years brought changes that seemed unimaginable in January 1989—far more than most leaders could have achieved in five or even ten years. And, I should add, the American embassy kept its eyes on the rapidly changing Soviet scene and revised its judgments in response to changes it observed. In July 1990, nearly a year and a half before the USSR ceased to exist, we advised Washington to make contingency plans for a Soviet collapse.[3]

Cold War End Confirmed

An assessment of U.S.-Soviet relations that lasted two or even three months might have been understood by the Soviet leadership. After all, Bush had hinted to Gorbachev in 1987 that he would be required to make statements during his campaign for the presidency that should be disregarded.[4] However, American policy remained in the "assessment" mode for most of 1989, and by summer both Gorbachev and Shevardnadze began to worry. Matters were moving with breakneck speed both in the Soviet Union and in Eastern Europe, and the United States seemed to be standing aloof —not hostile, to be sure, but at the same time not deeply engaged.

Despite Bush's apparent disengagement, Gorbachev from early 1989 hastened to defuse the arms race while pressing for fundamental internal reforms. He ordered the rapid demobilization of half a million soldiers as he had promised in his U.N. speech. He saw to it that the Soviet army left Afghanistan as agreed. The first contested elections since the ones aborted in 1918 were conducted in March 1989, and many Communist bosses lost their seats.* Boris Yeltsin, whom Gorbachev had expelled from political leadership in 1987, won a resounding victory in Moscow, despite the most strenuous efforts of the Communist Party machinery to defeat him.[5] Debates in the new legislature became the order of the day, and were conducted in full

---

*A "constituent assembly" had been elected in Russia shortly after the Bolshevik seizure of power in 1917. When it turned out that the Bolsheviks won a minority of the seats, Lenin ordered the assembly broken up by force when it met in January 1918.

view of the public. When too many people stopped working to watch the de-bates on television, the authorities started televising the day's proceedings only at night.

By summer, a non-Communist government had come to power in Poland; the Czechs and Slovaks used their "velvet revolution" to throw out the regime Brezhnev had imposed in 1968, and suddenly, in November, the Berlin Wall was taken down, piece by piece, by ecstatic Germans from both sides. By December, Romania was in the throes of a violent revolution that ended the rule of the Ceauşescu family.

The fall of the Berlin Wall symbolized, as nothing else could, the end of the Cold War division of Europe. When it is recalled by the Western media today, scenes of the Berlin Wall's destruction are usually preceded with a video clip of Ronald Reagan standing before the Brandenburg Gate in June 1987 and thundering, "Mr. Gorbachev! Tear down this wall!" The juxtaposi-tion leaves the impression that there was cause and effect; as the Scriptures tell us that Gabriel's trumpet brought down the walls of Jericho, so Reagan's challenge is presented as if it created a shock effect that, over two years later, liberated the residents of East Berlin and East Germany.

This is a false impression. The Berlin Wall did not come down because Reagan demanded it, and Mikhail Gorbachev did not tear it down. Gorbachev created conditions that allowed the Germans to remove the wall. He did this by insisting that the Communist-dominated governments of Eastern and Central Europe introduce reforms similar to his perestroika in the Soviet Union, and warning them that, whatever happened, the Soviet army would no longer intervene in their countries to keep them in power. Once the peo-ple in the Warsaw Pact countries realized that the Soviet Union was not likely to put down peaceful revolutions by military force (something that took a few months), they acted to remove their unpopular Communist leaders.

Most of this took place after Reagan's famous speech, but—if other factors had been the same—would have occurred even if Reagan had never visited the Brandenburg Gate and hurled his famous challenge. Gorbachev loos-ened the reins on Eastern Europe not because the United States demanded it, but because he understood that the old policies were not in the interest of a reformed Soviet Union, and also that military domination of Eastern Eu-rope was turning the population into enemies rather than friends. He had hoped, to be sure, that reform Communists like Alexander Dubček would replace the Warsaw Pact leaders, but when this did not happen, he accepted the non-Communist replacements with apparent alacrity.[6]

The point is not that Reagan's challenge was a mistake or that it did any damage. On the contrary, it was appropriate at that time. Reagan made the statement before it was clear that Gorbachev had discarded the Brezhnev Doctrine. He delivered it when he was recovering from the political blow inflicted by the Iran-Contra scandal. When serious negotiations resumed with Gorbachev in April 1987 and it appeared that a major arms control agreement might be possible that year—the Intermediate-Range Nuclear Forces (INF) Treaty that was signed in December—Reagan's advisers wanted to dodge the accusation that he was going soft on the Soviet Union, and on communism in general. The Berlin Wall was a legitimate issue, and had been ever since it was erected. It was useful in 1987, when curbs on the arms race seemed imminent, to remind Gorbachev that there were other important matters outstanding in East-West relations.

Nevertheless, the implication that Reagan's words brought down the Berlin Wall distorts what actually happened. The fact is that, in 1989, the year the wall came down, President Bush facilitated Gorbachev's policies in Eastern Europe by avoiding public challenges and allowing Gorbachev the political wiggle room to argue at home that he was acting in the interests of the Soviet Union (which he was) and not in response to American demands.

President Bush did little to engage Gorbachev personally during the first months of his presidency, but he did respond to signals from the Soviet leader. In July 1989, when Bush was planning a trip to Eastern Europe, Gorbachev took me aside at a social occasion and asked me to appeal to Bush to "be more considerate." Bush took the hint and avoided statements when he visited Poland and Hungary that could have been received in Moscow as putting pressure on Gorbachev. Shevardnadze informed me after Bush's visit that Gorbachev was pleased with the way the U.S. president had behaved.[7]

When Bush finally met Gorbachev in December on a Soviet ship in the harbor of Valletta, Malta, they discussed the situation in Eastern Europe in detail. They agreed that their countries were no longer enemies, and Gorbachev made a commitment not to intervene militarily in Eastern Europe to support Communist regimes. For his part, Bush assured Gorbachev that the United States would not claim victory if the Eastern Europeans were allowed to replace the Communist regimes that had been imposed on them. Furthermore, Bush and Gorbachev agreed not to continue arguments about "Western" and "Eastern" values, but jointly to promote democratic values.

These understandings helped Gorbachev make the liberation of Eastern Europe acceptable to key elements of the Soviet bureaucracy, since he could present his policy as serving Soviet long-term interests, not as capitulation to the West.

The ideological Cold War had ended the year before; now one of the most important causes of the Cold War was corrected: without an Iron Curtain kept in place by Soviet force, Europe was free to unite. The big question remaining at the end of 1989 was what would happen in Germany. The desire of the people in both German states to unite was clear, but how would this come about? The Soviets wanted a negotiation between the German Democratic Republic—up to then their puppet—with the German Federal Republic, as well as a commitment that the united Germany would leave the NATO alliance.

West German chancellor Helmut Kohl proposed that the provinces in East Germany simply adhere to the West German constitution as *Länder,* like the other constituent units of the Federal Republic. At first Gorbachev opposed this arrangement, but after the Christian Democrats (the ruling party in West Germany) won elections in the GDR in March 1990, he realized he could not stop the elected East German government from accepting Kohl's terms. But he could still insist on Germany leaving NATO—after all, he still had more than half a million Soviet troops and dependents stationed in East Germany, and the Soviet Union had a right to keep them there under the four-power agreements concluded at the end of World War II.[8]

In a brilliant stroke of diplomacy, Secretary of State James Baker convinced Gorbachev that it was in the Soviet interest to let a united Germany stay in the NATO alliance. A Germany in NATO would not be able to dominate its neighbors the way it had in the past, and a Germany in NATO could never in the future decide to acquire nuclear weapons. Gorbachev saw the logic, and, not wanting to be seen as the enemy of German unity, eventually agreed to end the postwar agreements that had kept the country divided. But he agreed to this under the impression that he had a promise that NATO jurisdiction and troops would not expand to the east.[9] He did not ask for a commitment in writing.

Outstanding arms control negotiations progressed rapidly. The main issues separating the parties regarding reduction of strategic nuclear weapons were settled by the end of 1989, although it took another eighteen months of quibbling over trivia before the Strategic Arms Reduction Treaty (START) was signed. A treaty between members of NATO and the Warsaw Pact to reduce conventional arms in Europe was concluded, following more than a decade of negotiations, in October 1990.

One important disarmament issue was handled privately. An international treaty to ban biological weapons had been concluded in 1972, following President Richard Nixon's announcement that the United States would end production and destroy stocks of such weapons.[10] The Soviet Union signed and ratified the treaty, the Biological Weapons Convention, but continued to maintain a large offensive biological weapons program in secret. The United States long suspected that such a program existed, particularly after an outbreak of anthrax near Sverdlovsk (now Yekaterinburg) in 1979 seemed caused by the accidental release of spores from a production facility. Nevertheless, the Soviet Union vehemently denied that it had a program to develop and produce pathogens and toxins prohibited by the 1972 treaty.

In 1989, a defector provided British and American intelligence with enough information about the program to prove that disavowals were lies. Instead of making a public issue of the question, President Bush and Prime Minister Thatcher decided to deal with the matter privately. Gorbachev at that point faced so many difficulties at home that it was believed that he could deal with the problem more effectively outside the glare of publicity.

British ambassador Sir Rodric Braithwaite and I were instructed to meet with Alexander Bessmertnykh in the Soviet Foreign Ministry, and then with Gorbachev's foreign policy assistant, Anatoly Chernyaev, to let Gorbachev know that we had evidence of an illegal program and to demand that it be terminated. Subsequently, President Bush, Prime Minister Thatcher, and Secretary Baker reinforced the message in private talks. At first the Soviet agency producing the weapons resisted acknowledging that the illegal program existed, but as U.S. and British pressure mounted, Gorbachev ordered an end to production of biological warfare (BW) agents. We learned only later that those managing the program contrived, without Gorbachev's knowledge, to preserve facilities with some production capacity.[11]

With Europe now whole and free, the Iron Curtain down, and arms re-duction proceeding apace, the only remaining major area of U.S.-Soviet geopolitical confrontation was in the Middle East. Saddam Hussein's sudden invasion of Kuwait in August 1990 provided a test of the developing U.S-So-viet relationship. Would Gorbachev use the Soviet veto power in the United Nations to protect his Iraqi ally? Iraq was armed with Soviet weapons and there were thousands of Soviet military specialists in Iraq to maintain the weapons and teach the Iraqis to use them.

Gorbachev, with Shevardnadze's urging, passed the test. Rejecting the ad-vice of Soviet Middle East experts, Gorbachev ordered the Soviet ambassa-dor to the United Nations to vote with the United States and other Western countries to condemn the invasion. Subsequently, he also agreed to vote in the Security Council to authorize the use of "all necessary measures" to force an Iraqi withdrawal. This provided the legal basis for the Persian Gulf War of 1991, when the U.S.-led coalition restored Kuwait's independence.

By the fall of 1990, the debris of the Cold War was largely cleaned up and was in the process of being carted off to history's garbage dump.

I have been criticized for characterizing the foreign relations of the first Bush administration as "cleanup" diplomacy. I do not mean it in a belittling sense. It was vitally important diplomacy, and it was conducted with skill. I call it cleanup diplomacy because the force of Cold War thinking had been drained from Soviet foreign policy before George H. W. Bush took office. We were no longer in a zero-sum game. Both American and Soviet officials recognized that there were serious problems: with the arms race, with the division of Europe, with the tensions in the world fueled by "superpower competition," and with human rights protection in the Soviet Union. We understood that it was in the interest of both our countries to solve these problems in a way that would not favor one side over the other, but empower the people living in the countries in question.

The diplomacy by President George Bush and his secretary of state, James Baker, achieved remarkable results despite the delay of nearly a year in engaging Gorbachev. They managed to prove without a doubt that Gor-bachev could implement the policy he proclaimed in December 1988. The Cold War was over, not just in theory, but in fact. Events of 1989 and 1990 confirmed what Ronald Reagan sensed when he and Gorbachev parted on

Governors Island in December 1988: that they were partners in building a better world.

Who Gets the Credit?

During his campaign for reelection in 1992, President Bush boasted, "We won the Cold War!" Others have claimed that Reagan won the Cold War. Some say he did it with his Strategic Defense Initiative. The argument is something like this (with only minor simplification): by proposing SDI, Reagan forced Gorbachev to recognize the fact that he couldn't afford to keep up and therefore decided that it was best to give up.[12]

This idea just doesn't fit the facts. First of all, Gorbachev did not have to match SDI to "keep up." He could easily defeat any practicable missile defense by building more missiles (which were cheap in the Soviet Union) and arming them with sophisticated decoys (even cheaper than real warheads). They could swamp any defensive system the United States could mount. And if, as many assumed, SDI meant the stationing of missile interceptors in space, the Soviet Union could easily bring down any orbiting weapons with antisatellite devices—which it had actually tested. Andrei Sakharov, the nuclear physicist and human rights champion, pointed out in the 1980s that it was much easier to take something out of space than to put it there. Antimissile weapons orbiting in space would be much more like sitting ducks than hovering hawks.

The reason Gorbachev wanted to stop SDI was that he and his colleagues thought it was part of a strategy that would permit the United States to attack the Soviet Union and remain immune from retaliation. Some Soviet leaders even thought it was a cover for a first-strike strategy or for placing nuclear weapons in space. These were not the objectives of SDI, but it was natural for the Soviet leaders to try to stop a program that they considered a mortal danger.*

Others argue that Reagan brought so much economic pressure to bear

---

*While Reagan tried to make it clear that he envisioned strategic defenses as necessary only if both sides eliminated their strategic nuclear weapons and also promised to commit the United States to share defenses with the Soviet Union, Gorbachev did not find these assurances credible.

on the Soviet Union that Gorbachev had no choice but to come to terms. They cite Reagan's arms buildup and the fall in oil prices, which they attribute in part to a deal with Saudi Arabia to flood the market.

These arguments also aren't convincing when you look at all the evidence. For example, Reagan's arms buildup (actually not much larger than the one Carter had proposed at the end of his term) was designed not to bring the Soviet Union down, but to convince the Soviet leader that he could not win an arms race. In fact it did that: by 1987 Gorbachev was telling the Politburo that the United States wanted to trap the Soviet Union in an arms race it would lose. So this part of the Reagan strategy worked: it showed Gorbachev that he had a stake in ending the arms race.

As for oil prices, ever since the OPEC-authored squeeze on supplies in the early 1970s, the United States has tried to moderate oil prices in its own interest. U.S. officials probably used the argument with the staunchly anticommunist Saudis that it would hurt the Soviet Union, an oil exporter, to make sure supplies were adequate to keep oil prices low. The real reason was to benefit the U.S. economy. Furthermore, low oil prices are not what brought the Soviet Union down economically, because it was not significantly dependent on foreign trade. One of the weaknesses of the Soviet system was its self-sufficient autarky. So long as it had enough exports to pay for the grain it needed to feed its people, it did not need a lot of foreign trade. Of course the Soviet Union made less money from its energy exports when prices were low, and this was painful. Painful, but far from fatal. It was not a major factor in Gorbachev's decision to cooperate to end the arms race.

The price of oil was also not a major cause of the collapse of the Soviet Union. Yegor Gaidar, the Soviet economist who became the first prime minister in newly independent Russia, has written: "The excuse for the profound economic crisis that provoked the collapse of a superpower [the USSR] was the fall of oil prices in the mid-1980s, which for all its significance is incommensurate with its consequences. Developments on the oil market were, for the Soviet economy, not the reason but the excuse for its collapse."[13]

While some give all the credit to Reagan or to Bush for ending the Cold War (and even for ending Communist rule in the Soviet Union and forcing its collapse), others give the lion's share of the credit to Gorbachev. This was the reasoning of the Norwegian Parliament when it awarded the Nobel Peace Prize to Gorbachev alone. What this decision ignored was the fact that the plan for ending the Cold War was developed and applied by Reagan, even before Gorbachev came to power. Gorbachev initially tried to end the arms race without the internal reforms or the change in ideology that would have put an end to the confrontations. Reagan's four-part agenda that tied internal reform to external behavior defined the negotiations necessary to end the Cold War confrontation.

Once Gorbachev understood that the Soviet Union could benefit from solving the problems the agenda addressed, it proved to be the key to ending the Cold War. The American agenda sought results that did not damage the interests of a Soviet Union willing to live in peace with its neighbors. It was not forced on Gorbachev, but circumstances made it desirable for him to accept this approach. There was no other practical way to put an end to the arms race.* And Reagan made it politically possible for Gorbachev to accept the agenda he proposed by not publicly claiming "victory."

If Reagan had not been willing to engage Gorbachev, the Cold War would likely have continued regardless of what Gorbachev did. Most important, without an agreement on the radical reduction of nuclear arms, it would have been politically impossible for Gorbachev to undertake the internal reforms he considered necessary.

It is difficult to imagine how the Cold War could have ended when and as it did if both Reagan and Gorbachev had not been in office at the same time. A Democrat or even a moderate Republican like George H. W. Bush could not have gotten a major arms reduction agreement through the U.S. Senate at the time Reagan did. But once he did, he opened the gate for others to continue the process. As we have seen, Bush, after some hesitation, continued the process Reagan started.

As for the USSR, no other possible leader in the 1980s would have attempted both to reorient foreign policy and to undertake a fundamental re-

---

*It can be argued, in the abstract, that Gorbachev could have called off the arms race by unilaterally disarming. In theory, at least, this should have enticed the U.S. Congress to reduce defense expenditures and slow the development of new weapons. But, given Soviet political reality at the time, it is highly unlikely that any Soviet leader would have been permitted to take this course.

form of the Communist-ruled system. In his willingness to take chances and to revise traditional ideology, Gorbachev was unique among his political peers.

It may seem unfair to argue that no other pair could have achieved what Reagan and Gorbachev did. Certainly there were other people in both countries who were capable of understanding what needed to be done. And there were politicians who could have come to power who might have been convinced that ending the Cold War would benefit their countries. But what plausible leader in either country had both the imagination to break with traditional policies and the political stature and skill to gain approval at home? I can think of none in either country. Good ideas come to nothing if they cannot be put into practice.

One other thing should be clear from a close look at the record: every agreement Gorbachev made was in the true interest of the Soviet Union. The Cold War ended, not in the victory of one side over the other, but in an agreed outcome that benefited both. Ronald Reagan never boasted, "We won the Cold War!" In fact, he wrote in his memoirs that "democracy triumphed in the cold war because it was a battle of values."[14] He did not consider the "triumph" as a military or quasi-military victory, but that of one idea over another, and he noted that Gorbachev was inculcating the superior idea in the Soviet Union as the Cold War came to an end.

Understanding the Cold War

Some historians deny that history contains any "lessons." Yet history, properly understood, represents experience. Can one seriously argue that experience teaches no lessons? If that is true, then it is inexplicable why we should value experience in selecting leaders. If you suddenly discover that you have an intrusive brain tumor, wouldn't you prefer—given the choice— a neurosurgeon who has operated successfully on brain tumors to one just completing his or her residency? Or, in selecting a lawyer to represent you in an important litigation, would you hire someone who just passed the bar examination last week if you could afford someone with more experience? Obviously, experience is not irrelevant, and neither is history, so long as we do not entertain a false view of what actually happened.

Nevertheless, those who deny that history contains lessons have a point. The fact is, in politics and in international relations, history never repeats itself precisely. Any lessons from history must be considered contingent. Even if we understand properly what worked (or didn't work) under a given set of conditions, what if next time some of the conditions are not the same? The approach that worked before might or might not work under different circumstances. Furthermore, historians are often appalled by the way politicians tend to misuse history by looking for superficial analogies and then defending a given policy with a historical reference that, upon objective examination, ignores significant differences in the two situations.

A striking example of this tendency was the argument, made by a succession of presidents and secretaries of state and defense, that the situation in Vietnam in the 1960s and early 1970s was analogous to that in Europe in the 1930s, when an aggressive Hitler was not stopped while he was weak, but was allowed to gain sufficient strength to plunge the world into the Second World War and commit one of the gravest crimes in human history, the Holocaust.

The Vietnamese Communists were viewed as part of a worldwide Communist conspiracy, which had to be stopped—as it had been in Korea—if the world was not to be plunged into a much wider and more costly war. This was an argument that, at the time, I supported. However, the analogy was simply not valid. Communist-ruled countries were not operating, as theory would have it, from a single center. The struggle for control of Vietnam contained tragic elements, particularly for those who, with good reason, opposed the Communist takeover. But it was one that American military force was unlikely to win, given the fact that the Vietnamese fighting against us were on their home ground and were willing to sacrifice much more than the United States could in order to prevail.

American motivations were moral, and the people who were sent to fight in Vietnam did so in good faith, and at great personal sacrifice. Nevertheless the war was a mistake by American's elected leaders—a mistake of judgment based on a misreading of history, then perpetuated by misleading but politically potent slogans, such as "There is no substitute for victory!"

Results always speak louder than intentions, and the U.S. military involvement in Vietnam did more damage to both countries than Ho Chi

Minh is likely to have inflicted if he had been allowed to replace the Japanese occupiers with a Vietnamese Communist regime in 1945 and 1946. Would that have condemned Vietnam to communist "slavery" for all time, or have spread the communist infection throughout Southeast Asia? Not very likely. The communist system does not, in fact, work very well and, left on its own, prevails only for a time. Vietnam today is shedding many features of communism, is adopting more and more features of a market economy, has friendly relations with the United States, and welcomes American investment, despite bitter memories of the past.

Is it an accident that the unreformed Communist regimes that remain today, like fossils in a developing and globalizing world—Cuba and North Korea—continue to exist with little change largely because of what their governments perceive as external military and economic pressure? Perhaps— but the correlation between trade and contact with the outside world on one hand and internal reform on the other is striking in most formerly Communist countries.

One of the most difficult exercises in policy analysis is to determine whether historical analogies are appropriate. We cannot expect dispassionate analysis from politicians; they (or, more likely, their staffs) will normally cherry-pick the evidence to provide the most persuasive case. And, in their eyes, persuasive means emotionally persuasive. When a president recommends a new course of action, nobody wants a lot of nuance and "on-the-other-hands," or a host of facts that do not produce a clear, unequivocal conclusion. (Henry Kissinger, who sometimes pretended to be more cynical than he was, once complimented a staffer's recommendation by saying that it was good since it was persuasive, "and has the additional virtue of being true.")

We cannot expect political leaders to offer finely reasoned, balanced analyses of the policies they recommend. What we should expect, however, is that a president (or presidential candidate) will examine more nuanced analyses before deciding on a policy. And, of course, journalists and scholars should be prepared to evaluate policy pronouncements on the basis of their cogency and accuracy, including the relevance of any historical analogies used.

When I was working at the National Security Council in 1986, a book appeared that described a set of techniques that can be used to assess policy choices. Written by two Harvard professors, Richard Neustadt and Ernest May, *Thinking in Time: The Uses of History for Decision Makers* illustrated the approach with a series of case studies of political decisions, most of them faulty in one respect or another. They pointed out that analysts needed first of all to understand the history of a problem, and to "place" the people principally involved, that is, to understand enough of their personal history and the culture of the institutions they headed to grasp how these people are likely to react to a given situation. Any good journalist or diplomat understands the need for both, but there still are not enough good ones to go around. *Thinking in Time* provides a useful checklist to sharpen skills in this regard.[15]

Neustadt and May went beyond advice on how to understand a problem and how to size up individuals and institutions. They suggested that, in analyzing a problem, a person should clearly categorize facts, unknowns, and assumptions. When this is done, thought should be given to what additional information would clarify the unknowns, and also what sort of things might happen to change some of the assumptions.

Since a policy maker never has as much information as he or she would like, and decisions have to be made before everything is clear, it seems obvious that one should pay close attention to the quality of the information and the inevitable assumptions that go into any analysis. And yet, obvious as the need is, it is rarely practiced in real life, at least not in the United States.

One of the serious mistakes President Kennedy made early in his presidency, when he approved the disastrous Bay of Pigs operation in Cuba, resulted from his failure to probe the assumptions the organizers of the operation made.[16] Their critical assumption was that if the Cuban refugees who had been trained and armed by the CIA at a secret base in Central America attacked Cuba, the population would rise up in support of the anti-Castro forces. When this did not occur, and Castro's forces were capturing and driving the attackers into the sea, Kennedy was faced with the choice of supporting the exiled Cubans with American forces or accepting their defeat. He chose the latter, but the Bay of Pigs operation itself cemented a military alliance between Castro and the Soviet Union and opened the door to the only serious nuclear confrontation of the Cold War. Obviously, Kennedy should have insisted that the sponsors provide more evidence that their assumption was correct, and also should have made sure that there was a workable "plan B" in case the assumptions were faulty. It would have been much less damaging to the United States to have called off the operation before it happened and failed.

Observations on the Cold War and Its End

All right. I'll be true to my conservative temperament. I'll refrain for the moment from writing about lessons from the Cold War. At this point I'll call them observations. We can consider later to what degree these observations are relevant to problems following the Cold War, and whether they contain lessons we need to heed now and in the future.

1. *The arms race was driven by political and psychological factors, not by military or defense necessity.* Both sides piled up many more weapons than they needed for defense because they feared that the other would use a perceived superiority to derive some political advantage. Arms races, once started, can be driven by a logic that transcends any realistic military objective.

2. *Arms races normally cannot be stopped by arms control measures alone, but only by solving the underlying political cause.* President Reagan liked to say, "Nations do not fear each other because they are armed; they arm because they fear each other." Maybe that seems simplistic and not always true, but George Kennan (whose views were closer to Reagan's than many suppose) expressed the same idea more elaborately when he wrote, "Armaments are a function and not a cause of political tensions. And no limitation of armaments on a multilateral scale can be effected as long as the political problems are not tackled and regulated in some realistic way."[17] The Cold War arms race did not end because agreements were reached to reduce weapons; those agreements were reached because the perceptions and policies that gave rise to the arms race changed.

3. *Not a single theory of international relations predicted the way the Cold War ended.* Each theory of international relations tells us something about how nations interact with each other. But theories are more useful for analyzing historical forces than for predicting what might happen in the future. One reason the end of the Cold War and the collapse of the Soviet Union came

as such a surprise to academic specialists in international relations is that neither event fitted easily into any of the theories that had been developed to understand international relations.

4. *International relations are ultimately controlled by people, not by impersonal forces.* Of course, objective circumstances matter. It makes a difference how powerful a country is, how productive its economy, how contented its people, whether neighbors are friendly or not. Political leaders are always constrained by circumstances, but they determine how they deal with these constraints. They can submit to them and continue the policies handed down to them, or—if they believe the traditional policies are not working, they can try to change them. Though some have argued that circumstances produce the leaders who can deal with them, history provides abundant evidence to the contrary. Not every political crisis is surmounted—otherwise there would be no fractured or failed states—and far from every commercial enterprise stays profitable, or else there would be no bankruptcies.

If we take the Soviet Union, we should recognize that when Gorbachev became general secretary of the CPSU, he was dealt essentially the same hand as that held by his two predecessors, Yuri Andropov and Konstantin Chernenko. In time, Gorbachev chose policies that neither of his predecessors would have embraced, even if they had lived longer than they did. They were of a different generation, had a vested interest in policies that were not working, and were incapable of thinking outside the box of Marxist-Leninist ideology. Gorbachev, it turned out, was different, but he did not have to be. He could have spent his time strengthening the control the Communist Party had over the country rather than loosening it. He could have been quick to suppress any incipient rebellion. This would have come at a cost, as the Soviet Union became less and less competitive in the world, but it could have been sustained for a long time, maybe even for Gorbachev's natural life span.

George Kennan made the point when he noted that there was little place for individuals in Arnold J. Toynbee's theoretical approach to history, and observed, with his usual eloquence, "Yet, at the bottom of all human experience, there lies, after all, the mystery of the individual personality—its ultimate autonomy of decision, its interaction with the mass."[18] Those who argued that Gorbachev, a product of the Soviet system, would inevitably be a leader with the same goals and prejudices as his predecessors missed this important insight. They seem to have assumed that Marx, Engels, and Stalin were right, that individuals are merely the products of the social forces that formed them, lacking any autonomy of mind and judgment.

5. *Culture matters.* American politicians often make the unconscious assumption that other people think as we would and have trouble understanding passions that seem impractical or irrational. But culture, religion (or ideology), social norms, and historical experience play a critical role in the way other leaders perceive events and react to them. In particular, every society has concepts of honor and prestige that are important for political leadership. Many countries have historical grievances that, even if more imagined than real, can arouse great emotion if stirred. Others have internal friction—sometimes actual, sometimes latent—between different ethnic, linguistic, religious, or economic groups. Some have powerful bureaucracies that resist policy change, particularly if they sense foreign pressure. All of these considerations inhibit political leaders' ability to form foreign policy on a strictly rational cost-benefit basis.

One of the keys to the success that Reagan, Shultz, Bush, and Baker had in engaging the Soviet leaders was their attention to this factor. Reagan may not have mastered every detail of every arms control negotiation (there were plenty of people in his administration who concentrated on that), but he spent as much time trying to understand Gorbachev's thinking and the political constraints on his behavior as he did studying the "substance" of the issues. George Shultz was acutely aware that Eduard Shevardnadze, a Georgian, was immensely proud of his cultural heritage. By showing interest in it and respect for it, Shultz was able to establish a degree of personal rapport with the Soviet foreign minister that helped them come to terms on issues that had resisted solution for decades. James Baker picked up where Shultz left off and continued the relationship that benefited both countries.

6. *Refusing to talk to an adversary is like turning into a dead-end street.* Avoiding communication with an adversary concedes the diplomatic initiative to the opponent and is usually a losing strategy. Every time the Soviet leaders withdrew from negotiations or from participation in the United Nations, they suffered a political defeat. West Germany's Hallstein Doctrine (refusal to recognize the German Democratic Republic as a sovereign state or to

maintain diplomatic relations with any non-communist country that established official relations with it) did not weaken the Soviet hold over East Germany; *Ostpolitik* (establishing official relations with East Germany), which replaced the Hallstein Doctrine, did. The U.S. refusal to recognize Communist China for years weakened American diplomacy and probably delayed the Sino-Soviet split. Andropov's withdrawal from arms control negotiations in 1983, intended to deny Reagan reelection, helped Reagan win in 1984. Reagan's policy of always accepting proposals to negotiate and refusing to walk away from negotiating tables eventually resulted in agreements and understandings that brought the Cold War to an end.

A refusal to communicate without preconditions actually plays into a dictator's hands, since dictators thrive on foreign hostility, real or imagined. A dialogue may turn out to be fruitless and accommodation impossible, but the very fact that the United States is in communication and trying to deal with a problem country limits the ability of hostile leaders to claim alleged U.S. hostility as an excuse for tyranny at home. Few things unite the people of a country more than the perception that a foreign power is trying to push them around. This means that it is normally unwise to demand "regime change" (that is, ouster of the existing government) as a precondition to negotiations, since this tends to strengthen rather than weaken dictators and ultimately leaves the demanding country the option of going to war or doing nothing.

7. *A large, well-funded intelligence agency doesn't necessarily make a government intelligent.* The Soviet Union operated probably the largest and most active network of spies any country ever has. Nevertheless, the leadership was rarely well informed about what was actually going on inside and outside its borders. It was not because Soviet KGB officers were incompetent: KGB external intelligence had moles in both the CIA and FBI from the late 1980s, and also had gotten crucial communications intelligence from the U.S. Navy and National Security Agency employees.[19] As intelligence agencies go, the KGB was spectacularly successful.

So why was the Soviet leadership not better informed? First, because Soviet intelligence agents were inclined to report what their superiors wanted to hear, not what they actually heard and saw. Second, because the Soviet leaders put more credence in secret intelligence than information available openly, even though the latter was often more accurate. Third, because the KGB chairman would tailor intelligence reports, sometimes actually fabricating "evidence," to support policy choices he favored.

In the end, the Soviet leadership's heavy reliance on slanted secret intelligence was a handicap rather than a source of strength. George W. Bush's administration's use of "tailored" and distorted intelligence to justify its invasion of Iraq showed that it had failed to grasp some of the lessons that might have been derived from a study of the Soviet experience.

8. *The same form of government does not translate into "friend" or "ally."* The Manichean worldview of Marxism-Leninism held that "imperialism" and state conflict were rooted in the competition of bourgeois states for power and resources. This struggle was to be replaced by a proletarian paradise that would abolish war and competition, since, having eliminated the bourgeoisie and established social justice, the proletariat would live in peace and harmony, without any need for the trappings and constraints of state structures and their governments. In this context, a country that had established "socialism" was automatically allied with other "socialist" countries.

In practice, it didn't turn out that way. Marshal Josip Broz Tito set up a Communist government in Yugoslavia once he chased the Germans out in the closing months of World War II, but in 1948, when he refused to bow to Stalin's dictates, was expelled from the Cominform, the organization Stalin founded to replace the Comintern. Similarly, Mao Zedong, whose Communist forces conquered mainland China with Soviet help in 1949, broke with the Soviet Union some ten years later, and even provoked military battles along the Chinese-Soviet border.

Stalin was unable to crush Tito, though he tried, and Khrushchev was not able to subdue Mao, but when Imre Nagy tried to take Hungary out of the Warsaw Pact and Alexander Dubček attempted to put a human face on "socialism" in Czechoslovakia, Soviet forces invaded to make sure governments totally subservient to Moscow prevailed.

By the 1960s, it should have been clear to informed observers on both sides of the Iron Curtain that Communist governments were not, in fact, automatic allies. Countries could be kept under Soviet control by the credible threat of military force, but not by the attraction of a common ideology or a similar form of government.

When we hear today that both peace and American power would be advanced by the spread of "democratic" governments, it might be well to keep the Soviet experience in mind. The world will doubtless benefit if more countries become democratic, but there is no reason to think that a convulsive change to democracy would be peaceful, or that another country would automatically ally itself with the United States just because it is a democracy.

As the Soviet government concluded agreements with the United States and its NATO allies to confirm that the Cold War had ended, it did so in the midst of a profound internal transformation. Gorbachev's attempt to bring democracy to the Soviet Union unleashed forces that weakened and, in a short time, destroyed the Soviet Union as a unitary state. Is there anything we can learn from that?

4
Regime Change:
The Soviet Union Disintegrates

NEITHER RONALD REAGAN NOR George H. W. Bush tried to destroy the Soviet Union. They wanted to change the behavior of its government but never posited "regime change" as a policy goal. Both were smart enough to know that such a goal would only strengthen the authoritarian tendencies of the regime and make any genuine accommodation impossible.

Gorbachev also did not set out to weaken the Soviet state, but only to improve the way it was governed. Even before he became general secretary of the Communist Party of the Soviet Union, he had become convinced that the country was headed in the wrong direction. Both he and Shevardnadze have written that they would tell each other in private, when both were provincial party leaders, "We can't go on like this."[1]

Gorbachev and Reform

At first, Gorbachev thought that the stagnation that had enveloped the Soviet economy could be overcome by some management changes and by reducing the drain on the economy that heavy spending on arms and the Soviet military had caused. He thought he could accomplish this without any basic change in the Soviet system—in fact, he believed that the Communist Party was the appropriate instrument for driving the changes that were needed. At home, he would improve industrial productivity by insisting on more efficient management and steadier work habits. He knew that both public health and labor productivity were damaged by rampant alcoholism. Therefore, he initiated an anti-alcohol campaign that severely restricted production not only of vodka and other spirits but even of wine and beer.

So far as military spending was concerned, he knew that it had to be curbed, but he could do this only with American cooperation. So long as an arms race was under way with the United States, he would be unable to reduce the economy-busting resources demanded by the Soviet arms industry. He was convinced by his advisers that the United States, and President Reagan in particular, were intent on gaining military superiority over the Soviet Union in order to secure an advantage, and perhaps even to attack the Soviet Union. If that was the case, the only way to deal with the United States effectively was to court America's European allies in the hope that they would bring pressure on it to moderate the arms race. That is why Gorbachev visited London and Paris before he met Reagan for the first time.

His views on most of these points changed between 1985 and 1987.

First, his limited domestic reforms failed miserably. The anti-alcohol campaign was carried out so clumsily and ruthlessly that it led only to a sharp rise in moonshining and bootlegging. (Later, Soviet experts on the United States asked me, "Didn't our leaders ever check with you about what happened during Prohibition?" Well, they didn't—and actually, Gorbachev faced greater obstacles than those the American authorities of the Gatsby era did, since, unlike the United States at that time, there was no widespread movement among the Soviet population in favor of restricting access to alcoholic beverages.) The attempt to force more output by reducing absenteeism—much caused by the need to stand in line to obtain essential food and clothing—also backfired, because it heightened discontent over shortages of available goods.

Second, Gorbachev was getting nowhere with Reagan by pushing for arms control alone, and by continuing to insist on agreements that would preserve Soviet advantages while eliminating those the United States possessed. Western European leaders—particularly Margaret Thatcher and French president François Mitterrand—assured him that Reagan was a man of peace who was willing to negotiate fairly. They also pointed out that Soviet policies and actions had given rise to Western fear and hostility. As he thought over Reagan's behavior during their meetings at Geneva and Reykjavík, Gorbachev realized that, despite their differences, Reagan had been struggling to find a way to reduce the threat of nuclear weapons. From February 1987, Gorbachev began to lecture the Politburo on the necessity of coming to terms with the United States, at times ridiculing the positions the Soviet Union had been taking in negotiations.

Third, Gorbachev recognized that Reagan's four-part agenda was consistent with the reforms the Soviet Union needed. From 1987, it became the unacknowledged framework for U.S.-Soviet negotiations. Anatoly Chernyaev, his foreign policy assistant, told a group of historians and former officials at a meeting in 1998, "Our policy did not change until Gorbachev understood that there would be no improvement and no serious arms control until we admitted and accepted human rights, free emigration, until glasnost became freedom of speech, until our society and the process of perestroika changed deeply."[2]

From 1987, agreements to reduce arms moved in tandem with accelerating political reform in the Soviet Union: glasnost (more openness in the media) morphed into perestroika (reconstruction), requiring broader and more fundamental change. In the summer of 1988 a Communist Party Congress endorsed wide-ranging democratic reforms, and contested elections were held in March 1989—neither totally free nor totally fair, they nevertheless resulted in the defeat of many longtime Communist Party apparatchiks and emboldened the populace to demand even more reform.

As the momentum of reform increased, opposition grew. One of the first public signs that some senior officials thought Gorbachev was going too far with internal reform emerged in March 1988, when Yegor Ligachev, then Gorbachev's number two in the party leadership, took advantage of Gorbachev's absence on a trip to Yugoslavia and authorized publication of a pro-Stalinist article.[3] Gorbachev and his allies in the Politburo, including Eduard Shevardnadze and Alexander Yakovlev, who had studied for a year at Columbia University and served ten years as Soviet ambassador to Canada, pressed ahead with their reform agenda. It became increasingly clear to Gorbachev, however, that he could not depend on the Communist Party to implement the reforms in good faith. By 1989, he had decided that if the Soviet Union was to become more democratic, he had to jockey the Communist Party out of total control of the country.[4]

To most observers, inside and outside the Soviet Union, the proposition that the head of the Communist Party of the Soviet Union would maneuver to diminish the party's control of the country seemed to be nothing more than a dangerous delusion. It was not a goal that Gorbachev could openly espouse—after all, he could hardly expect to lead the party over the political cliff if he let it be known where he was headed. So he often seemed to talk out of both sides of his mouth, as a hard-line Communist in one context and as a liberal democrat in another.

Step by step, taking advantage of the tradition that the proposals of the general secretary were automatically approved, he secured formal acceptance by the top party organs for sharing power, first by allowing contested elections, then by permitting the formation of public and social groups outside Communist Party control, then by eliminating the constitutional provision that made the Communist Party the only legal party in the country. By 1990, he had persuaded the quasi-elected legislature to create the office of president with an appointive council, which in effect could replace the CPSU Politburo as the ultimate policy-making body.

These moves shifted power from the Communist Party, which had ruled largely behind the scenes, to the institutions of constitutional government. Ultimate power then rested not with the general secretary of the Communist Party, but with the president of the USSR. Nevertheless, Gorbachev would cling to both positions until, following the aborted coup d'état in August 1991, he resigned as general secretary.

In 1990 and 1991 Gorbachev would say in private that Russia had always been ruled from the top down, but in the contemporary world, successful countries were ruled from the bottom up. Creativity and progress came from a free people permitted to rule themselves. But, he added, the Russian people had no experience ruling themselves. He could not reinvent the Russian people or their history, but had to take things as they were and change them step by step. "Our people are not yet politically mature," he would explain. "They need time to learn the responsibilities of self-government."[5]

There was much wisdom in Gorbachev's understanding of the political situation in Russia, and his tactics worked for a while. But he also had some blind spots in his understanding of the situation. Throughout this period, the Soviet economy experienced increasing difficulties. If the Brezhnev period had been one of stagnation, the Gorbachev period became one marked by deterioration, at first slow, but by 1990 a rapid decline threatening collapse. While Gorbachev had an acute understanding of political liberalism (although he used a different vocabulary), he had little understanding of economics, particularly market economics, and did little to encourage the institution building necessary for a market economy, or the development of laws and procedures to encourage successful entrepreneurship.

Gorbachev also had trouble grasping the importance of nationalist sentiments among the non-Russian population of the Soviet Union, which by 1990 exceeded the ethnic Russian population. He seems to have believed that ethnic nationalism had been largely superseded by Soviet patriotism. Therefore, he showed no sympathy with and little understanding of the nationalist movements that began in 1986 and 1987 in the western and southern regions of the Soviet Union. KGB reports did little to enlighten him about the nature of nationalist sentiments, since these reports usually pictured nationalist movements as small groups of troublemakers without extensive public support in their regions.

That is why Gorbachev seems to have been taken by surprise by Lithuania's declaration of independence in the spring of 1990 (more precisely, a declaration that its independence had been restored) and, although he huffed and puffed and briefly applied some economic sanctions, he refused to suppress the Lithuanians, or the Estonians and Latvians who were following the same course toward independence. The elected leaders of all three Baltic republics were permitted to stay in office and even fly their official planes into Moscow for meetings with the American secretary of state and other foreign dignitaries. Gorbachev's leniency in the face of what many Communist officials considered treasonous attempts at illegal secession stoked opposition to his leadership within the Communist Party, the KGB, and the military. From the spring of 1990, the conventional wisdom in Moscow was that Gorbachev would be removed if he allowed any of the Baltic countries to assert its independence. Shevardnadze, still foreign minister at the time, told me privately in March that he feared a successful coup against Gorbachev if the Lithuanians declared independence before Gorbachev had been installed in the newly created post of president.[6]

Though Gorbachev failed to understand the growing force of nationalism

in the Baltic area, he was remarkably successful as a tactician, maneuvering
the Communist Party out of the total power it had exercised since Lenin's
time. He reduced the size of staffs of local party organizations, making it
more difficult for them to control the local bureaucrats. There were contested elections in 1989, when several unpopular party bosses lost their seats
and many new faces appeared in the new legislature. Then, in 1990, he was
able to establish the office of president, in theory at least independent of
Communist Party control. He also persuaded the quasi-elected legislature to
rescind the notorious Article VI of the Constitution, which made the Communist Party the only legal political party in the country. But he made a serious error when he arranged to be elected president by the legislature, not
by the population as a whole.*

The Yeltsin Factor

By 1990 and 1991, Gorbachev also became caught in a struggle for power
with a former protégé, Boris Yeltsin. In 1985 party leaders had brought
Yeltsin from Sverdlovsk, a provincial capital in the Urals, to be Communist
Party boss in Moscow city, with instructions to reform the party organization
in the capital. Yeltsin did so with such vigor that he won the hearts of Mus-
covites but clashed with conservative elements in the party, and—equally
important—with Raisa Gorbacheva, who, unlike the wives of previous Communist Party leaders, took an active interest in political developments, pes-
tering senior officials with questions, suggestions, and comments.

When Yeltsin criticized Gorbachev for not moving fast enough on reform
and offered to resign his position in the Politburo in the fall of 1987, Gorbachev turned against Yeltsin with fury. Acting on a signal from Gorbachev,
speaker after speaker at the party meeting condemned Yeltsin, removing
him from the Politburo. A few days later, Yeltsin was forced from his sickbed
to attend a meeting of the Moscow Party Committee, which removed him as
its chief following a barrage of humiliating charges. Nevertheless, Gorbachev allowed Yeltsin to stay in Moscow in a politically innocuous position,
as first deputy chairman of the State Construction Committee. Some eigh-

---

*The initial term of office was to be six years, after which there would be a general
election.

teen months later Yeltsin managed to contest the Moscow seat in the new, elective parliament that Gorbachev's reforms had created. His popularity was such that he won more than 90 percent of the vote against a candidate backed by the Communist Party apparatus. In the minds of many Russians, Yeltsin became overnight the leader of a democratic opposition to Communist Party rule.

By 1990, Yeltsin had become a significant political force. He left the Communist Party with great fanfare, ostentatiously walking out of an all-union CPSU conference in full view of the television cameras. As yet unable to contest Gorbachev throughout the USSR, he set his sights on securing leadership of the largest Soviet republic, the Russian Socialist Federated Soviet Republic (RSFSR). Unlike the fourteen non-Russian republics, the RSFSR had not, until 1990, had its own Communist Party organization—it was ruled directly by the CPSU—and it had a less comprehensive governmental bureaucracy. For the most part, the USSR bureaucracy ruled it directly rather than through local bureaucracies that had been created in the non-Russian republics.

As Russians saw the Baltic peoples declaring independence and nationalist movements arising in the other non-Russian republics, many of them began to insist that the RSFSR have the same degree of autonomy from the central government as the other republics. Pressure to create a Russian Communist Party within the CPSU became irresistible, and one was formed in 1990 despite determined opposition by Gorbachev, who recognized the threat this could eventually pose to the Soviet Union as a unified state. The danger to Gorbachev's position increased when the Russian Communist Party elected leaders who stood in opposition to many of his reforms.

Yeltsin was anathema to the hard-line Communists who dominated the newly formed Russian Communist Party, but he took them on in the RSFSR legislature elected in 1990 in a relatively free election. After two inconclusive ballots, Yeltsin squeaked through to become the chairman of the legislature. From that point, he had a political base to mount a direct challenge to Gorbachev.

By the summer of 1990 close observers of developments in the Soviet Union realized that the future of the nation might well depend on the ability of Gorbachev and Yeltsin to cooperate. Gorbachev and Yeltsin began to meet at times and to make agreements, but then one or the other would back out of what had been agreed. Their views on reform of the economy varied, with Yeltsin favoring more radical measures and Gorbachev reluctant to move too rapidly lest the state-run economy collapse altogether.

Meanwhile economic conditions were worsening, with growing shortages of food and consumer goods, and efforts began within the Communist Party to force Gorbachev's resignation.

Gorbachev's "Feint to the Right"

Fearing that if he should be driven from his post as general secretary of the Communist Party he would not be able to retain control of the country, Gorbachev began in November 1990 to appease the opponents of reform by appointing some of them to important positions. Sensing that he no longer had Gorbachev's full support, Eduard Shevardnadze resigned as foreign minister in December, predicting that "a dictatorship is coming."

Gorbachev's moves to reassure his opponents in the party only emboldened them to more aggressive tactics. In January 1991, KGB chairman Vladimir Kryuchkov masterminded a rehearsal of the attempted coup against Gorbachev by organizing a shadowy Committee of National Salvation in Lithuania and sending an elite KGB military unit to take the television tower in Vilnius, killing seventeen people in the process. The operation seems to have taken Gorbachev by surprise; he condemned it, but he seemed unwilling or unable to move against the perpetrators. When I saw him in a private meeting shortly thereafter, he told me that the country was on the brink of civil war. To avoid it he had to zig and zag, but he asked me to assure President Bush that he had not changed his goal of bringing democracy to the Soviet Union.[7]

He may not have changed his goal (I am confident he had not), but he quickly lost whatever credibility he had with democratic reformers during 1989 and 1990. In February 1991, he gave a speech in Minsk accusing the reformers of attempting to overthrow the government, then, misled by KGB disinformation, brought troops into Moscow to prevent a mob assault on the Kremlin when only peaceful demonstrations had been planned. The economy continued to deteriorate and Yeltsin started withholding taxes from the union government. When Grigory Yavlinsky worked out a plan for radical economic reform that might have attracted Western help, Gorbachev shelved it in favor of trying to keep the state-run economy afloat—something no Western government was prepared to assist.

In the spring of 1991, Gorbachev tried to shore up his eroding authority by conducting a referendum on the desirability of preserving a union state. Although some republics refused to participate at all, the proposition won a majority of votes in those republics that held it, and also in the autonomous entities of the Georgian republic. However, it turned out to provide little assistance to Gorbachev's efforts to preserve the union, because the wording was ambiguous and varied in different republics.

Yeltsin agreed to hold the referendum in Russia, but he took advantage of it by adding to the ballot a proposition to establish the post of president in the RSFSR. This received overwhelming support, and shortly thereafter Yeltsin was elected president of the RSFSR by a wide margin in the popular vote. Nevertheless, he continued to negotiate with Gorbachev on the terms of a union treaty, and it appeared in early August 1991 that there was agreement with Russia and seven other republics to sign the treaty Gorbachev sought.

Bush Tries to Help

As much as the U.S. government wanted to see independence restored to Estonia, Latvia, and Lithuania, it did not want the Soviet Union to collapse.* Gorbachev's plans to establish a voluntary federation seemed to the Bush administration more in keeping with American interests than the sudden creation of twelve independent countries, most with no experience governing themselves, and several with stocks of nuclear weapons.

---

*Following the Bush-Gorbachev meeting at Malta in December 1990, there were rumors that Bush had agreed that the Soviet Union could keep the Baltic republics if it allowed the Eastern European countries to throw off their Communist rulers. There was no basis whatever for those rumors. At Malta, Gorbachev assured Bush that he would not use force to keep Communists in power in Eastern Europe, but Bush did not change the longstanding U.S. position that the incorporation of the three Baltic nations in the Soviet Union had been illegal and that these countries should be allowed to regain their freedom. Both President Bush and Secretary of State Baker met personally with the elected leaders of Estonia, Latvia, and Lithuania to support their efforts to achieve Soviet recognition of their independence. They also stressed to the Baltic leaders the importance of keeping their struggle for independence entirely peaceful.

Sudden independence also did not seem in the interest of most of the nations directly involved, assuming that the welfare of the people was considered more important than the continuation in power of Communist bosses. Although the Baltic peoples were responsible and entirely peaceful in their push for independence, violence was beginning to prevail in some other areas. Georgian leader Zviad Gamsakhurdia was conducting a military campaign against South Ossetia, an autonomous area in the Georgian republic, and tensions were rising in Abkhazia, another such area. Fighting had broken out between Armenians and Azerbaijanis following pogroms against Armenians in Sumgait and Baku. Fledgling democratic movements in the five Central Asian republics and in Belarus were dependent almost entirely on the protection of Gorbachev's government in Moscow. In a country full of grievances and with a history of ethnic conflict, it seemed obvious that a voluntary federation would provide a better framework for effective reform and democracy building than immediate independence.

That is why George Bush, following meetings with Gorbachev and Yeltsin in Moscow, traveled to Kiev on August 1, 1991, and appealed to the Ukrainian parliament to approve Gorbachev's union treaty. His address was caricatured by columnist William Safire, who called it Bush's "chicken Kiev" speech, but what did Bush in fact say? He said that freedom and independence were not synonymous and that freedom should take precedence. Subsequent events have proved the wisdom of his unheeded exhortation.

Cheerleading from Bush or any other foreign leader could not halt the progressive disintegration of the Soviet empire. There were too many ghosts coming out of too many closets, too many old scores to settle, and too much at stake for the individuals involved. Loss of a government position could mean losing one's livelihood, there being as yet no significant private sector where retired officials could take refuge and flourish.

Gorbachev also failed at times to help his own cause. He went to the meeting of the Group of Seven in London in June 1991, hoping to enlist support for the ailing Soviet economy, but did not have a reform plan worthy of support and therefore got little.

When I received a report of a conspiracy to remove Gorbachev and, on President Bush's instructions, tried to warn him, he laughed it off. I probably made a mistake by not naming the people involved, but since I could not confirm the report with certainty, I thought I should not finger individuals. I assumed, incorrectly, that he could figure out for himself who was probably involved. The names I had were those of the people who did try to remove him some six weeks after my attempted warning.[8]

The fact that Gorbachev himself had put in office the people who betrayed him in August 1991 illustrates another flaw in his leadership: he was a poor judge of people and had difficulty working with those who might someday outshine him with the public.

Too Little, Too Late

Gorbachev might have succeeded in cobbling together a federation of seven or eight republics if KGB chairman Kryuchkov had not organized an attempt to remove him on August 19, 1991, while Gorbachev was on vacation in the Crimea. The poorly planned effort collapsed in less than three days, after Boris Yeltsin defied the junta and Soviet military forces refused orders to move against Yeltsin, the elected president of the Russian republic. When Gorbachev returned to Moscow from his vacation villa, where he had been held hostage, his political authority was shattered. Yeltsin, who had saved Gorbachev by opposing the plot against him, humiliated him publicly and systematically undermined the powers of the central government, subordinating the key institutions of the USSR government to those of the Russian republic. After Ukraine, in the wake of the failed coup, declared its independence, Yeltsin conspired with Leonid Kravchuk, the Ukrainian leader, and Stanislav Shushkevich, the chairman of the Belarusian parliament, to abolish the Union of Soviet Socialist Republics as a legal entity and replace it with a loose commonwealth deprived of the attributes of a sovereign state.*

The elected president of Russia triumphed over the unelected president of the Soviet Union.

---

*Russia, Ukraine, and Belorussia, along with the Transcaucasian Republic, had been the founding republics of the USSR. Since the Transcaucasian Republic no longer existed in 1991, having been divided into three republics, Georgia, Armenia, and Azerbaijan, the three leaders asserted the right of the founders to dissolve the legal entity they had created. Their claim could be challenged logically, but there was never a practical possibility to do so.

In many respects, the collapse of the Soviet Union was, as political scientists would say, overdetermined. It had multiple causes, only some of which might have been sufficient to bring it down.[9] Gorbachev made his share of political mistakes, but the enemies who resisted his reforms made more serious ones. Their attempt to force the Soviet Union back into an authoritarian (if not totalitarian) cage so undermined the capacity of the president of the Soviet Union and its quasi-elected legislature to govern that dissolution of the union was probably inevitable, even if the president of Russia had not seen it in his interest to rid the country of his rival. But the fact remains that it was the elected government of Russia that rejected both Russian and Soviet imperialism and sloughed off most of the Soviet empire—which, before the Bolshevik Revolution, had been a Russian empire.

Many questions of detail about the Soviet collapse may still be unclear and debatable, but one conclusion is absolutely clear: *pressure from governments outside the Soviet Union, whether from America or Europe or anywhere else, had nothing to do with it.* The Soviet leaders did it to themselves. What pressure there was from the outside was intended to keep as much of the Soviet Union together as possible. Aside from the restored independence of Estonia, Latvia, and Lithuania, which the West had always favored, the disappearance of the USSR as a coherent modern state was a *defeat* for U.S. and Western policy.

Learning from the Soviet Collapse

We have looked at some of the conclusions that might be derived from the Cold War and the way it ended. Are there any we can apply today from the collapse of the Soviet state and the breakup of the Soviet Union? Some might conclude that since the Soviet system was in many ways the antithesis of American or European democracy, there is nothing applicable to us that we can learn from its demise. Nevertheless, though our systems are quite different, and the geopolitical situation facing the United States today is quite distinct from that of the Cold War period, I believe there are important lessons for us in the breakup of the Soviet state.

For example, does the Soviet experience not illustrate something about the process of democratization? The Soviet collapse occurred not when the

Soviet Union was most tyrannical, but when it had become open to the outside world and its leaders were trying to build democratic institutions. Shouldn't we pay attention to why these efforts failed to create a democratic federation? Also, even if the Soviet Union had not changed internally, is there anything in its behavior abroad that contributed to its downfall? If so, does that experience not serve as a potential warning, even for countries with a different type of government?

It will be best to treat these two types of experience separately. Let's take the effects of democratization first.

Evil Empire No More

When I wrote a book about the collapse of the Soviet Union, published in 1995, I noted at the conclusion that, unlike many others, I was unable to celebrate when the Soviet Union ceased to exist.[10] This was because, by December 1991, the Soviet Union had already become something quite different from the Communist-ruled totalitarian state it had been during most of my life. Not only had it given up its "external empire" in Eastern Europe and recognized the independence of the three Baltic countries Stalin had acquired illegally, but it was also in the midst of encouraging democratic reforms throughout its internal empire. Democratic leaders from Uzbekistan to Belarus had told me that local Communist bosses would have long since halted their activities if it had not been for the support they received from Moscow while Gorbachev was in power.

The fact was, for most of the non-Russian republics other than Estonia, Latvia, Lithuania, and those in the southern Caucasus, the local Communist leaders who resisted Moscow's continued control did so to prevent democratization and to preserve their rule over the economic assets of their republic. They were the enemies of most of what Gorbachev was trying to do, seeing accurately that his reforms would eventually remove them from total control of their satrapies. Many had supported or stayed passive during the August coup attempt against Gorbachev; once it failed and Yeltsin decided that the best way to remove Gorbachev was to destroy the Soviet Union, they were pleased to grab their piece of the shattered Soviet empire. Both democratization and meaningful economic reform ended in most of these erstwhile Soviet republics.

Few outside the Soviet Union understood these important nuances. Assuming that the Soviet Union was still the dictatorship it had traditionally been, most foreign observers could not contain their joy. "The wicked witch is dead!" seemed to be their triumphant cry. In fact, the most wicked witch had already been swept aside; the sudden Soviet collapse, among other things, empowered a coven of smaller ones.

The Soviet Union had never been precisely what the ideologists and theoreticians had imagined. It was not a "communist" state that Karl Marx would have recognized, or a "socialist" state that a Western European democratic socialist would recognize. It was, rather, a country of state-monopoly capitalism, with the government essentially a front organization controlled from behind the scenes by a giant conspiratorial mafia called the Communist Party of the Soviet Union. The Communist Party ultimately controlled all property in the Soviet Union; the official economy operated not on market principles but on the basis of dictated prices and allocations—a command economy. Consumer goods and services were supplied mainly through an unofficial black market that operated on market principles, but illegally.

Although the command economy could, at great human and material cost, mobilize resources to force rapid industrialization and to support a massive military establishment, it did so only at the expense of the population's living standards and technological progress. When people's expectations of a better life failed to materialize in the 1970s and 1980s, economic, political, and intellectual stagnation ensued. Most people wanted change, but they felt powerless to bring it about and hadn't given much thought as to what it might look like.

Gorbachev changed that. By permitting freedom of speech and opening up the media to accurate information about the world and about the past, he gave Soviet citizens the unaccustomed feeling that they could influence the way their country was governed. Most people outside the party apparatus, the military, and the KGB (and a few within those organizations) used this newfound freedom to press for radical change. As one young woman told a television interviewer before the 1989 election, she intended to vote "against everything we have now and for those who will change it."[11] Her sentiment was not new or unusual; the fact that she not only had a chance to vote in a contested election but could say these things with impunity and even have them broadcast on national television was not only new, it was figuratively —and, as it eventually turned out, literally—revolutionary.

A heady air of liberation pervaded much of the Soviet Union during the last years of Gorbachev's rule. The instruments of compulsion were visibly crumbling, and most of the stifling controls on information, travel, and human contact were being relaxed and, by 1991, abandoned altogether. But these newfound freedoms emerged as economic conditions deteriorated for the majority. And, as yet, the institutions that make a democracy and a market economy work had not been developed. Many people seemed to feel that "democracy" meant the absence of any restraints on behavior.

During a visit to the Crimea in 1990, the mayor of Yalta took my wife and me on a tour of the city. It was a warm, sunny day, and many people were on the beaches and swimming in the Black Sea. It was an idyllic scene in many ways, except that I noticed a large sign on one segment of the beach that warned in Russian: DANGER, NO SWIMMING. There must have been a score of frolicking swimmers in the prohibited area. I pointed to them and asked the mayor why the authorities did not enforce safety regulations. He shrugged and explained, "We have democracy now; we can't tell people what to do."

With that concept of democracy lodged in newly freed Soviet heads, one could anticipate trouble ahead. There were also areas, particularly in Central Asia, where the authorities still considered democratic activists dangerous troublemakers. As soon as those party bosses were off Moscow's leash, they made quick work of the fledgling democrats Gorbachev's perestroika had produced.

It may be true that people everywhere ultimately desire freedom, but they may interpret it in different ways. Democratic institutions, and those that make a free-market economy efficient, do not rise automatically from the debris of authoritarian collapse.

Imperial Overstretch

In 1987, Yale professor Paul Kennedy published a best-selling study titled *The Rise and Fall of the Great Powers* in which he expounded the concept of "imperial overstretch"—the tendency great powers have to let their appetite for control over other countries exceed their digestive capacity. At the time it seemed that Professor Kennedy considered the United States guilty of imperial overstretch, but events soon proved that the Soviet Union was the overstretched empire, and that the imperial nature of the Soviet state had played a key role in its collapse. So Kennedy may have been misunderstood when people assumed he believed the United States would be the next great power to fall victim to imperial overstretch, but he was certainly correct to point out that imperial burdens can bring about the fall of great powers.

Differences between the Soviet Union and the United States are many and profound, but the differences may not be the end of the story. Are there not features of the two societies that bear some resemblance, in function if not concept? How often do we hear that American security depends on maintaining a larger military establishment than any imaginable combination of other countries? Or that our intelligence services are too small, or too inept, or too restricted in function to protect us properly? Or, that we will only live in security in a world where most countries (some would say *all* countries) share our form of government? Or—following from the latter —that we will be insecure in the future if we do not use our military prowess to promote our form of government—"democracy"—in the world?

With all the differences in the two systems, the Soviet and the American, do we not find analogous claims, mutatis mutandis, made for the USSR during its existence? And, if we do—did these ideas help or hinder the Soviet Union to fulfill the mission its founders set for it, or even—if we postulate a more modest goal—to insure its continuation as a going concern? If we look carefully, without preconception, at some of the factors that weakened the Soviet Union and contributed to its final agony, I believe we will find some things that may apply to us as well.

Let's start with one of the most fundamental mistaken ideas that led to the Soviet collapse: *Control of territory and people equals power.*

No way! In the modern world, few things *weaken* a government more than an attempt to rule people who do not want to be ruled by that government. Stalin acted in accord with the illusion that control equals power when, following his deal with Hitler, he forced a vast swath of territory west of the then Soviet border into the Soviet Union: the three independent Baltic states, the eastern provinces of Poland, the eastern tip of Czechoslovakia, and Romanian Bessarabia, which he called Moldavia, a misnomer that revealed his lust for even more Romanian territory.*

None of the people in these areas, aside from tiny groups of Communists, had any desire to be part of the Soviet Union; in fact, they hated the idea and resisted as best they could (including, in some instances, siding with the Germans as a lesser evil). Stalin dealt with them brutally, particularly after Soviet troops reoccupied the area in 1944. Wholesale arrests were made of "bourgeois" elements who were executed or sent off to the gulag. Those few who managed to return home following Khrushchev's mass release of political prisoners after Stalin's death came back broken, physically, if not spiritually.

In western Ukraine, churches of the predominant Uniate religion, Catholics who recognized the pope in Rome but followed the Eastern Orthodox liturgy in their services, were forcibly turned over to the Russian Orthodox Church, itself suppressed in the Soviet Union, but allowed to exist in limited fashion. Stalin considered the Russian Orthodox Church less of a threat than a church with allegiance to Rome. The Uniate Church was declared illegal and its priests arrested if they tried to continue conducting services.

Thus, a vast expanse of territory with tens of millions of people became "integral" parts of the Soviet state. Almost to a person, the people living there were opposed, but what could they do? In Stalin's time, even the thought of opposition tended to be a death sentence.

As Gorbachev began to loosen the tight controls over public expression, nationalist shock waves, beginning precisely in the territories grabbed and plundered by Stalin, began to spread. People in the three Baltic republics, western Ukraine, and Moldova began to agitate, first for autonomy, then for independence. Georgia, Azerbaijan, and Armenia, invaded and absorbed following the Russian Civil War, followed suit. In addition, Estonians, Latvians, and Lithuanians organized a calculated campaign in every one of the non-Russian Soviet republics to press for independence.

---

*Bessarabia was only the eastern part of the principality of Moldavia. Therefore, in naming Bessarabia Moldavia, Stalin implied a claim to the rest of the historic principality.

If Stalin had not taken these territories formally into the Soviet Union and committed atrocities against their peoples, but had left them as independent states, or parts of other independent countries, Gorbachev would have had a much easier time keeping the Soviet Union together as a voluntary federation.

Stalin's policy of territorial aggrandizement was based on the conviction that one could create "facts on the ground" by force and intimidation that could be maintained indefinitely. If we look back in history we can find instances when this worked, at least for a few centuries. Most countries in Western Europe were formed out of smaller units that were united by military conquest or territorial acquisition without reference to the desires of those living in the territory. In Asia, both China and Japan were periodically united on such a basis, and often the unity lasted for centuries. Since life was usually better for most people when the country was united under a single ruler rather than divided among contesting barons or warlords, public opinion usually favored a single ruler so long as the rule was not overly oppressive.

Acquisition of territory by force worked in an age that considered monarchy a legitimate, heaven-ordained form of rule and states the patrimonial possession of a family of rulers who could legitimately buy, sell, trade, or simply take control of a territory when they were strong enough to do so. It does not work in the modern age, since people virtually everywhere on the globe have been infected with the idea that the people living in a territory should be able to choose how they will be governed and by whom.

Stalin, of course, did not claim the divine right of a monarch to augment Russian territory. He claimed the right bestowed by "history" to take possession of territory and the people on it in the name of the "proletariat," which history had decreed would supplant the bourgeoisie as the rulers of society. Marx and his followers had claimed to be atheists, but their faith in the forces of history imputed to it the same functions that a believer would attribute to the deity. Marxism, as Lenin and Stalin interpreted and applied it, was the functional equivalent of a religion, and the Soviet Union itself was a faith-based state. The problem was that neither the religion nor the faith it inspired were consistent with actual conditions. A state created and held together primarily by force and intimidation will last only so long as its leaders have the means and will to use whatever force is necessary to stay in power. The Soviet Union disintegrated as a unified state when Gorbachev was not willing (and, arguably, not able) to use force to keep it together.

This leads to a related thought, that *when one uses force to create a utopia, the opposite is the most likely result.* This has been a frequent observation of philosophers, and has been emphasized recently in a passionately argued book by the conservative British philosopher John Gray, *Black Mass: Apocalyptic Religion and the Death of Utopia.* As Gray points out, both Nazism and communism were secular religions despite their claims to the contrary. They, like some strains of Christianity and Islam, believe "that history must be understood not in terms of the causes of events, but in terms of its purpose, which is the salvation of humanity."[12] Once events are viewed in teleological terms, understanding of actual causes is obscured, distorted, and if necessary totally invented by true believers.

We can find abundant proof of this proposition in the views of people as diverse as Osama bin Laden and America's neoconservatives. A passionate faith in what is "right" or what is "God's will" serves as license to apply any method, including the most violent ones, to achieve a utopia, either on earth or in the hereafter.

A mistaken faith can lead one astray if it feeds a distorted comprehension of reality. A leader's judgment can also be crippled by false information. For decades, the gigantic Soviet intelligence apparatus had been conditioned to report what the leaders wanted to hear, not what was actually happening if that contradicted ideological presuppositions or was unflattering to those in power.[13] When Gorbachev's reforms progressed, however, the intelligence reports were tailored to fit the political aims of Vladimir Kryuchkov, the KGB chairman, who underestimated rising nationalist sentiment in the non-Russian republics, tried to demonize the growing democratic movement, and in particular sought to prevent any cooperation between Gorbachev and Yeltsin.

Gorbachev was often taken in by false reports. For example, he was convinced that Lithuania's very popular leader, Vytautas Landsbergis, was only a troublemaker with few followers. When democratic forces planned a large demonstration in Moscow in March 1991, the KGB convinced Gorbachev that the demonstrators had plans to "storm the Kremlin," which caused him to order troops into Moscow. (The demonstrations took place anyway but were peaceful, as their leaders had intended all along.)

I was personally involved in another piece of egregious KGB disinformation. When Secretary of State Baker met privately with Gorbachev in March 1991 and urged him to try to cooperate with Yeltsin, Gorbachev told him that he had received a report that Yeltsin had asked me what the United States would do if he, Yeltsin, came to power "by unconstitutional means." When he left the meeting, Baker asked me if there was anything to that. Of course, there was not. Yeltsin had never said anything to me that could be interpreted as an intention to seize power illegally. Anyone knowledgeable about Soviet conditions would know that this was a preposterous idea, since Yeltsin was hated by the KGB, the army, and the Communist Party apparatus. There was no conceivable way he could seize power without the cooperation of the very people who despised him most.[14]

The next day I called on Anatoly Chernyaev and told him that the report of Yeltsin's conversation with me was an utter fabrication. He accepted my statement, remarking that he had not seen the report Gorbachev had mentioned to Baker but that it was very important to set Gorbachev straight. Chernyaev assured me he would tell Gorbachev what I said, but he suggested that I clarify the matter with Gorbachev personally. I did so during my next appointment with him. Gorbachev accepted my explanation, remarking that the information he had received "came from Yeltsin's own people." I told him I had no idea where it might have come from; I knew only that it was not true. Within days, Gorbachev renewed negotiations with Yeltsin and other union republic leaders for a union treaty to replace the Soviet constitution.

Vladimir Kryuchkov, who subsequently organized the attempt to isolate Gorbachev and take command of the country from him, systematically used his control of both internal and external intelligence to promote those policies he favored—in this case, a crackdown on dissidence and, probably, orders to arrest Yeltsin and other leaders of the democratic movement. The result was that, in 1991, the American government was better informed about what was happening in the Soviet Union than was President Gorbachev. The U.S. government expected its diplomats and intelligence agencies to report what was happening, even if what they had learned did not fit preconceptions in Washington. In the Soviet Union, the KGB had been allowed to become a state within a state, and the political authorities had no mechanism to ensure that intelligence reports were accurate.

Although more accurate intelligence might have induced Gorbachev to make some decisions differently, it is unlikely that it would have saved the Soviet Union once democratic reforms began to take hold. In the twenty-first century, empires are no longer viable political entities. Losing the "external empire" in Eastern Europe did not help preserve the "internal empire," the Soviet Union itself.

Regime change occurred in the Soviet Union when political forces inside the country brought it about. It did not result from American or Western pressure. In fact, the Bush administration sought in vain to support Gorbachev's efforts to bring the twelve non-Baltic Soviet republics into a voluntary democratic federation.

Nevertheless, at the beginning of the twenty-first century, the son of the first President Bush headed an administration that ignored virtually every lesson that might have been derived from the end of the Cold War and the disintegration of the Soviet Union. President George W. Bush and the advisers he relied upon seemed to assume that America had "won" the Cold War by its military and economic superiority, that it could simply demand "regime change" and other governments would fall, that it could change "facts on the ground" and create American-style democracies by occupying other countries, that it could allow precooked and sometimes fabricated intelligence to guide decisions of peace and war.

5

A New World?

1992

BY THE TIME JANUARY 1, 1992, HAD dawned, it was obvious that communism was no longer a threat to the world order and the Cold War was definitively in the past. The post–World War II era, dominated by two nuclear-armed superpowers confronting each other, had ended. The United States was left as the preeminent military, economic, and political power in the world. It had become so not by defeating other countries, but by building a more productive society at home, regulating most disputes with others through negotiation, and attracting the support of other countries that shared the values of democracy and political freedom. The "hot wars" fought in Korea and Vietnam had ended for the United States either in a draw (Korea) or in defeat (Vietnam). As important as they had seemed at the time they were fought, they probably had not been necessary to end the Cold War. In the end, the Communist system in the Soviet Union defeated itself.

President George Bush had already come to understand some of the possibilities the Cold War's end created for the world community. He had no grand design, but he saw that the United States had an opportunity to guide the world toward a less violent international environment, one based more on cooperation and consent than on force. He called it a "new world order," but in fact his aim was not a new system of international relations that would replace the nation-state pattern that emerged from the Peace of Westphalia in 1648; rather, he envisioned a change in the way nation-states dealt with one another.* The Peace of Westphalia ended the Thirty Years' War between Protestant and Catholic states in north and central Europe with an agreement to eliminate religion as a reason for war.[1] Thenceforth, wars would continue to be fought in Europe, but not over religion; each ruler would determine whether his domain would be Protestant or Catholic, and other rulers would not challenge that choice. Wars did continue to be fought over territory, however, and by the twentieth century, the concept of "total war," whereby civilians were targeted almost as much as military forces, ravaged Europe through two large conflicts that involved much of the world outside Europe as well.

Steps to a Safer World

George Bush did not set out to overturn the nation-state system of international relations, but he and his close associates, Secretary of State James Baker and Assistant for National Security Brent Scowcroft, understood that the end of the Cold War created an opportunity to set precedents that, with luck, might lead to a more orderly, less violent international environment. They concentrated on three important areas: deterring aggression by states, reducing the threat of nuclear, biological, and chemical weapons, and avoiding involvement in local and regional disputes devoid of any compelling American interest.

Outlawing Aggression

Through most of human history, the world has accepted, sometimes explicitly and sometimes tacitly, the acquisition of territory by conquest. That includes the United States itself, since its expansion to the west of the North American continent was based on its ability to subdue the native inhabitants by military force and, in the Southwest from Texas to California, to force Mexico to cede territory. As a result of the Spanish-American War of

*Peggy Noonan, Bush's speechwriter who reportedly coined the phrase, was too young to remember that Hitler had called his regime the "New Order" (Neue Ordnung). Therefore, for many Europeans, the phrase carried unwelcome associations. But Bush, never comfortable with phrase making, and Noonan, ever adept with the punchy line, meant well.

1898, it acquired the Philippines and Puerto Rico as colonies in all but name and Cuba as a protectorate—a fancy name for a colony governed indirectly.

Nevertheless, in the twentieth century, it became clear, especially to Americans, that the destructiveness of modern war and the growth of nationalist sentiments made territorial acquisition by conquest a dangerous and unacceptable practice. Efforts were intensified to deter acquisition of territory by military force. This was the principal goal of the League of Nations, President Woodrow Wilson's brainchild. That effort proved a failure, however, in part because it had no effective enforcement mechanism, and in part because the United States itself refused to participate.

In the 1920s, further efforts were made to outlaw war as an instrument of national policy and to limit armaments, but since there was no effective means to enforce these commitments, they proved no barrier to Italian, Japanese, and German aggression in the 1930s. Trying to learn from the lessons of the past, the United States took the lead during the closing years of World War II to create, with its allies, a more effective institution to keep the peace, and thus the United Nations was born. One qualification for membership, which eventually expanded to be almost universal, was a commitment not to use force except in self-defense. But the greatest difference from the defunct League of Nations was the enforcement mechanism the United Nations Charter established: a Security Council that could authorize collective resistance to infractions of the peace.

During the Cold War, the United Nations seemed powerless to arbitrate disputes between the United States and the Soviet Union, since each could veto any action it disliked. Nevertheless, the organization was much more useful than many Americans recognized. When the permanent members could agree, or when the Soviet Union boycotted the organization, it could authorize collective action, as it did in calling for resistance to the invasion of South Korea in 1950. This enabled the United States to combat the incursion under the United Nations flag and thus escape, for most of the world, the stigma of fighting a war for imperialist purposes. It also enabled the United States to obtain the direct support of many other countries that sent forces to fight with the Americans.

The United Nations was also useful in several score local disputes, by providing mediators and peacekeepers—most from smaller countries that could not be suspected of imperial ambitions. The end of the Cold War and of the ideological and geopolitical competition between the United States and the Soviet Union seemed to restore to the United Nations the potential to perform the role its creators had intended. That role was never—as some of the more opinionated critics assert—one of action independent of its member governments. It has none of the powers of government; it is merely an instrument for the collective action of its members. It has no power to do anything except what its members decide and pay for. What it can do is to provide international approval for the use of force and authorize member states to use it.

The first Bush administration did the world a great service when it decided to resist Saddam Hussein's invasion of Kuwait. Many have said that the Gulf War of 1991 was essentially an attempt to ensure access to (or control of) the oil resources of the Persian Gulf area. This is not entirely incorrect. The energy resources of the region gave it a strategic importance matched by few other areas of the world. But the war would have been neither necessary nor justified if Saddam Hussein had not attempted to swallow up a small neighbor and appropriate its natural resources. Resisting Iraqi aggression was important to avoid permitting the law of the jungle to replace accepted norms of international behavior. To serve that purpose, however, the resistance to Iraq's aggression had to be seen by the world as enforcement of international law and not simply as a struggle over petroleum resources. President Bush took meticulous care to line up nearly universal international support and to assemble an overwhelming military force in the area before he began military operations against Iraq.

When Iraq invaded Kuwait in August 1990, Bush's first move was to seek a condemnation of the invasion in the United Nations Security Council. If the Cold War had still been raging, any such suggestion would have been vetoed by the Soviet Union, which had a close relationship with Iraq, had supplied most of its military equipment and trained its army, and hoped to gain a major stake in the development of Iraq's substantial petroleum resources. Secretary of State Baker, who had been in Mongolia, flew home via Moscow and, during a brief meeting with Shevardnadze in the VIP terminal at Moscow's Vnukovo Airport, persuaded Shevardnadze to instruct the Soviet delegation to the United Nations to vote to condemn the invasion.

This was not an easy decision for either Shevardnadze or Gorbachev, who approved it subsequently. Most Soviet experts on the Middle East were against formally condemning the Iraqi invasion. They argued that Soviet interests in Iraq required the Soviet Union to block any attempt by the United States to force the Iraqis out of Kuwait. Nevertheless, Shevardnadze told his staff, "Iraq may be our friend, but even so, if your friend does something wrong, you should tell him so." This was the opposite of the Cold War attitude, and it was clear evidence that the Cold War was over.

At first, the U.S. Congress was not pleased with the thought of military intervention. But the Bush administration worked hard to convince the public and key senators that it was important to be prepared to force Saddam Hussein to leave Kuwait if he refused to respond to the U.N. resolution and the demands of neighbors by withdrawing his forces from Kuwait. At the same time, Baker and his State Department colleagues worked feverishly to secure the support of NATO allies, Japan, and—most important—almost every Arab country in the area.

Even though the Soviet Union had voted in the United Nations to condemn the invasion of Kuwait, Gorbachev did not want to sanction a war against Iraq. But President Bush came to Helsinki, Finland, to meet Gorbachev and persuaded him to agree to a resolution that would authorize the use of "all necessary means" if Iraqi forces were not withdrawn from Kuwait.

As the diplomacy progressed—to the point that Baker had obtained assurances that others, mainly Kuwait, Saudi Arabia, Germany, and Japan, would pay the costs of any military operation—American forces and those of thirty-four coalition partners were moved to the Persian Gulf area. A force of more than half a million troops was available to General Norman Schwartzkopf when the order was finally given to liberate Kuwait. The battle lasted only forty-two days, until the remnants of Iraq's army of occupation were making their way, many on foot, up the road to Baghdad. Bush refused to authorize a "turkey shoot" of helpless Iraqi conscripts fleeing the battle, and stopped offensive operations, not trying to occupy Baghdad or to remove Saddam Hussein.

When asked why he did not order U.S. forces to proceed to the Iraqi capital, Bush pointed out that the U.N. Security Council had authorized "all necessary means" to liberate Kuwait, not to depose the Iraqi regime. Furthermore, if the Iraqi regime collapsed entirely, the United States and its allies (if any were left) would be faced with the difficult, perhaps impossible, task of governing the fractured country. To obtain the approval of Iraq's Arab neighbors, Bush had promised that the United States would not try to occupy Iraq, but only to ensure that Saddam Hussein was deprived of weapons of mass destruction.*

Planning, preparing, and conducting the Persian Gulf War as President Bush did took us a step closer to the new world order of which he spoke. The system of U.N. inspections imposed on Saddam Hussein, along with vigorous economic sanctions, forced the Iraqi dictator to end his nuclear weapons program and to destroy his stocks of chemical and biological weapons. Unfortunately, it took thirteen years and another war to convince skeptics that this was true.

Reducing the Nuclear, Biological, and Chemical Threats

President Bush took another stride toward a new, safer international environment when he signed two treaties dealing with strategic nuclear weapons (START I in 1991 and START II just before leaving office in January 1993), reduced reliance on tactical nuclear weapons, and took U.S. nuclear bombers off alert.† These decisions and agreements were not adequate in themselves to keep the world safe from the nuclear threat, but they were steps in the right direction. START I was a giant step, cutting by half the most destructive and destabilizing nuclear weapons, with reliable on-site verification to make sure neither side would cheat.[2]

In 1992 the Bush administration also began implementing a program, initiated jointly by Senators Sam Nunn (D) and Richard Lugar (R), to assist

---

*Without violating promises to allies, Bush could have done more to damage Iraq's Presidential Guard and to protect the Shia in southern Iraq from Saddam Hussein's retribution when they rose up against him.

†Bush announced on September 17, 1991, that the United States would eliminate its inventory of ground-launched tactical nuclear weapons and remove all nuclear missiles from surface ships and attack submarines. Gorbachev responded on October 5, 1991, promising to remove all categories of nuclear weapons from deployment to "central storage facilities." In January 1992, Yeltsin confirmed Gorbachev's statement and slightly expanded it in the name of Russia. (Issue Brief, NTI Research Library, http://www.nti.org/e_research/e3_10a.html)

Russia in securing its nuclear weapons and nuclear materials, and in providing employment to Russian nuclear scientists who might be tempted to take their expertise to other countries. This program was farsighted and met an immediate need, since the collapse of the Soviet Union also brought a collapse of the economy, a sharp increase in criminal activity, and a weakening of the security measures that had protected the Soviet nuclear weapons program from unintended leakage of materials and know-how. It would be important throughout the 1990s and beyond to fund and manage cooperative security measures with Russia.

Secretary of State Baker negotiated another key agreement in May 1992 when he persuaded Kazakhstan, Belarus, and Ukraine to sign the Lisbon Protocol, agreeing that all former Soviet nuclear weapons would go to Russia.[3] Later, the Ukrainian parliament threatened to depart from this agreement, requiring the Clinton administration to continue negotiations in order to ensure that all nuclear weapons stationed in Ukraine would be returned to Russia.

As important as these programs and agreements were, they fell far short of moving toward the Reagan-Gorbachev vision of a world free of nuclear weapons. To do that, the momentum of weapons reduction with strict monitoring and verification needed to continue. The START II agreement required ratification by both the United States and Russia, and the informal understanding to reduce tactical nuclear weapons needed to be formulated into treaty obligations with agreed measures to verify compliance. If the United States and Russia were unable to keep momentum in reducing reliance on nuclear weapons—as the Nuclear Non-Proliferation Treaty of 1968 required—it would be much more difficult to hold the line on the further spread of these weapons to additional countries.

No weapon is humane, but biological weapons are instruments of special horror. To spread a disease that produces an agonizing death and is highly contagious, incapable of distinguishing between soldier and civilian —in fact, more dangerous to civilians without the protective devices or inoculations that may be available to military forces—would be an act that the human conscience has difficulty accepting.

Gorbachev had ordered the Soviet program closed after the U.S. and Britain demanded it, but some elements were apparently still in operation in 1992 after the Soviet Union collapsed. President Yeltsin assured the world that all such facilities would be closed. Obviously, it should have been a high priority to make sure that production of pathogens and toxins did not continue in Russia, to verify that the weapons created had been safely destroyed, and to develop antigens for them in case some had escaped destruction.

There were doubtless programs to make biological weapons elsewhere, such as in Iraq and North Korea, which needed to be dismantled. Although it is extremely difficult to make sure that every country respects the ban on biological weapons, the American government should have placed a high priority on developing means to do so. Despite the attention given to the Iraqi and Soviet biological weapons, there is no evidence of a serious attempt by the Bush I administration to take the lead in creating international verification procedures to deter bioweapons research.[4]

The Chemical Weapons Convention, signed by most countries in January 1993, a few days before President Bush left office, was a signal achievement of his administration. Although it was negotiated by a team of specialists at the U.N. Conference on Disarmament in Geneva, the convention had long been a personal goal of George Bush. While he was still vice president, he had gone to Geneva to submit the American draft treaty requiring the destruction of all chemical weapons stocks. Negotiating a ban on chemical weapons was controversial in the Reagan administration: Secretary of Defense Weinberger opposed it, preferring to develop a new generation of chemical weapons for the American arsenal. But Reagan overruled Weinberger and authorized Bush to press the issue. Though it would take years for the requisite number of signatures and ratifications to bring the treaty into force, the hardest work was over when Bush Senior left office.

Avoiding Involvement in Local Conflicts

Bush had tried to assist Gorbachev in holding the core republics of the Soviet Union together in a voluntary union, but when it became clear that this was impossible, he and Secretary of State Baker moved adroitly to establish good relations with all of the suddenly independent Soviet republics and to open embassies in them.[5]

Bush and Baker also injected caution in extending American involvement in disputes that were not directly relevant to American security. As tensions arose among Yugoslavia's constituent republics, they tried to keep the United States aloof and leave the primary responsibility to America's European allies. Regarding the growing conflict in Yugoslavia, Baker was quoted as saying, "We don't have a dog in that fight." He has denied making that statement, but his policy was not to get directly involved. Baker also counseled Armenia and Azerbaijan to settle their differences peacefully, and he supported the mediation offered by Russia, Kazakhstan, and the Organization for Security and Cooperation in Europe.

These were decisions that pointed American diplomacy in the right direction for the post–Cold War world. It was no longer necessary for the United States to hold the line against Communist expansion; it was time to entrust regional security to countries in the affected region and to avoid American involvement when valid American interests were not directly threatened.

Fumbling the Economic Transition

In other respects, however, George Bush failed to take full advantage of the unprecedented opportunity Gorbachev offered to influence the evolution of the Soviet economy to market-based capitalism. Instead of organizing, early in the process—say in 1989, or 1990 at the latest—an international effort to advise and support the difficult transition, he in effect stood aside and waited until Gorbachev could devise a plan that merited support.

I do not mean to suggest that it would have been politically possible, even under a charismatic president with a vision, to resurrect the Marshall Plan. Nor, in fact, would a copy of the Marshall Plan have worked, for the problem in the early 1990s in the Soviet Union and Eastern Europe was not the same as that in Europe in the mid-1940s. The Communist countries had not been devastated by war (at least not since 1945), but they had been saddled with a dysfunctional economic system, one that was failing not because of physical destruction, chance, or neglect, but because it was designed to replace a market-based system. Lenin and Stalin gave a monopoly of both political and economic power to the political leadership.

Market economics, they believed, was simply an instrument of exploitation; by establishing a command economy, they claimed to be protecting workers from capitalists who would exploit them. But what they built was a system whereby the exploitation was conducted by the state itself. The Soviet system was responsive not to the needs of the population but to the perceived needs of the state—meaning, in practice, the interests of the political elite that controlled the state. The organs of the state, including the executive authorities, police, and judiciary, were structured to support the command economy and to suppress any attempt at individual initiative. Owning income-producing property was illegal, as was hiring labor, the latter being considered exploitation by definition.

To move from a totally state-owned, state-run command economy to a market economy based largely on private ownership was like trying to convert a submarine to an aircraft while keeping it functioning with the same crew throughout the process. Nobody had done it before, and there were no handbooks or manuals to show what to do and what to avoid. What they had wasn't working, and Soviet reformers realized that they needed a system that, in it basic features, was the opposite. They knew how the existing system was designed and had an idea of what its replacement should be like, but no sense of how to convert what they had to what they wanted.

As I contemplated, from my vantage point in Moscow, the dilemma Gorbachev and his supporters faced in 1990 and 1991, I was reminded of the story of the alpinist who is confronted with a crevasse too wide to cross with the equipment he has. He hears that there is a wise hermit at the top of the mountain who gives sage advice. So he climbs up and asks the guru how to get over the chasm. "You should sprout wings and fly across," the oracle advises.

"But how do I do that?" the climber asks in dismay.

"That's an engineering question; I only deal in policy!" came the reply.

I am ashamed to report that most of the advice—from the United States, at least—that Gorbachev got when he was seeking help consisted of theory devoid of the engineering required to put it into practice.

Instead of taking the lead in organizing an international effort to combine Western knowledge of how a market economy works with Eastern (Soviet and Eastern European) knowledge of conditions and habits in their countries, Bush opted to call on the International Monetary Fund and the World Bank to deal with the problem. These are two fine institutions, but they had next to zero expertise in dealing with command economies of the Soviet type. The learning curve was steep, and much of the initial advice was not only useless, but sometimes actually damaging.

Yegor Gaidar, independent Russia's first premier, described the situation as follows: "When reforms began, we were not members of the IMF, and it took some time to join; any sort of financial cooperation was contingent on membership. In the critical months between January and April of 1992 as little as a few hundred million dollars of available currency reserves would have allowed us significantly more room to maneuver, but we had no access to them. And by the time the paperwork was finished, our stabilization program was coming apart at the seams."[6]

The IMF finally granted a billion-dollar loan in July 1992, but it was too late to prevent the collapse of the ruble. Actually the IMF contributed to that collapse by trying for months to preserve a "ruble zone" including the former Soviet republics, which ran their printing presses unrestrained throughout the year.

A little more than a year earlier, the Bush administration had raised more than $40 billion from other countries to pursue the Gulf War. In 1992 it did nothing to assemble an international effort that could offer the support Russia needed to transform its economy to a market system in an orderly fashion. Gaidar identified the problem when he observed, "I don't think that the leaders of the major Western powers were unaware of the magnitude of the choices they faced. The trouble, in my view, was that there was no leader capable of filling the sort of organizing and coordinating role that Harry Truman and George C. Marshall played in the postwar reconstruction of Europe."[7]

In 1991, a full year before Gaidar faced the nightmare of financial and economic collapse, Margaret Thatcher, although no longer prime minister of Great Britain, had correctly understood the need for massive Western assistance to the Soviet Union in the midst of fundamental transformation. During a visit to Moscow in the spring of 1991, she asked me to send a message on her behalf to President Bush with an appeal to organize a major effort to help Gorbachev reform the Soviet economy. Her appeal had no effect. Subsequently, she persuaded her successor, John Major, to offer support, but without American backing Major did not have the resources required.[8]

Generally, most Western experts advised a clean break with the past and a transition to private ownership without delay. In other words: "The elevator is unreliable and you don't have time to walk down the stairs, so why not just jump out the window." If the recipient of the advice is on the twentieth floor, there is an important factor that the adviser has ignored.

Of course, the goal had to be a shift of the bulk of the economy to private ownership, but in pressing for an immediate transition, the theorists ignored the fact that *there was no legitimate private capital in the country*. So, how do you get quick privatization? Well, you let Communist Party officials, senior military and KGB officers, and other privileged insiders join the criminals who had been running a black market steal what they could, as fast as they could. This process had already started, but in limited fashion, while Gorbachev was in charge of the Soviet Union. It greatly accelerated and became the norm in Russia and most of the other successor states, such as Ukraine, from 1992.

Maybe nothing else would have worked well either. The Soviet economy was such a mess that it is hard to be sure that any strategy could have saved it from collapse. But even without the hindsight we have now, people familiar with Soviet reality would have counseled a more gradual approach, first freeing up trade and small business, with generous loans available to entrepreneurs as well as arrest and prosecution of the criminals who preyed on small businesses. Heavy industry, rail and air transport, and communications could have remained temporarily under state ownership, as corporations required to compete with other state-owned corporations. That way, a structure might have been created for a more gradual privatization as private capital accumulated legally.

My point is not that the Bush administration, or the Clinton administration that followed it, is responsible for the mistakes that were made as the Soviet Union abandoned the command economy and Russia subsequently created a market economy. They are not. Russians made the decisions and Russians have had to live with the consequences. However, it is clear that most of the assistance and advice given by the West was not particularly helpful. It was based more on free-market fundamentalism than on the real problems of creating a market economy out of a collapsed command economy.

I witnessed an example of the sort of advice Americans gave in 1992, when I joined a meeting at the Hoover Institution in California on entrepreneurship in Russia. Ilya Zaslavsky, a member of the Moscow city council whom I had met when I was ambassador, had asked for the meeting to discuss a plan he had developed to promote small business in his district of Moscow. Zaslavsky had been one of the leaders of the democratic movement in Moscow and had defeated a Communist official for a seat on the city council. He was determined to privatize the small commercial enterprises in his district and had developed a plan to offer long-term low-interest loans from the city budget to entrepreneurs willing to create new businesses or to take ownership of state-owned stores, bakeries, and repair shops. When he explained his idea, the Hoover economists objected, saying that he must not involve the government; the government, they insisted, had to be kept at arm's length. If the government provided loans or subsidies, that would be perpetuating socialism.

Zaslavsky was incredulous. "If the government doesn't help, where are our entrepreneurs going to get their seed capital?" he asked.

"It must be from private sources," was the answer.

"You mean from our criminals?" he inquired. "If they provide the capital, they control the business. That's not what we want to happen."

Advice by the Hoover economists, and that of many other Western experts who were sent to Russia to teach how a market economy works, was about as practical as the guru's advice to the alpinist to sprout wings. A policy that paid more attention to Soviet reality and less to generalized theory might have helped mitigate some of the serious problems that developed during Russia's transition.

Why was this important to the United States? After all, once the Cold War ended and the Soviet Union itself shattered into fifteen sovereign states, the United States faced no plausible threat from the wreckage, aside from the possibility that nuclear or biological or chemical weapons, or the expertise to make them, might leak to rogue regimes or terrorists.

What happened to the countries that were once in the Soviet Union, and especially what happened in the largest, Russia, was important because there was going to be no "new world order" unless Russia could make a successful transition to a government and economic system responsive to its people's needs, to a government that would see itself as a responsible partner in providing security, supporting economic growth, and curbing crime and violence. For that to happen, the Russian people had to have the feeling that throwing off communism was a good thing and that they were welcomed by the rest of the world as partners in dealing with common problems.

In failing to assist a "soft landing" for the Russian economy, the West undermined the efforts of Russian democrats to create a liberal democracy on the ruins of the Soviet empire.

America's Addiction

Since the late 1940s, when the United States began importing oil on a large scale, its dependence on foreign petroleum had grown steadily. Demand continued to increase even as domestic production, from 1972, declined. By 1992, more than 42 percent of the petroleum consumed in America was imported, most from Middle East sources.

The Iraqi invasion of Kuwait in 1990 had been only the latest in a series of conflicts that endangered petroleum supplies from the Middle East. The American reaction to dependency on this unstable area had typically been to curry favor with oil-producing states, whatever their form of government, so long as they were friendly. Close relations with Saudi Arabia went back to Franklin Roosevelt's time. When an elected prime minister of Iran, Muhammad Mossadegh, nationalized the British-owned Anglo-Iranian Oil Company in 1952, the CIA helped organize a coup, which restored Shah Muhammad Reza Pahlavi to power the following year. For the next twenty-six years the United States depended largely on Iran to protect its interests in the Persian Gulf region. However, after the shah was overthrown in 1979 and American diplomats in Iran were taken hostage, President Carter dispatched a naval task force to the Persian Gulf.

From that point, the American military presence in the area grew, since it seemed necessary not only to ensure the free flow of oil from the gulf, but also to deter possible Soviet advances into the area, fear of which grew following the Soviet invasion of Afghanistan in December 1979. In 1985 the Brookings Institution published a thoughtful book on U.S. military strategy in the area by Thomas L. McNaugher. In it he based most of the rationale for a continued U.S. military presence in the area on the need to deter Soviet military intervention.[9]

As it turned out, the threat to gulf oil resources came not from the Soviet

Union but from one of the states in the area. Iraq invaded and occupied Kuwait in August 1990, and the United States was able to assemble an extensive coalition of oil-producing states and consumers to repulse Iraq's conquest.

Dependence on petroleum from the Persian Gulf doubtless helped form the coalition to oppose Iraq's grab, and to persuade Germany and Japan to contribute to the costs of the military campaign. Nevertheless, Saddam Hussein *had* been the aggressor; the United States and its allies did not try to seize the oil fields but only to return them to Kuwaiti control, and no effort was made to occupy oil-producing areas in Iraq. Iraq's infraction of international law was sufficient to justify the war, even though a full explanation of why the United States and its allies chose to enforce international law at that time must take account of the world's dependence on oil from the region.

This brings us to a second flaw in the first Bush administration's groundwork for a more peaceful world order. Despite America's vulnerability to any disruption in the supply of imported petroleum, the Bush administration did nothing to start the country on the path of reducing dependence on foreign energy. Instead, it increased the permanent U.S. military presence in the area, using it to keep Saddam Hussein in check by enforcing "no-fly" zones in part of Iraq. Inasmuch as these deployments were financed by U.S. taxpayers, the federal government would be bearing the cost of security for oil supplies and thus subsidizing American consumers' deeper and deeper addiction to that product.[10] Prices paid by the consumer did not cover the costs of the military presence in the Persian Gulf, which was borne by the American taxpayer. The subsidized low price of petroleum products in the United States made it much more difficult to finance development of alternate energy sources, even as environmental concerns made it clear that nonpolluting substitutes needed to be found for a significant portion of the fossil fuels consumed.

(Mis)Understanding the World Following the Cold War

Journalists, pundits, and scholars rushed to explain what had happened to end the Cold War and why the Soviet Union collapsed—developments few had foreseen but for which all, it seemed, had an explanation. Most acknowledged that the political world had changed radically. Obviously, one needed to understand the nature of world politics following the Cold War in order to adapt. We can now look back and review the analyses of the international situation published in the early to mid 1990s and determine how well their characterizations and predictions fared over the decade or so following their publication.

"Twilight of Sovereignty"

In 1992, Walter Wriston, then chairman emeritus of Citicorp, published a book titled *The Twilight of Sovereignty: How the Information Revolution Is Transforming Our World*. He pointed out that the combination of computing and the worldwide network of instant communication had created an environment for the spread of information that governments could no longer control. Individuals would be empowered as never before. No future Stalin could deny his people knowledge of the outside world. Governments could no longer exert absolute control over financial flows and the exchange of goods.[11]

Wriston's predictions were prophetic in many ways, calling attention to the spread of technologies on which the globalization of the world economy in the late twentieth and early twenty-first century was based. Nevertheless, in emphasizing the benign effects of the information revolution, he paid less attention to the fact that these technologies not only empower individuals to resist tyranny but also empower those who would use violence against society and legitimate governments.

Economic Battle for Supremacy

Wriston may have been only half right, but another popular strain of speculation turned out to be totally wrong. That was the prediction that the 1990s would be marked by the rise of Japan and Germany as economic powerhouses, which would lead to fierce competition of both with the United States for economic primacy in the world.[12] These observers seemed to assume that security concerns would recede and international competition would shift to the economy. After all, had not Japan maintained a much higher growth rate than the United States in the 1970s and 1980s? Had not

Germany just been unified, allowing it to combine the productive assets of both West and East Germany and, for the first time since World War II, harness the legendary economic prowess of an undivided German nation? Plus, in 1992 the United States was experiencing a recession.

With the collapse of the Japanese boom and then the onset of the "Asian flu" in financial markets in 1997, it turned out that Japan's economy was not surging ahead of America's, but was stagnating—at least through the 1990s and beyond.* And Germany, required to pour enormous resources into its eastern *Länder,* saw its economy lose momentum and settle down to marginal growth rates. Politically and economically, German leaders were preoccupied not with grandiose plans to compete against the United States but with the practical challenges of European integration and the absorption of former Communist countries into the European Union.

The predictions of intense economic competition with Japan and Germany missed the mark, although in fact they did little harm. After all, any encouragement to maintain a productive and competitive economy can be helpful to U.S. policymakers.

End of History

It was easy for those who did not bother to read Francis Fukuyama's book *The End of History and the Last Man* to ridicule the thesis that there could be an "end to history." Of course he did not mean that events had stopped occurring; he was using a philosophical conceit based on the Hegelian notion that history is a search for the proper system of government. The collapse of communism and the Soviet Union illustrated, Fukuyama argued, that society had finally found the ideal political and economic system: liberal democracy, market economics, and capitalism. Phrased that way, there was more to Fukuyama's thesis than critics allowed. The collapse of the communist system in the Soviet Union certainly demonstrated that it was not competitive with the system prevalent in the West, but did it also prove that liberal democracy and capitalism are fated to triumph in the world and will not be challenged by something different?

Ernest Gellner, the British sociologist who died in 1995, also thought that

*The Japanese stock market had already tanked in 1990–1992. Between December 29, 1989, and August 18, 1992, the Nikkei stock market average lost nearly two thirds of its value—63.2 percent, to be exact.

liberal democracy was spreading in Europe from west to east and was likely to be attractive elsewhere in the world.[13] But he recognized that the more communal concept of the Muslim *umma* (stressing society as a whole rather than the individual) might turn out to be a competitor, particularly in the Islamic world. His concern in that respect turned out to be more prescient than Fukuyama's prediction that "history" had reached its goal.

Fukuyama's thought had a flaw more fundamental than failing to foresee Islamic ideas as competitors to Western secularism. His entire analysis was based on a teleological principle, the view that human events have a purpose and a goal. Therefore, while he recognized correctly that the collapse of communism in the Soviet Union demonstrated that the specific Soviet form of Marxism could not compete with liberal democracy and capitalism, the idea that the latter would become universal in the world is tainted with the sort of utopian thinking that has always misled zealots, whether Marxists, apocalyptic religious leaders, market fundamentalists, or the followers of Osama bin Laden.

British philosopher John Gray pointed out, "The communist collapse was a decisive falsification of historical teleology, but it was followed by another version of the same belief [Fukuyama's thesis] that history is moving toward a species-wide civilization."[14] Despite the refutation actual history has rendered to every utopian theory, the conviction that the world was destined to adopt a uniform system of government would reappear as official American policy in the early years of the twenty-first century.

The Great Game Redux: Power Politics Continued

For Zbigniew Brzezinski, President Jimmy Carter's national security assistant, the world had gone berserk and—he seemed to think—was reverting to a replay of nineteenth-century geopolitical competition. In his 1993 book, *Out of Control: Global Turmoil on the Eve of the Twenty-first Century*, he analyzed, as he had in earlier works, the failure of the Communist system and the Soviet Union in convincing terms. However, he treated the end of the Cold War as a victory by the United States rather than a negotiated end that suited both sides. Furthermore, and inexplicably, he considered the collapse of the Soviet empire to have created a giant "geopolitical vacuum" in Central Asia. Apparently he considered this a part of the world unable to rule itself and destined to be feasted on by predatory neighbors if the United States did not step in and provide protection and stability. He predicted that there would be massive migrations of people from the area, particularly ethnic Russians, and considered the greatest potential threat to the area a resurgence of Russian imperial power.[15]

Brzezinski's next book, *The Grand Chessboard: American Primacy and Its Geostrategic Imperatives,* took his geopolitical analysis one step further, adopting a variant of British strategist Sir Halford John Mackinder's "heartland" thesis, usually stated in shortened form as "He who rules the heartland (Eurasia), commands the world."* This is a thesis that most strategists abandoned long ago—if they ever entertained it. Admiral Alfred Thayer Mahan's view that control of the seas was the key to winning wars seemed to be much more relevant to the observed exercise of power in the world. After all, when did the master of the Eurasian heartland ever control more than the Eurasian heartland? Great Britain and then the United States developed a worldwide reach through the use of sea and air power, while Russia, at its greatest imperial extent, was defeated by the Japanese navy in the Far East and, in 1917, by the German army in the west. The Soviet Union was unable to dominate China even after it became Communist. He who rules the heartland rules the heartland, period. And only for a time, for empires of any type are obsolete.[16]

Overall, Brzezinski's predictions have proven to be more alarmist than subsequent events justified. The countries of formerly Soviet Central Asia have serious problems, many stemming from features of Soviet rule, but aside from Tajikistan, mired in a civil war for several years in the 1990s, there was more stability in this area than in many others in the world of the late twentieth century. Outmigration of Russian "settlers" from Central Asia, which Brzezinski considered a source of potential mass unrest, has oc-

---

*Mackinder expressed his ideas in a 1903 lecture, which was published by the Royal Geographical Society in London. Subsequently, he wrote a book in 1919, *Democratic Ideals and Reality,* intended to influence the negotiations at the Versailles peace conference, stressing the importance of controlling eastern Europe in order to control what he called the World Island—Eurasia. He stated his thesis as, "Who rules East Europe commands the Heartland; Who rules the heartland commands the World Island; Who rules the World Island commands the World."

curred, but it has been peaceful and beneficial to Russia, plagued with a looming demographic crisis. Even with the influx of ethnic Russians from Central Asia, the Russian population declined from about 148 million at the time the Russian Federation became independent to something like 143 million in 2005. Far more serious migration crises have occurred in the former Yugoslavia, Afghanistan, the Middle East (think Iraq, Iran, Lebanon, and Palestine), the Central Africa of Rwanda, Burundi, and Congo, the Horn of Africa, and Sudan.

The fact is, the fate of the world was never going to be decided by control of what Mackinder described as the heartland, and while Brzezinski described accurately many of the problems facing the world in the 1990s, his prescriptions for U.S. policy were a variant of the thesis that the United States must extend its hegemony in order to provide stability in the world. We will in due course look closely at the implications of this strategy.

Clashing Civilizations

Harvard professor Samuel P. Huntington published an article in *Foreign Affairs* in 1993 titled "The Clash of Civilizations?" which evoked more discussion than that journal had stimulated for decades. Three years later, Huntington presented his thoughts in greater detail in a book with the question mark omitted from the title: *The Clash of Civilizations and the Remaking of World Order.* The following three quotations summarize his principal theses:

· "In the post–Cold War world the most important distinctions among peoples are not ideological, political or economic. They are cultural."
· "Civilizations are the broadest cultural entities; hence conflicts between groups from different civilizations become central to global politics."
· "The key issues on the international agenda involve differences among civilizations."[17]

Huntington's theory, like most theories, contained nuggets of insight— culture does matter, and cultural differences can fuel conflict, particularly when combined with other causes. Marxism also contains accurate observations, such as the fact that there have been and probably will continue to be conflicts between economic classes. However, both Marx and Huntington, like many other theorists, got off track when they concocted general principles from select and disparate pieces of evidence, ignored facts that did not fit, then projected into a vision of the future the grand scheme that resulted.

If we take Huntington's propositions separately, we can spot the weaknesses of the overall theory and also distill some of his insights that are valid. Regarding the first, that *the most important* distinctions among people are cultural rather than ideological, economic, or political: how does one disaggregate "cultural" differences from the other factors, all of which are components of culture as most people understand it?

Is Osama bin Laden's opposition to Arab governments that cooperate with the West based on culture or religion? Did the Tamil Tigers conduct terrorism in Sri Lanka because of cultural differences or because they feel there has been ethnic discrimination? Why should the Kurds resort to violence against Turks and Arabs when they belong to the same culture and "civilization," as Huntington defines them? Do Shia and Sunni Arabs in Iraq fight each other because they come from different cultures? One could go on, citing massacres in Rwanda, the Shining Path guerrillas in Peru, hoodlum rule in Liberia and Sierra Leone, genocide in Darfur, warlordism in Somalia, and the rebellion in East Timor against Indonesian repression.

When one examines conflicts that have occurred since Huntington took the question mark off his thesis, there is scant evidence that "culture"— whatever that is—trumps everything else.

Now, considering Huntington's second assertion: have conflicts between groups from different *civilizations* become *central* to global politics? Huntington takes his definition of "civilization" largely from historian Arnold J. Toynbee, who viewed human history as the rise, breakdown, and fall of societies or civilizations. Toynbee's definition of a civilization was based largely on the "dominant religion," but he was not always rigorous in applying that principle. For example, according to Toynbee, the "Hellenic civilization" (in which he includes the Roman Empire) was replaced by two civilizations, the "Western" and the "Orthodox Christian," as a result of the split in the Catholic Church between those loyal to the pope in Rome and those who followed the Byzantine patriarch. However, he does not split "Western" civilization into Protestant and Catholic, or "Islamic" civilization into Sunni and Shia.[18] For this and other reasons, most historians have been reluctant to accept major parts of Toynbee's thesis, both his identification of the components of a civilization and also the idea that civilizations are comparable to organized entities—to states, for example. Huntington ignored the inconsistencies in Toynbee's analysis and treated the civilizations he defined as if they are super states with boundaries so precise that "fault lines" appear between them.

For a time in the 1990s, it seemed to some that the conflict in Bosnia was an example of "civilizational" struggle. After all, did not Catholic Croats, Orthodox Serbs, and Muslim Bosniaks belong to three distinct civilizations? Well, they differed in their traditional religion (many were actually more secular than religious), but not in language or ethnicity, and the struggle had more to do with common cultural traits than with some transcendental clash of civilizations. It was a struggle for power and dominance, led by demagogues who revived old prejudices and exploited common cultural traditions, such as that of the vendetta.

More recently, some have opined that jihadist terrorism is a symptom of civilizational clash and thus a vindication of Huntington's theories. Such an allegation reveals both a misunderstanding of Huntington's theory and a lack of knowledge about Al-Qaeda and similar terrorist organizations. Osama bin Laden leads what is essentially a rebellious movement *within* Islam. It attacks American and European targets because it sees Western influence in the Islamic world undermining its fundamentalist view of Islamic society, but it is equally prepared to use its terrorist tactics against Muslims who do not agree with it.

Many more conflicts in today's world occur within Professor Huntington's putative civilizations than between them. Though conflicts between groups from different "civilizations" do occur, they are far from *central* to global politics. It follows, then, that there is no convincing evidence to support the third of Huntington's propositions, that "the key issues on the international agenda involve differences among civilizations." Actually, the most serious security issues facing the world today—the spread of weapons of mass destruction, the competition for resources, disputed territorial claims, global warming and environmental degradation, organized crime, and the spread of disease—are all issues that transcend nations, states, and civilizations, however defined.

Even if we find the idea of a conflict of civilizations a misleading guide to policy making, there is an important insight that lurks under the rickety theoretical edifice: *culture matters*. Differences in culture can exacerbate problems arising from other sources. Differences in culture can lead to unnecessary and dangerous misunderstandings. We will be much more successful solving international problems if we have an understanding of where the people we deal with are coming from, emotionally and intellectually, than if we act on the implicit assumption that everybody thinks alike. In this sense, Samuel Huntington had a lot to teach us, even if we find his overall theory more confusing than enlightening.

Most of the analyses and predictions I have cited have not worn well in the years since the USSR was relegated to history. Most contain significant elements of truth, but often miss factors that turn out to be decisive in pushing the world in a direction different from the one predicted. Among the problems with most predictive interpretations are their oversimplification of complex phenomena, their tendency to project temporary trends indefinitely into the future, and their inability (which is inherent and inescapable) to account for the ultimate unpredictability of human beings. Life is never as understandable and predictable as theory pretends.

Other Perceptions

"Civilizations" may not be destined to clash in the sense that Samuel Huntington argued, but there is no question that different cultures create different perceptions, and different perceptions can cause foreign political leaders—and foreign publics as well—to see things in a different light than most Americans would. The analyses cited above were all by authors living in the United States. How did other people react to these events, and how different were their reactions from those common in the United States? Let us consider some illustrative examples of how people in the rest of the world viewed the end of the Cold War and the dissolution of the Soviet Union.

Europe

For most people in Western Europe there was relief and satisfaction that, following the better part of a century of conflict, confrontation, and division, Europe was whole and free. In Eastern Europe there was euphoria over having escaped Communist dictatorship, followed by some disappointment and considerable division over how to adjust their state-controlled economies to be competitive in world markets. Most Russians were enthusiastic about the possibility of becoming, once again, an integral part of Western civilization, but apprehensive that they might not be accepted and dismayed by the steep and sudden decline of morality and living standards following the Soviet collapse. In Western Europe there were already, in 1992, incipient fears that, with no USSR to provide a balance, an America with too much power might not be good for the world. There was little inclination to join the United States in battles against threats outside the continent of Europe.

China

While most Americans and Europeans greeted the collapse of the Soviet Union with a combination of surprise, disbelief, and relief, the Chinese Communist leaders considered it a disaster, not in the sense that it increased the external threat to China, but because it seemed a vivid illustration of what rapid democratization can do to an authoritarian society. The Chinese leaders had shown, by their massacre of student demonstrators in Tiananmen Square in 1989, that they were determined not to allow the gradual liberation of the economy to spill over into sudden political change. The collapse of the Soviet Union convinced them that they had been right to refuse to combine political with economic liberalization. For them, Gorbachev's perestroika served as a clear example of what *not* to do.

A few years ago, I took part in a conference in Beijing of historians studying Soviet history. During my presentation I stated that Gorbachev's refusal to use force to keep himself in power set the important precedent of a ruler yielding to a peaceful change of government. One of the Chinese participants responded, "We consider Gorbachev's refusal to use force his greatest mistake."

The collapse of the Soviet Union convinced the Chinese rulers that preservation of Communist Party control of the country was essential if China was to escape the Soviet fate, and thus reinforced the conviction that dissent had to be suppressed and that economic modernization had to proceed only under the close supervision of the Chinese Communist Party.

East and South Asia

Most Japanese were pleased to see Japan's traditional rival and erstwhile enemy, Russia, cut itself down to size. Many hoped that, in its current weakened position, Russia would return to Japanese control the islands north of Japan that had been occupied by Soviet forces following World War II.* Many Japanese businesspeople also hoped that the Russian Far East would present attractive investment opportunities, especially for oil, natural gas, and raw materials needed by Japanese industry. These were the principal subjects of conversations I had with Japanese diplomats and business leaders during several trips to Japan before and after the Cold War ended.

The two Korean states remained locked in a frozen conflict, but South Korea, shunned by the Soviet Union until late in the Gorbachev period, actively promoted exports to Russia. North Korea, on the other hand, faced almost complete isolation as its former Soviet ally disappeared and its Chinese neighbor opened to the outside world, seemingly determined to replace Maoism with capitalism. There were serious questions as to how the Stalinist North Korean regime could survive in the new international environment.

In Southeast Asia, most Cold War conflicts had come to an end by 1992. Even in Cambodia, which had been under Vietnamese occupation since the 1970s, an agreement had been concluded in October 1991 for Vietnamese withdrawal and for an end of the Cambodian Civil War under U.N. supervision. Much of the rest of Southeast Asia seemed poised for rapid economic development, with the exception of Burma, or Myanmar, which had fallen into the grip of a repressive military dictatorship. One relic of the Cold War in the area was the Russian naval base at Cam Ranh Bay in Vietnam, a holdover from the Soviet period.

---

*These comprised the Habomai archipelago and Shikotan, both within sight of northern Hokkaido, plus two larger islands often considered the southern Kuriles, Kunashiri and Etorofu.

Indians regretted the sudden Soviet collapse, having considered the Soviet Union a "friend" taking their side in India's disputes with Pakistan and China. The Pakistan government was relieved by the elimination of a regional competitor, and its government turned its attention to extending its influence in Afghanistan and training terrorists for Kashmir. Both India and Pakistan felt less constrained in their nuclear weapons programs than they had been when the Cold War was raging. A. Q. Khan, who had helped build the Pakistani bomb, was allowed to help other countries get on the nuclear bandwagon.

Middle East

Three events in 1991 seemed to transform the prospects for some sort of settlement between Israel and the Palestinians: the Gulf War, the first intifada on the Israeli-occupied West Bank, and the collapse of the Soviet Union. Actually, circumstances had changed radically even before the formal demise of the Soviet Union. It had supported resistance to Iraq's invasion of Kuwait and reestablished diplomatic relations with Israel. Gorbachev had agreed to co-host (with President Bush) a conference in Madrid of Arabs and Israelis, including representatives of the Palestine Liberation Organization (PLO). This meeting would, for the first time, provide a forum for Israeli officials and Palestinians to talk directly to each other. When the Soviet Union passed from the scene, President Yeltsin of Russia replaced Gorbachev as titular co-chairman of the Madrid Conference.*

Tensions between Israel on the one hand and its Arab neighbors and the Palestinians on the other had brought to naught all American and other outside efforts to encourage a settlement that would establish and preserve peace. Soviet military and political support for the PLO and the most recalcitrant Arab states had long served to amplify hatred and empower the enemies of Israel to block a settlement. Now that Soviet support had ended and Russia, the successor state, had an incentive to support peace rather than hostility, prospects for a settlement seemed more promising than they had been at any time since the creation of the State of Israel.[19]

---

*The co-chairmen were symbolic, since the foreign ministers of both countries actually chaired the meetings in Madrid.

Africa

One should not attribute the end of apartheid in the Republic of South Africa to the end of the Cold War; that profound shift in the governance of the most economically developed country in Africa was brought about by the inspired leadership of Frederik Willem de Klerk, South Africa's president from 1989 to 1994, and Nelson Mandela, his successor. However, if the Cold War had not been at its end in 1989 and 1990 and if the Soviet Union had still been considered a threat, it would have been more difficult for de Klerk to release Mandela from prison in February 1990. Many South Africans (and not only South Africans) had considered Mandela's African National Congress a Communist-dominated organization. The Soviet Union had provided support to the ANC and also military support to anti–South African forces in Namibia, Angola, and Mozambique. If that support had not been terminated, it would have been much more difficult for de Klerk to dismantle the apartheid regime and prepare the country for majority rule.

The end of the Cold War facilitated the steps necessary to move South Africa peacefully to majority rule and political stability. To point this out is to take nothing from the exceptional qualities of leadership both de Klerk and Mandela exhibited as they transformed the country from a shunned pariah to a respected democracy. In 1993, on the eve of Mandela's election to the South African presidency, the prospect that the political transformation then taking place in South Africa would radiate through the continent and strengthen democracy south of the Sahara seemed bright.

By 1993, the South African government had made another significant contribution to world peace by terminating its clandestine program to develop nuclear weapons. In 1989, de Klerk had decided to end the nuclear weapons program and to destroy the devices that had been produced. This was accomplished in 1991, but the facts were not disclosed publicly until 1993. In this way, South Africa became the first country voluntarily to leave the "club" of nuclear powers. (Others had terminated programs in their early stages, before weapons were produced. South Africa was the first—and so far still the only—country to end a program voluntarily once weapons had actually been produced.)

In some parts of Africa, violence had ebbed with the withdrawal of Soviet support for insurgencies and of American and South African support for resistance to them. Nevertheless, in many areas, peace was tenuous because of predatory governments, ethnic rivalries, spreading disease (AIDS in particular), and widespread, endemic poverty. Sierra Leone had fallen under a dictatorship, and conflict in Somalia prevented delivery of food to a starving population. Nevertheless, one could hope that the post–Cold War environment would foster more effective action to correct these ills than had been possible during the Cold War.

Latin America

By 1992, the main relic of the Cold War in Latin America was Fidel Castro's Cuba; there is no question that the end of Soviet economic subsidies and military assistance was a heavy blow to Castro. Even before the Soviet collapse, Gorbachev had withdrawn support for Cuban military activities abroad. Cuban forces, with the support of Soviet money and arms, had intervened in Nicaragua, Grenada, Angola, the Horn of Africa, and elsewhere, but these activities had ended before 1992. A Soviet-American agreement had helped end the civil war in Nicaragua by an agreement to respect the outcome of elections. Remaining insurgencies in Latin America, such as that of the Sendero Luminoso (Shining Path) in Peru continued without Soviet or Cuban support, and drug trafficking, particularly from Colombia, continued to be a serious problem, but on the whole, the Western Hemisphere was relatively quiet. Over the period of the Cold War, most countries in Latin America had replaced military dictatorships with elected governments, and although deep social and economic problems remained in many of the countries, prospects for further development had improved with the end of outside support for Communist-inspired insurgencies.

The role that contact, communication, and dialogue had played in bringing the Cold War to an end suggested that it would be wise to ease economic sanctions on Cuba and to promote increased contact between Americans and Cubans still living on the island. This would have improved the condition of ordinary Cubans and deprived Castro of an external enemy he could use as a pretext for further repression. The decision the next administration would make regarding relations with Cuba would be an indication of whether it grasped one of the key lessons that might be derived from the way the Reagan and Bush administrations helped bring the Cold War to a successful and peaceful end.

In sum, 1992 was a year of hope that the end of the Cold War and the breakup of the Soviet Union would usher in a new era in international relations, one given less to violence and more to international cooperation and economic development.

George Bush's administration did many important things right, such as negotiating the terms of German unification to permit a united Germany to stay in NATO, concluding three crucial arms reduction treaties, and persuading Gorbachev not to block the liberation of Kuwait. It did not do as much as it might have done to help the Soviet, then Russian, leaders to devise a "soft landing" for their economy—but this may have been an impossible task, whatever assistance had been offered. Overall, the aims Bush and Baker had for a "new world order" were reasonable, not utopian, and achievable without excessive drain on American strength. In most ways, they pushed America in the right direction to cope with the challenges the twenty-first century might present.

In psychological and political terms, however, President Bush planted a land mine under the future U.S.-Russian relationship when he claimed, during his losing campaign for reelection, "We won the Cold War!"

This was a claim Ronald Reagan had been careful not to make. He understood that the agreements Gorbachev made with the United States and other Western countries were in the Soviet interest. And they were. But now, President Bush's words reverberated throughout Russia, leaving the impression that Gorbachev had allowed himself be tricked.

PART TWO

MISSING THE POINT:

SIXTEEN MISDIRECTED YEARS

6

The Unipolar Delusion:
The 1990s

PERCEPTIONS OF THE STATE OF THE world varied in the 1990s, but one thing was clear to all: the United States was the predominant power and had no rival. Its military was more than a match for any conceivable combination of countries. Its economy was the most productive, its currency had become the world standard. It was, for most people in the world, the most admired country, and its youth culture, fads, and fashions spread throughout the world, often to the dismay of older generations.

This was power, power in all its forms: power to attract, power to persuade, power to coerce, power to destroy.[1] Used wisely, it could help transform world politics—not to the point of a conflict-free utopia or a one-world democratic state, or a U.S.-enforced Pax Americana, but to a world in which violence could be reduced and, when it did occur, contained, to a world that would more often use peaceful tools to adjust to inevitable change, to a world in which geopolitical rivalries could be balanced and attenuated by growing habits of cooperation.

Used unwisely, in ways that other countries would see as self-serving or contrary to their interests, this immense power could, in a relatively short time, be frittered away. And not only frittered away: unbridled use of military force without international sanction could create more enemies than it destroyed or intimidated. The very fact that the United States possessed unparalleled means to destroy suggested that it would have to refrain from using that power unilaterally lest it undermine respect for the international law required for a more peaceful world. Use of force without international sanction would also damage the institutions the United States had helped create to deal with international violence.

A robust economy, of course, is also a crucial element of power. Perhaps it is more important than military preponderance, for military superiority cannot be maintained without a productive and healthy economy—as President Dwight Eisenhower understood when, at the outset of his term in office, he ordered a sharp cut in defense spending. The Soviet generals also understood this when they supported Gorbachev's early moves to end the arms race.

In this respect, there were several yellow caution lights visible regarding the American economy in 1992 and 1993: (1) it had just experienced another recession, relatively mild, to be sure, but sufficient that President Bush did not feel empowered to do more to assist the economic transition under way in the crumbling former Communist empire; (2) the United States was afflicted with a growing fiscal deficit and a growing imbalance in its foreign trade; and (3) the United States was becoming dangerously dependent on foreign sources, many in unstable regions of the world, for its energy. Furthermore, evidence was already clear to any unbiased observer that the release of excessive carbon dioxide and other greenhouse gases was contributing to a gradual warming of the earth's atmosphere. If these emissions were not restrained and eventually reduced, they could bring about changes in climate and sea levels that could inundate some of the world's greatest cities and be catastrophic to many agricultural areas.

A third essential element of national power is political strength at home. I do not mean unanimity, but a political process that works to produce results, a political process that includes both competition and cooperation to reach needed objectives. Both Ronald Reagan and George Bush had been highly partisan in their campaigning—as had their opponents—but they maintained respectful working relations with the Democratic leaders.

Reagan would cooperate with Tip O'Neill, the Speaker of the House of Representatives, to get legislation through Congress; he would accept the quiet assistance Senator Edward Kennedy offered to establish communication with the Soviet leaders; he would be grateful for the unanimous support of Democratic senators for the treaties he signed with the Soviet Union, particularly when elements of his own party opposed him.

President Bush also worked with the opposition when he had to. As fiscal deficits continued to grow and interest rates rose to levels rarely seen in the United States, he yielded to Democratic pressure and accepted two tax increases.*

When William Jefferson (Bill) Clinton took the oath of office in January 1993, America's ability to retain its primacy in a world without the Cold War and without the Soviet Union as a presumed competitor would depend not only on its military strength and how it used it, and on its ability to maintain a healthy, productive economy, but also on the willingness of its political leaders to work together to achieve common objectives. Adherence to some ideal perfection in all these areas was not to be expected, and the United States had a lot of elbow room to make mistakes, but in time America's primacy could be maintained only if its government preserved the country's many assets, kept them strong, and used them prudently.

Understanding Threats: The Key Issues

An essential prerequisite to any coherent strategy is a realistic understanding of existing and potential threats. What can we say about the security threats that should have been perceived by American policy makers in 1993?

Nuclear Weapons

While there was no reason to fear that the United States might be the target of a deliberate strike of nuclear weapons from another country, or that any country could use a perceived nuclear superiority to blackmail the United States, nuclear weapons remained the most serious physical threat to Americans. In 1992 and 1993, the Carnegie Corporation of New York sponsored a study by three eminent persons: McGeorge Bundy, who had been the president's assistant for national security during the Kennedy and Johnson administrations, Admiral William Crowe, who had been chairman

---

*This cost him dearly with dogmatic elements that had begun to dominate the "base" of the Republican Party, but the growing fiscal deficit that these tax increases were designed to moderate was a principal issue raised by Ross Perot, who headed a third-party effort that may have prevented Bush's reelection.

of the Joint Chiefs of Staff during the Reagan administration, and Sidney Drell, a nuclear physicist from Stanford who had advised most recent administrations on nuclear and disarmament issues. The three summarized their conclusions with ten propositions, of which the first (and most basic) rephrased a thought that had dominated Ronald Reagan's thinking: "The United States should respect the reality that as long as there are nuclear bombs, there will be a danger that is unique in all history."[2]

Nuclear weapons, by their very existence, constitute a threat. Despite the treaties signed and ratified during the Reagan and first Bush administrations, thousands of nuclear-armed missiles remained on alert in the United States and Russia. A mistake or accident on either side could have caused a tragedy, even if the victim decided not to retaliate in kind. But this danger was probably not so great as the possibility that material and know-how to make the weapons, or even some weapons themselves, would leak to irresponsible parties—rogue regimes or terrorists.

Russia had poorly secured weapons and fissile material that could be used for bombs. Russia was awash with scientists who knew how to make nuclear weapons and were in 1993 virtually unemployed; even if they had jobs, many were not receiving regular pay. When the Soviet Union fragmented, nuclear weapons and materials were also located in at least three successor countries outside Russia: Belarus, Ukraine, and Kazakhstan. Making sure that these materials were secure and under responsible control was a high priority.

Even at the height of the Cold War, the United States and the Soviet Union had cooperated to restrict the spread of nuclear weapons to other countries. They had sponsored a treaty to prevent proliferation (the NPT) that promised countries assistance in developing nuclear power if they would pledge not to develop nuclear weapons. The treaty also contained a commitment by the five avowed nuclear powers at the time (China, France, and the United Kingdom, in addition to the United States and the USSR) to embark on a process of nuclear disarmament.

As we have seen, both Reagan and Gorbachev took this commitment seriously and tried to set the United States and the Soviet Union on a course that would lead eventually to a nuclear-free world. In 1993, the United States and Russia should have had no higher policy goal than maintaining the momentum of nuclear weapons reduction that had been established. They also needed to deal urgently with the many tasks required to ensure that existing weaponry, material, and know-how would not spread to irresponsible hands.

Biological and Chemical Weapons

By 1993, it seemed that Russia was on the way to terminating the extensive program to develop biological weapons that had existed in the Soviet Union. Nevertheless, in 1993 it was difficult in Russia—as it is in many other countries—for political leaders to ensure that their bureaucracy, especially police and military forces, behave as instructed. Therefore, it was important for the United States to work closely with Russian officials and scientists to make sure the Russian program was converted to one for defensive research alone. In fact, it would have been in both countries' interest to have a joint defensive program; obviously Russian scientists would be helpful in developing antigens for those pathogens they had developed. Also, it was important to ensure that the germs that had been developed and tested did not escape responsible control.

Of course, the potential threat of biological weapons was broader than that created by the remnants of the Soviet program. Iraq, for example, had developed biological weapons in secret before the Gulf War, and—most likely—other countries maintained concealed programs. For this reason, it was important for the United States and its allies to develop and agree on measures to verify compliance with the Biological Weapons Convention, and also to pay more attention to defensive measures that might be taken, such as the development of vaccines and the training of first responders.

As for chemical weapons, both the United States and the Soviet Union had signed an international agreement to destroy their stocks and to outlaw possession of these weapons. When Clinton took office, the principal task was to secure ratification of the treaty by the United States and other signatories and to prepare for the destruction of existing chemical weapons in a manner that would not endanger the environment. Since this treaty, even if implemented, could not ensure that terrorist groups would be unable to acquire toxic chemicals, attention needed to be given to steps that would be needed to respond to an attack on civilians in America.

Military Involvement in Local Disputes

Some of the most dangerous moments of the Cold War occurred when the United States and the Soviet Union provided military assistance to competing factions in regional or national struggles for power, or actually intervened directly. Both the Korean and Vietnam wars were essentially local contests over political control. The Soviet Union backed and, in fact, encouraged attempts by Communist forces to seize power; their Leninist ideology told them that this was simply the inexorable march of history toward a global communist society. The United States opposed aggression and armed insurrection by Communist or Communist-leaning groups in order to contain Soviet power.

The end of the Cold War removed most of the rationale based on self-interest for American military involvement in local or regional flare-ups. The breakup of the Soviet Union so weakened the military forces of the successor states, including Russia, that successful aggression across national borders was not feasible, certainly not in the short term. The United States had formal defense commitments to its allies in NATO as well as to other countries including Japan, South Korea, Australia, and New Zealand, and it was important to keep these commitments. But it was no longer desirable to become militarily involved, except as part of a U.N.-authorized coalition, in local contests for power that did not directly threaten either the United States or its formal allies.

Countries in each region needed to develop the capacity to deal with local disputes without expecting the United States to take on the duties of a world policeman. It would take time—years certainly, decades probably—to develop the capacity of international institutions to head off violent conflict and suppress it when it occurred, but America had an unprecedented opportunity to mentor and support regional efforts to deal with conflict in parts of the world distant from the United States.

"Rogue States" and "Failed States"

During the Cold War, conflict in the Third World often took on a strong East-West coloration. The Soviet Union frequently provided arms and political backing to insurgencies in countries viewed as pro-Western, and this provoked the United States to back countervailing forces. That competition largely ended in the closing years of the Cold War, and in some instances, such as Nicaragua, political solutions were found that ended most of the violence. Nevertheless, conflict continued in some areas, including the Horn of Africa, even after external involvement based on Cold War competition ended. Other conflicts developed without any help from either side in the Cold War: Sudan, Liberia, Sierra Leone, and Rwanda were already in the throes of civil war or showing signs of imminent internal upheavals.

Problems associated with the collapse of the Soviet Union added to the festering crises in Africa. Civil wars had broken out in newly independent Tajikistan and Georgia; Armenia and Azerbaijan were in a struggle over an area the Russians call Nagorny Karabakh; a portion of Moldova bordering on Ukraine had rebelled against the government in Chişinău. Furthermore, Yugoslavia had begun to fall apart, but, in contrast to the Soviet collapse—which occurred peacefully except on the southern fringes—with growing violence, especially between Serbs and Croats, and between Serbs and Muslims in Bosnia-Herzegovina and Serbs and Albanians in Kosovo.

Many other countries that had won independence since World War II had fragile governments and were beset with multiple challenges including ethnic or religious friction, widespread poverty, endemic corruption, and criminal activity. Predatory political leaders who milked the country's resources for their personal gain were more common than honest ones. Any one of these challenges, if not kept under control, could bring a government to a total breakdown and unleash unrestrained violence. Usually more than one, and sometimes all of them, were present.

Obviously, state failure could create humanitarian crises, but one might have questioned whether they constituted threats to American security. Initially—that is, when a gangster or warlord takes control of a distant small country—state failure might seem to be remote from any American security interest. Nevertheless, countries controlled by criminals can rapidly become centers of international criminal activity, whether in the illicit drug trade, the underground trade in arms, or the financing, training, and equipping of terrorists.

Finding ways to reduce and control the spread of violence in developing countries would be a priority task for the U.S. government in the 1990s, even if the breakdown of law and order in a distant country did not directly threaten the security of Americans at home.

Environmental Degradation

In the long run, the threat that could do the most damage to the economy and to the well-being of the American people is that resulting from pollution of the environment. Even during the Cold War, the United States and the world community as a whole had begun to respond to clearly defined problems. The warnings in Rachel Carson's *Silent Spring* were taken seriously and resulted in an international ban on the use of DDT, the persistent insecticide that was having a devastating effect on many species of wildlife and beneficial insects. When it was found that the use of ozone-depleting substances in spray cans was contributing to the reduction of the ozone layer in the stratosphere—a layer that shields the earth from ultraviolet radiation that can affect crops and oceanic plankton, and cause skin cancer in humans—an international treaty was concluded in 1987 and enforced so that by the late 1990s the gap in the ozone layer at the poles had been stabilized and was showing signs of closing. Laws had also been passed to reduce emission of polluting gases by automobiles and to reduce pollution of freshwater streams. There were, in short, multiple precedents for effective government action to reduce environmental degradation. In each case, however, industries that had contributed to the harmful pollution had fought against protective measures. When they were taken, however, the industries were not damaged to the extent they had predicted, and in most cases they were not damaged at all. It was equally profitable (sometimes more so) to produce safer, less polluting substances.

By 1993, it was already evident that growing emissions of carbon dioxide, in particular by motor vehicles and coal-fired electric power plants, were contributing to progressively higher atmospheric temperatures. Scientists had noted for years that there was a gradual warming of the atmosphere, but there was a dispute as to whether this was a natural temperature fluctuation that has occurred over the millennia of the earth's history, or whether human activity was contributing significantly to the warming. By 1993, it was clear to most scientists studying the question that greenhouse gas emissions from human activity were accelerating warming of the earth's atmos-

phere, and that such warming would, if not restrained and eventually reversed, seriously affect the climate of the entire earth.

Energy Dependence

The oil shortage and price shock of 1973–1975, when the newly created
Organization of Petroleum Exporting Countries (OPEC) agreed to limit production and forbid export to the United States and the Netherlands, demonstrated the vulnerability of the American and European economies to dis-
ruptions in the supply of imported petroleum.* A gasoline shortage in the
summer of 1974 produced long lines at pumps and widespread frustration
of commuters and vacation travelers alike. It led the Carter administration
to initiate a series of emergency steps to reduce demand for petroleum products. But once the economy had absorbed the higher level of prices, pressure
to economize dwindled and the country resumed its growing addiction to
imported petroleum, even though the taxpayer was, by 1992, paying a hefty
price by maintaining a large military presence in the Persian Gulf area in
order to keep supply lanes open.

The end of the Cold War and the disintegration of the Soviet Union had
ended any plausible threat that important Middle East petroleum reserves
could fall under the control of the other superpower. This opened an opportunity to serve a dual purpose: by initiating a comprehensive program to
replace imported petroleum with renewable energy, the United States could
both enhance its security and also begin to deal with the looming problem
of global warming. Reducing reliance on imported energy was both a security and an economic issue.

In enumerating the principal threats to American security that should
have been apparent in 1993, you may have noticed that I did not include terrorism. In the 1980s, particularly between 1983 and 1986, there had been
a rash of attacks on American embassies, military bases, and aircraft overseas, but then they tapered off. Terrorism continued to be a problem in several areas of the world, but serious attacks on Americans had not occurred

*The OPEC embargo was in retaliation for U.S. support of Israel during the Yom
Kippur War of 1973, when Israel was attacked by Syria and Egypt. U.S. planes flying
weapons and military supplies to Israel used Dutch airfields.

for four years—since December 1988, to be precise, when a bomb planted by Libyans brought down Pan Am flight 103 over Lockerbie, Scotland, killing all 259 people on board and eleven persons on the ground.

Although some American tourists and the U.S. embassy and Marine barracks in Beirut had been attacked, terrorism seemed to be something that happened elsewhere—in Northern Ireland, the Middle East, Africa, Latin America, Europe, Japan, or Sri Lanka. It was a problem, certainly, and the State Department had established an office headed by a senior diplomat to track terrorist acts and devise means of preventing them. Even so, most experts considered terrorism something for police forces and intelligence agencies to deal with. Germany and Italy had successfully eliminated the Baader-Meinhof gang and the Red Brigades. Terrorism did not seem to be a problem affecting American *national* security or one that might cause the United States to go to war with another country. Such was the view in 1993. It may have been shortsighted, but it was not irrational.

Granted that counterterrorism experts were capable of understanding that suicidal terrorists, with careful planning, might be able to hijack a plane and fly it into a building, they probably would have assumed that any country with competent intelligence and police resources could foil such a plot; it would have been a stretch for them to have imagined that American airline pilots, in the early twenty-first century, would still be instructed to deal with any attempted hijacking by complying with the hijackers' demands.

Threats to the Economy

A productive economy with benefits distributed in a matter deemed fair by society is essential to the health and political cohesion of any country. Although the U.S. economy was coming out of a mild recession, it was by far the strongest in the world. With the end of the Cold War, people expected a "peace dividend." Military expenditures could be reduced, it was reasoned, since the Soviet Union was no longer a threat, and the resources saved could be applied to domestic needs.

However, shifting resources is not nearly so simple as it may have seemed to many people. It was politically impossible to stop paying for unneeded military equipment abruptly and divert the money to such things as equipment in hospitals or facilities for public transportation. Much of the American economy depended on military production, and a sudden termination of contracts would have thrown hundreds of thousands, maybe millions, out of work. In time, the economy would have adjusted, but what about the people who lost their jobs and either had trouble finding new ones or were forced to accept much lower pay? Large shifts in government procurement need to be planned with effective assistance to the "losers" if unacceptable disruption of people's lives is to be avoided.

When I retired from the Foreign Service in 1991, Rebecca and I lived for two years in North Stonington, Connecticut, a bucolic area (at least until the Pequot Indian casino nearby was expanded) not far from the port of Groton, where America's nuclear-powered attack submarines are produced. With the end of the Cold War, the Defense Department canceled orders for two such submarines. This sent the entire area into a panic. No fewer than forty-five thousand jobs, most with high pay, depended on the production of the submarines. Sudden cancellation could throw eastern Connecticut and adjacent areas of Rhode Island into a sharp depression. Political pressures grew until the order for one of the submarines was reinstated—but not because the submarine was needed to protect America. The only reason for building it was to sustain the economy of an important region. It was, in effect, a public works subsidy, but for public works the nation didn't really need.

This is precisely one of the reasons President Eisenhower worried about the influence of the military-industrial complex in the United States. It was not that it would necessarily push us to war, but that it would distort the rational development of the American economy. Political pressure comes not only from defense contractors but from the many people who work for them and from the communities that are dependent on the money spent to produce armaments. Government money spent on military equipment can become as addicting for communities as oil has been for the country as a whole and tobacco or crack cocaine for individuals. Communities have as much trouble going cold turkey as an individual hooked on drugs would.

Bringing defense spending in line with the country's real needs in a different geopolitical environment was one of the most important challenges facing the Clinton administration.

Spending on arms and military forces is, furthermore, only one portion of necessary spending for defense. Coping with natural disasters (or major terrorist attacks) requires a properly trained, equipped, and coordinated force of "first responders," and plans for recovery that mesh government and private, as well as federal, state, and local, facilities and personnel. The best defense against possible biological or chemical attacks will be a robust public health system with the capacity to detect new diseases promptly, whether spread deliberately or naturally. The nation's infrastructure must be kept up to date; the collapse of a bridge on a busy interstate highway resulting from poor maintenance can do as much damage as an explosion set off by terrorists. And, of course, no defense based on advanced technology, as America's is, can be maintained for long without a superior educational system that produces the scientists, engineers, and technicians necessary to create, produce, manage, maintain, and use technically sophisticated devices.

In short, many so-called domestic issues cannot be divorced from the country's ability to flourish, compete, and defend itself. America's ability to maintain its preeminence and the safety of its people in a post–Cold War world would depend importantly on how successful its political leadership was in reorienting its spending to a balance between what was necessary for adequate military force and what was necessary to maintain prosperity and safety at home.

Human Rights

Protection of human rights was a major theme in U.S. policy toward the Soviet Union and other Communist countries. It also played some role in U.S. relations with non-Communist countries, particularly with apartheid South Africa, but it was usually soft-pedaled when the United States needed the support of an authoritarian regime in the Cold War competition. Thus, the U.S. did little to promote human rights or democracy in South Korea; changes there occurred as a result of internal developments, particularly the growth of a middle class and the institutions of a civil society.[3]

The end of the Cold War eliminated the necessity of tolerating human rights abusers in order to preserve their support on Cold War issues. Nev-

ertheless, the greater freedom of action did not provide an automatic answer to the question of where and how an American president should fit
protection of human rights into diplomacy. As Joseph Nye has observed,
"Human rights is an important *part* of foreign policy, but it is not foreign
policy itself, because foreign policy is an effort to accomplish several objectives: security and economic benefits as well as humanitarian results."[4]

The world witnessed serious human rights abuses during the years following the end of the Cold War. Though in theory the United States may
have seemed more empowered than it had been to deal with the problem,
prevention of atrocities and increasing respect for fundamental human
rights has remained one of the most wrenching problems for United States
foreign policy.

Using Opportunities and Dealing with Threats

In 1993, it seemed to most that, at least for the United States, the world
presented more opportunities than threats. In any event, both opportunity
and threat had changed in many ways. The United States needed to adapt
both methods and instruments of foreign policy to the new circumstances.

Methods

Methods matter. If you want to extract money from another person's wal-
let, you can offer to sell him something he wants at a price he can't resist.
You can ask him to make a contribution to a cause he supports. You can ask
him for a loan. Or you can try to do it by picking his pocket or putting a gun
to his head and demanding the transfer. All of these methods may work
some of the time, but only the first works all the time. Some of these techniques are not advisable if you want to keep the money and stay out of jail.

In some respects nations are not very different from individuals. They cooperate if they have something to gain, or if it is to further a cause they believe in. They may do favors if they think the favors will be returned in some
fashion. They also may sign on to a particular enterprise if they are tricked
by false claims or subjected to sufficient pressure. But, if tricked or forced,
they are likely to drop out at the earliest opportunity, and possibly shift their
support to others. Useful allies are voluntary. Enthusiastic ones have a stake

in the cause they support. Resentful ones can bring the whole effort to a halt. Ask Mr. Gorbachev about what happened to the Warsaw Pact.

What sort of methods were most likely to serve American security interests? All except two that I have mentioned required the cooperation of other countries. The United States, had it possessed leaders with foresight, wisdom, and political courage, could have reduced its dependence on imported energy in the decade of the 1990s without the active cooperation of any other country. The United States could also have moved to limit its involvement in local disputes without depending on others, although that needed to be negotiated carefully with its alliance partners. The other threats could be met only through cooperation with other countries. Cooperation did not necessarily require permanent international organizations, but it did demand methods that would attract the committed support of other countries.

Tools

Methods matter, and that axiom suggests that the tools of statecraft need to be adapted to the task and the methods chosen. A chainsaw may be the tool of choice for felling trees, but is of little use to a cabinetmaker. The military, diplomatic, intelligence, public information, and even economic tools available to the president in 1993 had all been developed during the Cold War and formed to assist the confrontation with communism and the Soviet Union. When the geopolitical world changed, the tools needed to be adapted to the new environment.

This was not easy for at least two reasons. First, there was no agreement regarding how the United States could best use its newfound preeminence, and second, every bureaucracy represents an interest group that tends to resist any change other than accretion of its size and authority. When these bureaucracies are tied to important domestic interests, whether defense contractors, ethnic communities, or corporations looking for tax breaks or licenses to exploit public lands or subsidies, it requires great political skill as well as keen judgment and insight to bring about the needed change.

In 1993 presidential leadership was needed to adapt America's military, diplomatic, intelligence, and public information bureaucracies to deal with the altered conditions in the post–Cold War world. Regarding defense, it required a shift from a military suitable for fighting another superpower to one that, while stronger than any putative adversary nation, would be effective in what military strategists call low-intensity conflict.

Since America's security would depend to a great extent on maintaining and extending alliances, the Foreign Service, America's diplomatic arm, needed strengthening, particularly by increased funding to allow more training, more modern means of communication, and a more secure work environment in dangerous areas. The Foreign Service had developed an extensive corps of specialists on Russia and the Soviet Union, but it was short of diplomats comfortable with languages like Arabic, Farsi, and Chinese—though it was much better off in this respect than the other government agencies involved in international relations.

Paradoxically, the Department of State, the country's first line of defense, had never been considered a "national security agency" for the purpose of funding. Therefore, at times of crisis, funding for the State Department often was kept static or reduced, even as the defense budget ballooned. The first step in correcting this situation would have been to consider State Department funding a part of national security.

So far as American intelligence collection is concerned, during the Cold War the emphasis had been overwhelmingly on collecting information regarding the Soviet Union, its allies, and its activities abroad. When there was no Soviet threat, collection needed to be reoriented to focus on other types of threats: proliferation of nuclear, biological, and chemical weapons, terrorism, criminal activity, "rogue state" behavior. This would require different targeting than that dominant during the Cold War, and also different linguistic skills and cultural competence. Penetrating terrorist cells required approaches different from those needed to recruit KGB officers during the Cold War. The end of the Cold War also opened up the possibility of collaboration with the intelligence services of former Communist countries against targets that were a threat to both, such as Islamic terrorists.

Competing with Communist propaganda by supplying objective, accurate information had been a major part of Cold War competition. With the Cold War over, it could be anticipated that there would be efforts to trim the resources available for public information. But it was very important to resist attempts to cripple public diplomacy or to turn it into propaganda. It was not that government information programs could or should replace the commercial mass media. They could not, and should not. However, a major effort by the government to get accurate information into the public domain was important to combat inaccurate stereotypes and false rumors.

Economic instruments are among the most powerful tools available to policy makers. They run the gamut from punitive measures, such as boycotts and sanctions (which rarely achieve important political objectives), to supportive measures such as foreign aid, investment promotion, or development loans from the World Bank (which, if given for political reasons, rarely achieve their economic objectives). Economic tools are only partly the province of government, for private investment, particularly by multinational corporations, exerts a significant influence on relations between countries.

During the Cold War, foreign aid was sometimes granted and investment encouraged primarily to stave off Communist influence. When done for that reason, it often did not make the contribution it should to the economic development of the recipient country. With the Cold War at an end, the temptation to preempt a potential rival was removed and should have led to foreign aid policies that focused primarily on benefit to the people in a given country rather than on bribes to its leaders for political support.

Investment by private business has a much greater impact on economic development abroad than foreign aid decisions. But not all private investment improves relations between the countries in question. Extraction of oil or other natural resources by foreign firms can inspire serious political instability if it seems that the local people derive few benefits while government officials in the far-off capital are living lavishly off payoffs disguised as consultancy fees.

The foreign policy challenge of the 1990s was not only to settle on an effective strategy and to select the appropriate methods to implement it, but to see to it that the government's tools were adapted and reconditioned to be most effective for the tasks at hand. There were no magic formulas or hard-and-fast rules to bring about these changes, most of which had to be defined and implemented in the rough and tumble of the domestic political process.

There would be a premium on political leadership, but the most important prerequisite was to get the strategy right, to set the right priorities, and to retune the instruments of power to do the task. With so many uncertainties in the political world of 1993, one could not expect clarity in every detail, but enough information was available to explain why one strategic approach should have been rejected.

The Imperial Temptation

Given a mindset that held that the United States had won a quasi-military victory over the Soviet Union in ending the Cold War, that Communist rule in the Soviet Union had buckled and shattered under superior American military and economic strength, and that the collapse of the Soviet Union as a unitary state was brought about by external pressure, it should not be surprising that both Americans and non-Americans became infatuated with the notion that the United States, the world's only remaining superpower, could do whatever it pleased with impunity so long as it was willing to use the unprecedented power it possessed.

Whether the United States was already an empire or an empire in the making or the opposite of an imperial power has been much debated of late by those members of the intellectual community who like to argue about foreign policy concepts. For those who thought it was already an empire, the question remained whether this was good or bad for the United States and good or bad for the world. For those who thought it was becoming an empire, similar questions arose: was it possible for the United States, by using its preeminent military and economic power, to create a Pax Americana? And—if this should be possible—would it be desirable, either for Americans or for the rest of the world?

What Is an Empire?

The words "empire" and "imperial" are now used so widely and so loosely that we must think about definitions if we are to get a better understanding of the issues these words raise. Some observers seem to define any spread of influence abroad, however voluntary, as imperial. Others deny that the United States has ever been or could be an empire. Still others will argue that world peace and justice can be brought about and maintained only if the United States is willing to acquire an empire, or maintain the one it has already acquired. There are those as well who dodge the issue by saying that, yes, the United States is (or has) an empire, but it is not a traditional empire

—rather, it's an empire of a new type. And, of course, there are those who argue that the United States can ensure its security and promote peace in the world only if it does *not* seek an empire.

Let's go back to the original meaning of the term. The Latin word on which "imperial" is based meant the power to command, what was later called the "sovereign" or ultimate power to govern. "Empires" were the realm in which that power was exercised. Nowadays, one standard definition of "empire" is "a state which governs a number of territories beyond its borders and comprises a diversity of peoples."[5] Others would omit the phrase "beyond its borders" from the definition, because that would not fit empires like the Austro-Hungarian or the Russian or the Chinese. To make a useful distinction between overseas empires and those made up largely of contiguous territory, some scholars have spoken of countries that *had* an empire (for example, Great Britain, Spain, Portugal, and France), and those that *were* empires (Austria-Hungary and pre-1917 Russia).* As we have seen, the Soviet Union was an empire that also had an empire.

One thing that the world should have learned in the twentieth century is that both of these traditional types of empire are obsolete. Spain lost all but remnants of its once vast empire in the nineteenth century, first by rebellions in its Latin American territories, then following defeat by the United States. The Germans lost their short-lived overseas empire to the British and French following their World War I defeat, but even though the British were among the winners of World War II and the French had the support of both the British and American governments to reassemble important parts of their empire, both Britain and France were forced—in part by circumstances, in part by American pressure—to relinquish their control over most of their overseas territories in the years immediately following World War II. Japan lost its empire when it capitulated to the United States in 1945. And then the Communist empire, which had been imposed on much of the former Russian Empire, imploded in 1991.

*For this argument, I will ignore the fact that, with the possible exception of Portugal, all of the "metropoles" listed in the first group were cobbled together in an imperial process: England conquering Scotland, Wales, and Ireland; Castile conquering Catalonia, Andalusia, Galicia, and other regions; the French king subduing Aquitaine, Brittany, Normandy, and other areas.

These events suggest that in the modern world, *empires are not worth the blood and treasure necessary to create and maintain them*. The nineteenth-century concept that great powers enhanced their power by extending their control over alien territory proved to be false. Multinational empires of both types contained the seeds of their dissolution in their very structure. People don't like to be ruled by foreigners, and in today's world of instant communication and easy access to deadly weapons, determined rebels against imperial rule will make that rule intolerably costly to any distant metropole.

America's Imperial Past

Most Americans today are reluctant to think of their country as an empire. Haven't we, throughout living memory, followed an anti-imperialist policy? We sought and obtained no territorial gains after our victories in two world wars; we encouraged the British, Dutch, Belgians, and French (except in Indochina) to dismantle their empires; we immediately recognized former colonies when they became independent and offered them both friendship and economic aid. The American position during the whole Cold War was, at its basis, a struggle against Communist imperialism, a struggle to prevent the creation of a Communist imperium by force, intimidation, and subversion.

So goes the reasoning of most Americans, if they think about the issue at all. This reasoning is not devoid of merit. Let's just say that it may oversimplify things and ignore some inconvenient facts, but it still contains more truth than falsehood. The United States did not set out after either twentieth-century world war to rule the world.

That was doubtless what Defense Secretary Donald Rumsfeld had in mind, a few days before the American invasion of Iraq in 2003, when he told an interviewer from the Al-Jazeera television network: "We're not a colonial power. We've never been a colonial power."[6] Niall Ferguson, a Glasgow-born historian who teaches at both Oxford and Harvard Universities, quoted Rumsfeld's statement in a recent book to refute it, arguing "not merely that the United States is an empire, but that it has always been an empire."[7]

Is Ferguson's claim really true? Well, certainly from the 1890s, specifically from the Spanish-American War of 1898, the United States followed, for a couple of decades, an avowedly imperial policy in the Pacific and in

the Caribbean. The Philippine Islands were taken from Spain and made a
U.S. dependency; Cuba and Puerto Rico were brought under American control; the Hawaiian Islands were annexed following a rebellion against the
indigenous government by American settlers and adventurers; a section of
the Isthmus of Panama was torn from Colombian jurisdiction, a client state
created, and a corridor of land between the Atlantic and Pacific was placed
under direct U.S. administration in order to construct and operate a canal
between the two oceans. Even before the United States entered World War
I, it was clear that it met the strict definition of a country with an empire: it
governed "a number of territories beyond its borders" that comprised "a diversity of peoples."

Therefore, in this instance, Donald Rumsfeld—along with probably most
Americans if they had been asked the same question—was wrong. It was incorrect to say that the United States has never been a colonial power. But—
does Ferguson have it right when he says that the United States has always
been an empire? Let's look closely at this question, because our founding fathers often used the rhetoric of imperial expansion.[8] Some of our states did
also. To this day, New York State dubs itself "the Empire State."

Our forefathers not only used the rhetoric of imperialism; they used its
methods, conquering territory from the native inhabitants in an inexorable
extension of settlement from the Atlantic coast to the Pacific. The methods
were imperial if viewed by Native Americans or (in today's Southwest) by
Mexicans, but did these imperial methods create an empire? Was the result
"a state which governs a number of territories beyond its borders and comprises a diversity of peoples?" Well . . . not quite. Circumstances and official
policies of the nineteenth century created a sense of shared nationhood
among the European immigrants that made up the overwhelming majority
of migrants in the westward movement. We still have on our money "E
Pluribus Unum," One (People) from Many. Additionally—and very important—the territories of European settlement were allowed to organize self-
governing communities, and then admitted to the Union with the same
rights as the other American states. Therefore, it seems correct to say that
although imperialist methods were used to expand the original United
States of America, the result was not an empire in the usual sense.

Also, it would be fair to note that the period of classical imperial rule did not last long. By 1934, with the Philippine Independence Act, the United States had promised the Philippines independence—a commitment it honored after it reconquered the islands from the Japanese in 1944. Arrangements with the other territories acquired during the McKinley–Theodore Roosevelt era also were changed, one by one, to a status other than that of typical colonies. The urge to establish sovereignty over distant territories ebbed following World War I when most Americans, disillusioned with the results of the war, favored isolationist policies.

Well, Ferguson and many others might argue that I am splitting hairs. After all, they concede that the American empire is a "different type" from the classical empires. But, if this is the case, why not find a suitable label for that "new type" rather than using an old one that doesn't really fit?

I started this discussion by stating my belief that in this century empires are not worth their costs, if they are possible at all. One might legitimately ask how it is that the United States followed an imperial approach in much of the North American continent and got by with it. If the product was not an empire, it nevertheless became the most successful political entity of the twentieth century. If it took imperialism to create that, it seems mistaken to say that imperialism won't work now on an even larger scale.

Those who argue that since imperialism helped create the United States it can be an instrument today for improving the world ignore some key facts: the imperial expansion occurred at a time when the settlers in North America could deal with the native inhabitants in a manner that later would be classified as genocide; they could also exercise the "right of conquest" to acquire territory from their weaker southern neighbor. Once the new territories were settled by migrants from Europe and the East Coast, the residents willingly accepted, indeed demanded, inclusion in the federal union. They needed the support of the United States to subdue the native inhabitants, while the federal authorities did not interfere in most everyday activities. The settlers retained a large measure of freedom and exercised self-government regarding most matters that touched their daily lives. They did not consider themselves a conquered people ruled by foreigners; they were instead themselves the conquerors.

Today it is impossible, morally, politically, and practically, to follow successfully the imperialist strategy that created the United States. Given the vast differences in societies, cultures, and psychology that exist in the world today, it is inconceivable that the United States could bring other countries, even if conquered and occupied, into a single federal union as states. That is what prevented nineteenth-century American imperialism from producing an empire on the North American continent. Nineteenth-century imperialist expansion is not an option for dealing successfully with the world in the twenty-first century.

Degrees of Domination

Thinking and communicating clearly about complex issues requires some precision in the use of terminology. It is an old trick of propagandists to demonize or sanctify a word or concept and then argue that any policy they don't like belongs to the first category, and those they do like to the second. But the world and America itself are much too complex for "either-or" thinking. There is an infinite number of intermediate points between "empire" and "isolation," and you cannot plot them on a straight line. Military involvement abroad is one thing, economic involvement another, political and diplomatic interchange a third, and contacts by private citizens a fourth, and even this doesn't complete a possible list of categories of involvement.

In each of these categories there are ranges of involvement. Military "involvement" might mean selling arms to a country, or offering training to its military personnel. It might also mean exchanging military liaison missions with the country—which can vary by size and scope of activity. It can mean operating military bases from a foreign territory. It can also mean occupying a foreign country and attempting to rule it. The other forms of involvement will also vary in scope, intensity, and degree of local acceptance. Some are obviously more intrusive than others, and some more coercive than voluntary.

If we are going to talk about America's role in the world, we need to be precise in the words we use. What do we mean when we use terms like empire and imperial, hegemon and hegemony, or leader and leadership? Sometimes these words are used almost interchangeably, but the word chosen both reveals the attitude of the speaker and affects the way the policy or activity is perceived by others.

The most insightful discussion I have found of the question as to whether the United States is an empire is in Harvard professor Charles Maier's *Among Empires: American Ascendancy and Its Predecessors*. He points out that "critics and cheerleaders alike have tended to focus on having an empire, not being one." There is a difference. As Maier explains: "States that are empires usually rule most of their territory according to one encompassing authoritarian regime which may, however, allow enclaves of semi-autonomy. Nations that have empires rule their possessions abroad by authoritarian methods while they often govern their homelands by representative systems."[9]

As a pragmatic observation about the nature of empires, Maier's descriptions are difficult to challenge. Nevertheless, they are generally ignored by those who argue that the United States has a duty to police the world and transform it in the American image.

Niall Ferguson, who was quoted as saying that America is and always has been an empire, is one of the champions of an imperial American role in the world, although he doubts that Americans are up to the challenge history has thrust upon them. He believes that the United States should continue to follow imperial policies on a worldwide scale. He summarizes his view of America's duty in the world as follows: "What is required is a *liberal* empire —that is to say, one that not only underwrites the free international exchange of commodities, labor and capital but also creates and upholds the conditions without which markets cannot function—peace and order, the rule of law, noncorrupt administration, stable fiscal and monetary policies —as well as provides public goods, such as transport infrastructure, hospitals and schools, which would not otherwise exist."[10]

Wow! Professor Ferguson doesn't expect much from the American soldier, diplomat, businessperson, and taxpayer does he? Let's ignore the fact that, by most definitions of empire, a *liberal* empire is an oxymoron. As Charles Maier explained, countries that *are* empires (remember the Russian Empire and the Soviet Union?) are ruled by authoritarian regimes or worse; countries that *have* empires (think British Empire) rule their possessions by authoritarian methods. It would seem that a liberal democracy cannot be an empire without becoming something else, or creating something else in its dependencies.

But let's put aside quibbles over definitions, and concede that all the goals

Ferguson lists are desirable and laudable. Does it take an *empire* to achieve these goals? Traditional empires brought about greater movement of commodities, labor, and capital within their imperial sphere, but rarely, if ever, was it a free or balanced exchange. Typically, empires set up privileged trading zones within the domains they ruled—privileged, that is, for the ruling country, but a disadvantage for the appendage. (George Washington, John Adams, and Alexander Hamilton could have told us something about that!)

Commodities moved from the colonies to the metropole, higher-value manufactured goods from the center to the colonies, and guess who benefited most. Empires promoted a certain movement of labor: of administrators from the mother country to the colonies, but rarely of administrators from the dependencies to the center. (One of the things that induced Benjamin Franklin to be a patriot rather than a Tory was his failure to secure an important position in King George's government in London.) As for capital, there was movement from the center to the periphery but hardly any from the periphery to the center. It is a real stretch to suggest that imperial practices in the past have led to a *free exchange* of any of these things. In fact, if history is any guide, truly free exchanges of economic goods on market principles are more likely to occur among countries with market economies, whether liberal or not, than within an imperial trading system.

But how about the "conditions without which markets cannot function"? For the sake of discussion, I will ignore the obvious fact that markets *do* function in the presence of many of the conditions Ferguson lists; maybe he means "without which markets cannot function perfectly"—as if they ever do. But let's set that aside and ask whether empires bring peace and order, the rule of law, stable fiscal and monetary policies, and an abundance of public goods. In the short term, even illiberal empires can produce some of these things. The Soviet Union created internal peace and a rigid order, an extensive transportation system, an unprecedented network of schools, hospitals, and clinics. The imperial Communist regime achieved nearly universal literacy, when other countries with market economies that were governed by elected governments—India and Pakistan (with an elected government occasionally in its history) come to mind—lagged far behind.

Oh, but wait—the Soviet Union was not a market economy; many of the "public goods" were the result of an authoritarian command economy. And the peace, law and order, and social stability that seemed to prevail for several decades following World War II were comparable to that of a prison.

All the goals Ferguson mentions are desirable, but hasn't he left something out? How about the human desire for freedom—personal freedom, not just market freedom—the need for respect, both self-respect and the respect of others? Are economic goods the only goods a person desires? A person who is hungry may indeed prefer slavery to starvation, and a person whose life is threatened by violence may prefer a police state to a pseudo-democracy riddled with violence and gross economic inequality. An oppressed people may welcome, temporarily, a foreign force that removes an oppressive regime, but that welcome is quickly dissipated. No country is content for long to be dominated by foreigners.

If human experience is any guide, then the economic "goods" Ferguson lists can be obtained only through international cooperation and not through the attempt of a single country, no matter how powerful, or how democratic, or how liberal, to set and enforce the rules. Other countries, whatever their internal governance, must have a part in making the rules and seeing that they are observed. Governments will do so over the long term only if they feel it is in their advantage to do so.

If Not Empire, What?

Some persons who argue that the United States must police the world because nobody else can do it avoid the words "imperialism" and "empire" and speak of the need for *hegemony*. Literally, the word simply means leadership, and sometimes it is used to refer to noncoercive leadership, as when a powerful country, or commercial entity, or other group sets rules and standards to which others comply voluntarily. The Greek historian Thucydides used the term to describe Athens' leadership of its colonies and allied Greek states during the war with Sparta. One might also speak of Microsoft's hegemony in the design of personal computer operating systems, or the hegemony of the American dollar in international financial flows.

Used in the latter sense, hegemony is not, in any direct way, coercive, and it can be challenged. If a challenger attracts a sufficient following, the challenger becomes the hegemon, just as, during the twentieth century, the dollar gradually replaced the pound sterling as the world's favorite currency for trade and international financial transactions.

The problem with using the term to mean a benign leader setting rules by example is that hegemony is often used to apply to rule setting by compulsion, and by the use of violent methods to establish dominance.[11] This is particularly true when it is applied to policies by nations. In that case, hegemony usually means control of another country's foreign policy, while empire would involve control of both foreign and domestic policy. However, even hegemony in its more limited sense is normally viewed as imperialistic if it is obtained by compulsion. The method used to secure the cooperation of other countries is the most important factor in determining whether a country's policy qualifies as imperialism. Forcing a country to submit is one thing; persuading a country to cooperate in its own interest or in return for protection is quite another.

Leadership is a more acceptable concept so long as it is used to mean leadership by example and consensus building, and not leadership by command. It is a tricky word to use in international discourse because foreign languages may lack exact equivalents and thus produce confusion of the two definitions. After all, "leader" is a favorite appellation of dictators: Hitler was *der Führer*, Mussolini, *il duce*, Stalin, *vozhd*. In North Korea, Kim Jong-il is the Korean equivalent of "Dear Leader." Furthermore, as Pavel Palazchenko, Gorbachev's interpreter, has pointed out, the usual translation into Russian of "U.S. global leadership" is *rukovodstvo mira*, which sounds to most Russians as meaning "control of the world."[12] In describing the policies and aspirations of the American government to people in other countries, there needs to be an awareness of the way the terms we use at home can be seriously misunderstood when they are carried abroad and translated into other languages.

Perhaps in time the forces of evolution or our intelligent designer (could they be one and the same?) will straighten out what Immanuel Kant called "the crooked timber of humanity," and make it possible to create throughout the world a form of liberal governance that would achieve the laudable goals Niall Ferguson lists.

When I was an undergraduate in the 1940s I was an active World Federalist; I met my wife at a United World Federalist meeting. We were convinced that if mankind did not create a world government, it was doomed to extinction in a nuclear holocaust. Then, as a graduate student of the Soviet Union, I realized that a world federation was not a practical possibility. We had to work with what we had—a disorderly, frequently irrational world— to make sure doomsday did not occur. Rule, or hegemony, by a single country can never guarantee all the benefits Ferguson listed, in part because no foreign country can deliver the noneconomic "goods" most people crave: freedom, respect, a feeling of pride—and, yes, a sense of responsibility for their own fate and participation in setting the rules by which their lives are regulated. There is a simple term for it: "self-government." Or, as Abraham Lincoln once described it, "government of the people, by the people, for the people."

To recognize this is not idealism, but realism. And realism suggests that a workable new world order can only be created by strengthening and expanding international law, strengthening the institutions that help arbitrate disputes, encouraging the development of governments responsive to their citizens' needs, deterring resort to violence, and cooperating with others to combat it when it occurs. It requires the development of regional security structures, with most of the responsibility for regional security resting with the nations in that region. The new world order cannot be an American empire, or based on a crudely applied American hegemony.

America's potential for helping transform the way power is exercised in the world had never been higher than it was when the Clinton administration took office in 1993. The choice should have been clear: to work toward an effective international order to deal with aggression and to encourage both respect for human rights and economic development, or to undermine the developing but still fragile international order by acting as a vigilante, not bound by the limitations of agreed legal procedure.

To put it bluntly, the world in 1993 was not a "unipolar world," as many people claimed; there was not even a "unipolar moment," when the United States, using its superior power, could alone rearrange world politics to its liking.[13] In many ways, the end of the Cold War and the end of the Soviet Union *reduced* rather than augmented American power.

Communism was not an attractive system either for people living under it or for people looking at it from the outside. The United States gained enormous influence in the world because it was seen as a protector of a country's independence, not as a threat to it. It gained great influence in the Soviet Union and other Communist countries because it was seen as a model of what people in those countries would like to have in their own country. Once there was no Cold War requiring superpower protection, and no Soviet Union that oppressed its own people, American influence receded. Attempts to use American power in the ways the Soviet Union had would induce many in the world to see the United States as a threat rather than a liberator.

The idea of unipolarity was a delusion that fed the temptation to act alone when the international structures that had been designed to bolster and augment American power failed to produce the immediate results the Clinton administration and its Republican opposition desired.

7

Hubris and Its Consequences:

1993–2000

BILL CLINTON DID NOT SET OUT TO remake the world in America's image when he assumed the presidency in 1993. He set out to pull the United States out of a mild recession, to stimulate growth of the American economy, to improve the health care system, and—above all—to ensure his re-election in 1996. In contrast to the preceding Bush administration, which prided itself on its foreign policy competence, the Clinton administration devoted more attention to domestic issues than to foreign policy, particularly in its early years. This was not necessarily bad, since the United States needed leadership not overly burdened with Cold War habits. Also, one should remember that Clinton had been elected, with Ross Perot's indirect help, on the slogan, "It's the economy, stupid."* It was to the economy and electoral politics that he devoted his keenest attention.

Clinton's Domestic Policy: Achievements and Failures

Clinton achieved more on the domestic front than in foreign policy, despite the failure to reform health care. These achievements on the whole strengthened the government's ability to conduct an effective foreign policy.

The persistent federal budget deficit had loomed large in the 1992 presi-

*Perot's third-party candidacy secured nearly twenty million votes. A majority of these would probably have gone to George H. W. Bush if Perot had not been on the ballot.

dential campaign and was one of the two major issues that fueled Ross Perot's third-party effort. Clinton managed to persuade Congress to raise taxes sufficiently to reduce the federal deficit and, by 1998, to produce a surplus, the first since 1957. The tax increases, it turned out, did not hamper the economy's growth, as the "no new taxes" crowd had warned, but in fact accompanied a surge in employment and economic productivity. There is no question that the budgetary surplus Clinton passed on to his successor created policy options that would not have been available if the budget had still been in deficit.

Clinton's second success was securing the ratification of the North American Free Trade Agreement (NAFTA), which had been concluded by George Bush in December 1992. If Clinton implemented one of Perot's campaign proposals by balancing the budget, he did the opposite when he persuaded enough Democrats to support the Republicans to pass NAFTA.* Perot had spoken of "the great sucking sound" of jobs flowing south if NAFTA should be implemented, but Clinton supported the view that it would benefit Americans as a whole by increasing the volume of trade. He worked actively to gain approval of the agreement, negotiating two supplementary accords to meet some of the objections and making it a legislative priority.

Other programs adopted during Clinton's presidency may have improved societal harmony, which strengthens the hand of any president in conducting foreign policy. Welfare reform ended some abuses and benefited the working poor without increasing costs; Clinton's appointment of more women to high government posts than his predecessors enabled him to draw from a larger pool of qualified candidates for responsible jobs than would have been available if he had relied primarily on male candidates.

These were important achievements, but any appraisal of their benefits must be balanced, at least in part, by failures. The attempt to reform health care failed; the long-term viability of Social Security and Medicare was not addressed; American dependence on imported energy grew; lip service to environmental concerns produced only marginal improvements and, though Vice President Albert Gore pressed for effective action to reduce the threat

*Both parties were divided on the issue, but although Republicans were predominantly in favor, they did not have enough votes to ratify the agreement without substantial assistance from the Democrats. The vote in the House was 234–200, with 132 Republicans and 102 Democrats in favor. The Senate vote was 61–38, with 34 Republicans and 27 Democrats approving the agreement.

of global warming, Clinton himself did little to support meaningful inter-national action. Defense procurement remained skewed in favor of the sort of weapons that had been necessary during the Cold War rather than those that would be of most use in the "low intensity," asymmetric struggles (with terrorists, drug dealers, and hoodlum regimes) that were already spreading in troubled areas of the world.

Foreign and Security Policy

President George H. W. Bush once noted, in a gesture of modesty, that he lacked "the vision thing." It is true that his style of leadership resembled that of a manager more than a crusader. Nevertheless, in many ways his idea of what would be necessary to create a "new world order" following the collapse of the Soviet Union was based on a sounder vision of reality than his successor demonstrated. In particular, Bush recognized that there were limits to American power and that the United States needed to exercise its leadership through appropriate international organizations if it was to be effective. That is why he and Secretary of State Baker spent as much time and effort as they did to convince Gorbachev that the Soviet vote on the U.N. Security Council should support the use of force, if necessary, to liberate Kuwait from Iraqi occupation.

Bill Clinton, in contrast, seems to have begun his presidency with few clear foreign policy goals, and more often than not he left the articulation of policy to subordinates. Much of the time he seemed to react to events rather than try-ing to shape them. As American politics became more polarized and vitu-perative, the public seemed to forget that foreign affairs mattered. When Clin-ton left office in January 2001, few noticed that the country was neither as safe nor as dominant in the world as they had assumed. The Cold War was over, but the contours of the post–Cold War world remained obscure.

Nuclear Weapons

Immediately after taking office, the Clinton administration took care of some of the most urgent tasks required to reduce the nuclear danger, but gradually seemed to lose interest in the topic. As a result, the momentum Reagan, Gorbachev, and Bush had imparted to nuclear arms reduction slowed during the Clinton administration to the point that Ambassador Avis

Bohlen, who played a key role in arms control negotiations during the 1990s, characterized the period as "the fall of arms control."[1]

One of the most immediate tasks Clinton and Warren Christopher, his first secretary of state, faced in 1993 was to make sure that the Lisbon Protocol, negotiated by Secretary of State Baker in 1992, was implemented. It required all Soviet nuclear weapons to be transferred to Russia. Belarus, having contracted an extreme public aversion to anything nuclear following the Chernobyl disaster, transferred the weapons on Belarusian soil to Russia without urging from abroad. It took a little longer to make sure that weapons and weapon-grade materials were removed from Kazakhstan and Ukraine, but American diplomats, working with their Russian counterparts, secured satisfactory agreements from both.* Also, the Clinton administration ramped up funding for the Nunn-Lugar program to improve the security and safety of nuclear sites in Russia and made that assistance part of the U.S. defense budget.

In other respects, however, the movement toward further reduction of nuclear weapons faltered. To judge from the comments at a press conference held by Defense Secretary William Perry and others in September 1994, America's nuclear doctrine at that time differed little from that during the Cold War.[2] The large number of nuclear weapons were justified by the alleged need to "hedge" against some future breakout by Russia. (Apparently, the Reagan-Gorbachev goal of eliminating the possibility of a breakout by eliminating strategic weapons themselves was either not considered or rejected.)

The Russian State Duma delayed ratification of the second strategic arms agreement signed by President Bush (START II), in part because some legislators felt that it required Russia to make greater concessions than the United States (in fact, it did). This objection might have been overcome if the United States had offered a follow-on agreement that corrected some of the imbalance and had refrained from actions that most Russians considered unfriendly, such as enlarging the NATO alliance and bombing Serbia without the approval of the U.N. Security Council.

As for existing strategic nuclear weapons, thousands remained on alert in both countries. Alert for what? This was never debated or even explained to the public, which seemed oblivious to the threat they represented. Suppos-

---

*At one point the Ukrainian parliament (the Supreme Rada) asserted Ukrainian ownership of strategic nuclear missiles on Ukrainian soil.

edly these weapons were not targeted at the other country, but such missiles can be retargeted in minutes, if not seconds. It was (and continues to be) a very dangerous situation, since the missiles might be launched by accident or as the result of a mistaken report. Any rational national leader should want to have ample time to consider a response if an attack by a nuclear weapon should occur. The last thing anybody should want would be an automatically escalating exchange that could result from keeping numerous weapons on alert status. Furthermore, under most hypothetical circumstances, the United States would have ample non-nuclear means to respond to any attack on its territory by another country.

So far as short-range, tactical weapons were concerned (the sort that would be of most use to terrorists if any should escape responsible custody), no apparent progress was made beyond the unilateral statements that had been exchanged between President Bush the elder and Presidents Gorbachev and Yeltsin. These provided a good start in dealing with a difficult issue, and there should have been immediate negotiations for a verifiable agreement to continue dismantling these weapons and removing those that were retained to a centralized location, distant from potential hot spots. Even this should have been an interim measure, since the goal should have been to progress from a bilateral U.S.-Russian agreement to one including other nuclear powers. Unfortunately, nothing was achieved to expand and verify the unilateral statements of 1991 and 1992.

The United States also had a strong interest in achieving a verifiable ban on further nuclear testing. The United States and Russia both knew how to make nuclear weapons and could even develop new types without further testing. Countries without nuclear weapons were not likely to develop a credible arsenal without some testing. Therefore, if avoiding proliferation of nuclear weapons was important to American security—as it certainly was—support for a verifiable test ban should have been a no-brainer.*

Would a comprehensive test ban ensure that no additional country would

---

*Critics argued that testing was needed to ensure the safety and "reliability" of nuclear weapons. But technical advances had made it possible to ensure safety without testing. Reliability should have been of lesser concern, since no country would attack the United States with nuclear weapons on the assumption that U.S. weapons had become so unreliable that they would not be effective deterrents. In any case, even reliability could be assessed with high confidence without further testing.

develop a nuclear weapons capacity? No, of course not. There is no way any single measure can give absolute assurance of success. But an international agreement to ban further nuclear testing would greatly strengthen the leverage the United States and its allies would have to deter testing by unreliable governments and to summon international support for measures to deter proliferation.

So, what happened? The Clinton administration worked with other countries to conclude the Comprehensive Nuclear Test Ban Treaty. Some 160 countries signed it. It was presented to the U.S. Senate for ratification in 1997, but the Republican-controlled Senate refused to ratify it. The Republican senators who voted against it should bear the primary responsibility for rejection, but many observers felt that the Clinton administration had not worked as closely with the Senate as it could have to explain and defend the treaty. Also, it should be recalled that the Senate's consideration occurred when the Clinton administration was distracted by the investigation by Kenneth Starr and the revelations about the president's relations with White House intern Monica Lewinsky.

Chemical and Biological Weapons

The treaty to ban chemical weapons that George Bush signed just before leaving office was ratified four years later, with President Clinton's support, just days before it came into force in April 1997. The treaty created the Organization for the Prohibition of Chemical Weapons, which, by 2008, had 183 member states and had made substantial progress in ending production and destroying existing stocks of chemical weapons.*

Progress in developing means to verify the ban on biological weapons (BW) was much slower, however, even though evidence mounted that the number of countries with active programs might be increasing. In 1994, the United States joined other countries that had accepted the treaty banning biological weapons in a conference to consider enforcement provisions. It

---

*According to the OPCW Web page (www.opcw.org), as of November 2008 the organization had determined that all declared chemical warfare production facilities had been inactivated. Furthermore, it had supervised the destruction of 30,130 metric tons of chemical weapons (42 percent of those declared) and 3.1 million weapons or containers of chemical agents (about 36 percent of the total).

was clear then that it would be much more difficult to verify the ban on biological weapons than it had been to ensure that commitments regarding nuclear and chemical weapons were carried out. It also was obvious that the world would be safer if there was a system of international inspection of facilities that might produce biological weapons. Therefore, the conference on biological weapons established an international working group, officially called the Ad Hoc Group, to negotiate a legally binding protocol for a regime of inspections that would deter attempts to make weapons out of germs. This group, headed by Tibor Tóth of Hungary, met periodically at Geneva but did not complete its work while President Clinton was in office.

The main opposition to a regime of inspections came from the pharmaceutical industry, which feared compromise of trade secrets if there was inspection of its facilities by international enforcement authorities. Countries that were suspected of continuing some BW activity, including Russia, were unwilling to accept inspections unless the United States did. One has the impression that the Clinton administration did not place a high priority on this effort, in part because it did not want to face down the pharmaceutical industry—whose fears were almost certainly exaggerated.

Dealing with the potential threat of nuclear, biological, and chemical weapons involved more than negotiating with foreign governments to control or eliminate the weapons and to verify that agreements were kept. It was also important to make preparations in case the worst happened and some of these weapons were used against Americans in their own country. During the Cold War, some of the so-called civil defense measures that were peddled by politicians from time to time were both useless and ill-advised. Frightening schoolchildren with alarms and teaching them to hide under desks created unnecessary anxiety. If there had been a nuclear attack, it would not have helped the hapless children to crawl under desks minutes before they were incinerated, nor would any position in the schoolroom protect them from lethal radiation if they were outside the blast zone.

However, if there should be the detonation of a nuclear device or radiological bomb by terrorists, or the release of a lethal chemical or a designer germ, there are things that can be done. Not, of course, for those killed in an initial nuclear blast, but for the many people who would be injured or at risk following the attack. Essentially, defense against such attacks would in-

clude devising and placing sensors able to detect and identify the weapons
or the lethal substances that might be released, prepositioning appropriate
equipment and antidotes, and training first responders. Since most of the
latter would be under the control of local or state governments, planned
training and a system of coordination would be essential. Though some
types of special equipment might be required, most of what needed to be
done to deal with a terrorist strike would be that needed to recover from a
natural disaster.

The Clinton administration made progress on some of these needs, but
in retrospect, it accomplished only a small part of what was necessary for
civil defense and disaster relief. Responsibility for any shortcomings in this
area, however, was shared by state and local authorities, who tended to resist federal guidance, and the Republican Congress, which opposed most
proposals made by the Clinton administration.

Military Involvement in Local Disputes

At first, it seemed that the Clinton administration would resist expanding
American obligations to defend other countries, but the pressures of humanitarian crises, the "war on drugs," residual Cold War thinking, and domestic politics led it to involvement in conflicts that were not threatening to
the United States. Lacking a strategy to reform the security architecture of
the post–Cold War world by bolstering international capabilities to deal with
local conflicts, the Clinton administration increasingly involved American
forces in what were essentially no-win situations. In doing so, it weakened
the international institutions so laboriously nurtured by previous administrations and walked away from some of the international legal commitments
that had helped the United States and its allies negotiate an end to the Cold
War and encourage democratization of Communist countries.

Environmental Degradation

Virtually nothing effective was done to continue the process of environmental protection that had made slow but unmistakable progress under previous administrations, with measures including the ban on DDT, the protection of the ozone layer, the reduction of acid rain, Superfund cleanup of
polluted soils and streams, and the so-called CAFE standards (Corporate Av-

erage Fuel Economy) for automobile mileage first adopted by Congress in 1975 to improve the fuel efficiency of cars sold in the United States. With oil prices relatively low, there was little economic incentive to find alternative sources of energy, and the Clinton administration did not take the lead in explaining the necessity of promoting nonpolluting technologies, the views of Vice President Albert Gore notwithstanding.

Toward the end of his second term, President Clinton signed the Kyoto Protocol, designed to reduce greenhouse gases, but it lacked sufficient support to secure ratification by the U.S. Senate.

Energy Dependence

The Clinton administration also failed to reduce dependence on imported oil. The expense of maintaining substantial military forces in the Persian Gulf in order to keep petroleum export lanes open and Saddam Hussein in check was not passed on to the consumer, thus subsidizing the real cost of imports. Proposals made in the early 1990s for a tax on gasoline or on imported oil faced substantial public opposition, and the Clinton administration made no serious attempt to explain how they might, in combination with other measures, contribute to American security by reducing dependence on imported oil and financing alternative sources of energy. During the Clinton presidency, U.S. imports of petroleum grew from 2.9 billion barrels in 1992, the last year of the Bush presidency, to 4.2 billion in 2000, the last year of the Clinton presidency, an increase of 45 percent. By January 2001, the United States was importing 12.6 million barrels of oil each day.[3]

New Threats

Terrorism did not seem to be on the short list of potential threats to the American homeland in January 1993. There had not been a serious attack against Americans or American installations abroad for four years. Only a few days after Clinton was inaugurated, however, a bomb in a van parked in a garage under the World Trade Center in New York exploded, killing six people and wounding 1,042. A little over three years later a bomb destroyed the Federal Building in Oklahoma City, taking the lives of 168 people and wounding over 600. Less than a year later a pipe bomb exploded in Atlanta during the Olympic games, killing one person and wounding 111. The same month a suicide bomber attacked a military housing facility in Saudi Arabia, killing nineteen U.S. military personnel and injuring hundreds of others. Even more serious bombings were to come: in 1998, U.S. embassies in Nairobi, Kenya, and Dar es Salaam, Tanzania, were attacked. Two hundred and ninety-one persons were killed in Nairobi, including nine Americans, and over 5,000 people were wounded. In Dar es Salaam, ten persons were killed, including one American. Two years later, the terrorists chose a much harder target when suicide bombers steered an explosive-laden boat into the destroyer USS *Cole,* which was in the Aden harbor for refueling. Seventeen sailors were killed and another thirty-nine wounded.

Although Osama bin Laden's Al-Qaeda was responsible for several of these attacks, it was not behind all of them. The bombings in Oklahoma City and Atlanta were conducted by Americans connected to, or sympathetic with, "Christian" white-supremacist groups. Their actions demonstrate that one should not attribute the resort to terrorism to adherents of one religion alone. Extremists of every religion and culture have at times indulged in violence against civilians.

The Clinton administration took these terrorist acts seriously. As Richard A. Clarke—an experienced civil servant who had worked in both the Reagan and first Bush administrations—detailed in the book he wrote after the attacks of September 11, 2001, both the president and vice president gave full support to the recommendations of their experts on terrorism.[4] American bureaucracies, however, were slow to do so. The Defense Department and the CIA were more adept at finding excuses for not striking Al-Qaeda bases in Afghanistan than in planning effective ways to do so. According to the 9/11 Commission, the FBI leadership refused to give the threat of terrorism priority attention. According to Clarke, FBI director Louis Freeh at times behaved—to say the least—unprofessionally.*

---

*For example, when a bomb exploded in Atlanta during the Olympic Games in 1996, FBI agents in Atlanta told Clarke that Freeh insisted on making Richard A. Jewell the prime suspect even though there was no evidence that he might be guilty. In fact, Jewell had been the security guard who spotted a suspicious backpack and warned people nearby to flee, thus saving many lives. Freeh was said to have acted on a hunch that Jewell was a wannabe cop who staged the incident to prove his bravery so he could get a

Despite the reluctance of the FBI to address seriously the terrorist threat inside the United States, by 1999 and 2000, the Clinton White House had come to the conclusion that terrorism was the greatest security threat to the United States. Unfortunately, it had not managed to change the attitude and the preparedness of the intelligence, law enforcement, and military arms of the federal government.

Key Areas

During the Cold War, the rivalry between the United States and its allies, on the one hand, and the Soviet Union and its captive nations on the other influenced and overshadowed developments throughout the world. To many, it seemed that the world was run by the superpowers, but this was never really true. Many things happened that were beyond the control of either. But this tended to be forgotten (if it had ever been understood) by those who felt that, since it was no longer a superpower, Russia didn't count and could be safely ignored by the United States and its allies in constructing a post–Cold War order.

There is no question that, in the 1990s, Russia was a mess in many respects. Its economy had collapsed with the implosion of the Soviet command system, and its military was in disarray.[5] It faced a demographic crisis. Having lost control of half the population of the Soviet Union, it was slowly losing what was left of it in the Russian Federation, with mortality exceeding the birth rate and net immigration. There was no reason to treat Russia as either a threat to the United States and its allies in Europe or as a competitor for world leadership, or a co-arbiter of the world's problems. But there was every reason to take it seriously, to make sure that the East-West divide did not recur, to enlist Russian support where it could be effective, as

---

regular job. His suspicions leaked to the press and not only damaged Jewell's personal reputation, but allowed the real culprit, Eric Rudolph, to escape and conduct two more bombings before the FBI put him on a wanted list. He went into hiding in the mountains of western North Carolina and escaped a manhunt led personally by Director Freeh that resembled a performance by Keystone Kops with helicopters. Two years later a county sheriff's deputy arrested Rudolph when he was rummaging for food in a garbage dump. (Clarke, *Against All Enemies*, pp. 109–110.)

in the Balkans, and to encourage development of a democratic, "European-style" government in Russia.

With all of its weaknesses, Russia continued to be vitally important to any new world order. It had an arsenal of nuclear weapons that equaled that of the United States in numbers. That is what had made the Soviet Union a superpower, since its economy was not competitive. Russia also had a productive capacity for military equipment second only to the United States. It had a permanent seat in the United Nations, so its vote (or abstention) would be required to make any military intervention legal in the world's eyes. Russia also controlled more land on the earth's surface than any other country, stretching over eleven time zones, and the land was full of resources—oil, natural gas, minerals of all types. It also had an educated population with a plethora of scientists and engineers. If properly employed, they could be an irreplaceable asset for economic development; if ignored or abused, they could help create weapons of mass destruction in any country willing to pay for their services.[6]

For all of its initial talk about a "partnership for reform," the Clinton administration dealt with Russia as if it no longer counted, even in European politics. Two decisions in particular turned Russian public opinion during the years of the Clinton administration from strongly pro-American to vigorous opposition to American policies abroad. The first was the decision to extend the NATO military structure into countries that had previously been members of the Warsaw Pact—something Gorbachev had understood would not happen if he allowed a united Germany to remain in NATO.[7] The second was the decision to bomb Serbia without authorization from the United Nations Security Council.

There was no need to expand NATO to ensure the security of the newly independent countries of Eastern Europe. There were other ways those countries could have been reassured and protected without seeming to re-divide Europe to Russia's disadvantage. As for the bombing of Serbia, if NATO had not been enlarged in the manner that occurred, Russia's government would have been much more willing to bring pressure on Slobodan Milošević to come to terms with the Kosovars, and—if unsuccessful in this effort—more willing to vote in the United Nations to authorize military intervention. In fact, tacit agreement with Russia in the mid-1990s to hold off any formal expansion of NATO so long as Russia cooperated to keep peace in the Balkans and refrained from threatening other countries would almost certainly have helped to reduce the violence in both Bosnia and Kosovo and could have ensured that whatever military action turned out to be necessary would receive Security Council approval.*

President Clinton managed, by personal diplomacy, to force Russian president Yeltsin, who desperately needed American support, to agree to arrangements that enraged Russian opinion leaders, particularly those in the bureaucracy, including top military officers.[8] Clinton's actions severely damaged the credibility of democratic leaders in Russia, who appealed in vain for a more considerate attitude toward Russian national interests, which in fact did not conflict with American interests.

The Clinton administration was deaf to these appeals, as well as those of George Kennan, the author of the successful containment policy, who warned that enlarging NATO in the proposed manner would be "the most fateful error of American policy in the entire post-cold-war era." He then explained why: "Such a decision may be expected to . . . restore the atmosphere of the cold war in East-West relations, and to impel Russian foreign policy in directions decidedly not to our liking. And, last but not least, it might make it much more difficult, if not impossible, to secure the Russian Duma's ratification of the START II agreement and to achieve further reductions of nuclear weapons."[9]

Why was the advice of most diplomats who had dealt with the Soviet Union and helped bring the Cold War to an end through realistic, muscular diplomacy swept aside? It is difficult to escape the conclusion that the decision to expand NATO was influenced by an assessment of domestic politics rather than by a careful analysis of America's interests abroad. It was well known that Americans of Polish, Ukrainian, and other Eastern European origins were strongly in favor of bringing their ancestors' countries into NATO. Many of them, though Democrats, had voted for President Reagan. President Clinton needed them to win the electoral votes in key states like Pennsylvania and Illinois in 1996. (Although the Senate vote to accept

---

*If Russia had supported authorization for military action, China probably would also have voted in favor, or else abstained, allowing the proposal to pass.

new members in NATO took place after the 1996 election, during the campaign Clinton pledged that the expansion was a matter of "not whether but when.") The domestic political argument was the only one that could be honestly made for enlarging NATO in the manner it was done.

Of course, these were not the arguments made. Rather, the public was told that we needed to expand NATO to "remove Cold War divisions in Europe." But those divisions had already been removed. Expanding the military organization that had maintained a defensive line in the middle of the continent was a good way to revive the division rather than to preserve a Europe "whole and free"—the objective of every American president up through George H. W. Bush.

The question should not have been "expand NATO or nothing," but rather to explore how the United States could give adequate assurance to countries in Eastern Europe that their independence would be preserved in the future, and at the same time to create a security system in Europe that would place the prime responsibility for the continent's future on Europeans. Moving NATO's jurisdiction to the east would not be as advantageous to the Eastern European countries as a Europe in which Russia played an active and constructive partnership role while the former Soviet satellites reformed their economies to make them eligible for membership in the European Union.

Choosing the politically advantageous route, the Clinton administration made a profound mistake, for, combined with rhetoric claiming "victory" in the Cold War, expanding NATO suggested to the Russian public that throwing off communism and breaking up the Soviet Union had probably been a bad idea. Instead of getting credit for voluntarily joining the West, they were being treated as if they had been defeated and were not worthy to be allies.

In fact, Russians did not even receive the consideration granted Germans after World War II, even though the Germans had started the war and had lost it. Once the Allied occupiers had removed Nazis from the West German government, Germans were welcomed into the Western alliance. The United States had, in effect, made reconciliation, a psychologically difficult task for the French, Dutch, British, and others, a condition for the Marshall Plan, and thus championed the inclusion of Germany in the Western alliance as a full partner. The Clinton administration, without any provocation, in effect repeated a fundamental mistake made at Versailles in 1919. By excluding Russia from the peace settlement when it was not even a defeated party but actually one of the victors over the Communist Soviet Union, the Clinton administration practically ensured that there would be no new world order in Europe, and that Russia would lose its incentive to reduce nuclear weapons, both of which should have been at the top of any American strategic priority list.

That is not the only mistake the Clinton administration made in its European policy. It was in the American strategic interest to bolster the ability of Europeans to keep the peace in Europe. There had been some attempts by our European allies to create European defense organizations as part of NATO. During the Cold War, the United States had usually discouraged these efforts, feeling that they undermined NATO unity. Following the Cold War, there was no reason to discourage a European force that could be used independently of the United States. In fact, the United States could only gain in the long run if it avoided the impression that it was trying to dominate the continent in its own parochial interest. Nevertheless, the United States continued to discourage European efforts to create a European defense community to supplement NATO.* This is one of the reasons (though not the only one) that the Europeans were unable to keep the contending forces in Bosnia from committing mayhem until Americans stepped in and Ambassador Richard Holbrooke knocked heads in Dayton, Ohio, and achieved a tenuous peace.[10]

My argument is not that all would have been sweetness and light in Europe if only the United States had been kind to Russia and encouraged the Europeans to settle their own problems, especially in the Balkans. I am aware that efforts to forge new habits of cooperation might well have fallen short, and that, in the end, there might have been no choice but for the United States to take part in military intervention to save lives in the former Yugoslavia.

*The British, with American support, vetoed a French proposal to bring the West European Union into the European Union as a European Security and Defense Identity (ESDI). In 1996, it was agreed that the ESDI would be developed only within the NATO framework.

My point is different: the United States should have made every effort to bring the European states, West and East, and including Russia, into a new security arrangement. Traditional NATO could have been part of the new European security architecture, but not a substitute for it. If the Europeans were unable to cope with the humanitarian crises accompanying the breakup of Yugoslavia, then at least we could have expected Russia to vote in the U.N. Security Council to authorize whatever military action was necessary to prevent genocide or mass "ethnic cleansing." That way, the United States could have avoided breaking international law in its action and behaving as if a military alliance could supplant the Security Council in authorizing war on a country that had not committed aggression against any NATO member.

The Clinton administration's action in bombing Serbia without U.N. approval not only enraged Russia and made close cooperation on nuclear issues more difficult, it also sent a message to other countries with policies or practices that met American disapproval: Better get nuclear weapons as fast as you can! Otherwise, you can become a target for the U.S. Air Force!

Middle East

Prospects for settling the conflict between Israelis and Palestinians seemed to have improved toward the end of the Cold War. Early in the Clinton administration, a promising breakthrough occurred: the Oslo agreement, reached by Israeli and Palestinian negotiators under Norwegian auspices. President Clinton lost no time arranging for the agreement to be signed in Washington, the occasion of a much-noted photograph of Palestinian leader Yasser Arafat shaking hands with Israeli prime minister Yitzhak Rabin. The Oslo agreement was the result of direct talks between Palestinians and Israelis and set a framework for future relations between Israel and an anticipated Palestinian state, but it left key questions still to be negotiated.

The ensuing negotiations made little progress, in part because the Israeli government continued to expand Jewish settlements in the occupied West Bank, thereby—in Palestinian eyes—attempting to preempt the territorial issues under discussion. President Clinton returned to active participation in the negotiations toward the end of his presidency, when meetings in October 2000 with Arafat and Ehud Barak at Camp David seem to have come close to agreement, but only renewed violence and heightened tension followed.[11]

The primary blame for failing to solve the Israeli-Palestinian conflict should not be placed on the Clinton administration. A peaceful settlement had eluded every effort before Clinton's presidency, and the situation has hardly improved since then. However, if there was any real chance that the Oslo agreement might lead to a long-term peace, Israel needed to hold off expanding settlements in the West Bank and Gaza and promptly make the sort of offer Prime Minister Barak did some seven years later at Camp David.[12]

Things might have worked out more favorably if President Clinton had given the matter closer attention early in his first administration and had exerted greater pressure on Israel to halt settlement activity outside Israel proper and on Yasser Arafat to curb violence and reduce the corruption in the Palestinian Authority. Expanding Jewish settlements was inconsistent with the commitment to recognize a Palestinian state and doubtless engendered violent resistance by the Palestinians—which in turn produced a swing to the hard-line "right" in Israeli politics and growing Palestinian support for militant groups such as Hamas. Despite Clinton's efforts late in his second term, the prospects for peace between Palestinians and Israelis seemed more distant when he left office than they had been at the beginning of his presidency.

So far as Iraq and Iran were concerned, the Clinton administration continued to enforce the sanctions placed on Saddam Hussein, but failed to open a dialogue with the Iranian leadership that might have eased relations —and indirectly undermined the ability of the mullahs to exploit anti-Americanism to keep themselves in power. The time should have been propitious. The United States had led a coalition to defeat Iran's main enemy and had so hobbled the Iraqi forces that they could be no threat to Iran. Iran still had not recovered fully from its losses in the war with Iraq and had good reason to welcome steps to end the sanctions growing out of the hostage crisis. It probably would have been willing to pay a price for normalization, so long as it was not trumpeted as a political victory by Washington.

Nevertheless, the Clinton team decided not to explore the possibility of improving these relations, choosing instead to lump Iran with its archenemy Iraq. This decision assumed that U.S. power was so great that America had no need to follow the classic geopolitical principle of keeping two hostile states at bay by balancing them against each other. The United States was believed to be powerful enough to keep both Iraq and Iran in check. Therefore, rather than talking to Iran to tighten the squeeze on Saddam Hussein, reduce the Iranian incentive to acquire nuclear weapons, and discourage Iranian mischief making in its neighborhood, the United States announced a policy of "double containment."[13]

It was as if the United States had learned nothing from its mistake in refusing for years to recognize Communist China—a mistake President Richard Nixon was wise enough to correct. Although we cannot be sure that an attempt to improve relations with Iran would have worked in 1993—a lot would have depended on *how* it was done—we can be certain that no real attempt was made, and that the Clinton administration seemed oblivious to the possibility of improving relations. Even when a more moderate government led by Seyyed Mohammad Khatami was elected in 1997 and sent signals that Iran wanted to improve relations, the Clinton administration decided not to embark on serious negotiations.[14]

South Asia

Both India and Pakistan unexpectedly exploded nuclear devices in May 1998. This should not have come as a shock, since it was known that both countries were well along in developing a bomb, but in fact the CIA was taken by surprise, demonstrating that it had not yet reoriented its intelligence capability to detect nuclear weapons proliferation. In building nuclear weapons, neither India nor Pakistan had broken any treaty agreement, because both had refused to sign the Non-Proliferation Treaty. (Israel, which developed a nuclear arsenal much earlier, was also not a party to the NPT.) Nevertheless, the decision of both governments to test nuclear weapons increased the possibility of further proliferation. The Clinton administration duly protested the nuclear tests, but failed to exhibit any clear strategy for dealing with the altered distribution of power in the world brought about by the enlargement of the nuclear "club."

Nor did it seem that much attention was devoted to developments in

Afghanistan—at least not during Clinton's first term. An extreme Islamist group, the Taliban, had seized power from the Northern Alliance that had received American support during and after the Soviet occupation. The Taliban had essentially been created by the Pakistan intelligence agency and had been funded in large part by Saudi Arabia. The Clinton administration seems to have paid little attention until Osama bin Laden took up residence in Afghanistan and opened terrorist training camps under Taliban protection. Following the bombing of American embassies in Kenya and Tanzania, President Clinton authorized military operations to capture or kill bin Laden, but neither the Defense Department nor the CIA found a way to implement the decision.

China, Japan, and East Asia

In East Asia, the Clinton record is better than it was in Europe, the Middle East, or South Asia. Japan's economic stagnation relieved the United States of the sort of intense competition some experts had predicted. China's economic transformation proceeded more rapidly than most had anticipated, and the Clinton administration decided not to let efforts to tie trade policy with protection of human rights prevent American participation in the accelerating Chinese boom. This was a wise decision because, given what happened to the Soviet Union, which the Chinese leaders attributed to excessive democratization, the United States did not have the leverage to force the Chinese leaders to adopt policies they considered tantamount to political suicide.

The North Korean regime presented the most serious security problem in Northeast Asia in the 1990s when it became apparent that it was using its nuclear facilities to develop materials suitable for bombs rather than for nuclear power plants, a violation of the Non-Proliferation Treaty, and that it was peddling nuclear weapons technology elsewhere. Threats of military action were not advisable, since the North Koreans had enough artillery in place to destroy much of Seoul, the South Korean capital, before they could have been taken out by American air power. Nevertheless, the situation seemed headed for a military showdown until former president Jimmy Carter traveled to Pyongyang and secured agreement that the North Koreans would halt their weapons activity in return for economic assistance and help in constructing nuclear power plants. It was not an ideal agreement, particularly given the North Korean history of duplicity and broken promises, but it seems to have slowed for a time the North Korean efforts to develop a nuclear weapons capability.

Latin America

The end of the Cold War should have liberated the U.S. government from its fear of Communist subversion and thereby enabled it to play a transformative role in the hemisphere by helping cope with the pressures of technological change and accelerated globalization. The Clinton administration achieved some individual successes: ratification of NAFTA and assistance to Mexico and Brazil in overcoming debt crises are among them.

Other policies and activities produced less than clear results. Military and police involvement in Colombia to combat the drug barons and affiliated terrorist organizations increased. There was a brief intervention in Haiti, approved by the United Nations. Immigration from Mexico, legal and illegal, continued and a law passed in 1996, designed to curb the flow of illegal immigrants, had little apparent effect on the steadily growing numbers of "undocumented" aliens in the United States.

The most significant missed opportunity could have been in relations with Cuba. An easing of sanctions on Castro's regime might have stimulated pressures on the island to weaken Castro's control and deprived him of an excuse for his regime's many failures. Nevertheless, Clinton, ignoring the Cold War experience with Eastern Europe, tightened the embargo on Cuba, apparently to curry favor with some of the more conservative elements of the Cuban exile community in Florida.[15]

In general, trade and the movement of people in the Western Hemisphere developed with governments playing little more than a marginal role. Violence continued in some areas but was usually connected with the drug trade rather than with pro-communist insurgencies.

Overall, Clinton policy in Latin America seemed to lack both sustained attention and a realistic vision of appropriate goals. Henry Raymont, the veteran journalist commissioned by the Century Foundation in New York to survey U.S. relations with Latin America, said: "Clinton's hemisphere policy was based not so much on an orderly, comprehensive weltanschauung, an understanding of the Latin American component in US history, but mostly was steered by the winds of circumstance."[16] As in Europe, domestic political expediency militated against adoption of a policy that would encourage needed changes in Latin America.

Africa

While Latin America during the 1990s created few new problems for U.S. policy, sub-Saharan Africa was beset with a most appalling series of reverses. The encouraging shift to majority rule in South Africa early in the decade did not bring clear benefits to countries farther north. The Horn of Africa was in turmoil, with gang rule in Somalia and a war between Ethiopia and Eritrea. In next-door Sudan, a war was in progress against the Christian and animist peoples in the south. By mid-decade, Rwanda erupted in a genocidal massacre of minority Tutsi by majority Hutu. Zaire virtually fell apart in civil and ethnic strife. Sierra Leone and Liberia fell for a time under the murderous sway of hoodlums. Meanwhile, throughout the continent, an AIDS epidemic spread, virtually unchecked.

Neither the United States nor the rest of the world was fully prepared, psychologically, politically, or militarily, to deal with the sort of crises that rapidly unfolded in sub-Saharan Africa. That was hardly the fault of the Clinton administration. Neither predecessors nor successor did any better. Many existing African governments were fragile and all too often run by cliques interested only in staying in power and using their position to convert to personal use whatever wealth could be squeezed from the population. Foreign diplomats on the scene normally understood this, but most capitals— including Washington—were preoccupied with other problems. Certainly there was no justification for the Clinton administration's decision to cut back economic aid to the continent, even though the way it was targeted and dispersed needed reform.

Looking at violence in Africa as if it were primarily a result of the Cold War had become a habit in many countries outside Africa. The Soviet Union and Cuba had usually supported insurgent groups and the United States and its European allies existing governments unless they were pro-communist, in which case the insurgents received American or European or South African support. If these interventions had been the causes of Africa's troubles, they should have ended, or at least subsided, with the end of the Cold War.

In fact, Africa's problems had not been caused primarily by Communist subversion. President Reagan acknowledged that fact in an address to the United Nations in September 1984, when he made it clear that he did not accuse the Soviet Union of creating conflicts in the world, but rather of trying to profit from them by providing arms and military help to one faction in a struggle.* He proposed that both the Soviet Union and the United States withdraw their support from rival combatants and encourage the parties to make peace. That is what happened in Angola for a short time. But even U.S.-Soviet cooperation did not suffice to bring peace to many places in Africa, and the 1990s witnessed struggles even more bloody and destructive than the "proxy wars" that occurred during the Cold War.

The Clinton administration took some steps to address the issue, such as creating a new office in the CIA to predict "humanitarian crises." The problems were daunting, particularly since most African states did not have military forces with sufficient training and discipline to be effective peacekeepers, and those that did (like South Africa) tended to avoid peacekeeping involvement in other African countries. Nigeria sometimes took on this role, with varying success, but there were few others able or willing to contribute.

Too often, the conflicts in Africa were "problems from hell," in Samantha Power's memorable phrase, and the Clinton administration faced strong opposition at home to risking American lives in such conflicts, especially after nineteen Americans were killed in Mogadishu, Somalia, in 1993 in the infamous "Black Hawk Down" incident.[17] That experience doubtless was one of the reasons both President Clinton and the Republican leaders in Congress opposed the use of U.S. troops later in Rwanda.

Would there have been a better record in dealing with humanitarian crises if the Clinton administration had given the issue more high-level diplomatic

---

*This is one of the issues on which he parted company with many in his administration. Several important aides, including Director of Central Intelligence William Casey, did consider Communist subversion the cause of most insurgencies. Reagan's view was more accurate and led to a negotiating strategy that removed most U.S.-Soviet competition from local conflicts as the Cold War came to an end.

attention? Perhaps, but we cannot be sure. It was probably sound reasoning to resist sending in the Marines or the Eighty-second Airborne Division whenever there was an impending or spreading ethnic conflict. Even if the United States could put enough military force in the area to stop the mayhem, what then? Who was going to reorganize the local administration or create one from scratch, make it effective, and keep the peace while coherent nations somehow evolved out of the chaos of warring clans and factions? It was far from clear that nationhood, as we normally understand it, is a feasible objective for foreign peacekeepers and would-be "nation builders."

There were real dilemmas for the U.S. government in the 1990s, and a reluctance to use American military force in humanitarian missions was not simply a matter of callousness or inattention. Nevertheless, the time was ripe to build more effective international instruments to deal with such problems. For example, why not think of creating a small force of volunteers from many countries, organized and trained to operate as a standing United Nations peacekeeping force? Units from the armed forces of member countries could be assigned to it for specific peacekeeping and nation-building missions. Advance attention to such matters as training, rules of engagement, relations with humanitarian organizations providing food, medical supplies, and other humanitarian support, along with financing for exercises in advance of crises, might have been possible, particularly in the early 1990s when it was easy for the United States to enlist widespread support.

In short, while it was understandable for the United States to resist being the sole "first responder," it should have been possible to do more than was done to organize and train people for an international effort to deal with natural and man-made humanitarian crises.

Tools of Foreign Policy: Adapting Bureaucracies to Change

With the Cold War behind us, it should have been an urgent task to reequip, retrain, and redirect American foreign policy instruments to meet the challenges to come. The Foreign Service, persistently shortchanged when it comes to appropriations, personnel, and modern equipment, needed more attention and resources. In 1992, its systems of communication were antiquated. The State Department had been slow to adapt to the computer age, in part because of a lack of funds, but also because its management failed to grasp the ways computer technology could improve communications and ease the burden of post administration.*

For example, telegrams from embassies and consulates, the basic form of communication before encrypted fax machines and secure voice connections, could be written only in capital letters, and there was no means of adding diacritical marks that are important in spelling names in many languages. (This is a critical issue in compiling accurate watch lists of criminals and suspected terrorists.) Personnel staffing was so tight that often key positions were left uncovered for months and it was impossible to provide adequate time for training. Although the Foreign Service was well equipped with people who could speak languages like Spanish, French, German, Portuguese, and Russian, it was short of those who knew Arabic, Farsi, Chinese, and Korean—to name a few. Regulations did not allow language training when there were no positions abroad designated for that language—which sounds reasonable until you realize that when there are no diplomatic relations (as with Iran after the hostage crisis) nobody gets trained in that country's language. In the late 1990s, there were only two or three fluent speakers of Farsi, the language of Iran, on active duty in the U.S. Foreign Service.

To meet the new, evolving challenges facing the United States, the Foreign Service needed to be treated as other instruments of national defense and given the funds and personnel to prepare for new tasks. Nevertheless, during the eight years of the Clinton presidency, the Foreign Service continued to be deprived of the resources it needed. State Department budgets were cut even more (in proportion to their size) than Pentagon budgets, even though the rapid globalization of economic activity in the post–Cold War world, combined with the breakup of states like the Soviet Union and Yugoslavia, increased the burdens on American diplomacy. When I was ambassador to the Soviet Union, we had one embassy in Moscow and two consulates general, one in St. Petersburg and one in Kiev, the latter with only a skeleton

---

*When I was appointed ambassador to the Soviet Union in 1987, the State Department not only refused funds to acquire a computer to handle invitation lists and financial accounts of the ambassador's residence—all unclassified—but even turned down an offer by IBM to contribute a computer for that purpose.

staff to prepare for a formal opening. When the Soviet Union fragmented, the United States opened an additional fourteen embassies and two additional consulates general in the Russian Federation. In Yugoslavia, also, the number of diplomatic posts was increased to cover the newly independent countries.

When embassies were attacked, funds would be appropriated to improve physical security, but support to permit adequate staffing, training, and retooling for new tasks was lacking. This is not entirely the administration's fault, because Congress normally cut even the austere State Department budget requests it received, but the problem started with the budget process itself, where the requirements of diplomacy were consistently underestimated.

The need for reorientation of intelligence collection was as urgent as strengthening the capacity for diplomacy. During the Cold War, the United States had developed superb instruments for collecting information on Soviet military equipment and dispositions. Satellite technology allowed us not only to count missiles and map military deployments, but even to estimate Soviet food production (often kept secret by the Soviet regime), so that the United States would have a heads-up on the impact Soviet grain purchases might have on world markets and thus on the American farmer. Much of the Cold War capability was no longer critically important. The Russian military was not a threat to the United States, and Russia had opened up sufficiently that espionage was no longer required to determine what was going on. A closed country had become, for a time at least, wide open to the outside world.

Although intelligence collected by technical means was far more important during the Cold War than that obtained from spies, technical devices would not be adequate to learn of threats from terrorists. Penetration of terrorist groups would be essential if the United States was to obtain the information necessary to anticipate attacks. Although the Foreign Service was short of speakers of several critical languages, the intelligence services were even more handicapped.[18] Nevertheless, I have seen no evidence that there was a concerted effort to recruit and train many more intelligence officers in languages spoken in the Middle East and South Asia, which are critical for penetrating and monitoring terrorist cells and understanding why people become terrorists. The CIA was slow to turn its focus to terrorist targets, and the FBI leadership seems to have paid only occasional attention, right up to 9/11. The National Security Agency was so short of translators who could understand Arabic that messages that might have alerted law enforcement to the impending Al-Qaeda attacks were translated into English only after the attacks occurred.

As for the military, it was an enormous challenge to reorient our defense establishment to the sort of warfare that was most likely to be required after the Cold War ended and the Soviet Union shattered. Each of the services had been focused on the Soviet threat and the need to be prepared to defend the United States from a nuclear-armed superpower. That threat had passed and no country, or even a group of countries, could begin to match American military power in 1993. But there was overwhelming momentum in the Department of Defense to continue doing what the armed services had been doing, and the department received strong support from the producers of missiles, planes, and ships. As Thomas P. M. Barnett put it in a study of Pentagon strategy: "In the 1990s, all four services were going out of their way to show how little their role in U.S. national security would change *simply* because the Soviets went away. If, five years earlier, they justified their budget primarily on the Soviet threat, now they went to great lengths to 'prove' that most of their past operations had little to do with the Soviets."[19]

In other words, professional military leaders, with notable exceptions, directed their attention not to what equipment they would need to meet new challenges, but to ingenious arguments to justify doing what they had been doing all along. It seems that not very much changed in the 1990s or even with the subsequent administration in its early years. When the United States invaded Iraq in 2003, its forces did not have vehicles hardened to withstand improvised roadside bombs and not enough body armor for the troops. In fact, army leaders had given little attention to the requirements for the sort of war American troops faced in Iraq.

As for public relations, the United States cut back sharply on information activities in the 1990s. Now that there was no Soviet Union, many failed to understand that America still needed to get its message out to the world. On the insistence of Republican senator Jesse Helms, the chairman of the Senate Foreign Relations Committee, the United States Information Agency was integrated into the State Department, a move that both the agency and the department opposed—and for good reason. USIA had been founded to provide objective news about America and its policies, and Senator William Fulbright, its principal sponsor, had insisted that it have independent status so that it would not be seen as simply a propaganda organ. The merger with the State Department was not a fatal blow, but budgets were cut and the move was seen by most U.S. officials as downgrading the importance of public diplomacy abroad.

In sum, although changing the direction of bureaucracies is always a slow, contentious, and politically sensitive process, an objective observer would have to conclude that the Clinton administration did little to improve the ability of American security and foreign affairs agencies to cope with the challenges of the twenty-first century.

My critique may seem unnecessarily harsh of Clinton's foreign policy, particularly since his record is unquestionably superior to that of the administration that followed. But the United States had such a breathtaking opportunity in 1993 to lead the world to a safer and more prosperous future that it is sad to realize that so many opportunities were ignored or passed up during the last decade of the twentieth century.

However we might assess Clinton's achievements and failures, we should recognize that his ability to implement many of his policies, whether foreign or domestic, was severely limited by the loss of control of Congress that the Democratic Party suffered in 1994. The elections in that year brought to Congress a large number of Republicans determined to force Clinton to reverse course on a number of key issues, hoping to lay the groundwork for their party's victory in the presidential elections of 1996.

Many of the new members had little knowledge of or interest in foreign affairs. Even when Clinton sent his senior foreign policy team—secretaries of state and defense, national security adviser, U.N. ambassador, and chairman of the joint chiefs of staff—to Capitol Hill to brief Speaker Newt Gingrich and the new members of Congress, the Republicans literally stood them up. After waiting an hour beyond the scheduled time for the meeting, the administration's representatives departed without seeing the people they had offered to brief.[20]

A stalemate with Congress ensued over the 1995 fiscal-year budget. Clinton vetoed the budget passed by the Congress, which, lacking the votes to override the veto, forced a shutdown of all nonessential federal government services. Within weeks, the Republicans in Congress learned that federal government services were more important to most people than they had imagined. The Republican tactics backfired, and although a compromise was worked out, this incident contributed to Clinton's success in the presidential election of 1996.

Even so, the polarization of American politics that intensified during Clinton's first term culminated during his second term in investigations of his activities while governor of Arkansas by Special Prosecutor Kenneth Starr and eventually a vote of impeachment by the House of Representatives, based on charges of false testimony to the special prosecutor. Although Clinton managed to avoid conviction by the Senate, the investigations and the impeachment process attracted so much public attention and so much time and energy of the president himself that it severely circumscribed his ability to steer the country in the still uncertain waters of the post–Cold War world. It was as if the leaders of both American political parties were cooperating to stage a public spectacle instead of dealing constructively with the looming problems facing the United States.

The leaders of both parties seem to have been intoxicated by a misplaced sense of what U.S. power could do and an assumption of American invulnerability. Who could imagine that the public interest would be harmed if its legislative and executive branches spent months indulging in a prurient farce that would cripple their ability to deal with both internal and external problems?* The whole impeachment episode was a clear indication that

---

*It was clear from the beginning of the impeachment proceedings against President Clinton that there were insufficient votes in the Senate to convict him. Furthermore, only a lawyer (in the most pejorative sense of the term) could devise a rationale that would explain why a private act between consenting adults, however reprehensible, could be considered among the "high crimes and misdemeanors" that, according to the U.S. Constitution, are grounds for impeaching the president. Of course, I am aware that the actual charge was one of false testimony, but then one must ask why the testimony was appropriate in the first instance, since the Paula Jones case, in connection with which the testimony had been required, was subsequently dismissed by the judge on grounds that, even if the allegations were proven, no crime would have been committed.

American politics had become dangerously polarized and trivialized. Oblivious to threats to the nation already visible on the horizon, the leaders of both parties chose political warfare over serious efforts to deal with the real problems facing the United States and the world.

When George W. Bush campaigned for the presidency in 2000, he called for a more humble and modest foreign policy and criticized Albert Gore, the Democratic candidate, for his support of nation building abroad. When Bush became president, despite having received fewer votes than his opponent, he appeared to reject everything the Clinton administration had done. This included the judgment that a terrorist organization called Al-Qaeda ("the Base," in Arabic), led by Osama bin Laden, was an immediate threat to the United States.

8

Asleep at the Switch:
9/11 and the "War on Terror"

THE ATTACKS ON THE WORLD TRADE CENTER in New York and the Pentagon in northern Virginia on September 11, 2001, could have been prevented. They very likely *would* have been prevented if a competent, alert administration had been in office in Washington.

That was not the explicit conclusion of the bipartisan commission established by Congress and the president to investigate the terrorist attacks on the United States.[1] But few people knowledgeable about the manner in which most presidents and their national security assistants react to intelligence warnings can escape the conclusion that President George W. Bush, Vice President Richard Cheney, and Assistant for National Security Condoleezza Rice were inexcusably negligent when they were warned repeatedly of an impending attack by Al-Qaeda.

As special assistant to the president for national security in the Reagan administration, from 1983 to 1986, I worked for three national security advisers: William Clark, Robert McFarlane, and John Poindexter. As a senior foreign service officer, I observed closely other assistants for national security, including Henry Kissinger, Zbigniew Brzezinski, Frank Carlucci, Colin Powell, and Brent Scowcroft. I cannot imagine that any of these persons would not have immediately called high-level meetings of the heads of all relevant government agencies to alert them that the Central Intelligence Agency had warned of an intended attack on American soil, and to discuss, with experienced counterterrorism experts, what form the attack might take and how it could be thwarted. I am also confident that, if the president, vice president, and national security adviser had conducted such meetings, steps could have been taken and probably would have been taken to prevent the hijackings. Even if they didn't succeed and some planes were hijacked, these steps would have prevented the planes being used as missiles against buildings.

This is a heavy charge, and I should explain why I make it.

Preventing 9/11

In his review of the 9/11 Commission report, Judge Richard A. Posner excused the administration for failing to heed warnings that Al-Qaeda was planning an attack, stating, "The idea that it [Al-Qaeda] would do so by infiltrating operatives into this country to learn to fly commercial aircraft into buildings was so grotesque that anyone who had proposed that we take costly measures to prevent such an event would have been considered a candidate for commitment."[2]

Grotesque? The CIA had warned President Bush repeatedly, in its daily intelligence briefs, that Al-Qaeda was planning an attack. On August 6, 2001, the president was warned that the attack was planned *in* the United States and could involve hijacked aircraft. Is it reasonable to call the idea of hijacked planes being flown into buildings grotesque? There had been a pattern of suicide attacks by explosive-laden trucks and also a ship (the USS *Cole* had been attacked the previous year), and plans had been thwarted to use aircraft for that purpose. There had been two failed attempts (in Morocco and Pakistan) to commandeer passenger planes and fly them into buildings.

If Judge Posner meant that it was "grotesque" to imagine that *four* planes would be hijacked almost simultaneously, then he might have a point. But it was only necessary to imagine that *one* might be hijacked in order to devise measures to prevent it. There was abundant evidence on the record to attach high probability to a hijacking.

Would measures to prevent hijackings have been costly? Not really. Three things could have been done, any one of which might have been enough to force cancellation of the hijack attempt and to foil the attackers if it did not.

First, the instructions to pilots could have been changed. For years, the Federal Aviation Administration had required pilots to do what hijackers demanded if a plane was commandeered. Yet there had been no hijacking in the United States for many years. If there was another, as the CIA report of August 6 clearly implied, it would probably not be to fly the hijackers to another country. It would most likely be for a suicide mission. Therefore, the FAA should have immediately instructed airlines to keep cockpit doors closed and locked during flight, to reinforce the doors if necessary, and to instruct pilots not to allow putative hijackers into the cockpit under any circumstances.

A review of instructions to airport screeners would have revealed that knives with blades up to four inches long could be carried aboard aircraft. One does not need to be a security expert to understand that determined hijackers can use knives of that size to attack members of the crew. Screeners should have been instructed immediately to allow no knives of any size in passengers' bags, and to publicize this prohibition. And, of course, the number of U.S. marshals assigned to long-range commercial flights—the most dangerous if used as missiles, because the planes would be carrying large quantities of combustible jet fuel—could have been increased.

The airline industry doubtless would have objected to some of these measures—especially the instructions to pilots—on grounds that they would alarm the public and deter some air travel. Nevertheless, the measures would not have been "costly" in any direct sense. And, in fact, if the news of these measures had leaked, as it undoubtedly would have, Al-Qaeda might have had to abort the mission because its chance of success would have been severely diminished.

How about the idea that it would have been "grotesque" to imagine that operatives might be "infiltrated into the United States" to learn to fly planes? Well, whether or not it would be hard to imagine it, one did not have to depend on imagination. Some FBI field offices had already raised alarms about this possibility, and the CIA actually had the names of some of the people involved in the 9/11 hijacking and knew that they were likely to be in the United States. Why was this not acted upon? In some instances, the CIA had failed to pass relevant information to the FBI; in others, the FBI leadership in Washington had failed to pay attention and act on information from its field offices. Of course it should have, but the attorney general failed to heed the warnings that the CIA had placed in the president's daily intelligence brief. The FBI director may not have even known about the warnings, since the content of the president's intelligence brief was such a closely guarded secret.

Experienced White House staffs understand that information does not flow easily or automatically from one agency to another, even when policy does not encourage compartmentalization—which it often does. Each department is, to a degree, a closed bureaucracy, jealous of its privileges and reluctant to share information and thus power with other agencies. One of the prime jobs of the National Security Council staff has been not only to advise the president on security questions, but also to see to it that bureaucratic compartmentalization and turf fights do not weaken America's defenses. This is exactly what Sandy Berger, President Clinton's national security assistant, did when there were numerous reports of possible terrorist attacks on the "millennium" new year of 2000.

According to Richard Clarke, Berger called numerous "principals meetings" (of the secretaries of state and defense, the attorney general, the FBI director, and the director of central intelligence) in 1999 to plan the response to reports of terrorist activity.[3] Thousands of FBI agents were put on alert; legal authority was obtained for additional wiretaps of suspect targets; and as Christmas 1999 and the new year approached, Berger held daily principals meetings. The attorney general, FBI director, and director of central intelligence gave specific reports on what their agencies had done over the previous twenty-four hours.[4]

Contrast Berger's activity with what appears to have been the studied inaction of the president's national security staff in the summer of 2001. Even before the CIA report of August 6, 2001, which spoke of an attack in the United States, possibly with hijacked aircraft, the president should have ordered an interagency review of what was known of Al-Qaeda operatives, particularly in the United States, and of what their plans might be. He should have instructed the CIA, Defense Department, State Department, and FBI to ensure that relevant information was shared, and given instructions to the FBI in particular to set up a special team to identify and track any suspected Al-Qaeda operatives in the United States. He should have ordered consultation with the Federal Aviation Administration, since aircraft hijacking was mentioned specifically in the president's daily brief of August 6, 2001.[5] Such instructions, enforced by the NSC staff, would have alerted all agencies to the urgency of the task and flushed out of the respective bureaucracies information relevant to preventing the attacks. *In fact, nothing was done by the White House to alert domestic agencies to the warnings the CIA was issuing.*

One should not lay all the blame, or even the primary blame, on the White House staff. What is clear from the record is that the president and vice president, as well as the attorney general, who had jurisdiction over the FBI, were remarkably complacent in the face of the CIA warnings. The president seemed not to grasp what the CIA warnings clearly suggested; he seemed more interested in finding excuses to invade Iraq than avoiding an attack on American soil. Attorney General John Ashcroft is reported to have ordered Thomas Pickard, the acting director of the FBI, to stop giving him reports on Al-Qaeda in July 2001, less than two months before the attacks.[6] Ashcroft did not take the threat seriously and did not want to be bothered by such trivia. (Apparently, he had more important things to worry about, such as ensuring that the exposed breasts of a female statue in the Justice Department entrance lobby were covered.) A competent assistant to the president for national security would have advised the president to insist that the attorney general and FBI director take the threat seriously and report to him personally on what was being done.

The 9/11 Commission Report

The conclusions set forth above are from a careful reading of the 9/11 Commission Report, my experience in working for national security advisers, and the information provided by Richard Clarke and other counterterrorism experts. Why didn't everybody else, including highly intelligent, well-informed people like Judge Posner, draw the same conclusions?

New York Times reporter Philip Shenon's book about the 9/11 Commission's work provides some of the answers.[7] In the first place, the commission's chairman, former New Jersey governor Thomas H. Kean, and vice chairman, former congressman Lee H. Hamilton, decided from the outset of the commission's work that they would not attempt to place blame on individuals but would focus on describing what had happened, discovering any weaknesses in the federal government's ability to deal with terrorist threats, and to recommend institutional changes to avoid such catastrophes in the future. They considered it important to produce a unanimous report, and since the commission was required by law to finish its work before the 2004 presidential election, it was clear that a report that pointed fingers explicitly at senior Bush administration officials would not attract unanimous approval.

Second, it is evident from the commission's experience that the Bush White House used every possible stratagem to avoid providing it with documentary material or testimony. Clearly, White House officials thought they had something to hide. White House counsel Alberto Gonzales—later attorney general—refused for months even to let the commission see the daily briefs the CIA had provided the president. It is a tribute to the commissioners that their persistence produced as much accurate information as it did.

Third, according to many commission staffers and Philip Shenon, who covered the commission's work throughout its duration, Philip Zelikow, the commission's staff director, was allowed almost total control over staff activities and communication with the commissioners, even though he had serious potential conflicts of interest.* Throughout the commission's work, he seemed to exert himself to deflect any direct criticism of the White House staff, and at times to skew the evidence to suit the administration's purposes —for example, by suggesting without convincing evidence that there was a link between Saddam Hussein and Al-Qaeda.

Under the circumstances, it is remarkable how well the 9/11 Commission and its staff did their job. The commissioners did finally force much information relevant to their task out of reluctant agencies and set forth the most important facts for the public to judge. The report made it clear that the Clinton administration had taken the terrorist threat more seriously than the George W. Bush administration, even though it might have

---

*Zelikow had worked with Condoleezza Rice on the NSC during the first Bush administration, co-authored a book with her, and then—most important—served on the transition team for the George W. Bush administration, at which time he advised demoting the White House official in charge of terrorism.

missed some opportunities to capture or kill Osama bin Laden. But the goal of producing a unanimous report in the midst of a hotly contested presidential election meant that the commission's statements had to be qualified so much that interpreting the real import of a judgment required the knowledge and ability to detect when a "balancing" statement really did not balance.

For example, Condoleezza Rice's explanation that the CIA warnings were largely "historical" and not detailed enough for action ignored the fact that the warnings were of an imminent attack in the United States and referred to airplane hijackings as a possibility. The historical data would have suggested the possibility of suicide missions and the World Trade Center as a likely target. Did she need dates and flight numbers to do something? Repeating statements to the commission as if it were simply a matter of "he said . . . she said" might have been necessary for the commission report, but this should not have misled impartial observers who studied and commented on the report.

One technique that Bush supporters used to neutralize criticism of the president and his staff was to vilify anyone who raised questions about their performance. Richard Clarke, the counterterrorism specialist whom Rice had sidelined, was ridiculed and treated as a virtual traitor by "right-wing" talk-show hosts when he had the gall to apologize for letting the attacks occur and described his futile efforts to persuade the Bush administration to take the warnings seriously. Attorney General Ashcroft, one of the most derelict of the Bush administration officials, made unfounded accusations against a member of the commission, Jamie Gorelick, to divert scrutiny away from his total inattention to the terrorist threat. This so infuriated all of the commissioners that President Bush apologized personally, assuring them that it should not have happened.[8] Nevertheless, Ashcroft's charges were mouthed and magnified by the usual suspects on the talk-show circuit to the point that Commissioner Gorelick received death threats.

Clarke's accusations were reported widely by the media, but when the commission report was published, even the "responsible" media did little to assist the public to understand what the report made clear: the Al-Qaeda attacks could have been prevented if the Bush administration had shown minimal competence in using the information the CIA had provided. Richard

Posner's description of the report in the *New York Times Book Review* was typical of most initial comment in purveying the false impression that it was unreasonable to expect any administration to anticipate something so "grotesque" as hijackers flying planes into buildings.

The first well-informed review of the 9/11 Commission report was by a former insider, Richard A. Falkenrath, who had been on Dr. Rice's staff before September 11, 2001, and was a special assistant to the president for homeland security thereafter, thus was in a position to have witnessed directly what had been done and not done by senior officials. He wrote his review after he left government employ and published it in *International Security*, a scholarly journal published by the Belfer Center at Harvard University.[9] His central criticism of the commission report was its failure to assign responsibility to individuals, which he felt reflected a "no-fault" theory of government behavior that was inconsistent with the report's narrative, which made clear where the faults lay.

Professor Zelikow and Harvard professor Ernest May, who had advised the commission on the report, responded to Falkenrath's review in the subsequent issue of *International Security* with a curious defense of the commission's "diagnostic finding that 9/11 shows the government to have lacked imagination." They wrote that they could not "explain in other language why there had been only desultory, low-level planning for the possibility of terrorists' using airplanes as weapons. After all, it was their practice to use vehicles as weapons—cars, trucks, boats. Why not airplanes?"[10] Well, precisely! The problem is that Zelikow and May seem inclined (at least in this instance) to excuse senior officials for ignoring the obvious on grounds that lower-level officials were not giving it sufficient attention.* Is it not the duty of senior officials to see to it that lower-level specialists are doing their job? It always was when I worked on President Reagan's NSC staff.

Replying to the comment by May and Zelikow, Falkenrath pointed out that, "in the end, politics won out over analysis in the commission's explanation of why the U.S. government failed to prevent the worst terrorist attack in history." Then he explained:

---

*Professor May did not hesitate to assign responsibility to specific officials for decisions they made or didn't make in his other studies, including in *Thinking in Time*, written with Richard Neustadt.

When the government fails to act in situations in which it has the legal authority to do so, it is almost always because specific and identifiable individuals made a decision—formally or informally—not to act. For all the various "paths not taken" in the 9/11 report—no use of force against the terrorist training camps in Afghanistan, no hardening of cockpit doors on civilian aircraft, no watchlisting suspected terrorists, and so on—there is a small group of government officials, who, for whatever reason, did not do what in hindsight seems like the right thing to do. In its analysis, the 9/11 commission chose not to name names, and indeed found less controversial and difficult explanations in disembodied concepts such as "imagination" and "management."[11]

I emphatically agree with Falkenrath that, in avoiding assessing the performance of specific individuals, the 9/11 Commission undermined the concept of personal responsibility and "sent the wrong message to future government officials and the people who train them." That message seemed to be that competence is not as important as personal loyalty, and that it is better to cover up mistakes than to admit them and correct them.

Instead of dealing with the mistakes made by senior officeholders, the commission recommended extensive and costly bureaucratic reorganization in the federal government. I suppose they had to recommend something, but revising bureaucratic "wiring diagrams" will not solve problems resulting from incompetent leadership.

The "War on Terror"

Once the Al-Qaeda attacks occurred, it was both proper and necessary to go after the organization and its leaders in the most vigorous way. After all, it had been Osama bin Laden who had declared war on the United States. If that was what he wanted, and the attacks on the World Trade Center and the Pentagon proved it, that's what he should have gotten. Acting with a speed that had few precedents, the United Nations Security Council approved a resolution on September 12 condemning the attacks and authorizing "all necessary means" to respond to them.[12]

Simultaneously, all NATO allies rallied to the American defense, declaring that the attack on the United States should be considered an attack on all. The Bush administration, in full accord with the U.N. resolution, demanded that the Taliban government in Afghanistan close Al-Qaeda terrorist camps and extradite bin Laden and his lieutenants for trial in the United States. The Taliban leader refused. The U.N. Security Council repeated its demands on the Afghan regime in a resolution on September 28.[13] These were ignored, and the United States began bombing targets in Afghanistan on October 7, 2001, less than a month after the hijacked planes had flown into the World Trade Center and the Pentagon.

American forces, with some help from allies, quickly removed the Taliban regime from Kabul and occupied most of Afghanistan. Nevertheless, more than seven years after the battle for Afghanistan began, American forces have still neither captured nor, so far as we know, killed Osama bin Laden and several of his key subordinates. Taliban forces have regrouped across the Pakistan border and continue to infiltrate into Afghanistan. Regional warlords, though opponents of the Taliban, have revived the illicit drug trade, which has become a threat not only to contiguous areas in the former Soviet Union, but also to Western European countries where the drugs are often sold.

Afghanistan remains a problem that I will discuss in a subsequent chapter, but I believe President Bush made the right decision to invade, and that initially he went about it in the right way. He was right to go after the Al-Qaeda leadership that had organized an attack on the United States, to eliminate terrorist bases that could be used for the same purpose in the future, and to remove the Taliban regime that had supported Osama bin Laden and his followers and thus was complicit in their crimes. It was done in the right way by obtaining in advance the approval of both the U.N. Security Council and that of America's NATO allies.

Furthermore, the Bush administration persuaded President Vladimir Putin of Russia not to oppose establishing temporary American military bases in former Soviet Central Asia to support the military effort in Afghanistan. Russian public opinion was very much opposed to the idea of U.S. bases in an area that was once part of the Soviet Union, but Putin gave his government's support to the American invasion of Afghanistan because he knew that the Taliban and Al-Qaeda were as great a threat to Russia as they were to the United States.

It was also wise for the American forces to make use of the Northern Alliance, led by the resistance fighters the United States had supported during the Soviet invasion of Afghanistan, to undertake much of the combat against the Taliban. While one can question subsequent American tactics in Afghanistan, particularly whether efforts were adequate to prevent the escape of Osama bin Laden and his lieutenants from their redoubt in Tora Bora, the decision to invade was sound and the political preparations for it were done well.[14] The effort in Afghanistan lost effectiveness later, when Washington shifted its attention to Iraq, diverting both troops and funds from the original mission, and the government of Pakistan proved unwilling or unable to deprive bin Laden of his base in the tribal areas of Pakistan.

Aside from invading Afghanistan, what should have been done to prevent more terrorist attacks in the United States? Al-Qaeda, after all, was not a country on which Congress could declare war, but an organization that propagated a religious doctrine. It had no highly organized hierarchy but encouraged imitators who could act independently of any central control. It was based on an idea, which, however pernicious, could not be eliminated by force alone.

Terrorism, the weapon Al-Qaeda and its imitators adopted since they were too weak to use any other, is an instrument, a technique of violent struggle. Dealing with it is not the same as going to war against a country with a military force that can be defeated by superior firepower, tactics, or martial skills. Dealing with terrorism successfully requires an understanding of what motivates terrorists and how they are organized. Only with that understanding can we devise effective means to protect ourselves.

The Bush II administration, unfortunately, seems to have rejected the idea that it could better protect the American people if it understood what it was fighting. The president at times acted like a prizefighter who bragged that he could put on blindfolds and still beat any opponent who dared to challenge him.

Understanding Terrorism

Presidential adviser Karl Rove, then deputy chief of staff in the White House, told a meeting of the Conservative Party of New York in June 2005, "Conservatives saw what happened to us on 9/11 and said: we will defeat our enemies. Liberals saw what happened to us and said: we must understand our enemies."[15] It should not take much reflection to detect the absurdity of Rove's statement. Put aside the obvious fact that virtually all Americans are determined to protect their country from terrorists. If there is a difference of opinion it is how to go about it most effectively and with the least damage to our democratic system of government. Disputes over what methods should be used cannot be plotted on a "conservative" to "liberal" gradation; they divide liberals, centrists, and conservatives, even those with crackpot tendencies. Furthermore, to imply that understanding terrorism is not consistent with fighting it is rather like saying that there should be no research on cancer because the researcher might end up sympathetic to it. Anyone who really wants to defeat terrorists better hope that their political leaders will make some effort to understand why people engage in terrorist acts and, with that understanding, will devise effective ways to protect the American people, and the rest of the world, from them.

Rove's inane comment is only one example of a persistent pattern of employing false and distorted imagery to achieve a political purpose. Since his boss, President George W. Bush, failed to take appropriate action when he was warned that Al-Qaeda was planning an attack on the United States, White House advisers needed to divert attention from that troublesome fact and convince people that the president, despite his obvious negligence, was more suited to defend the nation than his political opponents. In this instance, leaders of the Democratic Party inexplicably chose to help the president cover up his incompetence.

They, and the mainstream media as well, also let President Bush get by with his explanation for his inaction on 9/11. His favorite excuse was that "the world changed," as if there was nothing he could have done to prevent the attacks. Well, maybe *his* world changed, but that was because he had not bothered to pay attention to what was actually happening in the world. The plan to hijack planes and fly them into buildings had been in the works for years. American intelligence knew of Al-Qaeda's daring attacks in many other places and had warned that it was planning an attack in the United States. Bin Laden had announced publicly that his organization was at war with the United States. The world did not change on 9/11; only the policy of the Bush administration changed.

Al-Qaeda

Experts on terrorism in the U.S. government knew a lot about Al-Qaeda before the attacks on 9/11, but the public was largely ignorant, not only of the organization and its titular head, Osama bin Laden, but of the threat it posed to the United States. Since 9/11, several well-informed studies of the organization, its history, and its mode of operation have been published. One of the best is Lawrence Wright's *The Looming Tower: Al-Qaeda and the Road to 9/11*. Like other historians of the group, he makes it clear that Al-Qaeda is a faith-based movement that represents an extreme interpretation of Sunni Islam.[16] Its main objective is to restore the "purity" of the Islamic world, and its ultimate targets are the governments of most Muslim countries, which it holds to be irreligious, decadent, and subject to pernicious Western influence. They attack Americans and American establishments because they see them as instruments of religious apostasy. In other words, they attack us because we are there, present and active in the Islamic world, just as they attacked the Soviet forces in Afghanistan (with our support) because they were there, bringing what they considered infidel ways to the faithful. The attacks on the World Trade Center and the Pentagon were carried out as retribution for the influence the hijackers believed the United States exerted in Muslim countries. They were not trying to convert us to Islam (though in theory, like the Communist revolutionaries in 1917 Russia, they thought that eventually the world would be Muslim), but to keep us off what they considered their turf.

Another feature of Al-Qaeda that is often misunderstood is that it is nothing like an army, organized in a tight top-down command-and-control system. It encourages individual and small group initiative, using the Internet and other modern communication facilities to spot potential recruits, inspire them, and instruct them. Fighting Al-Qaeda and similar organizations is more like fighting cancer than fighting a conventional military organization: it is capable of metastasizing into numerous fragments, each of which becomes a source of violent activity, with or without coordination with others. Just as surgery alone is usually insufficient to cure cancer, military action alone will not defeat Al-Qaeda and terrorist movements like it. We need the political equivalent of radiation and chemotherapy to supplement the surgery of military action. We also need the societal equivalent of sound nutrition and preventive medicine if we are to have a robust society resistant to terrorism, whether of the Al-Qaeda type or that of Timothy McVeigh, or of people who plant bombs in abortion clinics, shoot children in school, send anthrax spores in the mail, or attack colleagues in their workplaces.

In his book *Violent Politics*, William R. Polk offers an insightful view of the role terrorism and the related techniques of guerrilla warfare have played over the past couple of centuries.[17] Irregular warfare has taken many forms, and the tendency to classify all as "terrorism"—as some do today—is misleading. In the past we have often supported and praised irregular fighters who oppose a dictator or a foreign occupier. We supported and praised the *maquis* in Vichy France that attacked not only German occupiers but also French officials and civilians accused of collaboration. We supplied arms and financial support to the Contras and similar combatants fighting pro-Communist forces in Central America, even though they frequently attacked civilians suspected of supporting "leftists." We need to remember that traditionally, one person's "freedom fighter" can be another person's "terrorist," and that terrorism is a technique used by the weak against the strong. That of course in no way justifies terrorism, particularly when it is directed randomly against civilians, but experience shows that outsiders have rarely been able to conquer insurgents fighting on their native turf by any methods short of genocide.

To be successful in an area, terrorists need a favorable "sea" in which to operate. If they are fighting a foreign force, the occupied country usually becomes a favorable sea. One cannot "drain the swamp" (or empty the sea) by just killing the terrorists. If they have the sympathy of the local people, more will come. Terrorists must be deprived of their apparent cause if the sea in which they swim refuses them the support they require to survive.

Nevertheless, it is important to understand that, while the leaders of terrorist movements may be motivated by political objectives, it is a mistake to think that all the "foot soldiers" are religious zealots or are what political scientists would call "political utility maximizers"—that is, people who rationally choose terrorism because they believe it is the most effective way to produce the result they seek. A study by Professor Max Abrahms of the University of California, Los Angeles, concluded that most terrorists are "rational people who use terrorism to develop strong affective ties with fellow terrorists."[18] In other words, rank-and-file terrorists bear some similarity to members of neighborhood gangs. Their motivation is to be a member of a

group and to prove their value to other members of the group by participating in violent action against outsiders considered competitive or hostile.
This insight should not be used to trivialize a serious security problem, but
it does suggest that, given the right techniques, Al-Qaeda operatives might
be easier to "turn" than one would suppose. Also, since much of the motivation is to prove one's loyalty to the group, terrorist cells are vulnerable to
efforts to sow distrust and suspicion among the members.

Those who have studied the Italian success in eliminating the Red
Brigades that operated in the 1970s report that the authorities did so by com-
muting prison sentences in exchange for actionable intelligence, infiltrating the terrorist organization, and then spreading suspicion and rivalry
among its members. Abrahms observed that the Italian approach is "the
sole counter-terrorism strategy that was a clear-cut success."

Metaphorical War or Real War?

The "war against terror" is clearly a metaphor, just as the "war on drugs"
or the "war on poverty" were, or Jimmy Carter's remark that energy con-
servation was "the moral equivalent of war." The use of the metaphor to justify extraordinary sacrifices to achieve an important end may be justified.
The metaphor is harder to justify if there is no call for sacrifice—even for
taxes to support the costs of war—on the part of the public as a whole. It is
a totally inappropriate metaphor if it is used to imply that the "war on terror" is comparable to a military conflict between nations.

Financier George Soros has observed, "War is a false and misleading
metaphor in the context of combating terrorism. Treating the attacks against
humanity as crimes against humanity would have been more appropriate.
Crimes require police work, not military action."[19] Some will immediately
object that "police work" is inadequate if it means only the detection and
prosecution of crimes once they occur. But that has never been a proper definition of police work, since the police should be as adept at crime prevention as at the identification and arrest of persons who have committed criminal acts. Furthermore, conspiracy to commit a crime is also a crime, so
there is no reason to suggest that police cannot act to prevent a terrorist attack before it occurs. Their ability to do so will depend to a great extent on
the quality of the intelligence they gather.

This brings us to "myth number 3" I listed in Chapter 1: that the Cold War was comparable to World War I and World War II. Both the two world wars were so obviously different from the Cold War, and the "war on terror" from any of the preceding, that this myth would hardly be worth mentioning if the idea had not been revived in a book by one of the founding fathers of modern neoconservatism, Norman Podhoretz. His *World War IV: The Long Struggle Against Islamofascism* not only pretends that both the Cold War and the "war on terror" are comparable to the two world wars—a logical absurdity—but argues that the challenge posed by Al-Qaeda's fanatical misfits is comparable to that posed by fascism, requiring a struggle of decades to overcome.[20] The idea that the struggle with terrorism is like any conventional war, let alone the two world wars, is not only a flagrant distortion of history; it is a prescription for perpetuating terrorism as a significant threat by exaggerating its potential and prescribing inappropriate methods to deal with it.

The Bush administration not only applied a misleading metaphor in its effort to combat terrorists, but went further astray by attempting to treat the war on terror as if it were the legal equivalent of a declaration of war by Congress, which would have granted the president extraordinary powers as commander-in-chief. This was a remarkable power grab for people who claim to be conservative and to believe in a strict interpretation of the United States Constitution. It also made it harder for the administration to defeat the terrorists it said it was fighting.

Combating Terrorism

Karl Rove's statement implying that there is no point in understanding terrorists does explain one fact: the George W. Bush administration failed to defeat terrorists because it went about fighting them with blindfolds on. Worse, it sometimes reacted precisely as Osama bin Laden wanted it to. One of the goals of terrorists is to provoke governments they oppose into self-defeating overreaction, just as a jujitsu master utilizes the opponent's strength and weight to bring him down. By using fear techniques with the American public following 9/11—remember all those color-coded warnings?—the administration built up the image of Al-Qaeda as a major force in the world.

Exaggerating bin Laden's reach and power was immensely useful to Al-Qaeda because it magnified its importance and popularized its image among Muslims who had a grievance (or thought they did) against some American policy or action. The abuse of prisoners at Abu Ghraib, detentions at Guantánamo under conditions contrary to the Geneva Convention, the illegal "rendition" of suspects to countries where they could be tortured, not only solidified Muslim anger but outraged the public in many of our key NATO allies.

The administration denied that it ever authorized or practiced torture, but the record is now clear that many of the practices used to interrogate suspects meet that definition. Vigorous efforts were made to cover up the evidence that malpractices occurred with the encouragement, if not the direct orders, of senior White House officials.

The most powerful reason for refraining from torture is that it is morally abhorrent and inconsistent with the behavior of any civilized nation, particularly one that claims to be democratic. The second reason is that it is illegal. It is barred not only by the U.S. Constitution and U.S. law, but by international covenants to which the United States is a party. (A ratified treaty is supposed to have the force of constitutional law in the United States, superior even to legislation.) The third reason is that it doesn't work. You cannot get reliable information as the result of torture, for the victim is inclined to say whatever he thinks you want him to say. If he is bent on "martyrdom" he may be even seeking death, thus inclined to provoke harsh treatment.

Studies of Japanese prisoners of war in World War II revealed that the United States was successful in obtaining useful information because it refrained from treating the Japanese POWs harshly. It was known that the Japanese were torturing the American prisoners they had captured, but Americans refused to behave in the same fashion. The Japanese prisoners were surprised that they were not tortured or killed, as they had been told would happen if they let themselves be captured, but were treated humanely. Interrogators were Japanese Americans who understood their culture and could talk to them directly in their own language.[21]

One does not have to go back to World War II and the interrogation of Japanese prisoners to understand that there are more effective ways than torture to elicit useful information from prisoners. The FBI had gathered valuable information from Al-Qaeda operatives like Wadi el-Hage, who had helped carry out the bombings of the U.S. embassies in Kenya and Tanzania in 1998, by treating him with respect and doling out some favors.[22]

Since April 2009, when the Obama administration released Justice Department memorandums ordering "enhanced interrogation techniques," more evidence has come to light refuting claims that these techniques produced useful information and saved lives. Apologists for torture had asserted that harsh methods produced important information from Abu Zubayda, a senior Al-Qaeda operative captured in Afghanistan. Ali Soufan, an FBI supervisory special agent who interrogated Abu Zubayda from March to June 2002, wrote in a *New York Times* article that "traditional methods" produced useful intelligence but the harsher techniques ordered by Washington subsequently were not only unnecessary but actually counterproductive. In Soufan's words, "There was no actionable intelligence gained from using enhanced interrogation techniques on Abu Zubayda that wasn't or couldn't have been obtained by regular tactics. In addition, I saw that using these alternative methods on other terrorists backfired on more than a few occasions."[23]

It is unlikely that any vital information has been obtained by torture; on the contrary, the resort to illegal techniques damaged the nation's ability to combat terrorists successfully. As Ali Soufan put it, "The short-sightedness behind the use of these techniques ignored the unreliability of the methods, the nature of the threat, the mentality and modus operandi of the terrorists, and due process." So much for Karl Rove's boast that terrorists could be defeated without understanding them. In fact, America's image, respectability, and capacity to lead other countries were severely damaged by practices that, in the eyes of the rest of the world, count as torture. Prompt moves by the Obama administration to end illegal practices and disclose past mistakes to the public have begun to repair the damage inflicted by the Bush-Cheney administration. The president's decision not to prosecute interrogators who followed legal advice from the Justice Department is understandable, but it is important to continue investigating the way decisions were made regarding the treatment of prisoners and who specifically was responsible for faulty legal advice.

The administration also seriously overstepped its authority when it came to eavesdropping on American citizens. Not that this should be prohibited if there is good cause—and it is not prohibited when it can be justified. But there are established procedures that require authorization by a court established by the Federal Intelligence Surveillance Act of 1978, known as the "FISA court." In an emergency, the authorization can be obtained after the fact of the intercept itself. Nevertheless, the administration violated the law by asserting that the president could authorize eavesdropping without reference to the legal requirements Congress had specified.

This was a clear overreach of presidential authority that was not necessary to protect American citizens. I have had no access to classified information since leaving the government in 1991, and have desired none, but while I was in government I had the opportunity to observe how electronic intelligence is collected, interpreted, and distributed. Computers may be able to calculate which lines should be monitored and identify patterns of communication. This can provide important leads for further investigation, whether regarding the communications among terrorists or the illegal flow of funds. But, at some point, the communications themselves must be read (or heard) by human beings. If we are dealing with terrorism, the bulk of the communications will be in a language other than English or the well-known European languages. They will also often involve code words and double-talk. They are not easily understandable, except by linguists with specialized training.

U.S. intelligence agencies have a very limited number of people who can make sense out of such communications. That means that intelligence agencies need criteria for deciding which of the millions of messages recorded need to be read, and in what priority. The criteria for selection would certainly be adequate to substantiate a warrant from the FISA court.

Bypassing this process is not only unnecessary, but in the real world of bureaucratic practice it is actually counterproductive. Without a compulsion to establish criteria and priorities that are consistent with the linguistic capabilities of analysts available, the tendency of bureaucrats in any agency is to cover themselves by collecting as much as possible, and passing it on, unread and unanalyzed, to another department or another agency. Then, if something happens and important information was not utilized in timely fashion, they can say, "We did our job. It's those other guys that screwed up."

Want some examples? Those messages intercepted just before 9/11 sig-

naling an impending attack that were not translated until September 13. Or
think about this description of the bin Laden unit of the CIA's Counterterrorism Center that a former CIA officer gave journalist Jane Mayer: "[It] was
just chaotic. There were piles and piles and PILES of untranslated intercepts."[24] The United States was already intercepting, legally, more messages
than it could translate and use.

National security gained absolutely nothing from the president's bypassing the legal procedures Congress had prescribed for authorizing intercepts
of communications involving American citizens. Nevertheless, I believe that
the telecommunication companies that followed Justice Department instructions should not be held liable, as some members of Congress have
demanded. If the companies were assured by the Justice Department that
the requests were legal, they should not be penalized for depending on that
advice. If there were infractions in the law, then those officials in the Justice
Department who authorized the wiretaps without the warrants required by
law, as well as anyone in the White House who instructed them to do so,
should be the persons held accountable.

The main result of the investigations that followed 9/11 was an extensive
rearrangement of organizational charts in Washington. A new Department
of Homeland Security was established, made up by tearing off parts of several other agencies and uniting them under a single head. An intelligence
"super-tsar" was created to oversee the various intelligence agencies. In
time, these bureaucratic realignments may produce better results than those
of the past, but it would be best not to count on it. The agencies in place before 9/11 had both the authority and the capability to prevent 9/11 if there
had been appropriate leadership. Reshuffling organizational charts will not,
in itself, produce more security. Proper leadership and competent management are the keys to effectiveness, whether with the old or new bureaucracies.

If Al-Qaeda masterminds another attack on the United States, its leaders
will presumably want the damage to be at least as spectacular as that of September 11, and possibly more so. Al-Qaeda does not have much to gain from
some suicide bomber blowing himself up in a supermarket or a football sta-
dium, although imitators could conceivably go for that. To serve Al-Qaeda's
purpose the attack would have to be big enough to kill a lot of people, eliminate some national symbol such as the Capitol or the White House, or crip-

ple the economy in a spectacular way. Since the terrorists can hardly get away with multiple hijackings again, they must look for something else—and that probably means the use of a nuclear device or a biological or chemical weapon, if they can get their hands on one and get it into the United States. It will be easier to sneak germs or poisons in than nukes.[25] Furthermore, there are credible reports that Al-Qaeda has developed a device for a poison gas attack in an enclosed space, such as a subway car or the ventilation system in an office building.[26]

It is manifestly impossible to inspect every container that enters the United States, so our security will depend importantly on cooperation with other countries to detect nefarious activity and to identify suspected terrorists. Our capacity for doing so has been much improved since 9/11, thanks to the quiet and largely unpublicized work of the CIA, the FBI, the National Security Agency, and the Treasury Department, which plays an important role in tracing funds moving to terrorist groups. There has been growing cooperation with foreign intelligence agencies, not only in Europe but also in Islamic countries, most of whose governments see Al-Qaeda-type terrorism as much a threat to them as to the United States.

Even so, it is obvious that the United States needs to continue improving its capacity to respond to disasters, whether natural or man-made. The deficiencies in dealing with the New Orleans flood were a wake-up call as to how far we needed to go to have an adequately organized response to a major emergency. The well-organized evacuations of New Orleans as Hurricane Gustav approached on Labor Day, 2008, and subsequent evacuations from Houston when another storm threatened, showed that we are now better able to evacuate people from those costal cities when a specific threat has been identified in advance. Nevertheless, complacency on this score is not yet justified.

Although Karl Rove talked as if fighting terrorism was a conservative monopoly, many of President Bush's actions were anything but conservative. Running up large deficits is not conservative. Bypassing legal procedures for no good reason is not conservative. Attempting to establish executive dominance over the legislative and judicial branches of government, and thus undermine the separation of powers required by the Constitution, is not conservative. Nevertheless, even with all of that, no decision President

George W. Bush made was *less* conservative or less helpful to the fight against terrorists than his decision to invade Iraq.

Don't take my word for it. Ask Patrick J. Buchanan, whose *American Conservative* ran some of the most persuasive articles arguing against the invasion of Iraq. One full-page advertisement in the *New York Times* pictured Osama bin Laden with the message: I WANT YOU . . . TO INVADE IRAQ. Or ask the scholars at the conservative Cato Institute in Washington, who made the same argument in greater detail. There is little question that bin Laden could only have been pleased by many of the actions taken by the Bush administration in the wake of 9/11.

By pretending that nothing could have been done to prevent the September 11 attacks and by exaggerating the threat of Al-Qaeda, the administration boosted bin Laden's prestige among Muslims opposed to American policies. By invading Iraq on specious grounds, the United States left the impression that it was an enemy of Islam, making it much more difficult to prevent the creation of terrorist strongholds in Pakistan. The occupation of Iraq also enhanced bin Laden's ability to recruit terrorists. By 2005, Al-Qaeda was creating mayhem in Iraq, where it had not existed before the American invasion.

Richard Clarke, one of America's most experienced counterterrorism experts, put it this way: "Nothing America could have done would have provided Al-Qaeda and its new generation of cloned groups a better recruitment device than our unprovoked invasion of an oil-rich Arab country. . . . It was as if Usama bin Laden . . . were engaging in long-range mind control of George Bush, chanting, 'invade Iraq; you must invade Iraq.'"[27]

The U.S. invasion and occupation of Iraq helped rescue Al-Qaeda just when it seemed to be on the ropes following the collapse of Taliban rule in Afghanistan. The attack on Iraq may also have encouraged other countries to seek nuclear weapons, and some to obstruct American efforts to track terrorists.

"Axis of Evil"

In his State of the Union address in January 2002, President Bush named three countries as part of an "axis of evil": Iraq, Iran, and North Korea. There is no question that all three were authoritarian regimes that denied their people basic human rights. But there were other nations that had at least an equal claim to the adjective "evil": the government in Sudan that for years had conducted a war against its Christian and animist citizens in the south and had begun a genocidal campaign against fellow Muslims in its Darfur province; the government of Burma (Myanmar) that had suppressed all political dissent for more than a decade and held the most popular political leader under house arrest when she was not incarcerated in jail; Somalia, a shambles as a result of fighting by competing warlords; Zimbabwe, where President Robert Mugabe was destroying the economy by encouraging the confiscation of productive farms by landless people and silencing, at times imprisoning, members of the opposition to his despotic rule. One could name others that, in terms of what they were doing to their own people, made them at least as "evil" as the three countries named. So, one might wonder: if we are talking about "evil," why just those three? Aren't there more?

All right, all three were bad, and maybe the president doesn't have to name everybody to make a point. But, in that case, why *axis* of evil? There was no discernable "axis" connecting the three countries named. I should mention for persons who came of age after World War II that the Axis Powers were Germany, Italy, and Japan, countries that were allied by formal treaty, all of which had declared war against the United States. In other words, it was a term for countries allied in a war against the United States.

Shortly after the president spoke of an axis of evil, I pointed out to Stephen Hadley, then deputy to the president's assistant for national security (subsequently her successor), that one could make a case for "evil," but not for "axis." He seemed surprised and remarked that he had not thought of the "axis" part. He then explained that the president was trying to call attention to "the nexus between nuclear weapons and terrorism."

At that time, in 2002, the country most active in spreading nuclear weapons technology was none of the three named—it was Pakistan. The CIA already knew that A. Q. Khan was peddling nuclear weapons technology throughout the Islamic world. But the president couldn't name Pakistan, because he needed the help of its dictator, President Pervez Musharraf, the army commander who had forced the last elected government out of office and the prime minister, Nawaz Sharif, out of the country.*

In many respects, countries are not that different from individuals in the ways they react. How do you regard someone who talks of high principle and ideals and then applies these principles inconsistently? The philanderer who prates of "family values" until he is caught? The hard-nosed prosecutor sniffing out white-collar crime who deals with a criminal gang to hire a prostitute? The president who, on his last day in office, pardons tax-evading felons who have enough money to contribute liberally to his presidential library? The governor who tries to sell a Senate seat?

When we learn we have been duped, we don't like it. We usually turn against the perpetrator, and so do countries if they feel they are being purposely misled. When the president of the United States called three countries evil and omitted others of equal or greater malignity, many foreign governments would conclude that there were ulterior motives behind the omission. Even if there were not, it's hard to expect the rest of the world to be convinced.

But the problem was greater than inconsistency. If the president of the United States proclaims that there is an "axis of evil" connecting three named countries, and then proceeds to attack one of them, what will the other two conclude? Are they being paranoid to think that they may be next? And—if they think they may be next—should it be surprising that they decide to resort to the only sure recourse to prevent a superpower from attacking them?

What is the only thing that keeps a regime safe? Some governments would conclude that only the atom bomb provides reliable insurance. The United States and the Soviet Union never fought each other during the Cold War because both had nuclear weapons. U.S.-led NATO would not have bombed Serbia over its treatment of Kosovo if Serbia had had the bomb. Most of the world did not want Pakistan and India to become nuclear powers, but treated them with greater respect once they tested weapons. With

---

*And, by the way, Nawaz Sharif was in power when Pakistan detonated its nuclear bomb. How complicated things get when you look closely at them! Pakistan went nuclear when it had a democratic government. Theories don't always fit, and "good" and "evil" get all mixed up.

nuclear weapons, a country is untouchable. Without them, a regime can be removed and the country occupied by foreigners. Such would have been the reasoning of rogue-state dictators.

But what was Saddam Hussein thinking? Having studied his role model, Joseph Stalin, carefully, I may have some insights.* I can imagine that Saddam's thinking went something like this: "I'm safe. Bush is after those other folks. I have gotten rid of my nukes, my germs, and even my chemicals. The Americans are smart enough to know that: they are just trying to scare off the others. They must understand that they need me to keep the Iranians in check, and that I have to create the impression that I have some special weapons so the Iranians don't come after me. So long as I keep clear of Al-Qaeda and that ilk, I should be home free. Americans may be a bit strange at times, but they are not stupid. If I am careful not to support their enemies, I should be OK."

Well, if that's what he was thinking, he was wrong. The Americans running the government in Washington were not as smart as he thought they were. It wasn't that they lacked intelligence; it was that they were living in a different world, in the imaginary world of superpower delusion.

Lord Acton famously wrote, "Power tends to corrupt; absolute power corrupts absolutely." Observing both the Clinton and George W. Bush administrations, I would paraphrase it to read, "Power tends to intoxicate; the illusion of absolute power intoxicates absolutely." The United States went to war in Iraq with the reckless abandon of an addict high on drugs.

---

*I once compiled a complete index to the thirteen-volume Russian edition of Stalin's *Collected Works.*

9

Tar Baby Iraq

ONE OF JOEL CHANDLER HARRIS's best-known Uncle Remus stories is the one about Brer Fox, Brer Rabbit, and the tar baby. Using his superior wiles, Brer Rabbit consistently eludes Brer Fox's pursuit, so Brer Fox decides to get even by taking advantage of Brer Rabbit's inordinate pride (a scholar of Greek might call it hubris). Brer Fox devises a lure that looks like a baby but is made of sticky tar. When the tar baby fails to respond to Brer Rabbit's greeting, Brer Rabbit decides to teach him to show proper respect by cuffing him. His paw sticks, so he hits the tar baby with his other paw, then kicks him, and soon Brer Rabbit is helplessly stuck, powerless to resist capture by Brer Fox.

The Uncle Remus stories were favorites of my generation when we were children. Had they passed out of fashion when President Bush the 43rd and his advisers were growing up, or were they just not paying attention? Probably the latter, for even as adults they had a habit of ignoring views and facts that didn't fit their preconceptions. In any case, the decision to attack Iraq was as ill-advised as Brer Rabbit's decision to slap the tar baby. Invading Iraq was probably exactly what Osama bin Laden was hoping the United States would do, but unlike Brer Fox, bin Laden did not create Tar Baby Iraq. George W. Bush and his most intimate advisers did.

Paul O'Neill, Bush's first secretary of the treasury, reported that the president had been thinking of invading Iraq from his first cabinet meeting, in January 2001, and that Vice President Cheney and Secretary of Defense

Donald Rumsfeld were looking for a pretext to invade long before the ter-rorist attacks on September 11.[1] Richard Clarke observed that the president's preoccupation with Iraq was one of the reasons he failed to pay attention to warnings that Al-Qaeda was getting ready to conduct an attack on the United States.[2]

It is still far from clear why, even before Al-Qaeda's attacks on 9/11, Bush and many of his close advisers were fixated (no other verb seems to fit) on removing Iraqi president Saddam Hussein. The Iraqi dictator was, to be sure, a tyrant. He had invaded other countries and massacred his political enemies, using at times even poison gas. He modeled his rule on Joseph Stalin's. But, in contrast to Stalin, he had lost the wars he started, had been effectively defanged, and even if he had still possessed his former military might, he had nothing like the potential Stalin possessed toward the end of his life to threaten his neighbors or the United States. In fact he posed no threat at all to the United States.

With what we know today, the idea that Saddam Hussein's Iraq was a se-rious threat to American interests at the beginning of the twenty-first cen-tury seems preposterous. The Iraqi leader had destroyed his biological and chemical weapons and abandoned efforts to develop nuclear weapons under the pressure of inspections authorized by the U.N. Security Council. His principal enemy was Iran, which had substantially recovered from the war following Iraq's invasion. Iraq was on bad terms with Saudi Arabia and other neighboring states, and was kept on a tight leash by international sanctions, even though they were—like most economic sanctions—leaky. He ruled his country with an iron hand, but the Kurds had established their autonomy in the north under the protection of the U.S. Air Force, and the Shia citizens in the south, though suppressed, were seething with discontent.

During his campaign for the presidency in 2000, George W. Bush gave no hint that he considered Iraq a threat to the United States so serious as to justify a war. In fact, in his second debate with the Democratic candidate Al Gore, Bush criticized President Clinton's nation-building efforts in Bosnia and Kosovo, stating, "I just don't think it's the role of the United States to walk into a country [and] say, 'We do it this way; so should you.'" Neverthe-less, once he became president, one of his first thoughts seems to have been how to find a way to do exactly that in Iraq.

We should pay careful attention to the thinking behind the president's decision to attack and occupy Iraq. At the most fundamental level that thinking was based on a misperception of historical experience going beyond caricature. Caricatures may distort an image by enlarging existing features out of proportion with the rest of the image. Stressing features that do not exist is not a distortion but simply a false image.

Rationalizing War

Kenneth M. Pollack, a former CIA analyst and member of the staff of President Clinton's National Security Council, published one of the most detailed and cogent arguments in favor of invading Iraq the year before the invasion commenced. I reviewed his book, *The Threatening Storm: The Case for Invading Iraq*, for the *New York Times Book Review* and gave my opinion that Pollack had made the best case possible but that his argument was still not convincing. For example, he asserted that Saddam Hussein had modeled his rule on Stalin's, and that a Saddam with nuclear weapons could not be deterred.[3] He seemed to have forgotten that we managed to deter a Soviet Union with tens of thousands of nuclear weapons. Why would it be impossible to deter Saddam Hussein, even if he had a few?

Another flaw that I found in the Pollack argument was that he postulated conditions for the invasion that I considered unlikely to be met: mobilizing at least three hundred thousand troops, United Nations approval, the backing of other states in the region, even a formal congressional declaration of war. All of these were reasonable conditions for invading another country, but even in late 2002 it was clear that the administration would not be able to meet all of them. In fact, it met *none* of them.

In my review, I did not challenge Pollack's flat statement that Iraq had an ongoing nuclear weapons program. After all, his positions in the CIA and the National Security Council presumably gave him access to information that justified the claim. But, on rereading his arguments with the hindsight of present knowledge, it is clear that many were flawed because they failed to distinguish between known fact and assumption, and gave no hint that there were unknown facts and factors that might alter a judgment. As I discussed in Chapter 3, Professors Neustadt and May set forth some thirty years ago a systematic method of thinking about historical evidence in making policy. It was based upon carefully distinguishing facts from assumptions, and identifying, to the extent possible, what was knowable but not known. The assumptions could be tested and thought given to what might happen to change them, and how some of the knowable unknowns might be clarified.

Kenneth Pollack would have none of this. Consider the following statement: "The only prudent and realistic course of action left to the United States is to mount a full-scale invasion of Iraq, depose Saddam's regime, and rid the country of weapons of mass destruction."[4] The assumption that Iraq had weapons of mass destruction was never questioned or qualified, and therefore the option of sending inspectors back to determine whether weapons of mass destruction still remained in Iraq was not considered.

The presence or absence of weapons of mass destruction in Iraq was a question of fact, though one difficult to establish beyond doubt. But when the author was talking of the future, he presented predictions without any qualification about the possible outcome. Here are a few examples: "Being rid of Saddam Hussein would be an enormous boon to U.S. foreign policy"; "Invading Iraq would ultimately allow us to reduce our presence in the Gulf region"; "Removing Saddam Hussein from power would sever the 'linkage' between the Iraq issue and the Arab-Israeli conflict."[5] The author does not discuss the assumptions that lay behind these predictions, and his failure to do so may explain why he was unable to foresee many consequences of the action he recommended.

Pollack's most far-reaching untested assumption was that an invasion could eventually reduce anti-American sentiment in the Arab world "if the United States were to build a strong, prosperous, and inclusive new Iraq state."[6] Yes, and if we could build a perpetual motion machine we could solve our energy problem. Maybe the author meant "if the United States could *help* build . . . ," but that is not what he wrote. How can any foreign country, with a distinctly different history and located in a totally different geopolitical environment, build a strong, inclusive state in a country with shallow national roots and fractured by ethnic and confessional cleavages its neighbors are inclined to exploit? Any assertion that it is possible for the United States, or any other country, to remake another country in its image is the stuff of dreams, not a sober analysis of realistic options.

This is not to say that Iraqis are incapable, in time, of developing a more prosperous, freer, and less threatening state, nor is it to say that the foreign policy of one country cannot influence the domestic policy of other countries, but effective policy makers must recognize the limits of their country's power. They also need to understand that democracy, good government, and restraint in resorting to violence must come from within a country and cannot be imposed from without.

I should, however, avoid laying stress on the holes in Kenneth Pollack's arguments, because the sort of reasoned analysis he presented, however flawed, was totally absent from the policy deliberations of the George W. Bush White House. (Pollack himself has been sharply critical of the way the Bush administration conducted the war in Iraq, though he still entertains extravagant ideas about the American ability to transform the region.)[7]

The evidence is overwhelming that the Bush White House was determined from the day the president was inaugurated to find an excuse to invade Iraq. The entire emphasis was to find or devise a pretext to remove Saddam Hussein. It did not seem to matter whether the casus belli was real or invented, so long as it would be accepted by enough of the American public to allow George W. Bush to seek reelection as a "war president," firm in defending American interests and honor.

Since the president's decision was not the result of faulty analysis by the foreign policy bureaucracy in the U.S. government, we should take a close look at the reasoning and attitudes that induced President Bush to become stuck in Tar Baby Iraq.

Enablers: The "American Supremacists"

Although the failure to prevent the suicide attacks on the World Trade Center and the Pentagon may have resulted more from incompetence and inattention than from a mistaken philosophy, subsequent decisions, including that to invade Iraq, were based on the illusion that American power was capable of reshaping the world by the application of force. The president and vice president may also have been motivated by a desire, conscious or perhaps unconscious, to divert attention from their failure to protect the country in September 2001. The reasoning, however, and the philosophical justification came from people who had most assiduously perverted the lessons of the Cold War to contrive a rationale for establishing American hegemony over the entire planet, including even "full-spectrum dominance" of the outer space beyond it.

Financier George Soros summed up this enabling philosophy as follows:

> International relations are relations of power, not law; power prevails and law legitimizes what prevails. The United States is unquestionably the dominant power in the post–Cold War world; it is therefore in a position to impose its views, interests, and values on the world. The world would benefit from adopting American values because the American model has demonstrated its superiority. Under the previous administrations, however, the United States failed to use the full potential of its power. This has to be corrected. The United States must assert its supremacy in the world.[8]

The group that embraced this train of thought is generally labeled neoconservatives, or neocons for short.

The Neoconservatives

When Leonid Brezhnev was complacently ruling the Soviet Union, Soviet citizens would sometimes joke about the two leading newspapers (when out of the range of KGB listening devices): "There is no truth in *Pravda* [Russian for 'truth'] and no news in *Izvestiya* [Russian for 'news']." It sounds cleverer in Russian than in English, but something similar can be said of the appellation "neoconservatives." There is really nothing new in their ideas, and they are anything but conservative, which may be why conservative thinkers like Patrick J. Buchanan prefer to call them neocons.[9]

Their intellectual roots go back to pre–World War II disputes on the extreme left wing of American political thinking; the original neoconservatives were Trotskyists who considered themselves anti-Stalin socialists. They subsequently broke with the American "left" over issues like the war in Vietnam and domestic social policy.[10] The appellation "neoconservative" was based on the mistaken notion that communism was left-wing and conservatism right-wing. Their philosophy was based on a stark, Manichean view of the world, which they considered an arena for a struggle between absolute good and absolute evil. When they discarded a variant of Marxism (the belief in world revolution), they merely redefined the contesting forces in the world. They were still seeking a utopia, but instead of viewing revolution by the proletariat as the means to fulfill the mandate of history, they looked to the power exercised by the strongest capitalist country in the world, the United States of America.

Those neoconservatives active in the Reagan administration consistently advised avoiding negotiation whenever possible, because they considered the Soviet Union immune to change and believed that it could be brought down only by applying maximum military, economic, and political pressure. Thus, they were ardent believers in stoking the arms race, skeptical about arms control, and—as Reagan refused their advice to avoid negotiation with Gorbachev—conducted a whispering campaign that Reagan was not really serious about dealing with the Russians but was only playing politics. When it turned out that Reagan was not only a serious negotiator but had actually succeeded in reversing the arms race, the neocons began to spread the word that he was going soft in his old age.

When Reagan's approach worked and the Cold War ended, the neocons simply misrepresented what happened and claimed that Reagan had followed their approach in dealing with the Soviet Union. Douglas Feith, who had been a senior official in Donald Rumsfeld's Defense Department, was quoted in early 2008 explaining that "during the Nixon presidency, and the George H. W. Bush presidency, the emphasis was on stabilizing relations with the Soviet Union. During the Reagan administration, the goal was to put the Communists on the ash heap of history."[11] This is a classic formulation of the myth the neocons have constructed about the past, and about Reagan's policy. The only shreds of evidence to support it are snippets of political rhetoric taken out of context. Reagan spoke at times about communism headed for the ash heap of history, but he did not propose that as the goal of American policy. Reagan's goal, as is evident from the official record and his own memoirs, was to change Soviet behavior.

Even some observers who are sharply critical of the neocon influence on the George W. Bush administration have been taken in by the myths they constructed about the Cold War. For example, Adam Garfinkle, the editor of *The American Interest* who served for a time as Colin Powell's speechwriter, observed in a recent article: "Yes, neoconservatives, *flush with having been vindicated by the West's victory in the Cold War* [emphasis added], lazily applied their creed to problems and places for which their experience was a poor guide."[12] Vindicated? In fact, Reagan and Bush the 41st succeeded precisely because they rejected neocon advice, engaging Gorbachev rather than trying to isolate him and shout him down. Most neocon advice was as bad during the Cold War as it has been since.

When the Soviet Union disappeared as a putative rival, the neoconservatives seemed desperate to locate an enemy that would justify maintaining a defense establishment as strong as that created to meet the Soviet threat. This was not easy, given the fact that the United States, even with the reduction of defense expenditures during the 1990s, was spending more on defense than the next most powerful seventeen countries combined. But this did not deter their search for enemies.

As Francis Fukuyama, once a neoconservative himself, observed, "Neoconservatives after the collapse of communism tended to overestimate the level of threat facing the United States. . . . After the breakup of the USSR, . . . many neoconservatives continued to see the world as populated by dangerous and underappreciated threats."[13] For a while, some looked to China as the next serious rival, but dreamed of dealing with both Iraq and Iran in the interim. Following 9/11, they latched onto Al-Qaeda and grossly magnified its power and reach by fusing the terrorist threat, which was real but manageable, with state failure and nuclear weapons proliferation. Norman Podhoretz, as I have mentioned already, went to the ridiculous extreme of calling the fight against terrorists "World War IV."

The Vulcans

In 2004, former *Los Angeles Times* correspondent James Mann published a study of the officials most influential during George W. Bush's first term titled *Rise of the Vulcans: The History of Bush's War Cabinet.* It focuses on Vice President Richard Cheney, Secretary of Defense Donald Rumsfeld, his deputy (for a time) Paul Wolfowitz, Secretary of State Colin Powell and his deputy, Richard Armitage, and Condoleezza Rice, Bush's assistant for national security. Most had served in the Bush I administration in varying capacities but, except for Powell and Armitage, had come to reject the elder Bush's stress on alliance diplomacy. They maintained contact with one another and with like-minded friends while out of office, developing a rationale for the unilateral use of American military power to transform other countries. They also embraced the idea of preemptive action; indeed, they were to go beyond it, conflating preemption of a tangible threat with preventive war against possible future threats.[14]

Some, notably Vice President Cheney and Secretary of Defense Rumsfeld, were devotees of new technology, convinced that new weapons systems would make it possible for the United States to preserve its military dominance without resort to tedious diplomacy, nation building, or much ground combat by soldiers. The creation of a missile defense became with them a quasi-religion, even though it was totally irrelevant to the sort of threat terrorists posed. In the dreams of the techno-freaks, the destructiveness and accuracy of the new munitions in the U.S. arsenal would create such a degree of shock and awe that countries subjected to it would cower in fright and others would rush to do American bidding lest they be next.

The group was not cohesive on all issues, and in fact both Powell and Armitage had more regard for the usefulness of allies and more caution about applying military force than the others. The more visionary voices, however, were those that prevailed with the president following the collective failure to prevent the attacks on September 11, 2001.

"Missionaries"

Another strain of thought, shared by some people who consider themselves staunch conservatives and some who are committed liberals, guides a diverse group of people that I call, for lack of a better term, political missionaries. They believe that the United States has a moral obligation to use its power to spread democracy in the world. They do not necessarily share the Manichean fantasies of the neocons, that everything is a cosmic struggle of good and evil and that evil can be eliminated in the world if only the United States will use its military power without hesitation. Nor do they necessarily share the vulcan (or—more exactly—Cheney-Rumsfeld) fixation on new technologies and the power of "shock and awe." But, for them, the fact that Saddam Hussein was a bad man who committed atrocities against his people was enough to justify a war against him, whether or not it was authorized by the United Nations Security Council. Their goal is to create democratic forms of government everywhere.

There are at least two problems with this approach. One is that it tends to assume that all one must do to build democracy in a country is to remove one impediment to it—the dictator. The other is that, to much of the rest of the world, an attempt to expand "democracy" by force is considered nothing more than pursuit of an imperial goal, the capitalist version of the infamous Brezhnev Doctrine.

Our evangelical democrats seem to assume that democracy is the natural state of mankind and that dictators are the exception. Even a superficial familiarity with world history should have taught us the opposite: over the millennia of human history, democracy is a new phenomenon in political organization, based on ideas growing out of the eighteenth-century Enlightenment.* Democratic governments are highly complex, and since executive authority is subject to checks and balances, for many purposes they are less efficient that authoritarian governments. Democracy is nowhere perfect and everywhere subject to setbacks. Every country that can be considered a relatively stable, liberal democracy has reached that condition as the result of internal evolution, not external compulsion.

"Missionaries" normally react to their critics by accusing them of denying that "people everywhere desire freedom." Well, of course, in the proper context, when they are assured of sustenance, shelter, and safety, most people do. But invasion by a foreign army, however benign in intent, usually exacts a greater immediate price than most people are willing to pay for the right to express their opinion and to vote for or against the people who will rule them. War can destroy the institutions and infrastructure needed to sustain a normal life, without which people have difficulty perceiving the virtues of political freedom. And, of course, there will always be some persons who seek freedom not to live in peace with their neighbors but in order to settle old scores or to suppress those neighbors of a different ethnic group or religious persuasion.

*It is true that the word originates with the ancient Greeks, but Athenian "democracy" would not be recognized as an authentic democracy today, since it disenfranchised the great majority of the people living permanently on its territory: slaves, persons without property, and women. It had no concept of human rights or the limitations of governmental power that are central to contemporary concepts of democracy.

A free society is one that lives by the rule of law and has effective institutions to protect citizens from arbitrary violence, whether by government officials or by fellow citizens. There is no one-size-fits-all structure of government that works in every society, and even if there were, it could not be imposed by force from the outside. Those missionaries of democracy who dream of doing good by eliminating evil in the world are placing an impossible task on the American military—and the American taxpayer. If a democracy invades a country that has not attacked it, the invader is far more likely to discredit democracy than to promote it. Much of the world will also interpret an attempt to impose "democracy" by force as a blatant effort to dominate the world, which should be opposed by whatever means available.

The Decision to Invade

If George Herbert Walker Bush did virtually everything right with the diplomatic and military preparations for the war to expel Iraq from Kuwait in 1991, his son seemed determined to do the opposite in the run-up to the invasion of Iraq in 2002. Perhaps this is one reason the results of the war that Bush started in 2003 have also been pretty nearly the opposite of the results of the first Gulf War.

Consider this: The United States emerged from the first Gulf War with its prestige high and its influence on world politics at a peak. That influence was great because the United States had led a broad coalition to enforce a U.N. Security Council resolution that was important to all the participating nations. America's potential for leadership was enhanced by the fact that it had shown restraint and avoided trying to occupy Iraq. It thus signaled that its intent was to deter aggression and to keep access to Persian Gulf oil open to all, not to extend imperial control over Iraq and its petroleum reserves. Furthermore, it did all of this without the costs becoming a burden on the American taxpayer. American goals were so much in accord with the interests of other countries that others were willing to defray the financial cost of reversing aggression.

Compare the situation in 1991 to the situation in 2009: The United States, still mired in an occupation of Iraq that has lasted more than six years, has lost prestige and influence everywhere. In the eyes of most of the world, the United States was itself the aggressor, invading Iraq without the sanction of the Security Council, and—illegality aside—created greater chaos than order in the region. Meanwhile, preventing mayhem in Iraq absorbed so many U.S. ground forces that there were not enough available to keep the Taliban from expanding its influence in Afghanistan, or to back up American diplomacy in other areas. The ability of the United States to meet the expanded security commitments it has undertaken is now hostage to the willingness and ability of Iraqi politicians to cooperate sufficiently to establish a viable state able to stand on its own. It is difficult to understand how a superpower would be so reckless as to put the future of its own security in the hands of squabbling and, more often than not, corrupt foreign politicians. Yet that is exactly what the Bush-Cheney administration did.

The difference in the two results is not caused simply by the fact that Bush the elder showed more wisdom and skill than his son—though there is no question that he did—but also that the first Bush understood that U.S. power was limited, even though the Cold War had ended and the Soviet Union was falling apart. He was careful to coordinate U.S. action with other countries with an interest in the situation, to make the effort to bring them along, to *lead* by persuasion. The first President Bush also showed infinitely better judgment in selecting advisers and deciding which to listen to.

One of the still unanswered mysteries, at least to me, is why President George W. Bush, in making decisions of war and peace, could ignore the advice of the only member of his cabinet who had actually fought in a war, commanded troops, and even chaired the Joint Chiefs of Staff during the successful Gulf War, in favor of armchair theorists who, like the president himself, had never participated in a military encounter. General Colin Powell, his secretary of state, had military experience that far surpassed that of all other senior members of his national security team combined. Powell also led the department of the U.S. government that was best equipped to understand the complexities of trying to rule Iraq. Yet he was, in effect, sidelined when the crucial decisions were made, and the experts in his department were ignored until the arrogant amateurs sent to rule Iraq had created a nearly hopeless mess.

In this respect, George W. Bush deviated not only from the practice of his father, who worked very closely with his secretary of state, but also from that of two presidents he reportedly admires: Ronald Reagan and Harry S. Truman. Reagan met regularly and frequently with George Shultz, privately whenever Shultz desired, and communicated with him on a daily basis. That way, Reagan was able to direct and utilize the resources of the Department of State and the Foreign Service to implement his policy choices. Harry Truman had George Marshall—a secretary of state with a profile very much like that of Colin Powell—and not only depended on him for advice, but allowed him to plan and take credit for one of the most innovative and successful foreign policy initiatives in the history of United States, the Marshall Plan, which revived Western Europe from the devastation of World War II and set its countries on the road to democracy.

President Bush told *Washington Post* journalist Bob Woodward more than once that he made his decisions on the basis of his instincts, his "gut," not as the result of analysis and reflection.[15] This was a remarkable boast from a person with scanty knowledge and experience and who, as many observers have noted, is basically uncurious about details. It contrasts with the governing style of Ronald Reagan, who also had only a sketchy knowledge of the details of many issues, but actively sought information from those who knew more than he did, and welcomed debate within his administration.

Historians will doubtless probe the psychological quirks that induced the president of the United States at the dawn of the twenty-first century to depend on his ill-informed instincts rather the advice of qualified advisers as he was making decisions on war and peace. Speculation about the source of George W. Bush's impulsiveness abounds. Was he psychologically competing with his father? Was he resentful of people with more knowledge and experience than he possessed? (He often spoke of his critics as "elitists.") Could he have been embarrassed that he had avoided service in Vietnam and uncomfortable with those who had fought there? Did he want to go to war with Iraq so he could run for reelection as a "war president"?[16]

I do not profess to know the answer to these questions, but I do know that one of the strengths of both Ronald Reagan and Harry Truman was their ability to use the services of people who knew more than they did on important issues without feeling diminished or not in command. Both knew they didn't know everything, were comfortable with that, and were eager to listen to those who were better informed or more experienced in a particular area of policy. Like George W. Bush, they had strong instincts, but they made sure their instincts were guided by facts and reason more than ideology and theory.

Bad Decision, Bad Implementation, or Both?

There are those who argue that President Bush's decision to invade Iraq in order to remove Saddam Hussein was appropriate and that the problems that subsequently arose were caused by defects in the execution of the decision—the failure to provide for security after the Iraqi armed forces were defeated, the abrupt dissolution of the Iraqi police and armed forces and wholesale removal of managers who were members of the Baath Party, the failure to suppress the growth of private militias and to secure the borders, the publicized abuse of prisoners in Abu Ghraib, and so on and so on.

These were real failures, for which identifiable people are responsible, but these failures of execution should not be allowed to obscure the fact that the decision to invade Iraq, under the conditions in which it was done, was wrong and did severe damage to America's ability to help create a more peaceful world. In fact, it was even more damaging than that, for it increased the threat to Americans by giving anti-American terrorism a new pretext, increasing the power and belligerence of Iran's mullahs, and absorbing military resources needed for missions elsewhere.[17]

The decision to invade Iraq was viewed as unprovoked aggression in most of the world. When Iraq was the aggressor against Kuwait, support for the coalition that restored Kuwait's independence was overwhelming, but in 2002 Iraq had attacked nobody. The administration tried to convince the Security Council that Iraq was harboring weapons of mass destruction in violation of its obligations following the 1991 Gulf War, but the evidence was not persuasive. The American people were told that Iraq was somehow involved in the terrorist attacks of 9/11—a blatant lie—but one that nevertheless became lodged in many American minds as if it were a fact.

The U.S. case for invading Iraq was so weak that even some of its closest allies—France and Germany in particular—went out of their way to persuade the United States not to attack without better evidence. The French position, supported by Germany and a majority of members of the U.N. Security Council, was that the United Nations inspectors should continue their work in Iraq to determine whether Saddam Hussein had in fact destroyed his weapons of mass destruction and terminated his nuclear weapons program. If illegal weapons were found, or if the Iraqi authorities refused to cooperate with the inspectors, the French argued, then serious consideration should be given to authorizing the use of force.[18] They were acting as friends trying to persuade a colleague who had overindulged from driving off before he had sobered up.

The Bush administration treated the critics not as allies who were trying to prevent a serious mistake that would cost America dearly, but as traitors. Some of our politicians proposed renaming French fries in the congressional dining room "freedom fries," which provides an accurate gauge of the quality of judgment displayed by Congress in what passed for debate over whether to invade Iraq. Anyone who takes the trouble to review what the French government actually said will find that most of the statements explaining why it was both unwise and illegal to attack and occupy Iraq turned out to be accurate.

Building respect for international law, which operates quite differently from domestic law, is an important prerequisite for a world order based on something other than perpetual conflict and the principle that might makes right. International law is best seen as a series of voluntary restraints that protect weaker powers from the arbitrary use of force by stronger ones, and stronger ones from the folly of trying to rule people who do not want them as rulers. International law does not forbid a country to defend itself, and even sanctions preemptive strikes against another country if there is a direct, immediate, and tangible threat.

Bush administration officials based their legal argument for the war on Iraq on this doctrine. The argument ran something like this: Saddam Hussein has retained chemical and biological weapons and is conducting a program to develop nuclear weapons in violation of the resolutions passed by the U.N. Security Council. The United States and other countries that wish to join it ("coalition partners") have a right, if not a duty, to enforce U.N. sanctions, even if the Security Council does not agree. Furthermore, administration spokespersons argued, we will not wait until we are attacked. We have a right to preempt possible future attacks.

The argument rested entirely on the allegation that Saddam Hussein was still harboring weapons of mass destruction. But by early 2003, senior administration officials should have realized that alleged evidence for an active nuclear program in Iraq was not solid. Furthermore—according to Ron Suskind—the head of Iraqi intelligence had told a British agent that Saddam Hussein had destroyed all chemical and biological weapons and terminated his nuclear weapons program, but did not want the word to get out to his enemies in Iran.[19] Standing alone, that report might have been dismissed, but it fit with everything else that was reliably known about the fate of weapons of mass destruction in Iraq.

Thinking back to our Cold War experience, I am reminded that Yuri Andropov, then KGB chairman, used a message from the KGB *rezidentsia* in Kabul to persuade his colleagues to invade Afghanistan. The message reported, without any evidence, that American marines had boarded an aircraft carrier in the Indian Ocean with orders to intervene in Afghanistan. (Presumably they would be granted overflight rights by a friendly Pakistan government.) Andropov must have known that the information was not true—it is a safe bet that he ordered the KGB in Kabul to report it—but used it to convince his Politburo colleagues that the United States would take over Afghanistan if they did not approve the invasion. I am also reminded that Soviet intelligence officers were so intent on pleasing their masters that they often avoided reporting unpleasant facts, and that Gorbachev was often misled about the strength of nationalist sentiment in his own country by KGB fabrications.

Few things are more dangerous for a country than having leaders who, either out of credulity or of calculation, accept illusion as fact. If President Bush and Vice President Cheney really believed that the evidence of a nuclear weapons program in Iraq was credible, they had lost the capacity of distinguishing fact from fabrication.* The "one percent doctrine" attributed to Cheney by Ron Suskind may be the explanation.[20] Cheney's insistence that a report must be acted on even it there is only a one percent chance of its being accurate means—if heeded—that ninety-nine percent of the government's activity would be useless or counterproductive.

*The code name for one of the sources of dubious reports was "Curveball," which should have tipped off even the most credulous official that his reports might not be accurate.

The claim that attacking Iraq was exercising a right of preemption lacked validity even if there had been some remaining weapons of mass destruction in Iraq. Under international law, preemption requires an imminent and tangible threat. Anything else is not preemption but preventive war, which is a thoroughly bad idea—and illegal as well. Why is it a bad idea? Because it can be used to justify any military attack. It is as if you could arrest someone because they might, in the future, break the law. It was this principle that Stalin and Saddam Hussein used in conducting purges of their associates. The victims were rarely active opponents; many were devoted supporters. The suspicion that they might at some time in the future oppose the dictator was sufficient for Stalin and Saddam to order their arrest and execution.

Is that the kind of world we want to live in? Can any country justify invading another by saying that it had to do it because sometime in the future the invaded country might commit aggression? Is it possible for anyone, particularly an outsider, to judge with certainty future intentions? Of course not—and the pretense that preventive war is justified under the cloak of preemption is one of the most dangerous doctrines that has gained currency from the way Iraq was attacked. Preventive war is *never* justified, and the world will become a much more nasty and dangerous place if it becomes an accepted practice.

The Conduct of the Occupation

The swift military victory over the Iraqi armed forces and rapid occupation of the country failed to have the effect proponents of the war anticipated— a rapid, Iraqi-led and financed restoration of order and establishment of a democratic government following elections. The coalition that quickly took control of the country did not have enough forces to keep even the most elementary order—virtually every government office aside from the oil ministry (which was protected), the national museum (an important symbol of national identity), and many private businesses were stripped by looters.

Most of the detailed planning for the occupation had been performed in the State Department, led by people familiar with Iraq and the region as a whole, but President Bush decided in January 2003 to entrust responsibility for the reconstruction of Iraq to the Department of Defense, which had

minimal capacity to deal with the internal workings of a foreign government. Secretary of State Powell apparently did not protest assigning responsibility for rehabilitating Iraq to his Cabinet rival. He knew that it would
be a messy and most likely hopeless task, and that the State Department
had not been given the resources to carry it out, and therefore did not want
his department to be blamed for failing to deal with a situation that should
not have been created in the first place.[21]

General Jay Garner, who was first assigned the task because he had
worked successfully with the Kurds in northern Iraq in the 1990s, never
had a chance. He was not given sufficient staff or time to plan the reconstruction of Iraq. Basic information about what was needed was not available; he assumed that he would be responsible for restoring facilities
damaged by the war, but was unaware that the Iraqi infrastructure had deteriorated to such a degree that almost everything had to be rebuilt. By the
time he was allowed to come to Baghdad with a small staff, the city was a
shambles. Not even the most experienced staff with realistic and detailed
plans could have restored essential services under those conditions.

It got worse. Shortly after L. Paul (Jerry) Bremer arrived with apparently
unlimited authority, he terminated Garner's mission and issued two orders
that practically ensured that the country would be unmanageable: one ordered the formal dissolution of the Iraqi army, and the other removed senior and mid-level bureaucrats who had been members of the Baath Party—
which meant virtually every official at the managerial level in the country,
since Baath Party membership was generally considered a prerequisite for
any position that had supervisory authority over other people.[22]

The reason given for these drastic acts was that the Iraqi army had already
disbanded and the majority of the people in the country would not accept the
military force and the bureaucrats who had supported Saddam. But American authorities in Baghdad had been informed that many soldiers would be
willing to come back, since they needed their pay to survive, and that they
were needed to back up the police and guard facilities from looters. None of
the government departments could work properly without the mid-level bureaucrats who had been forced to join the Baath Party. Many Iraqis argued
that it should be the responsibility of the elected Iraqi government, once it
was established, to weed out undesirable elements from the military and

the bureaucracy. They also noted that if Iraqis had primary responsibility for keeping order on the streets, the American presence would seem less like an occupation.

These considerations would seem self-evident to anyone not living in an imaginary world. Imagine: Jerry Bremer, acting on authority of the president of the United States (who possibly was not directly involved in the decision), makes it impossible for Iraqis to keep order in the country and to maintain essential services, even though he does not have the people or plans or resources to perform these vital jobs. Meanwhile, some million young Iraqi men with military training and easy access to arms—there had not been adequate coalition forces to secure them—were loose in the country without the means of subsistence. Where did they go? To sectarian militias, to criminal gangs, and to groups determined to harass the foreign occupiers until they left the country.

The Iraqi election in December 2005 was encouraging in many ways: over twelve million people representing nearly 80 percent of eligible voters participated. But the 20 percent who boycotted the election were largely Sunnis, the big losers from the American invasion, and that meant that they inevitably felt left out of the resulting government. Discontented Sunni Iraqis provided a supportive sea for foreign jihadists organized by Al-Qaeda to enter and survive in Iraq. They were active in organizing attacks against American and other coalition forces, and also in instigating Sunni retaliation against the Shia-led government. Saddam Hussein had kept the jihadists out of Iraq, except for a small group in a Kurdish area that he did not control. Now Al-Qaeda in Iraq suddenly became a major force, using the foreign occupation of the country and perceived Shiite repression of Sunni Arabs as recruiting appeals.

But then, Al-Qaeda in Iraq began to overplay its hand. Some two months after the election, in February 2006, Al-Qaeda-controlled jihadists destroyed the golden dome of the Al-Askari Mosque in Samarra, one of the most holy sites for the Shia, and kidnappings, killings, and bombings grew rapidly. Whole neighborhoods in Baghdad were ravaged by rival militias, and things got worse through 2006 and into the summer of 2007. An estimated two million people were forced from their homes and tens of thousands were killed.

A poll sponsored by ABC News and its media partners found that in late February and early March 2007, only 42 percent of Iraqis thought that life was better then than it had been under Saddam Hussein. A shocking 51 percent of Iraqis thought that violence against U.S. and coalition troops was acceptable—and in Sunni areas, nine out of ten people felt that way.

The deteriorating situation in Iraq became a dominant issue during the 2006 congressional elections in the United States, with most Democrats demanding a timetable for prompt U.S. withdrawal. President Bush strongly opposed these demands, threatening to veto any bill that contained them, including financing for the war. Serious doubts about the course of the war spread within the Bush administration, though these were not voiced to the public.[23] President Bush was careful to give no hint of his growing impatience with deteriorating conditions in Iraq, insisting that the United States must "stay the course" until the Iraqi government was able to bring order and exercise effective governance.

The combination of the pressure of a Congress controlled (though just barely) by the Democratic Party and dissatisfaction in his own administration over the course of the war caused Bush to change course. Instead of endorsing plans to reduce U.S. forces, he ordered—against the advice of the Joint Chiefs of Staff—an increase of five combat divisions in Iraq, bringing American forces to 160,000, and assigned General David Petraeus, a specialist on counterinsurgency warfare, to take command of coalition forces in Iraq. The additional troops were used to secure neighborhoods in Baghdad where sectarian militias were active and to combat the insurgency in some of the Sunni areas, such as Diyala and Anbar provinces, where foreign fighters controlled by Al-Qaeda in Iraq were operating.

A change of tactics in Sunni areas brought at least temporary success: U.S. commanders enlisted the help of tribal elders and paid Sunni young men to fight the foreign insurgents in their midst, thus, in effect, rehiring many of the soldiers Bremer had fired.* This was a risky strategy, since it was not clear that the Shia-dominated Iraqi government would be willing

---

*This is further evidence of the folly of disbanding the Iraqi army at the beginning of the U.S. occupation. The foreign insurgents would probably not have come to Iraq to fight an Iraqi force, and if Iraqis had been responsible for security, the foreigners could not have operated in a favorable sea.

eventually to absorb these forces into the Iraqi army. Potentially, they could become a local militia resisting Baghdad's control when and if the United States stopped paying them. As Peter Galbraith, a former ambassador to Croatia who has maintained close ties to the Iraqi Kurds, wrote in September, 2008:

> [Iraqi prime minister Nuri] Al-Maliki's agenda is transparent. The Kurds and Sunnis are obstacles to the ruling coalition's ambitions for a Shiite Islamic state. Al-Maliki wants to eliminate the Sunni militia and contain the Kurds politically and geographically. America's interest in defeating Al-Qaeda is far less important to him than the Shiite interest in not having a powerful Sunni military that could overthrow Iraq's new Shiite order.[24]

In other words, even if violence in Iraq is reduced sufficiently to allow the withdrawal of American combat troops, we may have created an Iraq less resistant to Al-Qaeda than it was when Saddam Hussein was in power.

The short-term effect of the change of tactics associated with the "surge" was, nevertheless, positive, because the Sunni fighters turned against the foreign jihadists (mainly from Egypt, Syria, Jordan, and Saudi Arabia) who had not only attacked U.S. and coalition forces but had tried to stoke conflict between the Sunni and Shia in Iraq.

By the spring of 2008, most foreign insurgents had been killed or flushed out of the Sunni areas. Those that survived retreated to Mosul in northern Iraq, a city in an oil-producing region with a mixed population of Kurds, Arabs, and other ethnic groups such as Turkmen. In May and June 2008, U.S. forces, supported by Iraqi and Kurdish military units, subdued the Al-Qaeda strongholds in the city. By the summer of 2008, therefore, the threat of Al-Qaeda in Iraq had been—it was believed—substantially reduced.

At this writing it is too early to judge whether, in fact, the battles of 2008 eliminated Al-Qaeda in Iraq as a significant force. One can hope that the foreign jihadists of the Al-Qaeda ilk will continue to be unwelcome everywhere in Iraq. But before boasts that the war in Iraq was necessary to combat Al-Qaeda are accepted, it should be remembered that there were no significant Al-Qaeda forces operating in Iraq under Saddam Hussein. They entered Iraq as the result of the American-led invasion and occupation.

Proponents of the war in Iraq argued, particularly during the elections of 2004 and 2006, "We are fighting the terrorists in Iraq so we don't have to fight them here." This was a bogus claim because the terrorists in Iraq never had the capability of fighting on American soil; they were recruited to fight a foreign occupier in a Muslim country. Nevertheless, the reduction in violence in Iraq overall and the improvement of security in several previously embattled Baghdad neighborhoods were welcome trends that reduced the prominence of the Iraq war in the election campaigns of 2008.

Damaging and Dangerous Precedents

Still stuck in the grip of Tar Baby Iraq, President Bush left to his successor the task of extricating the United States from his misadventure. Despite the claims of those who promoted the attack on Iraq that it would "transform the region" and create a democratic society that would radiate its benign influence throughout the Middle East, serious problems remained. Many of them seemed more dangerous and intractable than they had been when Saddam Hussein was in power.

Problems exacerbated by the war in Iraq included the prospect of nuclear weapons in Iran, the need for a settlement between Israel and the Palestinians and between Israel and neighboring Arab countries, the threat of a Taliban resurgence in Afghanistan and of Al-Qaeda and nuclear weapons in Pakistan. Iran's power in the region had been enhanced, and it could be expected to use its influence with the Iraqi Shia to obstruct reconciliation with Iraq's Sunnis. The invasion of Iraq and what was viewed as mistreatment of Muslims (such as the widely publicized harassment of prisoners at Abu Ghraib) had turned Pakistani opinion in a strongly anti-American direction. Public hostility to American policy hampered efforts to track down Osama bin Laden and the reinvigorated Al-Qaeda terrorists in the mountains along Pakistan's border with Afghanistan. Even if President Obama is able to leave a coherent, functioning government in Iraq as American forces withdraw, these problems will remain. The war in Iraq has made them more difficult to address, not easier.

The impact on the Middle East and South Asia is only part of the problem. Actions associated with the war in Iraq have also inflicted serious damage to American well-being, prestige, and power in many other ways. Here are just a few:

· The well-publicized mistreatment of prisoners at the Abu Ghraib prison still resonates not just in Pakistan but throughout the Islamic world and beyond. The extra-legal treatment of prisoners at Guantánamo has done severe damage to the confidence that America's allies have traditionally had in the fairness of its legal system. It may take years before the world regains confidence that the United States is a country that values and respects the rule of law.

· The use of civilian contractors not subject to local or U.S. law for security protection in Iraq has set a dangerous precedent, since it is bound to be viewed by Iraqis as the use of hired mercenaries.[25] If we are trying to establish a law-based democracy, the practice undermines the fundamental principle that law-enforcement agencies must be accountable for their actions. Hired mercenaries are also bad for morale among the uniformed military, because they are paid much more and are not subject to the discipline of military units. The development of private security firms to perform military service abroad has created a dangerous new segment of the American military-industrial complex. If not checked, it could prove a cancerous organ in the American body politic.

· No-bid contracts and sloppy accounting have created a growing segment of the American economy based on war. War profiteering has a particularly corrosive effect on American society, given the reduced taxes on high incomes introduced by the Bush administration.

· The ballooning federal deficit caused largely by the war in Iraq and the refusal to maintain tax rates from the 1990s on the most affluent Americans is forcing the federal government to go ever deeper in debt to stimulate the economy and rebuild a decaying infrastructure at home. Following the financial panic of 2008, runaway deficits are likely to cripple the American ability to dominate the world financial system as it has done since World War II.

· The attempt to deploy a large proportion of the U.S. Foreign Service to engage in nation building in Iraq without a concomitant increase in the resources for diplomacy has weakened the country's diplomatic arm at a time when effective diplomacy is vital to its future. Imperial powers have traditionally distinguished between their diplomatic services, suited to managing relations with other countries, and their colonial service,

trained to administer other countries. The attempt to convert a significant part of the U.S. diplomatic corps to what is in effect a colonial service
can only weaken American diplomacy in the future. Empires are obsolete and so are the civil servants who administer them.

I will have more to say about the liabilities the war in Iraq has engendered
as I discuss the future. At this point, it is enough to note that even the most
benign end to the U.S. occupation of Iraq will leave President Obama with
the task of repairing the damage the war in Iraq has done to American foreign and domestic policy. President George W. Bush left office with America's arms and feet still stuck in Tar Baby Iraq. As Bob Woodward observed
in concluding *The War Within:* "The next president will face a complex set
of organizational, military, political and leadership challenges because of
the Iraq war. It won't be solved with slogans or party doctrine, or through
wishful thinking."[26]

During the presidential campaign of 2008, the war in Iraq took a back
seat in public attention to the deteriorating domestic economy and the sudden financial panic in September and October. The failure of several large
banks and Wall Street investment firms caused a retraction of credit even to
credit-worthy enterprises and thus threatened to plunge the country, and
perhaps the entire world, into a prolonged depression. Understandably, this
crisis dominated public attention during the last weeks of the election campaign, and even past it as the president-elect struggled to fashion a strategy
to avoid the worst.

We should not close the books on the Bush-Cheney administration without taking a close look at how it dealt with problems in the nation and in the
world aside from combating terrorists and occupying Iraq. Did the sort of
decision making based on ideology and instinct that produced the war in
Iraq prevail in George W. Bush's approach to other problems? What should
we put on the bottom line of a balance sheet of achievements and failures
from January 2001 to January 2009?

10

Ideology Trumps Reality:
2001–2009

THE FINANCIAL CRISIS AND DEEPENING recession that gripped public attention during the final months of 2008 dealt a heavy blow to American primacy in the world financial system. Washington was forced to transcend
some of its dogma and to follow a European initiative as it struggled to cope
with the prospect that the financial meltdown could bring on a repeat of the
Great Depression of the 1930s.

The George W. Bush administration had been guided by an economic ideology that was peddled to the public with misleading slogans. George Soros
labeled the ideology "market fundamentalism"—the idea that markets can
solve all problems efficiently if left alone by the government—and warned
early in the Bush administration of its inherent dangers.[1] Slogans replaced
prudent analysis: "government is the problem," "starve the beast," "no new
taxes," "deficits don't matter," to recall a few.

Citizens were encouraged to borrow for current consumption, just as the
government did, and lenders to provide loans to people unable to repay
them. Bank regulation was lax, as market players devised financial instruments so complex that they could not be accurately valued yet were sold,
chopped up, recombined, and resold. Weak regulation permitted financial
institutions to leverage their capital far beyond reasonable prudence. Enforcement of securities law was so negligent that one prominent New York
broker and investment adviser, Bernard Madoff, managed to operate a clas-

sic Ponzi scheme for years, which may have cost his credulous investors more than fifty *billion* dollars.

Steps toward financial deregulation had been taken before the Bush II administration, but its officials carried the hands-off policy even further. In effect, the government, with bipartisan support, enabled and cheered on an immense housing bubble, which produced obscene profits for a few until it burst and thrust into bankruptcy or forced sale some of America's largest and most venerable financial institutions, as well as American International Group, the world's predominant insurance company.

To prevent a repeat of the Great Depression, the Bush administration was forced in its waning months to persuade a reluctant Congress to approve government intervention in the financial system on an unprecedented scale. At first, Treasury Secretary Henry Paulson asked for up to $750 billion to buy up bad debt, in an effort to bail out the banks that had made the questionable investments. Congress balked, and the authorization was changed substantially before authority was granted. But then, European leaders, principally British prime minister Gordon Brown and French president Nicolas Sarkozy, pioneered the idea of increasing the capital of banks by government purchasing of shares, a move that American market fundamentalists considered a step toward socialism if not socialism itself. Washington had no choice but to go along, and Paulson announced on October 12, 2008, that the Treasury would use up to $250 billion to buy shares in American banks; by the end of the year, the government held stock in 206 banks. In late December, the administration decided not only to underwrite the financial sector, but to stave off the bankruptcy of auto manufacturers General Motors and Chrysler with a $17.4 billion loan.

So much for "the government is the problem" and "starve the beast," slogans promoted by Grover Norquist and his Club for Growth, which had been mainstays of Bush administration economic philosophy. In fact, the "beast" had not been starved but fed by deficit spending, which meant that the economy could be bailed out only by borrowing even more money. As the world's largest debtor even before the financial crisis, the United States was in no position to dictate to its creditors. European leaders began to push for a new Bretton Woods, the arrangement pioneered by the United States at the end of World War II to manage international financial policy and currency exchange. This time, European leaders, it seemed, would be calling the tune, with China, Japan, Russia, India, and the oil-rich sheikdoms also influencing the outcome.

When Bush left office, the U.S. government was a substantial part owner of some the country's largest banks and the arbiter of the future of the automobile industry. Nevertheless, it was obvious in January 2009 that the bailouts engineered by Bush and Paulson would not be adequate to prevent a severe and prolonged recession. President Obama was faced with the necessity of providing a massive economic stimulus package.

In addition to profligate spending by the federal government on wars abroad and multiple subsidies to corporate interests, America's infrastructure had been neglected and was showing increasing strain.[2] Recovery from the New Orleans flood was slow and incomplete. In 2007 a bridge carrying Interstate Highway 35W over the Mississippi River in St. Paul, Minnesota, collapsed, killing 13 motorists and injuring 145, many seriously.[3] In a report released in January 2009, the American Society of Civil Engineers gave an average grade of "D" to the overall status of U.S. infrastructure and estimated that it would require $2.2 trillion of investment over the next five years to bring it up to acceptable modern standards.[4] The education system in much of the United States had fallen behind many other countries, particularly in training in mathematics and science.

Unemployment rose steadily through 2008 and accelerated in 2009. American industry was losing its technological edge. Although the United States still had the world's largest economy, government debt exceeded $10 trillion, more than a third of which was held by foreigners, mainly other governments.

As if the financial crisis, threat of recession, and mountainous debt were not enough, the nation also had an economy still addicted to imported petroleum and other fossil fuels. Emissions of carbon dioxide and other greenhouse gases could, within a few decades if not restrained, bring the world to a "tipping point" where global warming becomes practically irreversible and creates catastrophic damage—far more than terrorists, even with a nuclear device or two—could inflict.

If, in domestic policy, the Bush presidency did too little to curb excesses in financial markets and to keep America's infrastructure in sound and ef-

ficient condition, in foreign policy it tried to do too much, and often did it
in the wrong way. There was a disconnect between a stretched and heavily
indebted domestic economy and an assertive, costly, risk-prone foreign policy. This was true even though, during the latter part of his second term,
Bush allowed Condoleezza Rice to alter some specific policies, including negotiating strategy toward North Korea. Overall, such changes as were apparent in American foreign policy, though welcome, were too limited and
came too late to salvage a disastrous foreign policy record.

We need to look beyond Iraq, Afghanistan, and the war on terrorists if we
are to make a balanced assessment of American foreign policy over the first
eight years of the twenty-first century.

America Abroad

In 2009 it is hard to make the case that Americans are as secure as they
were in 2001, despite the fact that they had not faced a challenge from another superpower for nearly two decades and had not suffered a major terrorist attack since September 2001. In January 2001, the country was at
peace (though under a preventable threat from terrorists); in 2009 the war
in Iraq continued to smolder and the one in Afghanistan was flaming up
again. The continued occupation of Iraq and the growing threat of a resurgent Taliban in Afghanistan had stretched the capacity of the U.S. Army and
Marines. The leverage American military strength could give the nation's
diplomacy had been reduced.

The United States and Russia still had thousands of nuclear weapons deployed, even though there was no rational use for them. The agreement with
Russia concluded in 2002 to reduce the number of these weapons on station had no means of verification. Proliferation of nuclear weapons to other
countries, held in check during the Cold War, had become a heightened concern. The world had made no progress in negotiating steps to verify that a
country was not producing biological weapons. Al-Qaeda maintained a base
of operations in Pakistan, continued to recruit terrorists, and had begun to
penetrate Afghanistan again.

NATO had continued to expand its jurisdiction to the east, making the
United States less safe, not more. An expanding NATO had increased Amer-

ica's exposure to risk by adding countries to its security guarantee, had weakened NATO (because the more members it had, the more its unity was challenged by competing national interests), and had alarmed Russia and made it less willing to cooperate fully with the United States. Even though NATO supported the American invasion of Afghanistan, the willingness of NATO allies to contribute troops to the battle there waned as the fighting dragged on and serious questions about American strategy arose. Secretary of Defense Robert Gates was reduced to public pleading with our NATO allies for an extra thousand or two troops in the spring of 2008, and was rebuffed. By the end of the year, plans were developed to shift up to thirty thousand U.S. troops from Iraq to Afghanistan so that the heaviest combat missions would be conducted primarily by Americans.

In the Middle East, Israel and the Palestinians seemed even further from agreement than they had been when George W. Bush took office. In fact, a hot war, with casualties in the thousands, was under way between Israel and the Hamas leadership in Gaza in the final days of 2008 and the first weeks of 2009. The president gave little personal attention to the initiative launched in his name in 2007 to promote peace negotiations between Israel and the Palestinian Authority, and the effort came to naught despite numerous visits to the area by Secretary of State Rice.

Iran continued to enrich uranium, which in time could give it the capability of producing nuclear weapons. Nevertheless, the administration relied on threats and sanctions to deter Iran and refused direct talks on the whole range of issues, ignoring the recommendation of the Iraq Study Group that it convened in 2006.* Bush and his advisers unwisely passed up Iranian feelers in 2001 and what seems to have been an Iranian offer to settle a wide range of issues in 2003, when American leverage was high.[5]

The U.S. removal of the Taliban in Afghanistan and of Saddam Hussein in Iraq greatly increased Iran's relative power in the region. The best time to deal diplomatically with Iran would have been before those actions, particularly the invasion of Iraq, were taken, while the cautious reformer Seyyed Mohammad Khatami was president. Instead of seeing whether Iran was

---

*A bipartisan task force headed by former secretary of state James Baker and former congressman Lee Hamilton, its members included Robert Gates, the former CIA chief and soon-to-be secretary of defense.

prepared to moderate its policies in return for more normal relations with the United States, President Bush placed Iran in an "axis of evil," conveying a scarcely veiled threat to remove the regime by force.

The Bush administration's avoidance of direct talks probably strengthened the hard-liners among the Iranian clerical regime and contributed to the election of Mahmoud Ahmadinejad as president in 2005, when more moderate politicians were barred from competing. As Christoph Bertram, the former head of the German Institute for International and Security Affairs, observed in a study published in August 2008: "Since 1979, external pressure from the West has constantly strengthened the regime's hold on power internally. One reason for President Ahmadinejad deliberately opting for confrontation with the West is that this has now come to serve as a mainstay of the regime, diverting attention from the unsatisfactory state of the economy, justifying repression of dissidents and restraining reformist forces."[6] Upon his election, Ahmadinejad set out to solidify his power by anti-Israel and anti-American rants, and by insisting on developing Iran's capacity to enrich uranium, which could eventually give it the fissile material needed to develop nuclear weapons.

Ahmadinejad's reckless rhetoric was seized on by the neocons and American supremacists who were still roaming the world looking for monsters to destroy (to adopt the words John Quincy Adams used to describe what the United States of his day would *not* do). But once the United States was stuck in Iraq and desperate for adequate forces to quell a resurgent Taliban in Afghanistan, it was in no position to use force against Iran. In fact, Iran was capable of inflicting severe damage on American and allied interests if the United States or Israel decided to strike its nuclear facilities. Iran could, for example, make it exceedingly difficult (if possible at all) to move oil tankers safely out of the Persian Gulf through the Strait of Hormuz.

The net effect of neocon hysteria and the official policy of diplomatic isolation was to increase Iran's incentive to develop a nuclear weapons capability and to reduce the willingness of other countries to apply severe economic sanctions that would have raised the cost to Iran of continuing its development of uranium enrichment technology. The Ahmadinejads in Iran would probably welcome a military strike, because it would enhance the position of the most anti-Western elements in the country and provide a powerful argument for recruiting terrorists to attack American and Israeli interests.

Although problems abounded, some important changes took place in Bush's foreign policy toward the end of his second term. Although isolation of Iran remained official policy, Secretary of State Rice persuaded the president to reject Cheney's advice and alter tactics toward North Korea. Threats and a refusal to deal directly with the Kim Jong-il regime during Bush's first term resulted in North Korea creating and testing a nuclear device. Rice changed the approach the White House had dictated when she was the president's assistant for national security.* Instead of trying to isolate North Korea and force a "regime change"—implicit in Bush's 2002 reference to an "axis of evil"—she resumed direct negotiation with North Korea. Christopher Hill, one of America's most able professional diplomats, was assigned to take on the frustrating task of dealing with the erratic and frequently duplicitous North Koreans. His patient diplomacy brought about, for a time, an end to plutonium production in North Korea and a temporary halt to its nuclear weapons program.

Relations with China improved following the confrontations early in George W. Bush's first term. The administration handled the potentially explosive issue of Taiwan well. By discouraging Taiwanese efforts to declare independence from China but supplying some modern military equipment to Taiwan, the administration helped keep relations peaceful between the two antagonistic Chinese governments. Meanwhile, Beijing and Taipei made some progress in developing economic ties and increasing travel between the island and mainland China.

Relations with European governments improved during President Bush's second term, although publics in Western European countries remained skeptical of the war in Iraq, unqualified U.S. support for Israel, and the use of torture against detainees. When they were hit with the financial crisis in 2008, they—not entirely unfairly—blamed it on American mismanagement of the world financial system.

The United States received some credit in Africa for assistance to those

---

*The While House ordered the State Department to terminate negotiations with North Korea, rejecting the policy favored by Secretary of State Colin Powell.

fighting AIDS and for humanitarian assistance, but was unable to summon
effective international support to deal effectively with genocide in Darfur,
factional warfare and piracy in Somalia, civil war in the eastern Congo, or an
increasingly violent dictatorship in Zimbabwe.

Relations with Latin America as a whole were neither better nor worse
than they were when the Bush administration took office. President Bush
continued sanctions against Cuba that hampered human contacts and the
transmittal of money to relatives, and thus limited the possibility of American influence on the political transition that would follow Fidel Castro's
death. Hugo Chávez's Venezuela, Daniel Ortega's Nicaragua, and Evo
Morales's Bolivia were irritants, but they made little headway in their efforts
to build an anti-U.S. bloc in the hemisphere. All had serious disputes with
their neighbors and were weakened by internal divisions.

In sum, the positive alterations in U.S foreign policy toward the end of the
Bush administration slowed the decline of American influence to some degree, without compensating fully for the damage caused by the invasion of
Iraq and the other errors and excesses I have described. Even so, nothing
was more dangerous to future American security than the mismanagement
of relations with Russia. None of the steps that are essential for reducing
the threat nuclear weapons present to the world can be taken without the cooperation of Russia, yet the Bush administration dealt with Russia in ways
that made it difficult for any Russian leader to cooperate. As a result, U.S.
relations with Russia were at their lowest point since the end of the Cold
War when George W. Bush's second term ended.

The Russia Factor

The Clinton administration had done much to alienate Russian opinion with its policies of expanding NATO eastward and bombing Serbia
without Security Council approval, but President Bush tried, from his first
meeting with President Vladimir Putin in June 2001, to establish a comfortable personal relationship with the Russian leader. Following their
meeting, Bush told the press that he had "looked the man in the eye" and
"was able to get a sense of his soul." Subsequently, Bush was ridiculed for
his apparent naïveté, but those who scoffed ignored the fact that he had

praised Putin for such things as being "straightforward" and "committed to his country."*

Most journalists, along with the readers of their reports, seemed to have missed an important nuance: whenever political leaders speak of a "frank dialogue," as Bush did, it means they had arguments. And indeed, although both Putin and Bush praised each other following their meeting, they referred to serious differences of opinion on several issues. In Bush's case it was the war Russia was waging against separatists in Chechnya (where, incidentally, Al-Qaeda was active) and the restrictions on press freedom in Russia; in Putin's case it was NATO expansion, American plans for missile defense, and foreign criticism of Russia's internal policies.

Some three months later, on September 11, 2001, these differences seemed to be pushed aside. When the twin towers and the Pentagon were attacked, Putin was the first foreign leader to call Bush and offer his support in the fight against Al-Qaeda terrorists. He saw the attack on the United States as an opening that could be used to build a closer relationship with the United States. Al-Qaeda was as much an enemy of Russia as of the United States.

Putin was as good as his word, cooperating with the United States as it went after the Taliban and Osama bin Laden in Afghanistan, sharing intelligence, permitting military overflights, and not opposing temporary American bases in two of the former Soviet republics of Central Asia, bases that were needed to support the U.S. invasion of Afghanistan.

Putin went further to signal that Russia was prepared for more cooperative relations with the United States. He closed the Russian base in Cuba, which had been maintained throughout the 1990s, and also the naval base at Cam Ranh Bay in Vietnam.

What did he get in return? The United States continued to promote NATO expansion eastward, to the three Baltic countries, Slovakia, and Slovenia, and subsequently to Romania and Bulgaria. Then there were plans to move U.S. military bases from Germany into Romania and Bulgaria. The United

---

*The words quoted were spoken in the following context: "I looked the man in the eye. I found him to be very straightforward and trustworthy. We had a very good dialogue. I was able to get a sense of his soul; a man deeply committed to his country and the best interests of his country. And I appreciated so very much the frank dialogue." (White House press release, June 16, 2001)

States withdrew from the Anti-Ballistic Missile Treaty, which had been the cornerstone of the structure on which agreements to reduce nuclear weapons rested. It was not necessary to discard the ABM Treaty in order to develop missile defenses, since Putin had offered to amend the treaty to permit building such defenses against rogue states.

After leaving the ABM Treaty, the United States began deploying missile defenses and making plans to modernize its nuclear weapons and even develop some new ones. The Russians then announced that they, too, were developing new, improved nuclear weapons.

Although the Bush administration agreed that there should be further reductions of strategic nuclear weapons, it refused to conclude an agreement with verification provisions and announced that some missiles removed from active service would not be destroyed, as had been required in previous agreements, but held in storage in case they, or their parts, were needed later. The United States announced a national security doctrine that seemed to permit it to invade any country that it judged a potential threat and a space defense doctrine that spoke of ensuring U.S. dominance of outer space. It then invaded Iraq against Russian, French, and German objections, claiming falsely that Iraq still harbored weapons of mass destruction.

For a while President Putin took all of this with only occasional and muted complaints. Although he opposed the U.S. invasion of Iraq, he did not try to rally other countries against it as did French president Jacques Chirac. Putin recognized Russia's weakness and was determined to reassert Moscow's authority over the country and to end the downward economic spiral. He vowed to start Russia on a course that would allow it, in a few decades, to catch up with the European standard of living and to restore its ability to have a voice in decisions that affected its well-being and security. Successful integration into the globalizing world economy would require, among other things, joining the World Trade Organization (WTO). But negotiations were drawn out, with demands made on Russia, particularly by the United States, that exceeded those imposed on China, which had become a member in 2001.*

*In fact, the U.S. Congress developed a habit of moving goalposts it had erected. In 1974 Congress passed the Jackson-Vanik amendment to the Trade Act, which prohibited offering normal trade relations to any "non-market-economy country" that restricted emigration. The purpose was to force the Soviet Union to allow its Jewish citi-

The rapid increase in energy prices that occurred shortly after Putin became president of Russia in 2000 allowed him to restore much of Russia's economic clout without waiting for membership in the WTO or attracting as much private investment from foreigners as has flooded into China over the past decade. Russia became the second largest exporter of oil and Europe's principal supplier of natural gas. For eight years Russia maintained a highly favorable foreign exchange balance, a budgetary surplus, and an economy growing at something like 7 percent a year—at least until the financial crisis in 2008. The monetary largess from energy and other commodity exports enabled Putin to tighten his control over the nation and to bring Russia into world councils as a power to be reckoned with.

The first public sign that Putin was confident enough of Russia's restored power to speak in public about his frustrations with American policy occurred in February 2007, when he delivered a blistering critique of American "unipolar" behavior at a conference in Munich, Germany. He charged that the United States had "overstepped its national borders in every way," imposing on other nations its "economic, political, cultural and educational policies."

His words were particularly bitter regarding NATO enlargement: "I think it obvious that NATO expansion does not have any relation with the modernization of the alliance itself or with ensuring security in Europe. On the contrary, it represents a serious provocation that reduces the level of mutual trust." He asked, "What happened to the assurances our western partners made after the dissolution of the Warsaw Pact?" This time, he cited not James Baker's private words to Gorbachev and Shevardnadze, but a public statement by Manfred Wörner when he was NATO secretary-general. Putin recalled that Wörner had stated in a speech in Brussels in 1990: "The fact that we are ready not to place a NATO army outside of German territory gives the Soviet Union a firm security guarantee."

---

zens to leave the country if they wished. In the 1970s it may have helped increase Jewish emigration from the USSR, but from 1990 the Soviet Union removed the barriers to emigration, and the Russian Federation has never had such restrictions. Nevertheless, the Jackson-Vanik amendment is still on the books, and while it is, Russia cannot obtain membership in the WTO.

He also condemned U.S. plans to place elements of a missile defense system in Poland and the Czech Republic, warning that it could lead to a renewed arms race, and listed other grievances in regard to U.S. and Western policies, including attempts to cloak hostile acts under the cover of "democracy promotion." His speech was not entirely critical, however, since he partially balanced his complaints with praise for cooperation with the United States in such areas as production of nuclear fuel and efforts to prevent further proliferation of nuclear weapons.[7]

Secretary of Defense Robert Gates responded to the sharp tone of the Russian president's speech with the remark that Putin's words reminded him of the Cold War, and that "one cold war is enough." He vowed to go to Moscow and explain that American policy was not directed against Russian interests. In fact, he did so, but the policies that had angered Putin did not change. The problem with Russia was not lack of communication, but a refusal by the Bush administration to take Russian interests and attitudes seriously. Plans to deploy missile interceptors in Poland continued, and the United States vigorously pressed its NATO allies to approve "action plans" to bring both Georgia and Ukraine into NATO.

U.S.-Russian relations were subjected to a severe test in August 2008 when Russian forces invaded the Georgian republic, occupied the breakaway regions of South Ossetia and Abkhazia, and then gave them official recognition as independent countries. The Russian action was widely condemned as outright aggression against a small democratic country. Questions were raised, particularly in Europe and the United States, as to whether Russia aimed to reclaim parts of the erstwhile Soviet empire by force. Nevertheless, it soon became clear that the initial picture conveyed by Western media of the fighting between Georgia and Russia was incomplete, and in some respects distorted.

When we look carefully at the principal causes of U.S.-Russian friction we see that each issue has deep, intertwined historical roots that are often ignored in media reporting of events. We cannot make an informed judgment regarding the Russian government's intentions and capabilities without understanding the background of several issues that have influenced and will determine Russia's willingness to cooperate with the United States and its NATO allies. As Putin suggested in his speech in

Munich, the most important sources of Russian concern include relations of Georgia and Ukraine with NATO; missile defense, space weapons, and nuclear weapons policy; and the attempts by the United States to undermine governments in the former Soviet space under the cloak of "democracy promotion."

Georgia and Ukraine

When Russian forces invaded Georgian territory on the night of August 8, 2008, Western media reported it as if it were unprovoked aggression. Only later did the fact emerge in some of the media that Russian forces were responding to a Georgian attack on the South Ossetian capital of Tskhinvali the previous night. The Georgian attack violated a cease-fire and killed Russian peacekeepers who were stationed in the area by international agreement. Once they entered the fray, the Russian troops not only occupied South Ossetia and Abkhazia, the other separatist enclave, but continued well into the rest of Georgia. They substantially destroyed the Georgian armed forces, which had been equipped and trained by the United States. Their intervention was brutal, produced unnecessary civilian casualties, and resulted in uprooting tens of thousands of Georgians from their homes, at least temporarily.

I was deeply saddened by the sudden outbreak of this conflict because I know Georgia well, admire its people and culture, and have learned enough of its unique language—not related to any of the major language families of the world—to have read two speeches in it when visiting Tbilisi, the capital city. My wife and I have visited the country many times, during the Soviet era and since. We have close friends there and counted the former Georgian president Eduard Shevardnadze one of them. When we spent time with Mikheil Saakashvili in the 1990s, before he was elected president of Georgia, he had nothing but praise for Shevardnadze and, as a member of Georgia's parliament, seemed devoted to making sure that Georgia's new constitution and laws were fully democratic.

What shocked me in August 2008 was not so much the Russian invasion, which I deplored because of its unnecessary brutality, but the reckless decision by the president of Georgia to attack South Ossetia when it should have been obvious that this was precisely what the Russians were waiting for as an excuse to "teach a lesson" to the hostile Georgians—and to their American backers.

The fighting in South Ossetia brought back poignant memories from the winter of 1990–1991, when, from my post in Moscow, I learned that Georgian forces under their newly elected leader, Zviad Gamsakhurdia, had besieged Tskhinvali and forced tens of thousands of Ossetians to flee to their ethnic kinsmen in Russian North Ossetia. Nevertheless, the Ossetians managed, with help from other Caucasian peoples, to hold off the Georgians and retain control of those parts of South Ossetia populated largely by Ossetians.*

When the Georgians first attacked South Ossetia, the Soviet Union still existed, but Gorbachev was beset with so many problems—his opponents were already considering a coup to remove him—that he refrained from any attempt to bring Gamsakhurdia's rampaging Georgians under control.[8] But our embassy in Moscow reported to Washington what was taking place in Georgia, and that is why George H. W. Bush warned non-Russian republics against "suicidal nationalism" in his speech in Kiev on August 1, 1991. He had Georgia on his mind.

During the winter of 1991–1992, as the Soviet Union collapsed, the Georgian violence against South Ossetia morphed into a civil war of Georgians against Georgians. Gamsakhurdia was deposed by dissident Georgian forces, and when they were unable to bring order to the country they invited Shevardnadze, who was living in Moscow where he had been Soviet foreign minister, to return to Georgia and take charge. Shevardnadze was immediately elected chairman of the Georgian parliament, but he was unable to prevent Defense Minister Tengiz Kitovani from taking a Georgian force to Sukhumi, the Abkhazian capital, and attacking the Abkhazian parliament.

---

*The Ossetians speak a language unrelated to Georgian. Few know Georgian since their first language is Ossetian and their second language Russian. One of the Ossetian complaints was the attempt by authorities in Tbilisi not only to revoke South Ossetia's autonomy but also to make the Georgian language the sole official language of all areas in independent Georgia. During the Soviet period both Georgian and Russian were official throughout Georgia, and Ossetian was recognized alongside Russian and Georgian in South Ossetia.

The Georgians were then forced out of Sukhumi by Abkhazians supported by Chechens, other peoples from the North Caucasus, and Russian air force units near the border.* Following the expulsion of Kitovani's forces from Sukhumi, more than two hundred thousand ethnic Georgians were driven out of or fled from their homes in Abkhazia.[9]

From 1993 until 2008 there was an uneasy peace, marred at times by local fighting on the borders of both secessionist enclaves. While Shevardnadze was president of Georgia, the Georgian government refrained from making military threats but tried to regain control of the dissident regions by negotiation. However, when Saakashvili replaced him as head of state, he began a major expansion of Georgian military forces, with strong American support. Georgia's military spending went from $84 million in 2004 to $339 million in 2006 and reached a billion dollars in the budget approved in July 2008. Georgian relations with Russia deteriorated as its military spending grew and sporadic clashes occurred in Abkhazia and South Ossetia; Russia began to boycott most Georgian goods under one pretext or another and offered Russian citizenship to South Ossetians and Abkhazians who desired it.

By the time the brief Georgian-Russian war occurred in August 2008, none of the parties to the conflict could boast of clean hands. All had at times used force in ways that law-abiding democratic countries are supposed to avoid. Georgia had tried to do to its minorities what it accused Russia of doing to it. The view that the Russian invasion was purely a case of Russian aggression against small, struggling, democratic Georgia was as distorted and one-sided as was the Russian claim that it was merely repulsing criminal Georgian attacks against Russian peacekeepers and ethnic groups trying to exercise their right of self-determination.

The United States and its NATO allies had, in effect, set the stage over the previous decade for the Russian reaction. In 1999, NATO bombed Serbia over human rights abuses in its sovereign territory without U.N. ap-

---

*A "Confederation of Mountain Peoples of the Caucasus" had been formed by several non-Russian groups in the North Caucasus. Their aim was to form a republic independent of Russia, and they needed Abkhazia in order to have a port on the Black Sea. Several of these leaders subsequently led the Chechen rebellion against Russia.

proval. Then, in 2008, the U.S. and several of its NATO allies officially recognized Kosovo as an independent country, even though it was not independent in the full sense. It was, in fact, a ward of U.N.-authorized forces
from NATO and the European Union, which must still occupy it to keep
order. Russia protested plans to recognize the independence of Kosovo and
warned that Russia considered other "frozen conflicts," South Ossetia and
Abkhazia in particular, comparable situations. The Russian government
would argue that it has simply followed the example set by the treatment of
Kosovo and Serbia by the United States and its NATO allies in its treatment
of South Ossetia, Abkhazia, and Georgia.

According to public opinion polls, more than 80 percent of Russian citizens approved their government's action in invading Georgia. The intensity of feeling was fueled by the conviction, spread by the Russian media,
that the United States was using Georgia to establish its domination of the
southern Caucasus, with its energy resources and pipeline routes. Russian
foreign minister Sergei Lavrov stated that the Georgian attack on Tskhinvali
was the culmination of an "American project," and many Russians believed
that the United States was using Georgia to gain military control of the
strategic key to the Caucasus.

In fact, the State Department had attempted to dissuade Saakashvili from
reacting to Russian and Ossetian provocations, but one does not have to be
a conspiracy theorist to understand why it would seem to Russians that
Saakashvili was acting as an American pawn. He was educated in the United
States (law degree from Columbia University), had used American military
trainers for his American-equipped, rapidly growing army, and had participated in the American-led coalition in Iraq, sending two thousand troops to
assist in the occupation. Saakashvili visited Washington frequently and was
on close personal terms with both Bush and Cheney.

The Bush administration suspended implementation of an important
agreement with Russia for cooperation on nuclear fuel, but at the next meeting of NATO announced that it would not push for a decision at that time
regarding membership for Georgia and Ukraine because of the opposition
of Germany and other NATO allies. Meanwhile, the Russian government
remained unapologetic regarding its invasion of Georgia. President Dmitri
Medvedev made clear that Russia expected the world to acknowledge that it

had a right to a sphere of influence (sometimes called a "sphere of special interest") in the region.

Whether or not Russia could properly claim special rights in the former Soviet Union, it should have been clear that NATO membership was neither in NATO's interest nor in Georgia's. Within Georgia, opposition to President Saakashvili grew and was joined by several leading politicians who had been his supporters before the August war with Russia.

If it is unwise for Georgia to become a member of NATO, it would be tantamount to suicide for any Ukrainian government to do so unless NATO itself becomes a different organization. Well over half of Ukrainian citizens oppose the country's entry into NATO. To understand why, one must bear in mind that Ukraine's biggest security problem is not Russian "imperialism" but political, social, economic, and linguistic divisions inside the country.

A few years after Ukraine became an independent country, I traveled to Kiev (Kyiv in Ukrainian) with several other veterans of the National Security Council in Washington to advise Ukrainian officials on the way national security bureaucracies are organized. When we described the American system we were told that it would not suit Ukraine. Our Ukrainian interlocutors explained that whereas the National Security Council in Washington deals with external threats, in Ukraine the main threat comes not from outside the country but from inside. And then we were shown a map of Ukraine with the regions marked according to the vote in the previous national election. Most of the west of Ukraine, up to Kiev, was one color; the east and south, including the Crimean peninsula, was another.[10]

The political division in Ukraine was much more pronounced than that between so-called red states and blue states in American elections, where the breakdown might typically be 55 percent for one party and 45 percent for the other. In Ukraine, the western provinces tended to back one group of parties by 80 percent or more; in the eastern and southern areas the vote swang the other way, with 75 to 90 percent voting for members of the opposing coalition.

The differences go deeper than preferences for political parties and voting habits. The people in western Ukraine generally speak the Ukrainian language at home, while those in the east and south are more comfortable with Russian or a dialect that combines features of both. There are also religious divisions: Galicia in the west is predominately Uniate (the Eastern-rite Catholic church), whereas Ukrainians elsewhere tend to belong to one of the Orthodox confessions—if they are religious at all.

The sources of these divisions reach deep in Ukrainian history: the western provinces, where Ukrainian cultural nationalism is strongest, were never part of the Russian Empire. They were allowed to develop the Ukrainian language and national culture relatively unimpeded when they were part of the Austro-Hungarian Empire. When that empire was dismantled following World War I, the western provinces of Ukraine were included in Poland, until Stalin forced them into the Soviet Union following his pact with Hitler. People in the other areas of Ukraine have been under much heavier Russian influence for centuries and are more comfortable with it. In the Crimea, some 60 percent of the population is ethnic Russian, many of them descendants of the Russian settlers brought in after Catherine the Great conquered the peninsula from vassals of the Ottoman Turks in the eighteenth century.

There are also differences in the regional economies. The east had more industrial development during the Soviet period than the west, and the Black Sea littoral in the south lived off shipping, the naval base at Sevastopol, and tourism in the Crimean resorts, where both tsars and commissars passed their vacation time.

Ukraine became independent of the Soviet Union in 1991 by a massively favorable vote in both east and west (but only barely favorable in the Crimea), when the nationalist politicians in the west made common cause with the Communist *apparatchiks* of the east, who feared losing their control over the economy if Gorbachev's reforms continued. Ukrainian political disputes have congealed along these regional fissures ever since Ukraine became independent.

The Crimean peninsula is an area of particular sensitivity. The Crimea was considered an integral part of Russia from the late eighteenth century until 1954, when Nikita Khrushchev decided to transfer it from the Russian Socialist Federated Soviet Republic (RSFSR) to the Ukrainian Soviet Socialist Republic. Since the Communist Party ruled all the republics, this seemed at the time nothing more than a symbolic gesture, but it became the basis for including the Crimea in independent Ukraine. Ukrainian nationalists treat the Crimea today as if it had been sacred Ukrainian soil for centuries.

Despite political pressure in Russia to reclaim the Crimea, the Russian government, up to now, has consistently affirmed its respect for Ukraine's territorial integrity, including the Crimean peninsula. The Russian Black Sea Fleet shares Sevastopol as its base with the Ukrainian Black Sea Fleet, the two countries having divided the Soviet Black Sea Fleet between them. However, the Russian lease on the base is due to expire in 2017 and the current Ukrainian government has announced that it does not intend to renew it.

Ukrainian membership in NATO could cause the residents of both the Crimea and Russia to demand a return of the peninsula to Russia. Given the ethnic composition of the population and the economic value of the Russian base, it is likely that the Crimean population would opt for Russia if given the chance. Once again, as with Georgia, there is a potential conflict between two valid principles: territorial integrity and self-determination. It is in nobody's interest to stoke passions that divide rather than unite Ukrainian citizens.

Missile Defense and Nuclear Weapons

American plans to place ballistic missile interceptors in Poland and radars to guide them in the Czech Republic have also drawn strong opposition from Russia. This project is a bad idea that should be abandoned by the Obama administration. There are several reasons why it is not in America's interest to plan these installations at this time. First, the technology is not proven and it is not known whether it will work or not. Second, the alleged threat the missiles would counter—a missile attack on Europe from Iran— is highly dubious. Iran does not have missiles that can reach America's European allies, and even if it did, it has no motivation to attack countries in Europe. And third, Russia will probably refuse to continue reducing its nuclear weapons if the bases are established in Poland and the Czech Republic without its approval.

Russia has offered to cooperate in developing and deploying a defense to protect against missiles from "problem states" like North Korea and Iran. A cooperative defense located much closer to the countries that could be a threat will be much more effective than the handful of missiles planned for Poland. Among other considerations, one should bear in mind that it is much easier to intercept a missile when its rocket is in the slow-rising boost phase than later when the warhead separates from its booster. Russian territory and that of countries friendly to it are much closer to countries like Iran and North Korea than are Poland and the Czech Republic.

Deploying missile defenses in Eastern Europe will also militate against the sort of cooperation we need from Russia to continue to reduce nuclear arsenals in a reliable, safe, and verifiable way. With over 90 percent of the world's nuclear weapons, the U.S. and Russia will not be successful in stemming nuclear proliferation until they carry out their obligation under the Non-Proliferation Treaty to reduce their own arsenals. There is no more important security issue for the United States than reducing the threat of nuclear weapons, and it is folly to implement policies that, for no good reason, persuade the other major nuclear power not to cooperate.

Democracy or Hypocrisy?

One of the complaints former president Vladimir Putin and current president Dmitri Medvedev have made of the Bush administration, and of the American information media, has been their criticism of what has been called Russia's backtracking on democracy. There is no question that Putin and his circle in the Kremlin—many, like Putin, are former officers of the KGB—have increased their control over most newspapers and central television, made it difficult for political parties not allied with the Kremlin to operate, and kept key segments of the judicial system under political control rather than promoting its independence. These and other moves seriously damaged institutions necessary for a democracy to flourish.

It is not correct, however, to label these unfortunate developments a retreat from democracy. Russia's condition was closer to anarchy than democracy in the 1990s. It is also misleading to say, as some have, that Russia is returning to Soviet-style rule. That is not the case; many of the freedoms that were gained in the 1990s are still intact, including the rights to travel abroad and to own property.

Supporters of Putin and Medvedev point out that they won the support of some 70 percent of the voters in elections that were not fraudulent, even if not totally fair. It is inconceivable that any of the potential candidates who seemed more inclined to respect the rules of Western democracy could have won, or come close to winning, even the freest and most openly competitive elections. Most Russian citizens were turned off by the word "democracy" because it was used to label the chaotic, kleptocratic regime they suffered under in the 1990s. They sought stability, predictability, a stronger hand to curb excesses, and economic growth. Thanks to high energy prices, Putin was able to provide all four until the financial crisis of 2008. His success in this regard ensured his popularity—and Russian resentment when foreign politicians with far weaker popular support passed judgment on his policies.

I do not defend or excuse the authoritarian tendencies in Russian politics. I believe they ultimately will weaken Russia and hamper its development. But those are judgments for Russians to make, and it does not help if outsiders with different traditions and a different historical experience presume to tell Russians what is good for them. This annoys and offends rather than contributing to positive change.

It is particularly damaging if support for democracy seems invidious or hypocritical. Russians ask how it is that their "backsliding on democracy" has attracted so much more attention than the authoritarian rule of the Communist Party in China, which has been more oppressive than latter-day Russian authoritarians. Statements such as those by Vice President Cheney, who in 2007 criticized the lack of democracy in Russia but praised the state of democracy in Kazakhstan, struck knowledgeable persons as ludicrous. (President Nursultan Nazarbayev of Kazakhstan has suppressed his political opposition as thoroughly as the Russian government sidelined potential competitors. Nazarbayev tolerated the opposition, even encouraged it at times when Gorbachev was running the Soviet Union and he was the Communist Party chief in his republic, but suppressed all opposition as soon as Kazakhstan was independent and he had the power to do so.)*

To Russians, statements such as those the vice president made reek of hypocrisy and double standards—and not only that, but malevolence as well, for they seem to be designed to denigrate Russian national honor, to reduce

---

*I often met both with Nazarbayev and with opposition politicians in Kazakhstan when I was U.S. ambassador in Moscow. At that time, Nazarbayev seemed more inclined to support democratic movements than his predecessors in the Communist Party leadership.

Russian influence in former Soviet republics, and to curry favor with local rulers who sit on abundant hydrocarbon deposits.

Most Russians considered the "color revolutions" that swept Georgia, Ukraine, and Kyrgyzstan between 2003 and 2005 the fruit of conspiracies fomented by Western countries in order to replace Russian influence with that of the West. The sinister interpretation many Russians entertained was not in fact accurate. The demonstrations that led to political change were in response to real abuses, in most cases election fraud. Nevertheless, foreigners and local militants financed by foreign organizations played a prominent role in organizing demonstrations that brought down existing governments. In both Georgia and Ukraine, the winners proclaimed their allegiance to the West and began to talk of NATO membership. The Ukrainian coalition that triumphed in the elections following the "Orange Revolution" broke up within months amid charges of corruption hurled in every direction. Ukraine has not had a stable and lasting government since, with coalitions ruling for a few months and then falling apart. Elections may have become marginally more honest, but they have tended to divide rather than unite Ukrainians because they have been used by power brokers and oligarchs to promote their private agendas.

Given the history of the Brezhnev Doctrine, which Gorbachev discarded before the Soviet Union collapsed, it is easy to see why Russians (and many others) are skeptical of the American goal of promoting "democracy" everywhere in the world. To them, spreading democracy, particularly when force is employed, looks suspiciously like the Soviet effort to support "socialism" in order to create client states. When American policy seems to favor dictators if that is deemed convenient (think Egypt, Saudi Arabia, and Musharraf's Pakistan) and to use slogans of democracy to undermine governments it does not like, Russians, along with many others, will view the policy of "democratization" as nothing more than a cynical instrument to weaken and remove governments that resist American dominance.

Pitfalls of Democracy Promotion

Writing in *Foreign Affairs* during her fourth year as secretary of state, Dr. Condoleezza Rice argued eloquently that democracy promotion "must be an urgent component of our national interest," and that "in the broader Middle East, we recognize that freedom and democracy are the only ideas that can, over time, lead to just and lasting stability, especially in Afghanistan and Iraq."[11] This undoubtedly sounds good to most Americans: what can be a nobler task, or one more suited to America's many virtues, than spreading the benefits of democracy in the world, and in the Middle East in particular, where there is so much conflict and misery?

It sounds like a good idea if you don't give the question much thought, don't know much about the area where democracy is to be implanted, and have not given serious attention to how the United States is going to manage a transition to democracy in other countries without creating more problems than it solves. The problem with democracy promotion as a major goal of foreign policy is not merely that it can be misunderstood, as it perhaps has been by Russia, and therefore hampers protection of vital national interests, but that it encourages unfounded expectations and can be used to justify policies and practices that make the world less peaceful and less safe.

The problem begins with defining democracy. A cursory check of standard reference works will find no universally accepted definition. The Greek roots of the word we use means rule by the people, but how do you define "the people"? Is that everybody, or do some have more rights than others? Do they rule directly, as for example, in a New England town meeting where the residents will vote whether to spend tax money on tires for an old fire truck and whether to permit chicken coops in the backyards of people who live on Main Street?* Obviously, this form is impossible for political units much larger than a village, so normally we think of democracy as "representative," with representatives chosen by a vote. But then, who gets to vote, and for what level of representation? What powers will the representatives have? Majority rule is generally accepted as a basic principle, but are there limits on what a majority can do, or decisions that require more than a simple majority? What are the requirements, if any, for running for office?

Normally, these questions are set forth in a written document, a constitution, but not always. (Great Britain operates a democracy on the basis of

---

*These were actual issues at a town meeting in Norwich, Vermont, in which I participated when I was a resident in 1955. The propositions were sharply contested, but I voted in favor of both. One of the local farmers who opposed the zoning restriction spoke out bitterly after the vote was taken. "You professors are driving us out like we did the Indians!"

an unwritten constitution, dependent on the force of custom and precedent, which can however be overridden by Parliament.) How are constitutions drawn up, approved, changed? How much power does a majority have over a minority? How does a country ensure that its constitution is actually observed? (Stalin's constitution was, in principle, one of the most democratic in the world, but it was a meaningless facade obscuring the totalitarian system that operated behind the false front.)

This is only a start, for the questions are endless, and we are left with a variant of Justice Potter Stewart's observation about pornography: that he could not define it but he knew it when he saw it. Therein lurks the problem of subjectivity, for one's conception of democracy will be heavily influenced by one's culture and life experience. Americans assume that democracy is what they have: a representative government that protects the rights of individuals and minorities, limits the power of government, structures government in three independent branches, and elects by majority rule most of the people who make the laws and execute them.

Others may look at it differently or give different weight to the various principles. Does government have a role to play in providing equality of opportunity? To what extent should government be expected to promote and support social harmony and economic fairness? Most people will assume that democracy takes the forms they are familiar with if they are in a state that calls itself a democracy and it works to their satisfaction. If it doesn't work to their satisfaction, they will claim either than they do not live in a democracy, or that democracy itself is no good.

Democracy is, in fact, an amorphous concept, particularly since most (maybe all) democracies permit a relaxation of the normal rules in cases of national emergency, giving the executive something similar to autocratic power. And then there is the problem of what constitutes a genuine national emergency, and once again we are off in a mine field of conflicting principles. A functioning democracy is hard enough to achieve at home without trying to construct one that will work for others.

Concepts of democracy differ in different cultures, and no country measures up perfectly to any definition of democracy. In democracies, the most senior officials are elected, but is a country a democracy if its political system allows a candidate who received fewer popular votes than his opponent to become president? If the constitution of a democracy specifies that only the legislature can vote a declaration of war, is that country still a democracy if the president declares that the country is at war? Does a democracy knowingly and deliberately violate international covenants it has signed and ratified? If democracies do not do these things, then the United States itself has not acted consistently as a democracy during the Bush-Cheney administration, and also at many other times in its history.

We may concede that occasional temporary deviations from ideal democratic procedure do not invalidate a country's claim to be a democracy. Nobody and no country is perfect, and we can't let that stymie an effort to improve the world. As Secretary of State Rice would argue, the United States must promote democracy because only democracy will ensure that countries live in peace with one another and resolve their disputes without violence.

Political scientists call this the theory of the "democratic peace." Democracies don't fight other democracies, it is said. But is this really true? What is the evidence for it? How long has humanity been blessed with enough countries with democratic forms of government to test this hypothesis? Actually, not very many, and such evidence as exists is often based on circular reasoning. In other words, if two countries fight each other, at least one of them must not be a democracy.

Numerous projects by political scientists have tried to test the hypothesis of the democratic peace. Virtually all of them come to the conclusion that democracy is a gradual process and that countries are more prone to violence when they start democratizing than they were when they were under authoritarian rule.[12] This would suggest that promoting democratization— if a country can do that—would lead initially to more international violence rather than less. Also, a democratic country can backslide: there were few countries in Europe more democratic in the 1920s than Weimar Germany, but that did not prevent Hitler from coming to power legally, using democratic processes before he eliminated them.

There is also no evidence for the claim, which one often hears from neocons and American supremacists, that the spread of democracy "increases American power."* John M. Owen IV presented a typical argument in *The National Interest,* in 2006, when he argued that there was a "close connection between the growth of American power and the spread of democracy,"

*This seems to have been the thought behind Senator John McCain's proposal for a "league of democracies" to replace the United Nations in policing the world.

assuming, apparently, that correlation equals causation, the same way the Soviet leaders were convinced that the spread of socialism after World War II enhanced Soviet power.[13] Owen, to be sure, specified that he had in mind what he variously called "settled democracies" and "mature democracies," but he ignored the fact that mature democracies do not occur overnight or as the result of foreign promotional activity. Whether partial or mature, there is no evidence at all that democracies as such strengthen American power. Both France and Germany are settled democracies, but they did not make America more powerful when it attacked Iraq. Stable democracies may well make more useful allies than dictatorships, but they will not be allies unless American policy is consistent with their interests.

Of course, Americans would like to see people in other countries live in free societies with democratic governments. But if America wants to be helpful to democratic transformations in other countries, it will concentrate its effort on strengthening international structures to deal with instability, violence, and criminal activity. The United States must also be careful to behave in a way that is consistent with the values it cherishes. Is it a democratic value to invade and occupy another country that has not posed a direct and imminent threat? Is the torture of suspects consistent with democratic values? Do democratic countries abide by agreements they have signed, such as the Geneva Convention on prisoners of war, or ignore them if they find them inconvenient? Unfortunately, the claims of success in spreading democracy in the Middle East, such as those in Secretary Rice's *Foreign Affairs* article, are very likely illusory, because the Bush administration went about democracy promotion—if that was indeed its goal—in the wrong way.

Those who wish to see the spread of responsible government in the world should recognize that a democracy must be created from the inside in a manner consistent with the culture and historical experience of the country in question. As a rule, people do not approve of foreigners playing a direct role in their political process; foreign funding of American political campaigns is illegal, and direct foreign support for an American candidate would be a political kiss of death. Americans, therefore, should be able to understand that efforts to play an active role in the political process in other countries are more likely to backfire than to produce positive results.

Misunderstanding the Twentieth Century

How is it that the United States has gotten so seriously off track in its domestic and foreign policy? I have listed many mistakes of leadership: the hubris and destructive scorched-earth politics of the 1990s, and then the mindless aggressiveness of the Bush-Cheney White House, both abroad and at home, when questions of legality and the constitutional separation of powers were too often swept aside. I cannot help wondering whether Bush and Cheney were motivated following 9/11 by a subconscious feeling of humiliation that they had failed to protect the country from foreign attack. Unwilling to admit, even to themselves, their dereliction of duty, they exaggerated the threats faced by the United States and behaved in a manner unbecoming leaders of the world's most powerful democracy. As we have seen, many of those mistakes also were products of a mistaken philosophy, or rather a set of interlocked ideological concepts, some of which were based on a deliberate misrepresentation of the factors that brought the Cold War to an end.

The Bush administration made more than its share of mistakes, but America's problem is deeper than that caused by political leaders who led the country off in the wrong direction. The American people as a whole must assume a share of responsibility for their country's predicament in 2009. Too many Americans were receptive to slogans based on exaggerations of American power, American virtue, and the value of military solutions to the nation's problems.

I have referred repeatedly to the errors induced by unfounded myths arising out of the Cold War and the mistaken judgments caused by considering every paltry dictator a potential Hitler. As we consider the record of the forty-third president, an even more profound misunderstanding comes into view. As Tony Judt put it in his history of Europe since World War II, "In the U.S., at least, we have forgotten the meaning of war."[14] Americans, he argued, have not experienced all the horrors of war on their own territory since the American Civil War, while for Europeans twentieth-century wars "signified invasion, occupation, displacement, deprivation, destruction, and mass murder. Countries that lost wars often lost population, territory, resources, security, and independence."[15] But not only that, even the "winners" emerged as losers in many respects. More significantly, they sometimes lost the peace that followed, as when World War I was followed by fascism, Nazism, communism, and World War II.

The greater European sensitivity to the damage war can inflict, even on those who "win," provides a better explanation of the reason most Europeans opposed the American-led invasion of Iraq than that offered by armchair pundits like Robert Kagan, who famously labeled Europeans as from Venus and Americans from Mars.[16] Kagan attributed the European reluctance to join the United States in military operations abroad to their relative weakness. In so doing he exaggerated that weakness and also confused a reluctance to fight unnecessary wars with a reluctance to fight altogether.

What most European opinion opposed was the resort to war that violated accepted standards of international law and was based on fraudulent arguments. America's NATO allies all initially supported the war against the Taliban and Al-Qaeda in Afghanistan. They parted company with the Bush administration only when it came to the decision to invade Iraq, and later limited cooperation with the United States in Afghanistan when they saw evidence that American strategy was not working.

Kagan was also wrong in categorizing Americans as "from Mars." While it is true that Americans will defend themselves vigorously against an enemy, and also that a president can, by misrepresenting the evidence, persuade many people that a war of choice is actually one of defense, Americans as a whole are hardly domiciled on Mars. Only some of our theoreticians, most of whom have not actually experienced war, reside that far away from earthly reality. Nor are Europeans spiritually living on Venus, as anyone who has witnessed French troops dealing with a rebellion in the Ivory Coast can testify.

Most Americans and most Europeans consider war a last resort. If there is a difference it is that, having actually experienced total war in their own countries in living memory, Europeans are more skeptical about what it can achieve than are many Americans whose understanding of the consequences of war is more selective. The American experience in Iraq, however it turns out finally, is likely to move American opinion more in the direction of European opinion when it comes to questioning the utility of invading distant countries.

Actually, Americans should rejoice if Europeans are convinced that today's many problems and tensions can best be worked out by means short of war. After all, the twentieth century was marked by two world wars, both of which started in Europe. These wars not only came close to ruining all the countries involved, but also spread to affect the whole world. If peace has finally descended on the heart of Europe for the current century—as I believe it has—then that is a matter for rejoicing, not complaining.

Kagan's analogy was based on the assumption that the world is subject to a vast struggle of good and evil, and that neither Europe nor America will be safe unless "evil" is eliminated by resolute military action. It is a view that simultaneously exaggerates threats while it prescribes a self-defeating strategy for dealing with them. The solution lies neither with Venus nor with Mars but in policies based on the wisdom of Minerva. America needs a smart policy, not one of reflexive bellicosity.

It became clear by the end of 2008 that neither market fundamentalism nor the Ayn Rand brand of libertarian economics so beloved by Alan Greenspan would survive the financial crisis. Governments would be forced to intervene in and regulate markets. It also was clear that dreams of a Pax Americana were futile. Problems would have to be solved by developing cooperation and working within international organizations, however time-consuming and frustrating that might be.

The task of bringing American policy back in line with reality in the midst of a worldwide economic crisis and an international system that had proved dysfunctional in many respects was left to America's forty-fourth president. Since 1861, no newly elected American president had faced such a wide range of serious problems as those confronting Barack Obama when he took the oath of office on January 20, 2009. He had campaigned on a slogan of change; his challenge was to convert the slogan to a practical agenda and to see that it was implemented.

PART THREE

THE TASKS AHEAD

11

Course Change

PRESIDENT BARACK OBAMA RECEIVED A mandate for change not matched in American politics since Franklin D. Roosevelt was elected in 1932. He entered office with an overwhelming electoral vote in his favor and an incoming House and Senate with Democratic majorities. The nation's desire for change was so intense in the run-up to the 2008 election that both he and his opponent, Senator John McCain, competed over who was better suited to bring it about. Neither was willing to defend the outgoing Bush administration, which seemed in 2008 to have slipped into irrelevance many months before it was scheduled to leave office.

Obama's election sent a powerful message to the rest of the world. It demonstrated that the United States was not a nation of small-minded fanatics ignorant of the world around them allied with and used by armchair imperialists who dream of dominating it. Obama's campaign pledge to talk to adversaries as well as friends increased his popularity throughout the world. Even so, the challenges the new president faced were formidable. The deepening recession in the United States, burgeoning debt, and the shattered structure of the American-led financial world forced him to concentrate, first of all, on avoiding a worldwide economic collapse and a deep depression.

The financial crisis had been brought on by a series of "bubbles" in the economy: a housing bubble, a consumer credit bubble, a bubble of highly leveraged lending. While they were in progress, they gave the illusion of economic prosperity; when they burst, they threatened to take the world's economy with them. Governments throughout the world were forced to inject capital into their banking systems and sometimes to purchase or guarantee bad debt in order to avoid a total collapse of the system. The idea that unregulated markets would control themselves and avoid excess was exposed as a mirage, as was the idea that government participation in the economy must be avoided at all costs since that is, it was alleged, a form of "socialism."

In fact, all capitalist economies are mixed economies, with greater or lesser government participation; the main goal of the political process should be to find the right mix that will sustain healthy economic growth, dampen the extremes of boom and bust, and encourage a distribution of benefits that the society in question regards as fair.

Just as the financial and economic crisis of 2008 followed a bubble of spending, inflated prices, and debt, so the foreign policy of the Bush-Cheney administration reflected another sort of bubble: a bubble of illusory American power in the world. The way the administration went to war in Iraq showed contempt for the warnings of key allies and for international law. Mindless expansion of NATO and overreliance on military solutions to the terrorist threat expanded U.S. military commitments abroad. Furthermore, the Bush-Cheney administration promulgated official doctrines of military dominance based on the conviction that the end of the Cold War had left the United States the sole "superpower," able—if necessary—to rearrange the political map of the world by its own efforts. Its doctrine exaggerated threats and involved American forces in fights with no direct bearing on true American interests.

Domestic and foreign policy are intimately connected. Policies that are usually considered domestic (taxes, education, social security, immigration, law enforcement, and health care, for example) can either cripple or support foreign policy objectives. Whether it comes from tax receipts or loans, money spent on projecting power abroad and paying interest on the national debt is money not available for domestic needs. The political challenge is to get the balance right in the face of the determined resistance of groups defending special economic or political interests.

Accumulated domestic needs make it clear that America must reduce its military footprint abroad, curb direct involvement in local disputes, negotiate cooperative approaches with other nations to deal with common problems, and strengthen the diplomatic and intelligence tools at its disposal to protect its interests in the world. As it reduces its direct involvement in other peoples' squabbles, it should be able to achieve a better balance between defense expenditure and investment in America's development. Such changes will not only save money; they will also provide the United States with a more effective foreign policy.

Some people may protest that this is a counsel of isolation, even defeatism, that risks depriving the country of military victories in its grasp. They are wrong. There is no purely military solution to the wars President Obama has inherited, and reducing military involvement does not mean reducing America's involvement in the world. Military victories cannot solve the most serious threats to the well-being of Americans because the underlying problems are political, economic, and social.

The most fundamental task of the Obama administration is to return America to leadership by example and cooperation with others rather than by threat and use of force not sanctioned by international law. During the Obama administration, the United States must rebuild and enhance the capacity of the instruments of international cooperation to deal with common threats and take advantage of opportunities to work together. This will require adapting policy in existing institutions to accommodate rising powers and integrating military operations into a broader strategy that makes maximum use of diplomacy, "soft power," and development aid before resorting, if absolutely necessary for self-defense, to military action.

Instruments

The instruments available to President Obama are out of kilter with the country's needs for a successful foreign policy. The unnecessary war in Iraq has, like all wars, produced enormous waste. American military forces were equipped and trained to defeat another army, but they were inadequately prepared and staffed to win the peace by keeping order, protecting the population, and restoring essential services.

The demands of counterinsurgency in Iraq have led to significant changes in equipment procurement and training, but there is still a tendency, particularly in the air force and navy, to concentrate on expensive weapons suitable for fighting some latter-day Soviet Union. Robert Gates seems to have made progress in adapting the army and marines to the threats evident today and in restoring some measure of accountability to the command structure. He has also begun to cancel orders for expensive weaponry no longer needed. He will need strong White House and congressional support if he is to succeed in reducing waste, trimming fat, and ending procurement of weapons that are unnecessary in the current environment.

Every shift of emphasis tends to go too far, and there is a danger that a greater proportion of American armed forces than necessary will be designated, equipped, and trained for low-intensity conflict and nation building. American strategy should be to encourage responsible foreign governments to deal with conflict in their regions, with minimal use of American forces. Some American participation in policing and nation-building efforts may be necessary, but regional leadership in dealing with regional security problems should be the goal of American strategy. The wars in both Iraq and Afghanistan have demonstrated the problems any foreign occupier has in transforming the society and politics of a distant country. The United States must find a better way to protect itself, a way that does not involve long-term occupation of other countries by American armed forces.

The United States should also avoid making the armed forces the principal instrument of economic development abroad. That should be the task of the Agency for International Development. To entrust that work to the military is sending the wrong signal to recipient countries. For that reason, the recently created Africa Command (AFRICOM), a new four-star billet, and the Southern Command (SOUTHCOM), covering Latin America, should be eliminated and the limited military demands in Africa and Latin America entrusted to other commands.[1]

The Obama administration should instruct the secretary of defense to review carefully the extensive network of military bases the United States maintains abroad, with the goal of reducing their number and, whenever possible, the size of those that remain. The United States must make it plain that it is not attempting to rule the world, and—indeed—has no intention of serving as the default world policeman. It must continue to maintain the military capacity to support its alliances and to deal with those aspects of the terrorist threat that require a military response. For operations against terrorist training camps and terrorist command structures, a robust network of small special forces bases—whenever possible operated with the cooperation of host governments—should be retained and even extended if current facilities are not adequate to the task.

Whereas expenses for military operations should be reduced, those for diplomacy need to be expanded substantially. State Department budgets were cut in the 1990s even more (in proportion to their size) than the Pentagon budget, even though diplomatic tasks increased. This meant that many consulates outside capital cities—important for services to Americans, support for American business, and information on what is happening in a country as a whole—were closed. It also meant that the time available for training, including instruction in such critical languages as Arabic and Chinese, had to be curtailed. Personnel shortages meant that some positions were left unfilled for months. Although Colin Powell reversed some of the damaging trends after 2001, State Department budgets remained shockingly inadequate.

Condoleezza Rice tried shifting positions out of Europe and Washington to expand the presence of American diplomats outside capital cities in China and South Asia, but funds were not available for adequate support, and security and legal problems prevented full implementation of the program.[2] A significant proportion of the Foreign Service was forced to go to Iraq, whether or not the officers had the skills needed, most to operate out of the Green Zone under the escort of armed contract guards, to lend a hand for nation building. Foreign Service officers were sufficiently dedicated and disciplined to volunteer to staff the Baghdad embassy (now the largest American embassy in the world), but it is questionable how much real help they can be under the conditions that prevail in Iraq. Meanwhile, critical posts elsewhere are left understaffed because of the drain of resources for services in Iraq, which are likely to prove as quixotic as similar efforts were in South Vietnam in the early 1970s.

In 2008, with the support of Secretary of Defense Gates and the chairman of the Joint Chiefs of Staff, the State Department obtained additional funds for the Foreign Service and began recruitment to fill empty positions.* Nevertheless, it will take years to put the Foreign Service in a position to render

---

*It was revealed that there were more musicians in military bands than professional diplomats on active duty in the entire American Foreign Service—a revealing measure of the quality of budgetary judgment on the part of recent administrations.

optimum diplomatic support to the full range of American foreign policy objectives. Rapid expansion is not desirable. The Foreign Service has always been highly selective and should continue to be in order to maintain the personnel quality America deserves. It will take time to plan and open new posts, to train the officers, and to accumulate the experience that gives a diplomat insight into the thinking of people in other cultures and the skill to communicate effectively in the language of the country.

It is obvious that what makes a diplomat effective is his or her ability to understand the people and politics of another country, to interact with its citizens, and to explain to the home government how best to pursue its interests in regard to the country of assignment. The United States is equipped with a diplomatic service second to none in quality. Though the Foreign Service has often been shortchanged in support, a deeper problem that frequently occurs is the failure of American presidents to make full use of Foreign Service expertise and advice, as well as the more recent practice of imposing on it the duties of colonial administrators.

My thirty-five years in the Foreign Service provided me with abundant examples of how presidents and secretaries of state can benefit from making full use of embassies, and how they can stumble when they fail to do so.

As an example of full use I would cite my experience as ambassador to the Soviet Union. Presidents Reagan and Bush and Secretaries of State Shultz and Baker used the embassy in Moscow effectively as the American eyes, ears, and voice in the Soviet Union. The embassy was kept informed of Washington's thinking and consulted in advance when decisions were being made. Embassy officers were a part of every negotiation that took place in Moscow, even when the chief negotiator came from Washington. As a consequence, the embassy could follow up on commitments and answer questions from our Soviet contacts, literally on a daily basis. The embassy staff maintained contact with a wide range of Soviet officials and ordinary citizens, including those in the non-Russian union republics. Thus, the embassy was able to alert Washington to the rapidly deteriorating situation in the country well before CIA analysts fully realized that it was about to collapse. Embassy officers appeared on television or were quoted almost every day by the Soviet media on a range of topics. This played an important role in diminishing suspicion of the United States. Without trying, and without directly interfering in domestic politics, American diplomats played a transformative role, by explaining democratic values and democratic procedures when asked, as they often were when Gorbachev opened Soviet society to outside influences.

The embassy in Moscow, like many others, has not always been allowed to contribute to policy making, or even been kept fully informed of the thinking in Washington. Shortly after Jimmy Carter was elected, he prepared an ambitious proposal for "deep cuts" in nuclear weapons and sent Secretary of State Cyrus Vance to Moscow to sell it. The proposal was rejected out of hand, and Vance was sent away with nothing. I was the ambassador's deputy at our embassy in Moscow and witnessed the angry rejection, complete with accusations that the United States was reneging on commitments made earlier. Vance and his advisers were taken by surprise, since they had presented the proposal in good faith as a starting point for negotiations. But the Carter administration had made no effort to communicate its ideas to the embassy in Moscow before they were announced, or to seek the embassy's input on the probable Soviet reaction.

Subsequently, we learned from senior Soviet diplomats active at the time that Carter's proposal was, on its merits, negotiable, but it was rejected because it was presented in a manner that convinced Soviet leader Brezhnev that Carter was trying to humiliate him. Carter had begun his administration with strong public denunciations of Soviet human rights practices, yet had terminated the official dialogue that had been established to discuss the issues. Then he announced publicly that he would be proposing deeper cuts in nuclear arsenals than had been agreed earlier by Ford and Brezhnev. The combination of public denunciations and an abrupt change in the American negotiating position on the issue of the greatest importance to Brezhnev was enough to convince the Soviet leaders that Carter was playing politics and had no intention of concluding an arms control agreement acceptable to them.

How could this have been avoided? If Carter had instructed Secretary Vance to seek the advice of the American embassy in Moscow regarding the best way to present his proposal before making it public, he would have been told the following: Before making any mention in public of a new proposal, he should send a private message from Secretary of State Vance to

Foreign Minister Gromyko, which would (1) assure Brezhnev that Carter was willing to continue negotiations on the basis of what had been agreed with Gerald Ford at Vladivostok, but that he preferred a more ambitious goal, which he thought would be better for both countries; (2) present an outline of what the president wanted to achieve and solicit the Soviet reaction, with an offer to discuss the details confidentially in either Moscow (using the American ambassador) or Washington (with the Soviet ambassador); and (3) point out that Carter had a particular interest in improving the dialogue on protection of human rights and proposing to raise the level of the confidential talks that had been started.*

Additionally, the embassy would have advised the president to refrain from strong public criticism of Soviet human rights practices unless and until he found that the private channel was not working. It was clear to the American embassy in Moscow that the Soviets would not make improvements in human rights under American pressure unless they were convinced that the arms control negotiations were getting somewhere.

What would have been the probable outcome if Carter had sought and followed the advice of the American embassy in Moscow? Most likely, Brezhnev would have wished to conclude an agreement incorporating the principles he had agreed with Ford, since he had exerted considerable effort to secure Soviet military acceptance of the terms. However, in return for Carter's willingness to proceed on that track, he probably would have been willing to accept the Carter proposal, with only minor modifications, for follow-on negotiations. By consulting privately in advance, both sides could have reduced the suspicion that the other was more interested in playing to public galleries than reaching an agreement. Even if the original Carter proposal was never accepted, the United States would have been in a better position to fulfill its aim of completing an arms control agreement promptly if it had followed the course the embassy would have advised.

In sum, staffing embassies with competent, well-trained diplomats is important, and to do so the U.S. government must embark on a multiyear effort to strengthen the Foreign Service. However, even the most competent

---

*I know this because I would have been the person in the embassy who drafted the answer, but any of the diplomats in the embassy dealing with arms control would have given the same advice.

embassies will be unable to salvage American diplomacy if their advice is neither sought nor heeded by Washington. In pointing this out I am not arguing that foreign policy should be exclusively in the hands of diplomats. The president and secretary of state, with input from other cabinet members, have the responsibility for making policy. But if they ignore the advice of professionals, particularly regarding the mindset of foreign leaders, they risk being blindsided by unexpected opposition.

Although some ambassadors resent the use of special emissaries to deal with particular problems, at times they are necessary, particularly if the issue involves several countries or is highly technical.* Nevertheless, special emissaries and negotiators will be most successful if they keep the embassies in the countries they are dealing with fully involved in their negotiations. Secret negotiations behind the backs of those formally charged with maintaining a relationship will almost always create more problems than they solve. However, if the emissary from Washington works as a team with ambassadors on the spot and their staffs, the mediation or negotiation is likely to be more successful.

On the other hand, American diplomacy will suffer if diplomats are forced into roles for which they are not suited. Rice's campaign to make the U.S. Foreign Service an instrument of "transformational diplomacy"—an attempt to turn other countries into democracies—runs a serious risk of diverting American diplomacy from its main job.

As with other issues, we need to keep policy and practice consistent with fundamental principles: a diplomat's role is to represent one's country in another country, to protect the interests of the home country and its citizens, and to keep the diplomat's government informed about developments in the country of assignment. The primary role of diplomats has never properly been and cannot be to "transform" another country. Setting that goal makes American diplomats suspect as agents of subversion—organizers of fifth columns—in any country with a government that has differences with the United States.

How would the United States react to the representatives of a foreign gov-

---

*For example, President Obama's naming former senator George Mitchell to work on the Israeli-Palestinian problem, or sending Ambassador Richard Holbrooke to deal with Pakistan and Afghanistan.

ernment that proclaimed a goal of "transforming" its political system? When the Soviet Union tried, using the Communist International, the United States did not consider that a friendly act, and it was not. The whole idea of transformational diplomacy, no matter how well intentioned, will be considered in many other countries as a pretext for overthrowing sitting governments. The United States cannot turn its diplomatic service into a subversive force or colonial service and retain its diplomatic effectiveness.

This does not mean that the United States should not offer development assistance to other countries or that it should not adopt policies that encourage good, honest government elsewhere. Of course it should do those things whenever they are feasible and cost-effective, and it has done them throughout the post–World War II period, which has witnessed a remarkable expansion of democratic forms of government in many parts of the world. The United States has had much more success using normal diplomatic tools, along with its example at home, to encourage good government than it has by setting out overtly to "transform" other countries.

As for American intelligence services, the CIA and the FBI in particular, my impression is that both have had more success correcting pre-9/11 shortcomings than is generally recognized. The new National Counterterrorism Center should help prevent additional failures to share vital information across agencies. It is, however, too early to judge whether the creation in 2005 of a National Intelligence Directorate with an office of fifteen hundred employees to supervise and coordinate all U.S. intelligence agencies has improved the quality of intelligence. There is a danger that the additional bureaucratic layer will complicate rather than facilitate production of timely information. It would seem that any improvement in intelligence performance should be sought in the recruitment and selection of personnel rather than further realignments of organizational charts. The fact that there has been no major foreign terrorist attack on American soil since 2001 probably owes more to improved intelligence and police work, along with more effective cooperation with foreign police and intelligence agencies, than to the much more costly wars in Iraq and Afghanistan.

From its first days, the Obama administration set about ending any remaining illegal activities by the intelligence agencies, such as the use of torture and eavesdropping on Americans without judicial warrants. This should improve rather than diminish the intelligence product for reasons discussed previously. It will also help the morale of most professional intelligence officers, who understand that torture is unlikely to produce useful information and resent political pressure to employ it.

There is no question that both the CIA and the FBI need to continue to develop more expertise in non-European languages and cultures than they have traditionally possessed. This will take time. They also need to improve their analytical ability; collection of secrets helps little if the secret information is misleading or not accurately understood. Analysts must pay as much attention to open-source information as to secret reports in order to judge the accuracy and relevance of both. More must be done to make sure that information on hand is promptly available to those who need it. In this regard, the FBI has been slow to develop and update a computerized watch list of individuals who should be denied visas on security grounds. As late as 2007, it was still depending on laborious manual file checks that sometimes took months to complete, and had not purged its watch lists of Cold War relics that were not relevant to the terrorist threat.

Though American intelligence agencies have made mistakes, much of the criticism that has been directed at them has been overdrawn. As Professor Richard K. Betts of Columbia University pointed out in his insightful study *Enemies of Intelligence,* the larger problem is that policy makers typically expect more from intelligence agencies than they can reasonably deliver. When something goes wrong, the responsible officials tend to blame inadequate or misdirected intelligence when in fact it was their own faulty judgment that caused the failure. As Betts put it:

> In the best known cases of intelligence failure, the most crucial mistakes have sometimes been made by the collectors of raw information and the professionals who produce finished analyses, but most often by the decision makers who consume their products. . . . The use of intelligence depends less on the bureaucracy than on the intellects and inclinations of the authorities above it.[3]

Betts makes another point that supports the sort of change in foreign policy this book proposes: the more the United States tries to impose itself upon and change other societies, the more extensive, detailed, and accurate information it requires about other societies. This leads to unrealistic demands on intelligence agencies, which will never be able to produce "intelligence good enough to underwrite [the policy makers'] most ambitious attempt to shape the world to their liking. . . . Having a modest view of how well the intelligence system will ever work is only one reason to favor military policies more restrained than the United States pursued after the Cold War."[4]

President Obama has inherited the finest military, diplomatic, and intelligence instruments in the world today. Both economics and the requirements of international politics will require him to trim the resources allocated to the armed forces and reduce the American military footprint in the world. He can do so safely—though it will take determination and extraordinary political skill to avoid tripping over the barriers set by special interests—if he changes America's overall strategy from one of dominating the world to one of cooperating to achieve common interests. He will find that America's professionals, whether in the military, diplomatic, or intelligence arms of government, will be eager to assist him and his team. They will not speak with one voice, and should not, but if their advice is sought and respected, the Obama team can improve the prospects for bringing about the changes he has promised.

International Tools

A return to multilateralism, that is, cooperation with other countries, will mean increased reliance on existing international institutions, such as the United Nations and its specialized agencies, to deal with problems that arise. The United Nations itself is badly in need of reform, which however has proven to be extraordinarily difficult. For example, it is clear that the structure of the U.N. Security Council no longer reflects (if it ever did) political reality in the world. How is it that two members of the European Community (France and Great Britain) have permanent seats with veto power when countries of equal or greater size and importance (Japan, India, and Brazil are examples) have neither permanent seats nor the right of veto?

Obviously, there are historical reasons for these and other anomalies, but potential solutions tend to be either difficult politically or detrimental to the organization's effectiveness. It seems undesirable to grant veto power in the Security Council to additional countries, as well as unrealistic to expect any of the five countries that have this right to give it up. There have been proposals to add permanent members without veto power, but it is impossible as yet to achieve a consensus on which countries should be granted this role. Would Pakistan concede that India should, in effect, represent the subcontinent, or Argentina agree to have Brazil hold the "Latin American" seat? Not very likely.

The United States should remain flexible in its thinking about United Nations reform and lend support to reasonable proposals, but given the political complexity of achieving changes in the U.N. Charter, it should try to make the most of the organization in its present form. If U.S. policy is seen by the other members of the Security Council as seeking cooperation rather than enforcing a hegemonic policy, Russia and China are more likely to support American initiatives to deal with local and regional conflicts.

The Obama administration also needs to review the American position on a number of multilateral initiatives and return to negotiating tables that the Bush-Cheney administration abandoned. U.S. participation in the International Criminal Court would enhance the court's effectiveness and provide a tool for addressing some of the problems in dealing with failed states. Also, its jurisdiction might well be expanded to include crimes such as piracy and the production of offensive biological weapons. (The latter is illegal for governments, but there is neither an enforcement mechanism nor any basis for the prosecution of individual scientists who might be employed by rogue states or terrorist groups.)

Although the United States should be cautious about establishing new international bureaucracies, new institutions may be necessary to accomplish new tasks. The organization that monitors and enforces the chemical weapons treaty seems to be working well, and the one that supervises the Comprehensive Nuclear Test Ban Treaty is in place and able to enforce that agreement if the United States and other necessary countries ratify it. If a treaty to enforce the ban on biological weapons production can be negotiated, there will be a need for an organization to administer it.

In addition, we need creative thinking and political leadership to deal with the agonizing problems of failed states, international criminal activity, and the crimes of genocide and ethnic cleansing. Existing international structures are inadequate to meet these challenges, and ad hoc arrangements that authorize a given country (or group of countries) to take appropriate action cannot be relied upon if any of the permanent members of the U.N.

Security Council believe another is exploiting the situation for its geopolitical advantage.

The United States should take the lead in consultations with the European Union, Russia, China, and other key countries in an effort to improve the instruments available for intervention in troubled and violent areas without arousing suspicions of self-serving intent. As mentioned previously, one solution might be to establish a small international force under Security Council control to which specially trained units from small and medium-sized countries could be assigned for specific peacemaking and peacekeeping assignments.

Priorities

There is no question that the president's most immediate task is to manage a recovery of the economy, which has been brought to the brink of disaster by previous administrations motivated by misplaced faith in abstract theories that ignored what was happening in the real world. Everything else depends on the U.S. ability to avert a world depression and to end the current recession as rapidly as possible. Costly steps to cope with the economic crisis—not all effective—have been taken, but the economy will remain at the top of the president's list of concerns until there are clear signs that the financial system is in working order again and the recession is ending.

The terms of a new financial structure must be worked out in cooperation with other nations and therefore are unlikely to embody the degree of American hegemony that has prevailed in the world economy since World War II. The resulting global economy will not conform to the principles of market fundamentalism. Instead of leaving all to an unregulated financial market, the new system seems certain to embody a significant degree of government regulation and, in some key sectors such as banking and insurance, of state partnership—at least temporarily—in the capital structure of major international corporations.

Events in 2008 demonstrated that George Soros was prescient when he predicted six years earlier that markets "are not capable, on their own, of taking care of collective needs such as law and order or the maintenance of the market mechanism itself. Nor are they competent to ensure social justice."[5] The challenge will be not to overdo the role of government to the point that economic growth is stunted; the proper balance can be brought about only by a political process that gives appropriate weight to both public and private interests and seeks workable compromises rather than theoretically "correct" solutions, which tend to go from one unworkable extreme to its equally dysfunctional opposite.

Restoring growth to the economy is of prime importance to any American president who comes to office in a recession, but that does not mean that other issues can wait until the economy is healed. The United States is engaged in two wars, important nuclear arms agreements are set to expire in 2009 if not renegotiated, violence continues between Israelis and Palestinians, and genocidal conditions prevail in several parts of Africa. There is an urgent need for alterations in American policy in these and other areas, which cannot wait until the recession ebbs. Change will not come easily, despite campaign rhetoric. In foreign policy, prominent Democrats have been infected by some of the unfounded myths spread by neoconservatives and political missionaries and are likely to resist the degree of change current conditions require. Every existing policy has special interests that have profited from it and will fight against any real change.

During the 2008 political campaign, most of the debate touching on foreign affairs avoided the most fundamental issues. Only the Republican hopeful Ron Paul made a strong case during his primary campaign that the United States was overextended in the world and needed to reduce its military commitments abroad. Others seemed to avoid discussing the question lest they be charged with being "soft" or "naive" on defense issues. In fact, President Obama must find a way to reduce the defense budget. The preponderance of U.S. military power is now so great that it can be cut back substantially and still be adequate to protect America and support an effective diplomacy.

Obama is committed to more use of diplomacy and has promised to talk to everyone. This does not mean immediate summit meetings with Hugo Chávez or Mahmoud Ahmadinejad.* However, it does mean that there should be communications, without prior conditions, with lower-level offi-

---

*Ahmadinejad's verbal attacks on Barack Obama within days of the president's inauguration suggest that the Iranian leader fears the impact that a dialogue with the United States would have on public opinion in his country. American public hostility strengthens radical nationalists like Ahmadinejad.

cials. It will help if the president makes public statements that appear conciliatory without obscuring real problems in the relationship. The comments could be paraphrases of "With all our differences, we have important common interests, and we should seek a way to cooperate when both countries can benefit from it." The spirit of Reagan's January 1984 speech on cooperation with the Soviet Union could be applied to relations with most countries. The message would be the opposite of identifying an "axis of evil" or insisting on "regime change" as the only acceptable solution to a problem.

Simply talking, to be sure, is not magic and will not automatically solve problems. We must also listen, even when we don't and shouldn't agree. To hold promise, talks must cover the issues each side considers important. We are likely to get nowhere if we insist on talking about *a* but not *b* and *c* if the other side considers *b* and *c* important. We must be willing to engage other countries in a dialogue regarding the way each country views the strategic and security situation in the area in question as well as specific concrete issues in the relationship, such as aid to terrorists or nuclear weapons programs.

Security Issues

As we consider specific decisions that must be made, we need to keep in mind America's fundamental interests in the world and determine whether current policies are consistent with them. Often, when a policy is not achieving its goal, we need to step back mentally and consider whether a different approach might hold more promise. The idea is much like "zero-based budgeting," an approach occasionally adopted by new administrations in compiling a budget. Each department or agency is expected to start from zero and justify its budget request in relation to its actual functions and goals, not simply on the basis of past budgets. The argument that "we need *x* percent additional appropriation because of inflation if we are to do our job next year"—always works to perpetuate a bureaucracy, since it does not examine whether the organization is still performing a necessary or useful service, and whether it is doing so efficiently. The former approach, starting with zero, in theory requires a discussion of what the agency does, why it does it, and why it needs the specified sum to do it. In the budgetary process the zero-based approach does not always work as it should because special interests (for example, defense contractors) use their political influence to hijack the process and skew it in their favor. Nevertheless, when it comes to policy, renewed attention to fundamental goals can be a useful first step in opening the mind to policies capable of overcoming dangerous stalemates.

Homeland Security and Terrorism

The greatest threat posed by terrorism is not the damage that occasional acts of terrorism inflict—serious as that doubtless is—but the self-defeating reaction it often stimulates. All reasonable measures to deter and prevent terrorist attacks must of course be taken, but it is also important to avoid the temptation to overreact in ways that provoke more terrorism and at the same time undermine our own society's values and strengths. To consider the struggle to prevent terrorist acts comparable to a world war has been a dangerous diversion. A vigorous effort to defend the United States and other countries from terrorist attack is necessary, but it must be planned and executed so that it does more good than harm.

President Obama's decisions to close the detention center at Guantánamo and to forbid torture of detainees will do much to regain the world's respect and cooperation in the fight against terrorism. U.S. intelligence and police agencies are much better prepared to preempt future terrorist attacks than they were before 9/11, and the Obama administration's stimulus package directed at renewal of the American infrastructure will make the country more resilient in the face of both natural and man-made disasters.

Reducing the American military presence in the Middle East and the Islamic world in general will diminish incentives for terrorist attacks on the United States. For this reason among others, American forces ought to be withdrawn from Iraq as rapidly as can be done responsibly, and diplomatic solutions should be sought to prevent Al-Qaeda and its affiliates from operating training camps and command headquarters in either Pakistan or Afghanistan.

Nuclear Weapons

Nuclear weapons remain high on any list of threats because, in the numbers that now exist, they comprise the only plausible existing threat to our national existence. If a substantial portion of the weapons deployed today were ever used, civilized life on the planet would become difficult, perhaps impossible, to maintain. For some time, our attention has been focused on preventing dissemination of nuclear weapons to countries not already possessing them rather than reducing, under strict verification, the number that now exist. Actually, we must do both, for without the latter, we shall be unable to achieve the former.

Biological Weapons

Like nuclear bombs, these are horrible, inhumane weapons without any rational military use. With the advances in genetic engineering, the potential threat becomes much greater than it has been in the past, since it is now possible to engineer pathogens not subject to human immune reactions. Developing effective measures to verify compliance with the treaty ban on biological weapons should be among the highest priorities of any U.S. government.

Environmental Degradation

It is a longer-term threat than the previous two, but a deteriorating environment is potentially equally destructive of our prosperity and way of life. Further delays in dealing effectively with climate change and environmental pollution can be more damaging and costly in the long run than terrorist attacks, even if the terrorists acquire a nuclear device or two. The Kyoto Protocol was flawed, but the Bush administration's eight-year delay in proposing something better not only undermined America's ability to lead, it has also increased the future costs to the world community in dealing with the threat of atmospheric warming and the climate changes it entails.

Missile Defense and Space Warfare

As yet, we are fortunate not to be in a full-scale arms race in space, but we may be on the brink of starting one. If an arms race should occur in space and bring about a breach in the prohibition on placing nuclear weapons or other weapons of mass destruction in orbit, the United States will face another existential threat. Missile defense is a separate but overlapping issue, depending on the type of interceptors envisioned. These programs must be made subject to international agreement and international cooperation. The United States should take the lead in negotiating an international treaty to prohibit the militarization of space, just as it did earlier to keep weapons out of Antarctica and off the Moon, and to prevent placing nuclear weapons in outer space.

Cyber Warfare

Both our civilian economy and military effectiveness are heavily dependent on computer-controlled systems for communication, global positioning, weather prediction, intelligence collection, financial transactions, and data storage, to name only some of the most prominent uses. So far, cyber attacks on computer networks or databases by individual hackers have been more a costly nuisance than a serious threat, but a sophisticated cyber attack on facilities that are vital either for military operations or the economy (some are the same) could be much more dangerous. We must not wait until there is a successful cyber attack on essential services before we negotiate international standards to help protect the integrity of digital communications.

Energy Dependence

The scale of America's addiction to imported petroleum products increases its vulnerability as a nation. The need to ensure reliable supplies from some of the most unstable areas of the world has not only required costly military deployments, but also has limited leverage over countries whose actions support and encourage terrorism. The United States will not be able to implement an effective foreign policy in the Middle East until it reduces substantially its dependence on imported oil, and it will not be able to do its part in preventing global warming unless it sharply reduces its reliance on fossil fuels for energy.

Competition for Resources

We are already seeing the distorting effects of rising world demand on static and sometimes dwindling natural resources. China's rapidly growing need for petroleum products was one of the major factors in the sudden price increases in 2007 and 2008. Competition for access to resources also reduces the leverage the world community can exert over the behavior of ill-tempered oil-producing states, particularly Iran, Sudan, and Venezuela. Prices of other commodities are also rising rapidly. As global warming continues, the struggle for access to fresh water will intensify in many areas, including parts of the United States such as the Southwest.

Indebtedness to Foreign Countries

It used to be said that the national debt was of little importance, since it was only money we owed ourselves. But, if this was ever true, it is no longer so. Our ballooning fiscal and trade deficits have made the United States the largest debtor country in the world—to the tune of more than $3 trillion owed to foreigners, for the most part foreign governments. If this trend continues—and the financial bailouts and stimulus packages will make it worse before it can get better—we face one or both of two possible outcomes: foreign dollar holders will buy an increasing share of America's productive assets, or there will be a shift out of the dollar as a reserve currency, which would devalue further the already weak dollar, fueling runaway inflation at home. Our unabated appetite for oil is by itself enough to put us in the international poorhouse.

Human Rights and Democratization

Readers who have gotten this far have probably already asked: Where are human rights on the list of priorities? Have we no responsibility in that regard? Isn't it true that we were not able to end the Cold War with the Soviet Union until Gorbachev began to improve the protection of human rights in his country?

Yes, that is true. But Gorbachev did not take steps to provide better protection for human rights because of American threats. He did so because he became convinced that protection of human rights was important to his country's future development. He might not have come to that conclusion if the United States and its European allies had not pressed hard for the Soviet Union to respect its commitments in the Helsinki Final Act of 1975. It probably would not have been politically possible for him to rein in the KGB and other repressive elements if Reagan and then George Bush had not pressed the issue privately rather than relying on hostile public rhetoric.

Therefore, while it is true that respect for human rights was an important part of the American agenda in dealing with the Soviet Union, American and other Western leaders used persuasion, not threats.

There was no way that the United States or NATO could threaten the Soviet Union with military action if it reverted to the sort of wide-scale repression that had been characteristic of much Soviet history. But even "carrots" would have been of little avail if Gorbachev had not been genuinely convinced that his country's future depended on opening the society and cultivating a "bottom-up" system of governance.

One of the most difficult tasks I had as American ambassador to the Soviet Union was explaining to representatives of Lithuania, Estonia, and Latvia that, although the United States did not consider their countries legally part of the Soviet Union, we could not recognize their governments as independent until they were in fact. Furthermore, I had to explain that if the Soviet government cracked down on the Baltic independence movements, even brutally, there was nothing the United States could do directly to protect them. We could not risk a nuclear war by offering military protection. This meant that it was vitally important for the three Baltic nations to keep their drive for independence entirely peaceful. They did, in spite of provocations and pressure within their own movements to resort to violence. Nevertheless, the Baltic patriots prevailed in the end when even the Soviet Congress of People's Deputies recognized their independence following the unsuccessful coup against Gorbachev.

As it turned out, the practical inability of the United States to use force to protect legitimate human rights, including the right of self-determination, was a blessing. It eliminated any temptation on the part of Baltic nationalist movements to take or threaten violent action in the hope of Western support. The Soviet response to an uprising in the Baltics would have produced results that halted any reform in the Soviet Union for decades.

Human rights is an important cause, but one that governments, particularly powerful ones like the United States, must promote with discretion and understanding of the probable consequences of their words and tactics. There are genuine dilemmas, but it is important to resist the emotional reflex to "do something," particularly if that something is military action. Governments should abide by the physician's adage, "Above all, do no harm."

Precipitate action or public threats will often make the situation worse. Not only that: economic sanctions can harm the people as a whole more than the elite that victimizes them.

So, what is left? Do governments have to sit by and ignore serious human rights violations by other countries? No, but they should make sure that whatever the action taken, it is viewed as legal—that is, authorized by an appropriate international body—and not likely to make the situation worse. Second, governments, along with human rights organizations, must consistently counsel human rights activists to keep their opposition to abuses peaceful. Every minimally competent government will put down riots brutally; foreigners can best protect human rights activists by counseling them to avoid violence.

Foreigners can also be most effective if their efforts on behalf of human rights are seen as fair and principled. One of the problems the United States created for itself during the Bush-Cheney administration was the perception that the United States was preaching standards for others to which it was itself unwilling to adhere. In other words, many perceived that the country was acting hypocritically in a self-serving way, guilty of aggression and practicing torture while insisting that others were obligated to adhere to higher standards.

Potentially, one of the most powerful instruments for protecting human rights is the International Criminal Court (ICC), which was established in 2002 precisely for the purpose of making government officials accountable for egregious human rights violations such as genocide, crimes against humanity, and war crimes.[6] Unfortunately, the United States, along with Russia, China, and India, refused to participate in the ICC.* The Obama administration should take the lead in reopening negotiations on the treaty establishing the ICC, in an effort to introduce amendments to make it acceptable to the U.S. Senate and other major countries not yet participating.

An additional approach used in Europe may eventually be applicable in other areas. Though it was criticized at the time as being ineffectual and an

---

*President Clinton signed the treaty but did not submit it to the Senate for ratification. President George W. Bush rejected the treaty altogether and made no effort negotiate a replacement that might be more acceptable to the U.S. Senate.

unnecessary concession to Soviet interests, the Helsinki Final Act of 1975 proved to be the most important single instrument that brought about better protection for human rights in the Soviet Union. Leonid Brezhnev and his captive colleagues from Eastern Europe doubtless signed the document without serious intent to respect its provisions, but their endorsement of specific human rights standards turned out to be exceedingly important. The United States and its NATO allies could argue that the Soviet Union and other Communist-dominated countries should adhere to international standards, standards their governments had formally endorsed. This turned out to be a more effective argument than making protection of human rights a one-sided demand.

Governments in power will never protect human rights if they feel that human rights advocates are out to replace the government. There usually is no effective alternative to working peacefully within the system, unless the regime in question is already disintegrating as an viable government. When that happens, successful intervention by outsiders may depend greatly on the capacity and willingness of countries in the region to support and participate in peacekeeping operations.

Encouraging respect for human rights is not the same thing as democracy promotion. Respecting internationally defined human rights is an obligation of all governments, whether democratic or authoritarian. Some governments that are democratic in form are human rights offenders. A majority from one race, ethnic group, or religious persuasion can deny equal rights to residents not of that group—a situation that prevailed in the United States for most of its history.

Furthermore, as we have seen, an official policy aimed at changing the form of foreign governments risks being viewed as an imperial policy with the goal of reducing other countries to colonial dependency. If we wish other countries to become more democratic—and we should—we can best help not by active proselytizing, but by setting an example.

In its early months, the Obama administration began reorienting U.S. policy in many areas to attract cooperation from other countries rather than trying to intimidate and control them. Nevertheless, the problems facing the United States in the world were daunting and there were no obvious keys to success. It was one thing to believe that there should be more communication and use of "soft power," and another to define exactly what should be done in which instance, and how to go about it.

Each threatening situation in the world is in many respects unique, requiring a custom-designed strategy, not some off-the-shelf, theory-inspired generic approach. An effective strategy will be flexible enough to adjust in response to changes on the ground or discovery that some initial assumptions are invalid. To cope successfully with the problems the nation faces, President Obama and his team need not only to discard failing policies but also to design policy approaches that conform to the demands of each individual situation. We should now consider a few examples of how policy might be crafted to meet some of the specific problems confronting America abroad.

12

An Agenda, Not a Doctrine

JOURNALISTS AND SCHOLARS WILL BE eager to identify a phrase to character-
ize President Obama's foreign policy, the "Obama doctrine" or some such,
and members of his staff may be tempted to play along. It may not be best
for them to do so. We faced the problem of labeling policy in the Reagan administration and found a different solution.

As we prepared the speech on U.S.-Soviet relations that President Reagan delivered on January 16, 1984, members of the White House staff and
the State Department discussed at length what they would call Reagan's policy toward the Soviet Union. (Journalists had already adopted "Reagan doctrine" to mean only one subsidiary part of a larger policy—resistance to
Communist subversion in the Western Hemisphere—but this was not the
main thrust of Reagan's policy.) Some staffers thought that he should call his
policy toward the Soviet Union "constructive engagement," to emphasize
that he intended to engage the Soviet leaders in serious negotiations. Others objected, pointing out that "engagement" means engaged to be married,
and that was not what we had in mind. Another participant pointed out that
"engagement" could carry the opposite connotation, as in a military engagement, a battle. In sum, we could not find a phrase that conveyed un-
ambiguously what we were trying to express.

Unable to recommend a word or phrase for the idea, we asked the president what he wanted to call his policy toward the Soviet Union. He questioned why we needed a label and suggested that we just tell people what we

have in mind and how we plan to do it. Thus was born the "four-part agenda"—the what—and the "three-part approach"—the how. The agenda was specific to relations with the Soviet Union. (Its four parts were: reduction of weapons, particularly nuclear weapons, to the lowest possible levels; withdrawal from military confrontation in third countries; protection of human rights; and creating a better working relationship—a euphemism for lifting the Iron Curtain). But the approach—how to go about it—is applicable to many situations. We summed it up in just three words: realism, strength, dialogue.

When asked to explain what these three words meant, we said something like the following: realism means that we will take a hard look at a situation and make a judgment based on what we see, not on some preconceived idea; strength means that we will maintain adequate resources to negotiate successfully, including military capacity, economic health, and a strategy backed by the American people; dialogue means that we will stay in communication with everybody, including adversaries, listening to their point of view and searching for areas where we can cooperate as we simultaneously identify practices or intentions that we must deter or counter. Dialogue becomes negotiation when we determine that there is sufficient mutual interest in a particular outcome to make it worthwhile to try to agree on the terms of settlement.

This approach worked, and though there is no guarantee that it would work in any other situation, it will probably be useful as the default initial approach to most problems: we should at least try it first and stick with it long enough to make sure it is not working. If it doesn't work, then there will be time to consider how it might be adapted or changed. If we don't try it first—if we insist on "regime change" or refuse to talk until our counterparts agree with us on the matter under dispute—we will never know whether the problem could have been solved at less cost than forceful action. We would be making a mistake similar to the one Andropov made when he terminated negotiations on nuclear weapons in November 1983 in response to the deployment of American intermediate-range missiles in Europe.

As for the substance—the agenda—this will vary with the issue in question and the country with which we are dealing, but one feature of the Reagan agenda should be of use in other situations. Every issue was presented to the other side in the context of cooperation, not as demands for unilateral action. "We must cooperate to reduce arms . . . we must cooperate to protect human rights . . . ," and so on. Of course, to reach equality, the Soviet Union had to destroy more arms than the United States because it had more; so far as human rights were concerned, more radical changes were required in the Soviet Union than in the United States. But the question had to be posed as a matter of cooperation, to emphasize that a solution was in the interest of both countries. No political leader will submit willingly to a public demand by an adversary that is considered one-sided or demeaning. An unwilling submission—which may occur if sufficient force is brought to bear —normally turns out to be of little use in the long run, because the offended party will wiggle out of any forced commitment as soon as he or she can.

Once President Obama has made it clear that the United States does not seek to dominate the world but rather intends to cooperate with other countries in dealing with the political and economic problems that confront us all, how does his administration apply this vision? A change of words will net the American government very little if it does not move promptly to put the words into action.

Without attempting a comprehensive and exhausting tour of American policy throughout the world, I shall select a few pressing issues and describe ways to approach them that are consistent with a policy of cooperation rather than one of domination.

The Hot Wars

The wars in Iraq and Afghanistan are among the most urgent issues facing President Obama. The fundamental American interest is to end both in ways that will prevent Al-Qaeda or like-minded groups from using the sanctuary of either country to organize another terrorist attack on the United States or on American interests and allies elsewhere. Ultimately, ending American (or NATO) military occupation of both countries should reduce the ability of Al-Qaeda to recruit anti-American terrorists.

Given the agreement concluded with the Iraqi government in November 2008, which requires removal of U.S. troops by 2011, winding down the military presence in Iraq may be politically easier than dealing with the growing Taliban insurgency in Afghanistan. If there is a surge of violence in Iraq, the administration should resist prolonging the deployment of American troops for combat missions and instead force the Iraqis to deal with their internal problems. Once American troops leave Iraq, it would seem that no major faction there would have an incentive to play host to Al-Qaeda, even if many political tensions within the country continue—as seems likely. Nevertheless, military withdrawal from Iraq should be accompanied by regional consultations with Iraq's neighbors, including Iran, concerning the geopolitical future of the region.

The prospects for Afghanistan, in contrast, are not bright in 2009. It is far from certain that the additional U.S. troops transferred to Afghanistan will be able to turn the tide against the Taliban. Given Obama's promises during the campaign to shift forces from Iraq to Afghanistan, it may be considered a political necessity to try to make the increased military effort work. This will require a change of strategy to emphasize cooperation with tribal leaders (instead of depending primarily on a weak and corrupt central government) and more effort to avoid civilian casualties.

The odds are that even a modified strategy will fail to stabilize Afghanistan unless and until Pakistan is able and willing to eliminate the Taliban's free run of the border areas and the Taliban leaders are willing to deny Al-Qaeda a safe haven. The sad fact is that, even though the current civilian government of Pakistan may wish to bring the Taliban and Islamic fundamentalists under control, it may not have the capacity to do so. In 2009, it was not even clear that Pakistan could keep supply routes to Afghanistan open for NATO forces.

The United States needs a Plan C, to be implemented if, by 2010, conditions in Afghanistan have not improved substantially. That plan should evolve out of strategic consultations with other countries in the region, including Iran, Russia, and the Central Asian "stans."

If we consider geopolitical fundamentals, we will see the following: not a single country in the region, aside from some elements in Pakistan, wants to see the Taliban back in control of Afghanistan. Even less do they want to see Al-Qaeda or similar terrorist organizations gain the sort of base they had in 2001 for recruitment and training of terrorists. The irony, however, is that they also do not want to see a large and obvious American military presence. The widespread suspicion in the area, bolstered by Bush-Cheney administration statements and policy, is that the United States intends to establish permanent military control in order to exploit the region's natural resources. So long as American and NATO forces are viewed as occupiers, they will lack the full cooperation of the local people, without which they are unlikely to succeed.

The United States can gain a certain leverage by making it clear that it does not intend to maintain a military occupation indefinitely, and actually threatening to withdraw, leaving the problem of the Taliban to the Afghan tribal leaders and surrounding countries.

How dangerous would this be to the United States? Actually, not very. The capacity to track the movement of would-be terrorists in and out of South Asia and the Middle East has improved greatly since 2001, and there is no significant base within the United States from which terrorists can operate, even if some should sneak in. The alternative to trying to remake Afghanistan would be to "quarantine" Taliban-controlled areas of Afghanistan and Pakistan. All movement could not be stopped, of course, but it should be possible to track most would-be terrorists who come to the area for training or instructions as they move in and out. Also, Al-Qaeda camps and training grounds could be targeted for strikes from the air or by special forces. Taliban hospitality for Al-Qaeda could be strained by a variety of open and covert methods, such as those used by the Italian authorities against the Red Brigades in the 1970s.

The people of Afghanistan would be the losers if NATO forces leave and the country falls once again under Taliban rule. That would be most unfortunate for them. However, the Taliban was expelled from the country by the end of 2001, and if Afghan political leaders have not been able to organize themselves to resist the Taliban while under American and NATO protection, they bear much of the responsibility for their current predicament. We cannot save them from themselves, and we should make it clear that we do not intend to persist indefinitely unless there is more cooperation from within Afghanistan and Pakistan.

Israel and the Palestinians

There seem to be only two possible ways to end the conflict between Israelis and Palestinians that do not involve the physical removal of one or the other from the areas they now inhabit: the creation of two viable states living side-by-side in peace, if not necessarily in friendship; or the establishment of a single democratic state in all of Palestine that guarantees equal rights of all residents.* The latter could be neither a Jewish nor an Islamic state, but rather a secular democracy.

If current attitudes in Israel and in the Palestinian areas persist, it would appear that neither of these possibilities is feasible despite the fact that a "two-state" solution has been endorsed by both the Israeli government and the Palestinian Authority, as well as by the United States and its European allies. Unfortunately, the political process in Israel and in the Palestinian areas has been controlled at crucial times by extremists determined to prevent creation of two independent states—Israelis who insist on establishing settlements on the occupied West Bank with the obvious (though not always avowed) aim of incorporating all of Palestine into Israel, and Palestinians who dream of forcing the Israelis out of the area altogether.

The United States does Israel no favor in supporting Israeli policies that exacerbate the hatreds in the area and, in the long run, will pose a mortal threat to the Jewish state. The demographics are not in Israel's favor, since the birth rate among Arab Palestinians is much higher than that of Jewish Israelis, and net immigration to Israel from elsewhere has virtually ceased. Nevertheless, each time there has been progress toward a peace settlement, Israeli actions have undermined the process. Responsible Palestinian leadership has also been lacking, but as the stronger party by far, and as the one whose existence ultimately depends on the ability to live peacefully in the neighborhood, Israel should have done more to achieve peace and less to block Palestinian aspirations for self-government.

It was in Israel's interest to support the development of a responsible Palestinian leadership and help create the possibility of a viable Palestinian state on the West Bank and Gaza, with a capital in East Jerusalem. Instead, with its settlement activity and intransigence regarding the status of Jerusalem, it has followed a "divide and rule" policy that prevents any Palestinian leader from organizing a viable state. Practically speaking, Palestinians have been confronted with a choice of emigrating or else living on those

*The possibility of returning the West Bank to Jordan and transferring Gaza to Egyptian sovereignty seems unacceptable both to the Palestinians and to the countries in question.

of their ancestral lands not already incorporated in Israel in subjugation to Israeli military authority. It is not a choice that encourages a friendly attitude toward the Israeli state.

The basic problem is that Israel is seeking the impossible: absolute security for itself, which means absolute insecurity for everybody else in the neighborhood. Israel has invaded Lebanon twice and occupied the southern part for years (turning the Shia residents of the occupied areas into sworn enemies), and as recently as January 2009 invaded the Gaza Strip, having blockaded the heavily populated area since Hamas took control following an election that it won. The excuse was that rockets continued to be fired into southern Israel from Gaza, and this had to be stopped.

Firing rockets into Israel from Gaza was indeed unacceptable and, in terms of Hamas's interests, absolutely stupid. But these rockets did little damage to Israel, and it is not certain that the Hamas leadership had complete control over the perpetrators. Though there was supposed to be a cease-fire at the time, Israel had refused to open the border crossing points into Gaza, as the cease-fire required, and continued an attempt to blockade the entire Gaza Strip, depriving the residents of normal means of livelihood. The Israeli attack on Gaza in January 2009 produced more than a thousand Palestinian casualties, many civilians and children, far in excess of the few people killed or injured in Israel by the Hamas missiles. Much of the world has been horrified by the extent of civilian casualties in Gaza and the degree of Israeli callousness their military actions reveal.

The Israeli attempt to destroy Hamas's military capacity has failed, just as the 2006 invasion of Lebanon did not deprive Hezbollah of its Iranian-supplied weapons. The invasion of Gaza has, moreover, made it more difficult to create conditions in which Israel can live in relative security. In Israel's own interest, the United States must end automatic support for the most extreme hawkish policies that emerge from Israel's political process, and use its influence to convince Israelis that their future depends on their ability to make a reasonable peace with the Palestinians, not on attempts to eliminate enemies by military action.

Of course, with American support, Israel may possibly live for years as a garrison state with a population that considers itself under siege. But that cannot be a successful state, and young Israelis may increasingly look for a future elsewhere rather than be part of a militarized society engaged in chronic low-intensity warfare with its neighbors.

The basic outline of a reasonable peace agreement has been clear for at least forty years: an Israeli state within the borders recognized by U.N. Security Council Resolution 242 (subject to negotiated adjustments), with some provision of resettlement aid for Arabs forced out of Israel in 1948 and subsequently.

The possibility of a settlement seems remote at this time. Many observers will ask if organizations like Hezbollah and Hamas would ever, even under the most generous Israeli terms, give up the idea of putting an end to the Israeli state. The answer is that there is no way to know unless Israel makes a credible offer to allow and respect a Palestinian state on the land conquered in 1967 and convinces its neighbors that it is prepared to respect the human rights of Palestinian Arabs. It was an error to refuse any official talks with Hamas when it won an election in which it was legally entitled to participate.

While there is no assurance that either the Israelis or the Palestinians have political leaders capable of making peace, it would be unforgivable for the United States not to make a serious and sustained effort to put some new life in the peace process. There must be an end to blocking negotiations by raising the wrong questions. For example, one often hears that Israel cannot negotiate with Hamas or Hezbollah because they refuse to recognize Israel's "right to exist." That is the wrong question. No state has an inherent "right to exist." A state either exists or doesn't exist.

According to international law and custom, diplomatic recognition does not imply that a given state exists by virtue of some abstract "right," but only that it exists. King George III would never have agreed that his American colonists had a right to rebel and set up a separate state. He was not asked to do so. In the Treaty of Paris that ended the American Revolutionary War, the king's government recognized that the North American colonies were independent. The United States and many other countries would never have agreed that the Bolsheviks had the right to take power in the Russian Empire and establish a Soviet state. When they recognized the Soviet Union, they simply acknowledged that the Soviet government was the effective ruler of the country and therefore the entity through which relations with that country would be conducted.

Of course, no state will negotiate about the fact of its existence, but it is foolish and ultimately self-defeating to argue over whether creation of the state is the exercise of a "right." What Israel should seek is the recognition that the Israeli state exists as a sovereign political entity. To gain that recognition, Israelis must be willing to define the borders of the state they wish to be recognized. Most of the world has already accepted the borders approved by the U.N. Security Council. Is Israel willing to live within them? To most Palestinians, Israeli actions seem to say no, and if that is indeed the case, a peaceful outcome is certain to remain elusive.

Given the intense emotions on both sides of the Israeli-Palestinian conflict, a peaceful solution is probably not possible without the active involvement of the United States, and therefore it is encouraging that one of the first moves by President Obama was to name former senator George Mitchell as his representative to seek a negotiated settlement. But the Obama administration must also reverse the habit of the Bush-Cheney administration of endorsing even the most extreme and aggressive Israeli actions. This has helped neither Israel nor the peace process.

Though it will be politically difficult, President Obama needs to find a way to help Israeli citizens understand, in their own interest, what they need to do if they wish to live in peace in a Jewish state. More effort should be made to explain to American citizens, who are naturally and deeply committed to support the state of Israel, that the right-wing policies of expansion and military domination serve neither Israeli nor American interests.[1] Israelis in the peace movement understand this very well and are perplexed that so many of Israel's friends in the United States have been induced to support policies that ultimately could lead to the destruction of the Jewish state from within.

Nuclear Weapons Proliferation

The Bush-Cheney administration initially justified its invasion of Iraq by the charge that Saddam Hussein still had weapons of mass destruction and an active program to develop nuclear weapons. As it turned out, however, Iraq had ended its nuclear weapons program following the Gulf War in 1991. Therefore, the administration's efforts to prevent further proliferation centered on Iran and North Korea, both of which had been included with Iraq in President Bush's alleged "axis of evil." Pakistan and India, both of which had tested nuclear weapons in the 1990s, were courted by the administration, not condemned, even though Pakistan had been active in spreading nuclear technology clandestinely to several other countries. All three countries pose serious problems for the Obama administration.

Iran

The possibility that Iran could acquire a nuclear weapons capability figured prominently in the American political campaigns of 2008, with all candidates agreeing that it would be unacceptable to tolerate the Iranian regime's possession of nuclear weapons. Some candidates explained their position by speculating that Iran was trying to secure a nuclear arsenal to use against Israel, either directly or through terrorist surrogates.

If the history of nuclear weapons in other countries and a sober assessment of the Iranian government's most vital interests are guides, the speculation that Iran seeks nuclear weapons to attack Israel is almost certainly false. It would be suicidal for Iran to launch a nuclear attack on Israel or to supply weapons to others for that purpose, because Israel has enough nuclear weapons to obliterate Iran. The Iranian government knows this and is not suicidal.* In considering policy choices we should stick to facts and reasonable inferences from them, not hysterical speculation.

The facts are: (1) Iran is rapidly developing facilities to enrich uranium, ostensibly to fuel nuclear power plants. (2) Under the Non-Proliferation Treaty, Iran has a right to enrich uranium for peaceful purposes. (3) The Iranian government claims that it has neither plans to build nor desire to possess nuclear weapons, but is interested only in an assured supply of fuel for nuclear power plants. (4) Iranian activities, however, raise serious questions about Iranian intent. Inspectors from the International Atomic Energy Agency (IAEA) have been denied access to some facilities, and the CIA has reported that Iran had an active weapons program until it was ended in 2003. It could easily be started again. (5) If current enrichment facilities

---

*The Israeli weapons, possession of which Israel does not officially acknowledge, are reportedly on submarines and thus not vulnerable to a disarming first strike.

continue production and are expanded, Iran will soon have the capability of producing weapons-grade fissile material, giving it the option of resuming a weapons program.

There are several factors entirely apart from hostility to Israel that could motivate an Iranian regime to desire nuclear weapons. The most salient are (1) nuclear weapons provide insurance against a military attack by another country, and (2) they increase a country's prestige and political clout by conferring membership in an exclusive nuclear club.[2]

Although there is evidence that nuclear policy has been controversial in Tehran, it is a reasonable assumption that all factions wish to preserve a future option to develop weapons. Iran sees itself both as the standard-bearer of Shiism within the Islamic world and as a defender of Islam as regards the world outside. One of its neighbors, Pakistan, has a Sunni-dominated government with a nuclear arsenal. The main perceived enemy of Islam in the region is Israel, also a nuclear state. The main outside powers whose influence is resented, the United States, Great Britain, and Russia, have over 95 percent of the world's nuclear weapons. The other nuclear states seem to have accepted Pakistan's nuclear status, despite its record of proliferation, so, Iranians probably ask, why are they so opposed to Iran following suit? Many Iranians are likely to believe that the only reason the United States and its allies are intent on denying Iran a nuclear weapons capacity is to keep it vulnerable to military attack.

As distorted as these perceptions may be, they are real in many Iranian minds and provide a rationale for acquisition of nuclear weapons that has little to do with Israel. Threatening Iran with a military attack probably increases rather than undercuts its incentive to acquire nuclear weapons. Governments that have given up nuclear weapons programs in the past, including South Africa, Brazil, Iraq, and Libya, have done so when they were convinced—for quite different reasons—that they would be more secure without the weapons than with them.

The fact that the Iranian government still claims that it has no intention to build nuclear weapons provides an opening for negotiations, which should aim to make the nuclear power industry in Iran as transparent as possible and subject to enhanced inspection by the IAEA. Demanding that Iran stop all enrichment activity as a precondition for negotiations has obviously not worked, and needs to be revised. The United States needs to engage Iran in both bilateral and multilateral negotiations, but with a broader agenda than the nuclear issue alone.

Not all U.S. and Iranian interests are incompatible. Iran does not want to have a Taliban regime control Afghanistan once again. The Iranian mullahs do not support the version of Islam preached by Osama bin Laden and have given no support to Al-Qaeda. They probably do not want Iraq to become a battleground of neighboring states. The combination of the international financial crisis and the drop in the price of oil, Iran's principal source of income, is likely to produce greater unrest in Iran, which has, behind the facade of clerical control, an extensive civil society and more actual diversity than exists in many of the ostensibly "moderate" Arab countries.

The Obama administration needs to follow the example President Reagan set when he began negotiations with the Soviet Union by identifying issues on which the two countries share an interest. The U.S. should specify the steps both countries need to take to permit an eventual normalization of relations. Unless the Iranian government is convinced that the American government is not trying to overthrow it, it will not cooperate on the nuclear issue, or, for that matter, on any other. If U.S. terms are reasonable, the process of negotiation would itself weaken the radical elements in Iran that support Mahmoud Ahmadinejad and supply weapons to Hezbollah and Hamas.

As Bill Luers, Tom Pickering, and Jim Walsh suggested in a February 2009 article: "If President Obama is to dissuade Iran from building a nuclear bomb, as well as develop a successful regional strategy in Iraq and Afghanistan, he will have to develop an integrated approach toward Iran that addresses all three issues."[3] The authors then added, in words reminiscent of Reagan's agenda in dealing with the Soviet Union, that both the United States and Iran must recognize that these issues are connected and that progress in one can build trust and create confidence in others. They also noted that the U.S. should consult in advance with other countries, both those that are permanent members of the U.N. Security Council and Iran's neighbors in the area. And finally, they noted that there needs to be a continuing forum to allow the various countries with a stake in these issues to consult on a regular basis.

These proposals seem to me a creative and appropriate transposition of the elements of strategy used to end the Cold War with the Soviet Union to the specific conditions of relations with Iran.

Widespread protests followed Supreme Leader Ali Khamenei's declaration that Mahmoud Ahmadinejad had won the July 2009 presidential election despite evidence that Mir-Hossein Mousavi received more votes. Though the demonstrators were suppressed brutally, the election controversy seems to have split the clerical establishment that has ruled Iran since the fall of the shah and weakened both Ahmadinejad's government and Khamenei's authority. The Obama administration was wise to avoid endorsing the Iranian opposition, since that would have been used against its leaders in Iran. Even if Ahmadinejad manages to remain in office, the Obama administration should make it clear that it is prepared to engage whatever Iranian authorities are in office. The current Iranian government's political weakness at home may make it more amenable to reasonable accommodation than it was before the disputed election.

The greatest danger that Iran's acquisition of nuclear weapons would pose is the incentive it would give other countries in the area to follow suit, thus encouraging another round of proliferation, but also neutralizing any political advantage Iran might derive from its status as a nuclear-armed state. That is why the United States needs a strategy to persuade Iran that it is not in its interest to yield to the nuclear temptation. Only one thing would be more dangerous to the region and the world than an Iran with nuclear weapons: a military attack on Iranian nuclear facilities by either the United States or Israel. An attack would virtually ensure that Iran would covertly develop a nuclear weapons capacity. It would also greatly increase the possibility that Islamic militants in Pakistan could acquire some of Pakistan's weapons to use against the country that had, once again, attacked a Muslim country.

Pakistan

At the moment, nuclear weapons in Pakistan pose a greater danger than the prospect that Iran may have them sometime in the future. Pakistan is also the key to defeating the Taliban in Afghanistan and eliminating the threat of Al-Qaeda—issues that will doubtless preoccupy Ambassador Richard Holbrooke, whom the Obama administration has dispatched to the area.

There seems no prospect whatever that Pakistan could be persuaded to give up its nuclear arsenal, given the tensions with India. Therefore, American efforts must initially concentrate on helping the Pakistani government keep the weapons and nuclear materials and technology out of the hands of terrorist organizations. This will be a difficult task if the Pakistani government continues to be unable or unwilling to take control of the border areas where the Taliban is strong, gives protection to Osama bin Laden and Al-Qaeda, and is extending its control over ever larger areas of Afghanistan. Pakistan's decision in February 2009 to release from house arrest Abdul Qadeer Khan, who organized the sale of nuclear weapons technology to North Korea, Libya, and Iran, has increased doubts about the government's commitment to facing down the radical elements that support terrorism and nuclear proliferation.[4]

The ability of the Obama administration to improve cooperation with Pakistan to reduce the terrorist threat will depend to a great extent on changing Muslim attitudes toward the United States. President Obama's efforts to reach out to the Islamic world early in his presidency were steps in the right direction, but they are likely to be tested if the Taliban continues its offensive in Afghanistan and there is no progress in making peace between Israelis and Palestinians.

North Korea

The Bush-Cheney administration made a major error early in its first term by abandoning negotiations with North Korea over its nuclear activities. While North Korea had not been negotiating in good faith, the absence of negotiations allowed it to develop and test a nuclear device. Subsequently, U.S. policy changed and engaged the North Koreans both multilaterally (in the "six-party" talks that included China, Japan, South Korea, and Russia) and bilaterally. Halting progress was made in ending plutonium production in North Korea, but the talks frequently stalled when the North Koreans reneged on agreements or made additional demands.

There seems to be no promising alternative to continuing efforts, however frustrating, to engage the North Koreans, even though they resumed missile testing in April 2009 and announced that they would resume plutonium production. Since their earlier test of a nuclear device was a fizzle and the rocket test a failure, the international community may have exhibited more public alarm than necessary. Perhaps the North Korean antics should be treated more as the attention-getting stunts of a rebellious child than a mortal threat to neighbors. If the North Korean leaders see that their behavior is not frightening their powerful neighbors, it may be easier to induce them to behave.

The U.S. hand can be strengthened by maintaining the support of the other countries in the six-party talks, particularly China, which has the greatest leverage over North Korea. Ultimately the United States will need to define a route to normal relations with North Korea that would permit removal of U.S. military forces from South Korea and a verified end to Pyongyang's nuclear program.

Nuclear Arsenals: The Reagan-Gorbachev Vision

The Obama administration should restore the Reagan-Gorbachev vision of ending the threat of nuclear weapons by continuing to reduce the size of U.S. and Russian nuclear arsenals. Ultimately, the international community will not be able to prevent further proliferation of nuclear weapons if the countries that now possess most of these weapons insist on keeping thousands of them operational.

Few Americans seem to realize the threat inherent in the massive American and Russian nuclear arsenals that have survived the Cold War. The United States and Russia still maintain thousands of weapons on operational alert. It is as if the Cold War had never ended. An accidental launch or a false alarm could result in more damage than terrorists with a crude nuclear device could inflict.

The slowdown in reducing the numbers of Russian and American nuclear weapons obviously impedes efforts to prevent further proliferation. The Non-Proliferation Treaty, which is the legal basis for restraining the spread of nuclear weapons, stipulates that the signatory countries that possess them are obligated "to pursue negotiations in good faith on effective measures relating to cessation of the nuclear arms race at an early date and to nuclear disarmament."[5] The process of verifiable reduction, begun by Reagan and Gorbachev, has not only slowed, but in 2002 the Bush-Cheney administration abandoned the verification procedures in earlier treaties and concluded an agreement without any means of ensuring that its provisions would be implemented. It also failed to negotiate an extension of the START agreement, which was scheduled to expire at the end of 2009 if not renewed in some form.

A bipartisan group of former U.S. officials organized by George Shultz and Sidney Drell called public attention to the urgency of doing more to reduce the nuclear danger in articles published in the *Wall Street Journal* in January 2007 and January 2008. They called for a revival of the spirit of the 1986 Reagan-Gorbachev summit meeting in Reykjavík, when both leaders pledged to put the world on a course to eliminate the nuclear danger. They recognized that this could not be done overnight, but specified a number of steps to restore the lost momentum in nuclear weapons reduction. These steps included extending key provisions of the 1991 START agreement, negotiating a cooperative multilateral missile defense, discussing within NATO and with Russia ways to eliminate tactical and "theater" nuclear weapons, and renewing efforts to ratify the Comprehensive Test Ban Treaty and to bring it into effect.[6]

There was no evident progress on any of these proposals until President Obama took office. As a candidate, he endorsed the proposals of the Shultz group, and he reiterated his support in a speech in Prague in April 2009. Negotiations began with Russia on a replacement for the START treaty, with ceilings for strategic weapons lower than those pledged in the 2002 Moscow Treaty. Russian president Dmitri Medvedev announced, however, that Russian cooperation on the various nuclear issues would require a change in American plans to station missile interceptors in Poland. He made clear that Russia is unlikely to agree to reduce the size of its nuclear arsenal if it feels threatened and in confrontation with the United States and NATO.

Even though changes in policy may be required to secure Russian cooperation where it is needed, that is not the main reason the United States should review and alter Bush-Cheney policies. These policies need changing because it is in the American interest to do so, entirely aside from the Russian reaction.

Take the matter of Georgian and Ukrainian admission to NATO. Neither country meets normal NATO criteria for membership, Georgia because it has unresolved territorial issues and Ukraine because the majority of its citizens do not wish for it to belong to the alliance, and some are likely to try to block NATO activities on Ukrainian soil. It is also not in Georgia's or Ukraine's interest to join NATO. Entering a military alliance that Russia considers hostile would increase Russian incentives to subject them to political and economic pressure. NATO membership could even lead to a split of the Ukrainian state from within, since Russian-speaking Ukrainians in the east and south (including especially in the Crimea) do not wish to be in an alliance that Russia opposes.

The plan for missile defenses in Poland and the Czech Republic, supposedly to defend Western Europe from Iranian missiles, also seems ill advised. Reliable interceptor missiles have not yet been developed, and Iran does not yet have the capability of attacking Western Europe. What would even a hostile Iranian government achieve by launching attacks on Western Europe? It is a stretch to think that there is a plausible potential threat. If there should be a threat from Iran, then a missile defense system developed jointly with Russia would be more effective.

The fundamental point is that there is a direct connection between the development of missile defenses and the possibility of reducing the numbers of nuclear missiles. This was recognized as early as 1972, when President Nixon signed the ABM Treaty, which remained in force until the Bush-Cheney administration withdrew from it. When Reagan argued with Gorbachev over his Strategic Defense Initiative, he made it clear that he did not intend to deploy a missile defense system unless and until both nations eliminated their strategic nuclear weapons. He offered to share any defenses that might be developed. If Gorbachev had offered a joint program to develop anti-ballistic missiles, Reagan probably would have accepted, so long as the Soviet leader agreed that both countries would eliminate their strategic nuclear weapons as the defensive systems were developed.

The rush to deploy missile defenses not yet proven effective both in the United States and in Europe has more to do with abstract theory and interservice rivalry than with the defense needs of the United States.* American

---

*The U.S. Army campaigned for deployment of missile defenses in Alaska under its command because, otherwise, the U.S. Navy and the U.S. Air Force would have controlled most missile technology. The navy resisted using Aegis-class cruisers for boost-phase defense against rogue-state missiles since it feared its missile cruisers would be vulnerable to attack from nearby land.

"supremacists" have long been enamored of missile defense, apparently imagining that a system is possible that would effectively defend the United States from attack, and thus would allow the U.S. to bring military pressure on other countries and even invade them with impunity. However, even if the United States can develop interceptors that are reliable—it has not done so yet—they could not protect the nation either from a terrorist attack (unlikely to be by ballistic missiles) or from an attack by another major nuclear power, which could easily swamp any defensive system with decoys. Any space-based interceptors can be shot down from space more easily than placed in orbit.

There is a persuasive argument that it would be useful to have a defensive system that could intercept missiles launched by rogue states in their boost phase, as they move slowly, rising into orbit. Technically, this could be done with interceptors based on land or sea and fairly close to the launch sites. For defense against Iranian or North Korean missiles, Russian territory is ideal. Russia also has advanced technologies relevant to missile defense.

For all these reasons, it makes most sense for the United States and Russia to develop missile defenses cooperatively, and eventually with Chinese and European participation. This would allow all to defend their territory against rogue states, but would not stand in the way of the continued reduction of offensive weapons.

The bureaucracies in both the United States and Russia are likely to resist joint efforts in an attempt to protect "sensitive" technology. Their resistance, however, has a bureaucratic basis rather than one based on genuine dangers to national security. Both countries have mastered advanced missile technology and there is no reason for secrets between them unless one is planning an attack on the other—which would be a suicidal absurdity. Nevertheless, it will take strong political leadership in both countries to force their military-industrial establishments to share information in a spirit of true partnership.

One of the obstacles to cooperation on missile defense and to the further reduction of nuclear weapons is the doctrine of maintaining U.S. dominance of space, proclaimed by the Bush-Cheney administration. That must be revised, because it is untenable in the long run. The Chinese action in bringing down one of their decommissioned satellites by an anti-satellite device should be a wake-up call that China, along with Russia and probably other countries eventually, will not submit to unilateral American control of space.

We need an international treaty to regulate the proper use of space, which would inter alia ban placing weapons in space and limit the use of anti-satellite devices—which may be useful at times to remove clutter from orbit.* Discussions with Russia, China, and the European Union should be undertaken promptly in order to prepare for an international treaty to deter an arms race in space. Too much of today's economy depends on unimpeded access to satellites, particularly for communication and navigation, to endanger space-based assets with an arms race.

These are examples of urgent security issues that will require a radical change in the American approach if they are to be solved. Others that come to mind are policy toward Cuba; some of the economic sanctions that weigh primarily on the Cuban people should be eased and a dialogue with the Raúl Castro leadership initiated. Decades of boycott and exclusion have not weakened the Castro grip on the island but have provided excuses for continued oppression. The United States needs to put forth a clear and fair agenda of issues for discussion and eventual negotiation that could lead to more normal relations, even with the Castro regime still in place. President Obama's small first step, allowing Cubans in the United States to send money to relatives in Cuba, was timely, but a reversal of the travel ban and further relaxation of economic sanctions will be required before a tangible effect on Cuban policy can be expected.

Relations with European countries will improve if the Obama administration, as is expected, offers to implement practical measures to reduce the emission of greenhouse gases. As for the continent's security, the United States needs to encourage European solutions to European problems, and to support economic cooperation among the European Union, Ukraine, and Russia. If serious talk of bringing Georgia and Ukraine into NATO ends, it should be easier to forge the economic ties that would be beneficial to all. In East Asia, the rising power of China must be accommodated in realistic fashion, along with that of India in South Asia, while preserving the close ties with Japan and South Korea.

The world is changing radically, and any policy designed to perpetuate

*Nuclear weapons are already banned from space by international treaty.

the status quo is doomed to fail, particularly since the Bush-Cheney administration grossly overextended American commitments abroad, commitments that cannot be terminated abruptly but must be replaced over time with something that imposes a smaller drain on American resources and attention.

As is the case in dealing with the economic crisis at home, correction of the foreign policy errors that have put America on the defensive may take years to show unambiguous results. The complexity of the issues and the time it takes to turn defective policy around will test the political skill of the Obama administration to the utmost. Given the situation Obama has inherited, in some cases he will risk blame whatever he does. As *New York Times* correspondent David E. Sanger pointed out in his book *The Inheritance: The World Obama Confronts and the Challenges to American Power,* "If Obama honors his pledge to commit more forces to stabilizing and rebuilding Afghanistan . . . he risks getting bogged down in a country more fractured, more complex and more ungovernable than Iraq."[7] Similarly, if he continues raids in Pakistan, he will be accused of continuing Bush's policy and alienating a potential ally. If violence in Iraq increases as American forces leave, Obama will be blamed by some even if he follows the timetable Bush negotiated with the Iraqi government.

Ultimately, President Obama's ability to bring about the changes America needs in its domestic and foreign policy will depend on the American public's resistance to the false myths and the false ideologies that led both the Clinton and—to a much greater degree—the Bush-Cheney administrations astray. Although the United States will possess for a long time the most powerful armed forces in the world and—for a few more years, at least—the largest economy, it is not and has never been a "superpower" in the sense that it can alone rearrange the world to its liking. As David Sanger put it, "We have to adjust to a world that Bush could never accept—one in which new power centers arise, one in which America does not always set the rules and sometimes has to heed rules set by others."[8]

If President Obama can make that adjustment, replacing attempts to enforce hegemony with efforts to cooperate to achieve common purposes, America will emerge both stronger and more secure than it has been since the beginning of this century.

In 2007, when I began writing this book, the prospect that America would change its erratic and self-defeating course did not seem bright. Three years earlier, the American people had reelected a president who had plunged the country into a costly and unnecessary war and had converted a budget surplus to the largest deficit the U.S. Treasury had ever experienced. And yet, he was sold to the American people as a conservative. Even the Republican defeat in the 2006 election had brought only marginal changes in the way the U.S. government dealt with other countries and with the growing problems at home. Too many American voters, hypnotized by misleading slogans, seemed unable to distinguish truth from artfully concealed falsehood.

The presidential election in 2008 has given renewed hope to those of us who understand that our nation must change course if it is to retain its primacy in the world and its capacity to work with other peoples to keep the peace, spur development, and improve the quality of life. President Obama is not only an inspiring speaker and, to judge by the efficiency of his election campaign, a talented manager, but a pragmatic leader, guided not by abstract theories divorced from real life, but by an acute sensitivity to the effect policy choices have on people's lives.

It will probably surprise readers accustomed to judging politicians by their party affiliation when I say that the president whom Barack Obama most resembles is Ronald Reagan. Not all their policies are the same, but their leadership qualities are strikingly similar. One of the reasons I wrote this book was to refute the distortions of Reagan's foreign policy record perpetrated by the superpower illusionists so active in the Bush-Cheney administration.

One of Reagan's characteristic refrains was "It's morning in America," the dawn of a new day. His confidence in America's basic decency and potential for leading the world by example was unbounded. And though he talked of ideology, he was at heart a pragmatist, an adherent of that quintessentially *American* philosophy that also guides our current president.

We have come through a long night, but a new day is dawning. This book, which I began in a mood close to despair, ends in one of encouragement and hope. If the nation can face up to its mistakes and correct them, it will prove that the faith in America shared by Ronald Reagan and Barack Obama is not misplaced.

NOTES

Chapter 1. Myths and Realities

1. *Cold War* (1998), shown on CNN, http://www.cnn.com/SPECIALS/cold.war/.
2. "The Man Who Beat Communism," *The Economist*, June 12, 2004.
3. Francis Fukuyama, *The End of History and the Last Man* (New York: Free Press, 1992).
4. Clifford Levy, "What's Russian for 'Hacker'?" *New York Times*, October 21, 2007, Week in Review section.
5. One of the earliest and most voluminous of the "revisionist" histories was D. F. Fleming's *The Cold War and Its Origins*, published in 1961 by Doubleday and Company. (His penultimate chapter, "Why the West Lost the Cold War," illustrates the hazard inherent in writing instant history.) Regarding the claim that the Cold War might have ended earlier had U.S. policy been different, see—for example—Richard Ned Lebow and Janice Gross Stein, *We All Lost the Cold War* (Princeton: Princeton University Press, 1994).
6. André Fontaine, *History of the Cold War: From the October Revolution to the Korean War, 1917–1950* (New York: Pantheon, 1968), p. 26.
7. George F. Kennan, *The Decision to Intervene* (Princeton: Princeton University Press, 1958).
8. Norman Saul, *War and Revolution: The United States and Russia, 1914–1921* (Lawrence: University Press of Kansas, 2001), pp. 390–391.
9. Winston Churchill, radio broadcast on October 1, 1939, as quoted in the *Oxford Dictionary of Quotations*.
10. See Constantine Pleshakov's masterly *Stalin's Folly: The Tragic First Ten Days of World War II on the Eastern Front* (Boston: Houghton Mifflin, 2005).
11. Rodric Braithwaite presents an unforgettable picture of popular heroism and leadership incompetence in *Moscow, 1941: A City and Its People at War* (London: Profile, 2006).

12. The full text of Kennan's message is available in Kenneth M. Jensen, ed., *Origins of the Cold War: The Novikov, Kennan, and Roberts "Long Telegrams" of 1946* (Washington, D.C.: United States Institute of Peace, 1991). George Kennan commented on the telegram in his *Memoirs: 1925–1950* (Boston: Little, Brown, 1967), pp. 271–297, with an extended excerpt on pp. 547–559.

13. *Colliers* magazine, October 21, 1951. The issue showed an American military policeman with "MP–Occupation Forces" on his helmet and a map of the western Soviet Union in the background. The cover contained two headlines: "Preview of the War We Do Not Want," and "Russia's Defeat and Occupation, 1952–1960." It contained articles by many prominent journalists, scholars, and politicians of the day, including Robert Sherwood, Arthur Koestler, Edward R. Murrow, Alan Nevins, J. B. Priestley, and Senator Margaret Chase Smith.

14. David Holloway, *Stalin and the Bomb: The Soviet Union and Atomic Energy, 1939–1956* (New Haven: Yale University Press, 1994).

15. Edvard Beneš, *Paměti: Od mnichova k nvové válce a k novému vítězství* (Prague: Orbis, 1947).

Chapter 2. Framework Diplomacy

1. For this chapter I have drawn on the discussion in Jack F. Matlock, Jr., *Reagan and Gorbachev: How the Cold War Ended* (New York: Random House, 2004), and on my essay "Ronald Reagan and the End of the Cold War," published in *Ronald Reagan and the 1980s: Perceptions, Policies, Legacies*, ed. Cheryl Hudson and Gareth Davies (New York: Palgrave Macmillan, 2008), pp. 57–78.

2. Ronald Reagan, *An American Life: The Autobiography* (New York: Simon and Schuster, 1990), pp. 272–273.

3. Anatoly Dobrynin, *In Confidence: Moscow's Ambassador to America's Six Cold War Presidents* (New York: Random House, 1995), p. 493.

4. All of these ideas were expressed explicitly or implicitly in an address that Soviet minister of defense Dmitri Ustinov delivered on behalf of the Politburo in November 1981, the first year of the Reagan presidency. (Text in *Pravda*, November 7, 1981.)

5. Christopher Andrew and Vasili Mitrokhin, *The Sword and the Shield: The Mitrokhin Archive and the Secret History of the KGB* (New York: Basic, 1999), p. 243.

6. Published in *Pravda* and *Izvestiya*, September 29, 1983.

7. Oleg Gordievsky, then the KGB resident (i.e., station chief) in London, who provided information to British and American intelligence before his defection, informed the British and American governments that the KGB had placed high priority on collecting information that might indicate an impending nuclear attack on the Soviet Union. He warned that the KGB Center had been particularly alarmed by a NATO communication exercise in November 1983, code-named "Able Archer 83." Although Reagan had given instructions to try to arrange a summit meeting with the Soviet leader before he received this information, Gordievsky's report gave him an additional incentive to redouble efforts to con-

tact the Soviet leader and reassure him of Reagan's peaceful intentions. Gordievsky described the KGB program in Christopher Andrew and Oleg Gordievsky, *KGB: The Inside Story of Its Foreign Operations from Lenin to Gorbachev* (London: Hodder and Stoughton, 1990), pp. 502–503.

8. The full text was published in the *Weekly Compilation of Presidential Documents*, vol. 20, no. 3, pp. 40–45, and by the Department of State as *Current Policy*, no. 537, "The U.S.-Soviet Relationship." For a scholarly analysis, see Beth A. Fischer, "Toeing the Hard Line? The Reagan Administration and the Ending of the Cold War," *Political Science Quarterly*, vol. 112, no. 3 (1997), pp. 477–496.

9. "Vystuplenie R. Reygana," *Izvestiya*, January 17, 1984.

10. Korniyenko was the first name Gromyko mentioned when he discussed his replacement with Gorbachev; Mikhail Gorbachev, *Memoirs* (New York: Doubleday, 1996), p. 180. Alexander Bessmertnykh told me later that he had the impression that Korniyenko expected the appointment and was crushed when he learned that Shevardnadze had been chosen.

11. In my book *Reagan and Gorbachev*, I reported that Reagan had "dictated" this note to his secretary (pp. 150–153). That was my understanding at the time, when I was shown a typewritten copy, corrected in Reagan's hand. However, since then I have learned that in fact he wrote the memorandum by hand, had his secretary type it, then made a significant correction. The handwritten memorandum, without the correction, was quoted in Edmund Morris, *Dutch: A Memoir of Ronald Reagan* (New York: Random House, 1999), pp. 545–546.

12. Reagan reproduced the text of the letter in his memoirs, *An American Life*, pp. 642–645.

13. Ambassador Thomas W. Simons, Jr., who was a deputy assistant secretary of state at the time, described it as "a visionary program for eliminating all nuclear weapons by the year 2000," and considered it related primarily to Gorbachev's need to build a more solid constituency in the Communist Party Central Committee; Thomas W. Simons, Jr., *The End of the Cold War?* (New York: St. Martin's, 1990), pp. 79–80.

14. Reagan, *An American Life*, p. 550.

15. Frances FitzGerald traced the development of Reagan's thinking about nuclear weapons in her brilliant *Way Out There in the Blue: Reagan, Star Wars, and the End of the Cold War* (New York: Simon and Schuster, 2000).

16. Reported from notes taken during meetings with General Yazov.

17. Jack F. Matlock, Jr., *Autopsy on an Empire: The American Ambassador's Account of the Collapse of the Soviet Union* (New York: Random House, 1995), pp. 121–123.

18. Reagan included a lengthy excerpt from his speech at Moscow University in Reagan, *An American Life*, pp. 713–714.

19. Personal communication from Svetlana Savranskaya, National Security Archive, Georgetown University, Washington, D.C.

20. Reagan, *An American Life*, p. 720.

21. I quoted Politburo notes of the December 1988 meeting in Matlock, *Reagan and Gorbachev*, pp. 309–310.

22. These turned up in the reports of columnists Rowland Evans and Robert Novak, and also in the *Washington Times* newspaper.

23. Reagan, *An American Life*, p. 707.

24. U.S. Institute of Peace, "The USSR/U.S. Dialogue on Human Rights, 1986–1990," July 6, 2006.

25. In his memoirs, published as late as 1990, Caspar Weinberger complained that Gorbachev's skill at public relations "obscured the unchanging nature of the Soviet system"; Caspar W. Weinberger, *Fighting for Peace: Seven Critical Years in the Pentagon* (New York: Warner, 1990), p. 332. This was after the Soviet Union had conducted the first contested elections since the Communists consolidated their power, released political prisoners, ended censorship of the media, reduced its armed forces unilaterally, and allowed most Eastern European satellite countries to throw out their Communist rulers!

26. Note, for example, the contemptuous attitude toward summitry Kenneth Adelman displayed in *The Great Universal Embrace: Arms Summitry—A Skeptic's Account* (New York: Simon and Schuster, 1989). He pictures Reagan as a bungling amateur who would have been bested in every encounter with Gorbachev if Adelman (who actually had very little influence on Reagan's policy) and his friends had not saved the day for him.

Chapter 3. Cleanup Diplomacy and Conclusions We Can Draw

1. Interview on ABC's *This Week with David Brinkley*, January 22, 1989.

2. "The Soviet Union over the Next Four Years," 89 Moscow 2962, February 3, 1989; "Soviet Foreign Policy over the Next Four Years," 89 Moscow 3850, February 13, 1989; and "U.S.-Soviet Relations: Policy Opportunities," 89 Moscow 4648, February 22, 1989, declassified cables available at the National Security Archive at George Washington University, Washington, D.C.

3. The message, "Looking into the Abyss: The Possible Collapse of the Soviet Union and What We Should Be Doing About It," was drafted by Political Counselor Raymond Smith; 90 Moscow 23603, July 13, 1990, declassified February 28, 2007.

4. Pavel Palazchenko, Gorbachev's English interpreter, reported that Bush told Gorbachev, as he accompanied him to the airport following the Washington summit meeting in December 1987, that he intended to run for president the following year and that, in political campaigns, "things are sometimes said that we all regret afterward, and they should be disregarded." He then assured Gorbachev that if he was elected, he would continue a policy of cooperating with the Soviet Union. Pavel Palazchenko, *My Years with Gorbachev and Shevardnadze: The Memoir of a Soviet Interpreter* (University Park: Pennsylvania State University Press, 1997), pp. 79–80.

5. Matlock, *Autopsy on an Empire*, pp. 207–210.

6. I draw these conclusions from many conversations with senior Soviet officials that took place as the events occurred, and also from the comments of persons

like Zdeněk Mlynář, an ally of Alexander Dubček, who was also Gorbachev's roommate during their student years at Moscow University. The reminiscences of both, recorded in *Conversations with Gorbachev on Perestroika, the Prague Spring, and the Crossroads of Socialism* (New York: Columbia University Press, 2002) cast light on the evolution of Gorbachev's attitude toward Marxism and the Soviet system, and particularly on the impact the Prague Spring had on his thinking.

7. I recounted in detail the way this occurred in Matlock, *Autopsy on an Empire*, pp. 197–199.

8. Soviet troops in East Germany were withdrawn at the same time they were being transferred from other Warsaw Pact countries. It is estimated that about 650,000 Soviet citizens (500,000 military personnel and 150,000 dependents) were repatriated from the GDR, Poland, Czechoslovakia, and Hungary as the result of agreements reached in 1989 and 1990; William E. Odom, *The Collapse of the Soviet Military* (New Haven: Yale University Press, 1998), p. 275.

9. Philip Zelikow and Condoleezza Rice, *Germany Unified and Europe Transformed: A Study in Statecraft* (Cambridge: Harvard University Press, 1995), especially pp. 187–188.

In his memoirs, Gorbachev quotes Baker as proposing during the meeting on February 9, 1990, that a united Germany be allowed to remain in NATO "with the guarantee that NATO jurisdiction or troops would not extend east of the current line"; Mikhail Gorbachev, *Zhizn' i reformy* (Moscow: Novosti, 1995), vol. 2, p. 167. Gorbachev's account coincides with my notes of the conversation except that mine indicate that Baker added "not one inch." (The Russian translator may have omitted the phrase since "inch" is not a common measure in Russian and it would have been awkward to say "not even by 2.5 centimeters.")

Subsequently, Baker has explained that he made the statement with the territory of East Germany in mind, and that when he found that excluding East German territory from NATO jurisdiction would be legally impossible, he had the statement corrected. It was finally decided, in the "two plus four" negotiations, that the territory of East Germany would fall under NATO jurisdiction but that NATO troops, other than German troops, would not be stationed there.

The problem with this explanation is that Bush's initial statement to Gorbachev did not specify that he had only the territory of the GDR in mind. To the best of my knowledge, Gorbachev is correct when he states that he was never informed directly that Baker intended the original statement to be limited to the GDR. Therefore, both he and Shevardnadze assumed that they had assurances that NATO would not replace the Warsaw Pact in Eastern Europe. After all, that would have been a direct violation of the understanding at Malta that the United States would not "take advantage" of a Soviet military withdrawal from Eastern Europe.

10. Jonathan B. Tucker has provided a useful account of the considerations and bureaucratic maneuvering that preceded Nixon's decision in "Farewell to Germs:

U.S. Renunciation of Biologic and Toxin Warfare, 1969–1970," *International Security,* vol. 27, no. 1 (Summer 2002), pp. 107–148.

11. The most comprehensive published account of the Soviet biological weapons program is in Ken Alibek with Stephen Handelman, *Biohazard: The Chilling True Story of the Largest Covert Biological Weapons Program in the World—Told from Inside by the Man Who Ran It* (New York: Random House, 1999).

12. See, for example, the argument in Peter Schweitzer, *Victory: The Reagan Administration's Secret Strategy That Hastened the Collapse of the Soviet Union* (New York: Atlantic Monthly, 1994).

13. Yegor Gaidar, *Collapse of an Empire: Lessons for Modern Russia* (Washington, D.C.: Brookings Institution Press, 2008), p. 249.

14. Reagan, *An American Life,* p. 715.

15. Richard Neustadt and Ernest May, *Thinking in Time: The Uses of History for Decision Makers* (New York: Free Press, 1986).

16. Neustadt and May, *Thinking in Time,* pp. 134–156.

17. George F. Kennan, *Around the Cragged Hill* (New York: Norton, 1993), p. 183.

18. George F. Kennan, *At Century's Ending: Reflections, 1982–1995* (New York: W. W. Norton, 1996), pp. 315–316.

19. Victor Cherkashin with Gregory Feifer, *Spy Handler: Memoir of a KGB Officer* (New York: Basic, 2005).

Chapter 4. Regime Change

1. Shevardnadze recalled in his 1991 memoir that he and Gorbachev would take long walks in the evening when they met at resorts in Georgia or the Stavropol region and discuss deficiencies in the way the Soviet Union was ruled; Eduard Shevardnadze, *Moy vybor: V zashchitu demokratii i svobody* (Moscow: Novosti, 1991), p. 62.

2. Anatoly Chernyaev, Statement at a conference on understanding the end of the Cold War, Brown University, May 7–10, 1998.

3. *Sovetskaya Rossiya,* March 13, 1988. This incident is discussed in detail in Matlock, *Autopsy on an Empire,* pp. 119–121.

4. Robert D. English described the development of the ideas that lay behind Gorbachev's "new thinking" and perestroika in *Russia and the Idea of the West: Gorbachev, Intellectuals, and the End of the Cold War* (New York: Columbia University Press, 2000).

5. Paraphrased from notes made during a meeting with Gorbachev.

6. Matlock, *Autopsy on an Empire,* pp. 322–327.

7. Matlock, *Autopsy on an Empire,* pp. 468–473.

8. Matlock, *Autopsy on an Empire,* pp. 539–546. Mayor of Moscow Gavriil Popov, the source of my report, told me later that my warning to Gorbachev, which became known to KGB chairman Kryuchkov when President Bush mentioned it in a telephone conversation monitored by the KGB, may have undermined the success of the attempted August coup. According to Popov, Kryuchkov must

have realized that there was a leak in his plans to remove Gorbachev and therefore was unable to plan the coup properly. In fact, the coup leaders had not obtained in advance the support of some key military leaders, such as General Alexander Lebed, who refused orders to move against Yeltsin and thus contributed to the coup's failure.

9. For a detailed analysis of the collapse, see Dick Combs, *Inside the Soviet Alternative Universe: The Cold War's End and the Soviet Union's Fall Reappraised* (University Park: Pennsylvania State University Press, 2008).

10. Matlock, *Autopsy on an Empire*, p. 672.

11. Recorded in my journal when I watched the interview on television.

12. John Gray, *Black Mass: Apocalyptic Religion and the Death of Utopia* (New York: Farrar, Straus and Giroux, 2007), p. 5.

13. For a vivid illustration of the Soviet propensity to tailor diplomatic and intelligence reports to fit the prevailing ideology, one can take the telegram Soviet ambassador Nikolai Novikov sent to Foreign Minister V. M. Molotov in September 1946 explaining postwar American policy. Novikov's report begins with the following sentence, "The foreign policy of the United States, which reflects the imperialist tendencies of American monopolistic capital, is characterized in the postwar period by a striving for world supremacy." He then speculated that the United States considered Great Britain its "greatest potential competitor" but also a potential ally, which led it to agree to a temporary division of the world between them. Reactionaries, including columnists like Walter Lippmann and "conservative" newspapers like the *New York Times*, according to Novikov, were campaigning for a war against the Soviet Union. Kenneth M. Jensen, ed., *Origins of the Cold War: The Novikov, Kennan, and Roberts "Long Telegrams" of 1946* (Washington, D.C.: United States Institute of Peace, 1991), pp. 3–16.

14. Matlock, *Autopsy on an Empire*, pp. 489–491.

Chapter 5. A New World?

1. The Peace of Westphalia was actually two treaties, signed in Osnabrück and Münster on May 15 and October 24, 1648.

2. George Bush and Brent Scowcroft, *A World Transformed* (New York: Knopf, 1998).

3. James A. Baker III, with Thomas M. Defrank, *The Politics of Diplomacy: Revolution, War, and Peace, 1989–1992* (New York: Putnam, 1995), pp. 658–665.

4. The issue of bioweapons verification is not even mentioned in the memoirs of Bush, Scowcroft, and Baker, although they refer briefly to the Soviet and Iraqi programs.

5. Baker provides a vivid account of his contacts with the leaders of the Soviet republics in *The Politics of Diplomacy*.

6. Yegor Gaidar, *Days of Defeat and Victory* (Seattle: University of Washington Press, 1999), pp. 152–153.

7. Gaidar, *Days of Defeat*, p. 152.

8. I described the advice she asked me to give President Bush in Matlock, *Autopsy on an Empire*, pp. 537–539.

9. Thomas L. McNaugher, *Arms and Oil: U.S. Military Strategy and the Persian Gulf* (Washington, D.C.: Brookings Institution, 1985).

10. These issues are discussed in detail in Michael T. Klare, *Blood and Oil: The Dangers and Consequences of America's Growing Dependency on Imported Petroleum* (New York: Holt, 2004).

11. Walter Wriston, *The Twilight of Sovereignty: How the Information Revolution Is Transforming Our World* (New York: Scribner, 1992).

12. For example, see Jeffrey E. Garten, *A Cold Peace: America, Japan, Germany, and the Struggle for Supremacy* (New York: Times, 1992), and Lester C. Thurow, *Head to Head: The Coming Economic Battle Among Japan, Europe, and America* (New York: Morrow, 1992).

13. Ernest Gellner, *Civil Society and Its Rivals* (London: Hamish Hamilton, 1994).

14. Gray, *Black Mass*, p. 75.

15. Zbigniew Brzezinski, *Out of Control: Global Turmoil on the Eve of the Twenty-First Century* (New York: Scribner, 1993).

16. Zbigniew Brzezinski, *The Grand Chessboard: American Primacy and Its Geostrategic Imperatives* (New York: Basic, 1997); Alfred Thayer Mahan, *The Influence of Sea Power Upon History*, was published in 1890.

17. Samuel P. Huntington, *The Clash of Civilizations and the Remaking of World Order* (New York: Simon and Schuster, 1996). The three quotations are taken respectively from pp. 21, 128, and 29.

18. Arnold J. Toynbee, *A Study in History: Abridgment of Volumes 1–6*, by D. C. Somerville (New York: Oxford University Press, 1947).

19. Dennis Ross, who played a leading role in dealing with the Israeli-Palestinian issues in the Reagan, Bush, and Clinton administrations, described the diplomacy in lucid detail in *The Missing Peace: The Inside Story of the Fight for Middle East Peace* (New York: Farrar, Straus and Giroux, 2004). He describes the run-up to the Madrid Conference at pp. 46–87.

Chapter 6. The Unipolar Delusion

1. Joseph S. Nye, Jr., classified types of power into "hard power" (military and economic), which can compel, and "soft power" (values, culture) that attracts people; Joseph S. Nye, Jr., *The Paradox of American Power: Why the World's Only Superpower Can't Go It Alone* (New York: Oxford University Press, 2002).

2. McGeorge Bundy, William J. Crowe, Jr., and Sidney D. Drell, *Reducing Nuclear Danger: The Road Away from the Brink* (New York: Council on Foreign Relations, 1993), p. 77.

3. David I. Steinberg, "U.S. Policy and Human Rights in the Republic of Korea: The Influence of Policy or the Policy of Influence," in *Implementing U.S. Human Rights Policy: Agendas, Policies, and Practices*, ed. Debra Liang-Fenton (Washington, D.C.: United States Institute of Peace Press, 2004), pp. 167–216.

4. Nye, *The Paradox of American Power*, p. 148.

5. Vernon Bogdanor, ed., *The Blackwell Encyclopedia of Political Institutions* (Oxford: Basil Blackwell, 1987), p. 203. There are, of course, other definitions. Michael Doyle offers the following in his book *Empires* (Ithaca: Cornell University Press, 1986), p. 19: "Empires are relationships of political control over the effective sovereignty of other political societies. They include more than just formally annexed territories, but they encompass less than the sum of all forms of international inequality. Imperialism is the process of establishing and maintaining an empire."

6. Donald Rumsfeld, interview, February 27, 2003, press release, Department of Defense.

7. Niall Ferguson, *Colossus: The Price of America's Empire* (New York: Penguin, 2004), p. 2.

8. Richard van Alstyne, *The Rising American Empire* (New York: Oxford University Press, 1960).

9. Charles S. Maier, *Among Empires: American Ascendancy and Its Predecessors* (Cambridge: Harvard University Press, 2006).

10. Ferguson, *Colossus*, p. 2.

11. This is the sense in which Noam Chomsky uses it in *Hegemony or Survival: America's Quest for Global Dominance*. Chomsky's analysis is questionable in many respects, particularly his stress on economic factors, but he illustrates the tendency to use "hegemony" as a synonym for imperialism.

12. "There's more to leadership than you think," comments on the blog "Russia Beyond the Headlines" (http://rbth.ru), posted April 29, 2009.

13. Charles Krauthammer, "The Unipolar Moment," *Foreign Affairs* (Winter 1990–1991), pp. 23–33.

Chapter 7. Hubris and Its Consequences

1. Avis Bohlen, "The Rise and Fall of Arms Control," *Survival*, vol. 45, no. 3 (Autumn 2003), pp. 7–34.

2. Jonathan Schell, *The Gift of Time: The Case for Abolishing Nuclear Weapons Now* (New York: Henry Holt, 1999), pp. 28–29.

3. U.S. Energy Information Administration.

4. Richard A. Clarke, *Against All Enemies: Inside America's War on Terror* (New York: Free Press, 2004).

5. Odom, *The Collapse of the Soviet Military*.

6. William Zimmerman, *The Russian People and Foreign Policy: Russian Elite and Mass Perspectives, 1993–2000* (Princeton: Princeton University Press, 2002).

7. James M. Goldgeier, *Not Whether but When: The U.S. Decision to Enlarge NATO* (Washington, D.C.: Brookings Institution, 1999).

8. Strobe Talbott, *The Russia Hand: A Memoir of Presidential Diplomacy* (New York: Random House, 2002).

9. George F. Kennan, "A Fateful Error," *New York Times*, February 5, 1997.

10. Ivo H. Daalder, *Getting to Dayton: The Making of America's Bosnia Policy* (Washington, D.C.: Brookings Institution, 2000).

11. Both Clinton (in his autobiography *My Life*) and his principal negotiator, Dennis Ross (*The Missing Peace*), place the blame on Arafat for the failure at Camp David. Others, such as Clayton Swisher (*The Truth About Camp David*), have challenged that conclusion, judging that Arafat in fact made more concessions than did Israel.

12. Aaron David Miller has written a most revealing, insightful, and moving account of diplomacy during this period—and also before and after it—in *The Much Too Promised Land: America's Elusive Search for Arab-Israeli Peace* (New York: Bantam, 2008).

13. Martin Indyk, the new special assistant to the president responsible for the Near East on the National Security Council, outlined the policy in a speech at the Washington Institute for Near East Policy in May 1993.

14. Trita Parsi, *Treacherous Alliance: The Secret Dealings of Israel, Iran, and the U.S.* (New Haven: Yale University Press, 2007), pp. 202–222.

15. Henry Raymont, *Troubled Neighbors: The Story of U.S.-Latin American Relations from FDR to the Present* (Westview, 2005), p. 284.

16. Raymont, *Troubled Neighbors*, p. 307.

17. Samantha Power, *A Problem from Hell: America and the Age of Genocide* (New York: Perennial, 2003).

18. When American diplomats were taken hostage in Iran in 1979, not a single employee of the Central Intelligence Agency in that country spoke Farsi, its principal language; Mark Bowden, *Guests of the Ayatollah* (New York: Grove, 2006), p. 178.

19. Thomas P. M. Barnett, *The Pentagon's New Map: War and Peace in the Twenty-First Century* (New York: Berkeley, 2004), p. 139.

20. Derek Chollet and James Goldgeier, *America Between the Wars: From 11/9 to 9/11; The Misunderstood Years Between the Fall of the Berlin Wall and the Start of the War on Terror* (New York: Public Affairs, 2008), p. 111.

Chapter 8. Asleep at the Switch

1. *The 9/11 Commission Report: Final Report of the National Commission on Terrorist Attacks upon the United States* (New York: W. W. Norton, 2004).

2. Richard A. Posner, "The 9/11 Report: A Dissent," *New York Times Book Review,* August 29, 2004.

3. Clarke, *Against All Enemies*, pp. 211–214.

4. Clarke, *Against All Enemies*, p. 213.

5. The PDB of August 6, 2001, reported: "FBI information . . . indicates patterns of suspicious activity in the country consistent with preparations for hijacking or other types of attacks, including surveillance of federal buildings in New York"; *9/11 Commission Report*, p. 262.

6. When Thomas Pickard, the acting FBI director, mentioned CIA warnings of an Al-Qaeda attack to Ashcroft on July 12, 2001, Ashcroft was reported to have said, "I don't want to hear about that any more. There is nothing I can do about that." Quoted in Philip Shenon, *The Commission: The Uncensored History of the 9/11 Commission* (New York: Twelve, 2008), p. 247.

7. Shenon, *The Commission*.

8. Shenon, *The Commission*, pp. 342–343.

9. Richard A. Falkenrath, "The 9/11 Commission Report: A Review Essay," *International Security*, vol. 29, no. 3 (Winter 2004–2005), pp. 170–190.

10. Ernest R. May and Philip D. Zelikow, "Sins of Commission: Falkenrath and His Critics," *International Security*, vol. 29, no. 4 (Spring 2005), pp. 208–209.

11. *International Security*, vol. 29, no. 4 (Spring 2005), p. 211.

12. United Nations Security Council Resolution 1368, September 12, 2001.

13. United Nations Security Council Resolution 1373.

14. According to Ron Suskind, a CIA briefer warned the president and the vice president in November 2002 that the "backdoor" to the Tora Bora redoubt was open, and that a contingent of U.S. Marines should be moved there immediately to close it. The advice was ignored. Ron Suskind, *The One Percent Doctrine* (New York: Simon and Schuster, 2006), pp. 58–59.

15. "Deputy White House Chief of Staff Rove Delivers Remarks to the New York Conservative Party," *Newsmaker Transcripts*, White House, June 22, 2005.

16. Lawrence Wright, *The Looming Tower: Al-Qaeda and the Road to 9/11* (New York: Knopf, 2006).

17. William R. Polk, *Violent Politics: A History of Insurgency, Terrorism, and Guerrilla War, From the American Revolution to Iraq* (New York: HarperCollins, 2007).

18. Max Abrahms, "What Terrorists Really Want: Terrorist Motives and Counterterrorism Strategy," *International Security*, vol. 32, no. 4 (Spring 2008), pp. 78–105.

19. George Soros, *The Bubble of American Supremacy* (New York: Public Affairs, 2004), p. 18.

20. Norman Podhoretz, *World War IV: The Long Struggle Against Islamofascism* (New York: Doubleday, 2007).

21. Ulrich (Rick) Straus, who served as a Japanese language officer during the postwar occupation of Japan, has written a fascinating and revealing study of the treatment of Japanese prisoners of war during World War II, *The Anguish of Surrender: Japanese POWs of World War II* (Seattle: University of Washington Press, 2003). Japanese POWs were treated humanely and were usually interrogated by Japanese-Americans who understood both the language and the culture. The prisoners had been told that they would be killed if captured, and when they were treated decently they became more willing to talk. The interrogators understood that they needed to take their time and establish a rapport with each prisoner, and in time, they provided much "actionable intelligence." Straus summarized his conclusions in "When More Humanity Meant More Success," *International Herald Tribune*, December 23, 2004. The treatment of prisoners at

Guantánamo and Abu Ghraib is another example of the consequences of failing to learn from historical experience.

22. Suskind, *The One Percent Doctrine*, pp. 114–115.

23. Ali Soufan, "My Tortured Decision," *New York Times*, April 23, 2009. The information Zubayda provided before he was tortured led to the capture of Jose Padilla, the "dirty bomber," and also helped identify one of the top Al-Qaeda leaders, Khalid Sheikh Mohammed, who had hidden under the pseudonym Mukhtar, or "the Brain."

24. Jane Mayer, *The Dark Side: The Inside Story of How the War on Terror Turned into a War on American Ideals* (New York: Doubleday, 2008), p. 16.

25. Col. Randall J. Larsen, director of the Institute for Homeland Security, makes this point and others in his informative book, *Our Own Worst Enemy: Asking the Right Questions About Security to Protect You, Your Family, and America* (New York: Grand Central, 2007).

26. The CIA is reported to have found, on the hard drive of a computer used by Al-Qaeda operatives in Afghanistan, the design of a crude but potentially effective device to produce and deliver hydrogen cyanide, a gas that is lethal when inhaled. Suskind, *The One Percent Doctrine*, pp. 194–195.

27. Clarke, *Against All Enemies*, p. 246.

Chapter 9. Tar Baby Iraq

1. Ron Suskind, *The Price of Loyalty: George W. Bush, the White House, and the Education of Paul O'Neill* (New York: Simon and Schuster, 2004).

2. Clarke, *Against All Enemies*, p. 30–33.

3. Kenneth M. Pollack, *The Threatening Storm: The Case for Invading Iraq* (New York: Random House, 2002).

4. Pollack, *The Threatening Storm*, p. 334.

5. Pollack, *The Threatening Storm*, p. 337.

6. Pollack, *The Threatening Storm*, p. 338.

7. See Max Rodenbeck, "War and Peace" (review of *A Path Out of the Desert*, by Kenneth M. Pollack), *New York Times Book Review*, August 24, 2008, p. 1.

8. Soros, *The Bubble of American Supremacy*, pp. 3–4.

9. Patrick J. Buchanan, *Where the Right Went Wrong: How Neoconservatives Subverted the Reagan Revolution and Hijacked the Bush Presidency* (New York: St. Martin's, 2004).

10. Garry Dorrien, *The Neoconservative Mind: Politics, Culture, and the War of Ideology* (Philadelphia: Temple University Press, 1993), pp. 2–8.

11. Quoted in Geoffrey Goldberg, "After Iraq," *Atlantic* (January–February 2008), p. 76.

12. Adam Garfinkle, "Bye, Bye Bush: What History Will Make of 43," *Foreign Affairs*, vol. 82, no. 2 (March–April, 2008), pp. 151–152.

13. Francis Fukuyama, *America and the Crossroads: Democracy, Power, and the Neoconservative Legacy* (New Haven: Yale University Press, 2006), p. 62.

14. James Mann, *Rise of the Vulcans: The History of Bush's War Cabinet* (New York: Viking, 2004).

15. Bob Woodward, *The War Within: A Secret White House History, 2006–2008* (New York: Simon and Schuster, 2008), pp. 430–434.

16. A former official told Michael Gordon and Bernard Trainor that Karl Rove had predicted, as preparations were being made to invade Iraq in 2003, that the war "could be a boon to the president's re-election effort"; Michael R. Gordon and Bernard E. Trainor, *Cobra II: The Inside Story of the Invasion and Occupation of Iraq* (New York: Pantheon, 2006), p. 174.

17. One of the best summaries of the reasons the war in Iraq was a mistake from the beginning and not just a failure of planning or execution can be found in a policy analysis issued by the Cato Institute on February 13, 2008, "Learning the Right Lessons from Iraq," by Benjamin H. Friedman, Harvey M. Sapolsky, and Christopher Preble. The authors conclude that "what Iraq demonstrates is a need for a new national security strategy, not better tactics and tools to serve the current one."

18. See, for example, the address of French foreign minister Dominique de Villepin to the U.N. Security Council on February 14, 2003.

19. Ron Suskind, *The Way of the World: A Story of Truth and Hope in an Age of Extremism* (New York: HarperCollins, 2008), pp. 183–184.

20. Cheney is quoted as saying, "If there's a one percent chance that Pakistani scientists are helping Al Qaeda build or develop a nuclear weapon, we have to treat it as a certainty in terms of our response"; Suskind, *The One Percent Doctrine*, p. 62.

21. Gordon and Trainor, *Cobra II*, p. 171.

22. Ambassador Bremer described his reasons for these decisions in *My Year in Iraq: The Struggle to Build a Future of Hope* (New York: Simon and Schuster, 2006).

23. Described in detail in Woodward, *The War Within*.

24. Peter W. Galbraith, "Is This Victory?" *New York Review of Books*, October 23, 2008, p. 76.

25. See, for example, Jeremy Scahill, *Blackwater: The Rise of the World's Most Powerful Mercenary Army* (New York: Nation, 2008), and Robert Young Pelton, *Licensed to Kill: Hired Guns in the War on Terror* (New York: Crown, 2006).

26. Woodward, *The War Within*, p. 437.

Chapter 10. Ideology Trumps Reality

1. Soros pointed out, for example, that while unregulated free markets on a global scale are good at creating wealth, they also have a negative side in that many people are hurt by globalization and markets are not good at meeting social needs. Furthermore, global financial markets are crisis prone. These are problems "market fundamentalists" ignore when they resist a government role in

meeting social needs. *George Soros on Globalization* (New York: Public Affairs, 2002).

2. David Cay Johnston provides numerous examples in *Free Lunch: How the Wealthiest Americans Enrich Themselves at Government Expense (and Stick You with the Bill)* (New York: Portfolio, 2007).

3. Gray, Plant, Mooty, "Investigative Report to Joint Committee to Investigate the I-35W Bridge Collapse," May 2008, available at http://www.commissions.leg .state.mn.us/jbc/GPM_Report/InvestigativeReport.pdf.

4. None of the fifteen infrastructure categories received a grade higher than C+, and only one rated that high (Solid Waste). Five received a D- (Drinking Water; Inland Waterways; Levees; Roads; and Wastewater). "ASCE 2009 Report Card for America's Infrastructure," available at http://www.asce.org/reportcard /2009/.

5. For discussion of the U.S.-Iranian contacts in 2001 and 2003, see Parsi, *Treacherous Alliance*, pp. 223-257; Barbara Slavin, *Bitter Friends, Bosom Enemies: Iran, the U.S., and the Twisted Path to Confrontation* (New York: St. Martin's, 2007), pp. 194-208; John W. Parker, *Persian Dreams: Moscow and Tehran Since the Fall of the Shah* (Washington, D.C.: Potomac, 2009), pp. 235-238.

6. Christoph Bertram, "Rethinking Iran: From Confrontation to Cooperation," *Chaillot Paper,* no. 110 (Paris: European Union Institute for Security Studies, 2008), p. 46. See also Ali M. Ansari, "Iran Under Ahmadinejad: The Politics of Confrontation," *Adelphi Paper,* no. 393 (London: Institute for Strategic Studies, 2007).

7. The quotations are from an English translation of the speech on the Web page maintained by the Russian presidency, http://www.kremlin.ru/eng/text/speeches /2007/02/10/0138_type82912type82914type82917type84779_118123.shtml.

8. American political scientist Robert English was in Georgia at this time. He described in detail Gamsakhurdia's brutal treatment of Georgia's minorities in "Georgia: The Ignored History," *New York Review of Books,* November 6, 2008.

9. Jack F. Matlock, Jr., "Success Story," *New York Review of Books,* September 25, 1997.

10. I discussed this feature of Ukrainian politics in Jack F. Matlock, Jr., "The Nowhere Nation" (a misleading title supplied by the editors), *New York Review of Books,* February 24, 2000.

11. Condoleezza Rice, "Rethinking the National Interest: American Realism for a New World," *Foreign Affairs,* July-August 2008, pp. 2-26.

12. Professor Arthur A. Goldsmith of the University of Massachusetts, Boston, reviewed the relevant research in "Making the World Safe for Partial Democracy? Questioning the Premises of Democracy Promotion," *International Security,* vol. 33, no. 2 (Fall 2008), pp. 120-147.

13. John M. Owen IV, "Democracy, Realistically," *The National Interest,* Spring 2006, pp. 35-42.

14. Tony Judt, *Postwar: A History of Europe Since 1945* (New York: Penguin, 2005).

15. Tony Judt, "What Have We Learned, If Anything?" *New York Review of Books,* May 1, 2008, pp. 16-18.

16. Robert Kagan, *Of Paradise and Power: America and Europe in the New World Order* (New York: Knopf, 2003).

Chapter 11. Course Change

1. David Passage, "AFRICOM and SOUTHCOM: Reliquaria from an Earlier Age," *Foreign Service Journal*, February 2009, pp. 12–15.
2. Shawn Dorman, "Global Repositioning in Perspective," *Foreign Service Journal*, January 2009, pp. 18–30.
3. Richard K. Betts, *Enemies of Intelligence: Knowledge and Power in American National Security* (New York: Columbia University Press, 2007), pp. 19–20.
4. Betts, *Enemies of Intelligence*, pp. 192–193.
5. Soros, *George Soros on Globalization*, p. 6.
6. United Nations Treaty Collection, *Rome Statute of the International Criminal Court*.

Chapter 12. An Agenda, Not a Doctrine

1. John J. Mearsheimer and Stephen M. Walt described many of the reasons the policies followed by Israel's Likud and other right-wing parties have been in neither Israel's nor America's interest; *The Israel Lobby and U.S. Foreign Policy* (New York: Farrar, Straus and Giroux, 2007). I find most of the authors' judgments convincing, but would take issue with the title of the book. It should be "The Likud Lobby," because that lobby, though powerful and well financed, does not represent the true interests of Israel.
2. I discussed motivations in greater detail in my essay, "Regional Animosities and Nuclear Weapons Proliferation," in *Reykjavik Revisited: Steps Toward a World Free of Nuclear Weapons; Complete Report of 2007 Hoover Institution Conference*, ed. George P. Shultz, Steven P. Andreasen, Sidney D. Drell, and James E. Goodby (Stanford, Calif.: Hoover Institution Press, 2008).
3. Bill Luers, Tom Pickering, and Jim Walsh, "How to Deal with Iran," *New York Review of Books*, February 12, 2009, pp. 45–48.
4. Salman Masood and David E. Sanger, "Pakistan Frees Nuclear Dealer in Snub to U.S.," *New York Times*, February 7, 2009.
5. From Article VI of the Treaty on the Non-Proliferation of Nuclear Weapons.
6. *Wall Street Journal*, January 4, 2007, and January 15, 2008. The articles were signed by George P. Shultz, William J. Perry, Henry A. Kissinger, and Sam Nunn and endorsed by a number of other former officials who participated in conferences at the Hoover Institution. These op-ed pieces from the *Wall Street Journal*, along with sixteen articles discussing in detail various aspects of reducing reliance on nuclear weapons, are included in Shultz et al., eds., *Reykjavik Revisited*.
7. David E. Sanger, *The Inheritance: The World Obama Confronts and the Challenges to American Power* (New York: Harmony, 2009), p. 448.
8. Sanger, *The Inheritance*, p. 457.

ACKNOWLEDGMENTS

MANY PEOPLE HAVE CONTRIBUTED DIRECTLY or indirectly to this book. While writing it, I profited from meetings at the Hoover Institution dealing with nuclear issues organized by George Shultz and Sidney Drell, who were subsequently joined by Henry Kissinger, Sam Nunn, and William Perry, and from a conference at Harvard University organized by Mikhail Gorbachev and Graham Allison. I also participated in task forces dealing with U.S.-Russian relations and other foreign policy issues organized by the Century Fund in New York (co-chaired by Senator Gary Hart), the Washington office of the Council on Foreign Relations (co-chaired by Brent Scowcroft and William Perry), and by the Nixon Center in Washington (chaired by Dmitri Simes). Several meetings of former ambassadors to and from the Soviet Union and Russia, organized by Ambassador James Collins of the Carnegie Endowment for International Peace and Dr. Sergei Rogov of the Institute for Study of the USA and Canada in Moscow have contributed significantly to my understanding of both Cold War and current issues.

In my study of the Cold War I benefited from lengthy interviews with former president Mikhail Gorbachev, former president of Georgia Eduard Shevardnadze, former Soviet foreign minister Alexander Bessmertnykh, and Anatoly Chernyaev, Gorbachev's foreign policy adviser. Pavel Palazchenko of the Gorbachev Foundation was invariably helpful in answering questions about the development of Soviet foreign policy. Tom Blanton and Svetlana Savranskaya of the National Security Archive at George Washington University also assisted me by providing documents from the Cold War period.

A number of friends and colleagues read portions of the manuscript in various stages of its preparation and offered suggestions. They include Ambassadors Willard A. DePree and Thomas Simons, retired Foreign Service officer Dick Combs, whose study of the Soviet collapse was published in 2008, Professors Allen Lynch, Robert English, and Hugh Ragsdale, Reverend Donald E. Schomacker, journalist Bruce van Voorst, and Dr. Frances Mautner-Markhof.

Members of the staff at Yale University Press were patient with my delays in completing the manuscript. I would like to thank, in particular, Jonathan Brent, who encouraged me to write the book, my editors, William Frucht and Phillip King, who have helped greatly in improving the presentation, and Sarah Miller, whose support throughout has been exemplary.

Members of my family have helped in many ways, just as they have throughout my diplomatic and academic careers. My daughter, Nell Matlock Benton, tracked down sources for some of the quotations I used. My eldest son, James G. Matlock, compiled the index. My other sons—Hugh, David, and Joseph—took a lively interest in the topics I discussed and made useful suggestions throughout the period when I was thinking about the issues in this book and putting the ideas in a digital file. Most of all, my wife, Rebecca, made an indispensable contribution by reading the entire manuscript several times in its various stages of preparation and advising me on style and presentation. If the reader finds infelicitous expressions in the book, that is probably because at times I failed to take her advice.

INDEX

Abrahms, Max, 201–202

Abu Ghraib prison, 204, 226, 234, 235, 326n21

Abu Zubayda, 205, 326n23

Acton, Lord, 212

Adamishin, Anatoly, 50

Adelman, Kenneth, 318n26

Afghanistan, 118, 259, 304, 312; Northern Alliance in, 177; Al-Qaeda in, xi, 168, 196–198, 205, 234, 240, 245, 264, 285, 295–296, 304, 305, 326n26; Soviet invasion of, xv, 24, 27, 30, 31, 112, 228; Soviet occupation of, 50, 177, 200; Soviet withdrawal from, 9, 41, 45, 59; Taliban in, 177, 224, 234, 240, 241, 242, 297, 305–306; U.S.-led war in, 245, 272, 295–296

Africa, 137, 140, 272; Soviet policies toward, xv, 23, 125–126; U.S. policies toward, 179–180, 243–244, 272, 283

Agency for International Development (AID), 272

Ahmadinejad, Mahmoud, 242, 283, 283n, 304, 305

Al-Qaeda. *See* Qaeda, Al-

Andropov, Yuri, 34, 35–36, 52, 73, 75, 228, 294

Angola, 23, 50, 180

Anti-Ballistic Missile (ABM) Treaty (1972), 22; U.S. withdrawal from, 246, 309

Arafat, Yasser, 174, 175, 324n11

Argentina, 281

Armenia, 47, 88, 107, 137

Armitage, Richard, 220, 221

arms control agreements, 57, 134, 275; Anti-Ballistic Missile (ABM) Treaty (1972), 22, 246, 309; Comprehensive Nuclear Test Ban Treaty, 164, 281, 308; Intermediate-Range Nuclear Forces (INF) Treaty (1987), 61; Lisbon Protocol, 105, 162; Moscow Treaty (2002), 307–308; Nuclear Non-Proliferation Treaty (NPT), 105, 134, 176, 256, 302, 307; Strategic Arms Limitation Treaty (SALT), 22; SALT II agreement (1979), 24, 30, 162; Strategic Arms Reduction Treaty (START I, 1991), 63, 104–105, 307–308; START II agreement (1993), 104, 105, 162, 171; Vladivostok Agreement, 22, 275–276

arms control negotiations, 21, 294–295, 307–308; during Carter administration, 276; during Clinton admin-